AUTHORSHIP

AUTHORSHIP: FROM PLATO TO THE POSTMODERN

A Reader

Seán Burke

EDINBURGH UNIVERSITY PRESS

For Pat

Introduction and editorial matter © Seán
Burke, 1995
Individual essays © individual authors.
See Preface, pp. ix-xiii.

Reprinted 2000, 2003, 2004, 2006

Edinburgh University Press Ltd
22 George Square, Edinburgh

Typeset in 11/13 Linotron Bembo
by Photoprint, Torquay, and
printed and bound in Great Britain

by CPI Antony Rowe, Eastbourne
Transferred to digital print 2008

A CIP record for this book is available
from the British Library

ISBN 0 7486 0618 1

Contents

Preface

Like all Readers, this particular collection hopes to address a deficiency. While there is no theory of literature or the text which does not imply a certain stance towards authorship, there are yet very few texts outside film theory which address the issue of author in anything like a systematic or comprehensive fashion. Always pertinent, the theory of authorship has arisen peripherally and as an offshoot of more general positions.

Omitting works is doubtless more dismaying to the compiler of a collection than to its readers, and I have for the most part favoured monographs over the practice of editing larger works down to a single theme. The exclusion of Lacan, for example, does not indicate that I underestimate his significance in this context, only that his so very performative work precludes extraction.

The material collected here is divided into two parts, followed by a coda representing curious instances of the autobiographical. The first part deals with the aesthetic/theoretical debate (and could equally be intercalated with the section 'Writing the Self' to give a broader view of the history of attitudes to authorship), while the second concerns the political implications of authorship. In coming to the author question for the first time, my immediate sense was that the issues it raised were largely political. On the other hand, I felt that it was necessary to (re-) establish that authorship is a relevant category of contemporary thought, before enquiring into its political ramifications. The initial critique was therefore intended as a prolegomenon to the broader issues of authorship, even if those intentions were not as clearly expressed as they might have been.

My introduction proceeds on the assumption that the political may be reached through weaknesses in the aesthetic position. I realise, however, that this assumption is open to challenge from those who would begin from the political, and recommend Donald Pease's 'Author' – included below (pp. 263–76) – as an alternative to my own construction. In a similar vein, the second part of the book may well be read as a critique of the first, and the first as a conceptual contextualisation of the second. I make these observations, however, according to my personal conviction that these approaches should be finally complementary as attempts to unravel the conceptual and political complexities of authorship and the criticism which it produces.

Having been accused of effacing myself from my earlier book, it has seemed indispensable for me to say, if not who I am, then at least where I stand in relation to authorship. I am opposed to all unilateral determinisms – including that of the author – and wish to affirm that while the author-function varies in fact and principle from one historical context to another, it never disappears – least of all in those moments when it is concertedly attacked. I believe also that the inability of theoretical models to encompass the disruptive enigmas of authorship strengthens rather than weakens its claim on our attention. Just as I would argue that authorship is profoundly attractive to those who would wage war upon it, so too the Death of the Author fascinates me as gloriously baroque meditation on authorship. Which is to say that, for all its ostensible engagements, the argument is ultimately directed against the readers of the Death of the Author rather than its authors. The latter unfold in the extracts.

Permission given for the reprinted extracts by the following copyright holders and authors is gratefully acknowledged.

Plato, from *Ion* and *The Republic*, in *The Collected Dialogues of Plato*, ed. Edith Hamilton and Huntington Cairns (Princeton, NJ: Princeton University Press, 1961).

A. J. Minnis, 'The Significance of the Medieval Theory of Authorship', in *Medieval Theory of Authorship: Scholastic Literary Attitudes in the Later Middle Ages* (London: Scolar Press, 1984). Copyright © 1984 Ashgate Publishing Ltd.

Sir Philip Sidney, from *An Apology for Poetry*, ed. Geoffrey Shepherd (Manchester: Manchester University Press, 1965). © Thomas Nelson and Sons Ltd and Geoffrey Shepherd, 1965.

Edward Young, from 'Conjectures on Original Composition', in Edmund D. Jones (ed.), *English Critical Essays: XVI–XVIII Century* (Oxford: Oxford University Press, 1992).

Percy Bysshe Shelley, from 'A Defence of Poetry', in *The Norton Anthology of English Literature*, 5th edn, vol. 2.

Stéphane Mallarmé, from 'Crisis in Verse', in T. G. West (trans. and ed.), *Symbolism: An Anthology* (London: Methuen, 1980). Copyright © 1980 Methuen & Co. Ltd and T. G. West.

Sigmund Freud, 'Creative Writers and Day-dreaming', in idem, *The Standard Edition of the Complete Psychoanalytical Works of Sigmund Freud*, vol. ix, trans. and ed. James Strachey (London: The Hogarth Press, 1959). Copyright © 1959 Random House UK Ltd and

T. S. Eliot, 'Tradition and the Individual Talent', in idem, *The Sacred Wood* (London: Methuen, 1960). Copyright © 1960, by Methuen & Co. Ltd.

Boris Tomašeskij, 'Literature and Biography', in Ladislav Matejka and Krystyna Pomoroska (eds), *Readings in Russian Poetics: Formalist and Structuralist Views* (Cambridge, MA: MIT Press, 1971). Copyright © by The Massachussetts Institute of Technology.

W. K. Wimsatt Jr and Monroe C. Beardsley, from 'The Intentional Fallacy', in W. K. Wimsatt Jr, *The Verbal Icon: Studies in the Meaning of Poetry* (Lexington, KY: University of Kentucky Press, 1954). Copyright © 1954 by the University of Kentucky Press, and Methuen & Co. Ltd.

George Poulet, from 'Criticism and the Experience of interiority', in Richard Macksey and Eugenio Donato (eds), *The Structuralist Controversy: The Languages of Criticism and the Sciences of Man* (Baltimore, MD: Johns Hopkins University Press, 1972).

E. D. Hirsch Jr, from *Validity in Interpretation* (New Haven, CT: Yale University Press, 1967). Copyright © by Yale University.

Jacques Derrida, 'The Exorbitant. Question of Method', in idem, *Of Grammatology*, trans. Gayatri Chakravorty Spivak (Baltimore, MD:

Molly Nesbit, from 'What Was an Author?', *Yale French Studies*, 73 (1987). Copyright © 1987 by Yale University.

Donald E. Pease, 'Author', in Frank Lentricchia and Thomas McLaughlin (eds), *Critical Terms for Literary Study* (Chicago, IL and London: University of Chicago Press, 1990).

Máire ní Fhlathúin, 'Postcolonialism and the Author: The Case of Salman Rushdie'. Copyright © 1994 Máire ní Fhlathúin.

Seán Burke, 'The Ethics of Signature'. Copyright © 1994 Seán Burke.

Richard Rorty, 'Taking Philosophy Seriously', *The New Republic*, 11 April 1988. Copyright © 1988 The New Republic, Inc. Reprinted by permission of *The New Republic*.

Michel de Montaigne, from *Essays*, in *The Complete Works of Montaigne*, trans. Donald M. Frame (Hamish Hamilton: London, 1948).

René Descartes, 'Second Meditation', in idem, *Meditations on First Philosophy*, trans. John Cottingham (Cambridge: Cambridge University Press, 1986). Copyright © 1986 Cambridge University Press; English translation Copyright © 1986 John Cottingham.

Friedrich Nietzsche, 'Why I Am a Destiny', in idem, *On the Genealogy of Morals and Ecce Homo*, trans. Walter Kaufmann (New York: Random House, 1969).

Jorge Luis Borges, *Labyrinths* (Harmondsworth: Penguin Books, 1970): 'Pierre Menard, Author of the Quixote'; 'Kafka and His Precursors'; 'Everything and Nothing'; 'Borges and I'. Copyright © 1962, 1964 New Directions Publishing Corporation. Reproduced by permission of Penguin Books Ltd.

I would also like to thank all those who work at Edinburgh University Press for their patience, good cheer and unfailing courtesy. In particular I would like to express my gratitude to Jonathan Price, whose charming and erudite presence has made this project a positive pleasure. My thanks are also due to colleagues in the English Literature Department at Durham University, in particular to Agnes Delanoy and to Michael O'Neill for whom no enquiry – however trifling or trying –

was too much trouble. As ever, my thanks are to John, June, Tracey and Kevin for their enduring support, and to Nick Browne for spiriting the most recondite articles to my table in minutes. I would also like to thank Joe Emonds, *maître de langue* and master of friendship. Most of all, I express my gratitude to Patricia Waugh, whose intellectual companionship extends beyond the letter.

Introduction

Reconstructing the Author

Once Zhuang Zhou dreamed of himself being a butterfly; he was really a butterfly fluttering around, happy and comfortable, knowing not that he was Zhou. After a while, he woke up, and he was surprisingly Zhuang Zhou himself. It was not clear whether it was Zhou who had dreamt of being a butterfly or it was the butterfly who had dreamed of Zhou. Yet there must be differentiation between Zhou and the butterfly, and this is called the transformation of things.

Zhauangzi, i, pp. 53–4

Do we dream or are we dreamt? Might we dream and be dreamt? When an author writes or thinks to be writing, is that author simultaneously written? Does creative imagination guide the composition, or is the writer like the scrawl of an alien power trying out a new pen? Are the 'great authors' masters in the house of language, or its privileged tenants? Is the author the producer of the text or its product? Do we speak language or does language speak us? Does the author reflect culture and history, or is the author constructed in culture and history?

These questions have been raised in a myriad tongues and lexicons throughout the history of Western thought, and every attempt to decide the issue one way or the other has only served to rejuvenate the debate, to play it out in a different key. Authorship, like cosmology, remains a source of fascination for believers and non-believers alike since the issues which it raises reflect any given society's sense of being in the world, and construction of itself in relation to discourse, knowledge and tradition. Notions of the self, creativity, psyche, origin, source, theology, onto-theology, agency, free will, determinism, consciousness, causality, gender, cultural identity, objectivity, subjectivity, ownership, authority (scarcely to exhaust the list) are implied not only by the question of authorship but also by theories of the absence, death or disappearance of the author. The very movement against the author precipitated in 1968 by Roland Barthes's 'The Death of the Author' served, albeit antithetically, to remind us of the extent to which the history of our thought is bound up with conceptions of what it means to author a text. With unavoidable irony, the theory of authorial absence no more signalled a disengagement with issues of authorship than iconoclasm attests to the dwindling of the icons, or negative theology reflects an indifference to Divinity. The ancient chimeras of origin and authorship reassert themselves in the very gestures that seek to have done with origin and authorship.

Harold Bloom avers that 'meaning . . . cleaves more closely to origins the more intensely it strives to distance itself from origins', and the putative emptying-out of the authorial subject has been caught up in an asymptotic cycle of resistance to the transcendental presuppositions which it sought to erase.[1] The project of radically impersonalising discourse has obvious precedents in the mimetic tradition which, in both its idealist formulation and in the quasi-scientific literary naturalism of Zola and others, implies the total absenting of authorial subjectivity in the interests of an unmediated representation of objective reality. Barthes refers to this tradition as 'the castrating objectivity of the realist novelist' and redefines modern impersonality in anti-mimetic terms as 'that point where only language acts, "performs", and not "me" '.[2] However, while this position easily avoids the disinterestedness of Platonic and naturalist objectivity, it admits of very little distinction from the inspirational tradition of Classical, Patristic and Medieval theory. Within the Medieval view of the book, the author (or *auctor*) was the scriptor through whom the Divine script was performed. As the exegete Nicholas of Lyre (c. 1270–1340) puts it:

> In the act of prophesying, God (touching or elevating the mind of the prophet to supernatural knowledge) and the mind of the prophet (touched or illuminated in this way), concur. It is necessary that the moving action and the thing moved should coincide . . . God concurs as the principal agent, and the mind of the prophet as the instrumental agent.[3]

Within the Medieval view, the human author of Scripture has no power to originate, and his text derives from the creativity and authority (*auctoritas*) of God. Thus when Foucault describes the Mallarméan author as 'an executant in a pure ceremony of the Book in which the discourse would compose itself', the distinction between such a role and that of the Scriptural *auctor* resides only in the designation of the alterity by which the recipient is overtaken.[4] Similarly, the impersonal scribe with whom Barthes would replace the author only differs from the *auctor* in that language is sacralised in the wake of the Divine *auctoritas*:

> the modern scriptor . . . is not the subject with the book as predicate; there is no other time than that of the enunciation and every text is eternally written *here and now* . . . For him, on the contrary, the hand, cut off from any voice, borne by a pure gesture of inscription (and not of expression), traces a field without origin – or which, at least, has no other origin than language itself, language which ceaselessly calls into question all origins.[5]

We need only for 'language' substitute 'God' here to replicate precisely the dominant Medieval view of the *auctor* who, 'borne by a pure gesture of inscription (and not of expression), traces a field without origin – or which, at least, has no other origin than God Himself, God who ceaselessly calls into question all origins." The notion of a divided authorial psyche – and the consequent inability of the writing subject's intentions to become fully present to themselves in the text – is also resplendently anticipated in the Classical and Medieval traditions. While Plato and the writer known as 'Longinus' emphasised that poetry found its wellsprings in a frenzying visitation inaccessible to consciousness – the former perhaps ironically, the latter with conviction – Biblical exegesis, seeing Scripture as emanating from that most radical of alterities, the Divine Will, fully accepted that authorial intention (*intentio auctoris*) could be at most a concause in the texts, coming into being. Nonetheless, Christian exegetes developed sophisticated and intricate critical apparatuses to allow for a complex interplay of multiple determinants – including the role of the *auctor* – in the constitution of the Scriptural text. Seen from this vantage, the contemporary deployment of the various declensions of 'otherness' developed within theory – the unconscious, cultural or political forces, écriture, differance, etc. – distinguishes itself from the Medieval tradition mainly through an inability or unwillingness to acknowledge the overdetermination of a textual scene which encompasses alterities *and* the participant role of the author.

Indeed, the very term *auctor* (from which *author* is derived) was very late to garner the connotations of originality with which it is today (dis)credited.[6] Of the four terms from which *auctor* is held to derive, the three Latin verbs do not imply any sense of textual mastery. *Agere*, 'to act or perform', is close to the Medieval and Barthesian ideas of the scriptor as acting through a text which in some sense precedes its performance; *augere*, 'to grow', for all its organicist resonances, does not suggest that the text originates with its author. *Auieo*, 'to tie', derived from the poetic lexicon and referred to the connective tissue (metre, feet, etc.) by which poets such as Virgil structured their verses – in which regard it is more prefigurative of the structuralist notions of bricolage and authors as assemblers of codes than the concept of the author as a creative potency. Only the fourth root, the Greek noun *autentim*, 'authority', is suggestive of authorship as hegemonic, and even here the idea of authority is entirely remote from that of autonomy since the ancient authors received their authority (*auctoritas*) in the first instance from their relation to tradition and ultimately from the *auctoritas* of God as manifested inspirationally and in the Scriptural canon. If the Medieval view of the book could be unanchored from its theological moorings, it is unlikely that anti-authorial theories would find much to contest in this structural placement of the author.

Many theorists have of course been aware that the contemporary repudiation of the author echoes the ancient view – Barthes even talks of the 'modern scriptor' – but tend to appropriate the older view of authorship in order to celebrate the void of the abolished humanist author rather than to consider how our notions of authorship might be productively revised. What distinguishes premodern conceptions of authorship is their assumption that discourse is primarily an affair of public rather than private consciousness. The various imitative models – in their mimetic, didactic and technical senses – all affirm literature's connection with the public domain, whether that domain consists in an objective reality renderable by language, a shared vision of how the social should be restructured, or in terms of public conventions and traditions for the production and reception of discourse. The inspirational model assumes still more strenuously that discourse neither originates nor culminates with the individual since the author functions as an avatar of a Divine writing addressed to all humankind – hence its evangelical emphasis on wide dissemination, be it written or declaimed. So far from endorsing an interiority that feeds from itself back into itself, the inspirational tradition affirms that discourse is not a private intuition but a public revelation. Were it possible, in Barthes's famous phrase 'the birth of the reader must be at the cost of the death of the author', to take 'reader' as a synecdoche for 'public' and 'author' for 'interiority', then the movement against the author would gain greater coherence in cultural and political terms as well as a clearer sense of historical mission.

The movement against the author did not present itself in such terms, however, instead advocating a 'Reader' no less ambiguous and mystified than the 'Author' whom it sought to supplant. Given then that anti-authorial theory neither develops significantly upon the ancient conception of authorship nor returns discourse to the public sphere, I would suggest that the crucial historical change in conceptions of authorship did not occur in the theoretical upheaval of the last thirty years but with the romantic revolution and the eighteenth-century philosophical and aesthetic discourses upon which it drew. I would also suggest that it is to the very romantic tradition against which theory aligns itself that the Death of the Author belongs, even if it should do so inadvertently, and as its final term.

THE TRANSCENDENTAL AND THE IMPERSONAL

All too often, the idea of a 'break' or 'rupture' in thought asserts radical discontinuity in place of the subtler modes of realignment by which an age or epoch inherits traditional categories while decisively modulating their relations. It would, for example, be no more true to say that the mimetic impulse declines in romanticism than to claim that authorial originality or a concern with interior consciousness arose unprecedented in the late eighteenth century. The notion of a writer defying or transcending tradition – evident in the Renaissance celebration of Genius[7] – had been clearly prefigured in work of Edward Young, William Duff and others who championed original productions over neo-Classical imitation. Similarly, the subjectivist strivings of Montaigne for self-representation, along with the exploration of interior consciousness in Descartes and the thinkers of the Enlightenment, defy reduction to any such comfortable periodic tablature even if these untimely meditations had yet to pervade aesthetic awareness. What makes these continuities appear under the sign of epistemic discontinuity, however, is the power newly assigned by the romantics to individual consciousness in the creation of a world which it had hitherto been assumed to mirror or represent. The work of Young, Duff and others will seem to us 'preromantic' since their model of originality is defined reactively via tradition rather than in terms of a theory of interior consciousness as constitutive of the reality which it seeks to represent. Such a recognition – which required the most radical restructuring of the relation between consciousness and its objects – only became possible with Immanuel Kant, whose 'Copernican Revolution' asserted that the only world we know is the world we construct through innate mental categories.

For Kant, the world we perceive is only made possible to us through the operations of a transcendental ego which imposes the *a priori* categories of space, time and causality upon the ultimately inaccessible objects of experience. While Kant developed transcendental idealism in strictly epistemological terms, however, the concept of a subjectivity which originates the world given to it in consciousness promoted dynamic, if not always precise, analogies with artistic creativity. In what was perhaps the inaugural move of romantic idealism, Fichte and Schelling sought to make aesthetically and metaphysically substantive what was in Kant an epistemological postulate. Kant's demonstration that the world of experience is not in itself given to consciousness served to problematise the mimetic subordination of author to nature; the constructive function of the transcendental ego, on the other hand, invited at least metaphorical extension into the aesthetic realm via a model of imagination as shaping and (re)creating the world in poetic language. Shelley, for one, was to make the brightest claims for this function of the imagination: 'It creates anew the universe after it has been annihilated in our minds by the recurrence of impressions blunted by repetition'.[8]

Within a poetic cosmogony wherein mind becomes the cause in part of what it represents, the older categories of imitation and inspiration do not disappear but rather find themselves redistributed within the new economy of subjectivity. The mimetic role of poetry remains pronounced in Wordsworth, for example, but is now in consort with an unprecedented emphasis on the reciprocal fecundity of the imagination in what he calls 'an ennobling interchange/Of action from within and from without'.[9] Nature is no longer simply given but is in need of aesthetic completion. 'How exquisitely', Wordsworth declared, 'the individual Mind / . . . to the external World'

> Is fitted: – And how exquisitely, too . . .
> The external world is fitted to the Mind;
> And the creation (by no lower name
> Can it be called) which they with blended might
> Accomplish . . . [10]

Nature is now dependent upon the epiphanic power of the creative imagination for its poetic reproduction. The imagination is therefore needed to supplement nature, to reveal the truth of a nature which cannot precede its imaginative representation. Given that mind must therefore represent itself in the act of representing reality, the exploration of interior consciousness becomes a calling no less Olympian and sublime than the Miltonic theme of Creation and Fall:

> Not Chaos, not
> The darkest pit of lowest Erebus,
> Nor aught of blinder vacancy, scooped out
> By help of dreams – can breed such fear and awe
> As fall upon us often when we look
> Into our Minds, into the Mind of Man –
> My haunt, and the main region of my song.[11]

This radical exploration of the interior recesses of mind could not but reveal areas of intuition alien to consciousness or artistic control, with the result that questions of inspiration and alterity arduously reasserted themselves within romantic aesthetics. The renewed interest in inspiration did not, however, present itself as disjunct with the emergent category of imagination. The very idea of an 'inspired creator' resonated in romanticism with far fewer of the oxymoronic tensions which we would today discern in such a conceit: inspiration was set alongside rather than against the creative, originating imagination. Even a poem such as 'Kubla Khan', with its extreme weighting towards the unconscious, closes by hearkening for a state of inspiration mastered, and the productive reconciliation of the subject and alterity. Whether indeed inspiration is bounded by the self in the form of a Wordsworthian 'inner voice', or treated in Shelleyan terms as adnascent with the creative imagination, it is always in some sense thought of in terms of the individual subject and never as the radical alterity of the Patristic and Medieval traditions. Coleridge in fact makes of the reconciliation of the subject and alterity a famous formula:

> The IMAGINATION then I consider either as primary, or secondary. The primary IMAGINATION I hold to be the living Power and prime Agent of all human Perception, and as a repetition in the finite mind of the eternal act of creation in the infinite I AM.[12]

The ancient association of human and divine creativity is maintained but has been subjected to an unprecedented reversal. The author is no longer a privileged reader of the Divine script in nature, nor an elect who inspirationally mimes the Divine discourse, but is now seen as imitating the act of creation itself. Such a reversal is registered perhaps too crudely in Herder's assertion that 'The author is become a Creator-God',[13] but emerges influentially in Schiller's celebration of the objective cast of Classical (naïve) authorship:

> without intimacy [the naïve poet] flees the heart that seeks his, flees the desire that would embrace him . . . The object possesses him entirely, his heart does not lie like a tawdry alloy immediately beneath the surface, but like gold waits to be sought in the depths. Like the divinity behind the world's structure he stands behind his work; *he* is the work and the work is *he*; to ask only for *him* is to be unworthy of it, inadequate to it, or sated with it.[14]

The transcendence of the author here carries a concomitant impersonality. This dual stress has much in common with the subject of Kantian idealism which is both transcendent of the world and ontologically hollow. It can also be retraced – as M. H. Abrams suggests – to the theological tradition which portrays God as both transcendent of, and omnipresent within, creation.[15] As translated into literary terms, the author can be identified with the entirety of the work while being nowhere visible within the work. The will to impersonalise literary creation, though often downplayed in cursory constructions of the Romantic period, is also to be discerned in Keats's idea of negative capability – an empathetic act which requires the emptying-out of all personal concerns in poetic composition – as well as in Coleridge's insistence that 'to have a genius is to live in the universal, to know no self . . .'.[16] It is also a central edict in later German romantics such as K. W. F. Solger for whom artistic creation is requisitely objective, ironic and impersonal.[17]

One might of course ask why these seemingly contradictory impulses – towards subjectivity on the one hand, and impersonality on the other – should coincide at the very outset of the era of subjectivity. A possible explanation, I would suggest, is that impersonality functioned as a guard against the potentially nihilistic implications of Kant's subjective idealism, as an attempt to preserve something of the Enlightenment notion of disengaged reason in an era which could no longer see truth as mimetically grounded or divinely sanctioned. Precisely this vigilance informs Kant's *Critique of Judgement*, which proceeds from the recognition that the determining ground of judgement can be no other than subjective, to the injunction that such judgements involve 'detachment from all interest' and thereby lay claim to 'subjective universality'.[18] Impersonality, like disinterested-ness, would seem then to arise as a reflex or defence in simultaneously acknowledging the ascendance of subjectivity while guarding against its more destabilising ramifications.

This very same need to defend against the subjectivist turn in modernity informs modernist reactions against personality. The notion of literature as a revelation of personality had dominated criticism in the latter half of the nineteenth century and – bolstered by the emergence of popular psychology – served to justify a mixed and rhapsodic discourse which saw no contradiction in uncovering an author's personal life at the same time as lauding that author's transcendent genius. However, while the modernist aesthetic quite rightly countered this development, the strongest arguments of Eliot, Hulme, Pound and others often reclaim the higher romantic ground in the process of declaring their anti-romanticism. Schiller's depiction of the impersonal Author-God reappears with scarcely discernible modifications in the proto-modernist reflections of Flaubert, for whom '[t]he author in his work ought to be like God in the universe, present everywhere, and visible nowhere', which were in turn to form the blueprint for the image of the modernist writer as disinterested artificer.[19]

T. S. Eliot's theory of impersonality likewise calumniates one strand of the romantic movement even as it corrects another. His famous dictum that poetry 'is not the expression of personality, but an escape from personality'[20] has the clearest affinities with Schiller's celebration of the poet who 'flees the heart that seeks his, flees the desire that would embrace him'. Similarly, Eliot's insistence that 'the more perfect the artist, the more completely separate in him will be the man who suffers and the mind which creates'[21] not only echoes Keatsian negative capability but must also recall Coleridge's praise of Shakespeare in terms of the 'utter aloofness of the poet's own feelings, from those of which he is both the painter and analyst'.[22] No less than within romanticism, the reaction against subjectivity once more shows that its terms are governed by the era of subjectivity.

A similar structure of continuity in resistance emerges in the general reading of the New Criticism's development of impersonalist theory. Given that a transcendental/impersonal subject is not figured within the text, it is a long historical but short conceptual step to displace the autonomy of the subject into the text itself. In both romantic and modernist aesthetics, impersonality had for the most part described a mode or mood in which an author achieved aesthetic transfiguration. According to the dominant (though often problematic[23]) reception of the New Criticism – whose lineage combines modernist impersonality with the Kantian stricture of aesthetic disinterestedness – the refusal to confine criticism within a model of literature as self-expression trans-poses itself from an issue of writing to one of reading. Objectivity becomes not so much a matter of how the text is constituted but of the responses which it should properly provoke. Poetic autonomy thereby preserves the autonomy of the author in the same gesture by which it evacuates the author. The impersonal reflex comes to dominate the scene of reading as well as that of writing, and once more arises as a reactive inversion of the transcendental dynamic in which it is con-stituted.

In this light, one could read 'The Death of the Author' as the latest instance of the impersonalising tendency in modernity whereby 'writ-ing' rather than the lone text of Anglo–American formalism now becomes the privileged category which serves to distance the text from its authorial subject. The very manner in which 'The Death of the Author' oscillates between the performative and the descriptive, between viewing itself as the moment of the author's death and its contrary urge to establish precedents, attests to an anxious sense of continuity. The 'requisite impersonality' which Barthes champions is distinct from the realist canon of objective mimesis, but clearly cannot distinguish itself from the impersonalities of a Flaubert, Mallarmé or Valéry and hence from the high romantic conception of disinterested subjectivity. Indeed, as Michel Foucault betimes declared: '[*écriture*] has merely transposed the empirical characteristics of an author to a transcendental anonymity'.[24] Clearly, Barthes's essay does not escape from the transcendental/impersonal impasse of modernity by its extreme weighting to the latter term. While, however, we cannot read 'The Death of the Author' on its own terms as a step beyond the subjective horizons of high modernity, we might see it as a *crisis within* the impersonalising tradition, as the point where impersonality so oversteps the mark in the direction of the *reductio ad absurdum* as to force its own breach and to beckon something other than itself into being.

But what might that 'something other' be? The foregoing would seem to suggest that there is no way out of the play of transcendence and impersonality beyond that of making an unlikely and unwelcome return to biographical positivism or unreflective humanist models. I would suggest, however, that late modernity's profound unease about the subject can only be addressed through the subject and in terms which respect many of the objections made to the humanist author. I would also suggest that the only way of fulfilling the implicit demands of the Death of the Author consists in returning to the question of the author. Such a return implies further that the ontologies of the author and the subject might provide a positive space for those general crises in thought that announce themselves as the postmodern. Certainly, it is only through reciprocal enquiry that the dilemmas of postmodernism and subjectivity can arrive at fuller senses of themselves; less clear is the question as to which of these spaces waits in greater need of the other.

SITUATING THE SUBJECT

The first vigorous challenge to the Kantian notion of a transcendental subject came in the work of Friedrich Nietzsche, who advocated a return to the body against impersonal or disembodied consciousness. For this reason, among others, Nietzsche has been taken up as the most significant precursor of both postmodern and theoretical critiques of Enlightenment modernity. While Nietzsche's deconstruction of trans-cendental subjectivity is assumed as the starting point for contemporary thought, very little heed is paid to the procedure which made such a critique possible in the first place. So far from asserting an anonymity of discourse against the Cartesian and Kantian subjects, Nietzsche disputed the model of transcendence through his assertion that dis-course is inalienably personal, that philosophical authorship operates in the mode of self-erasure via rhetorical and conceptual strategies which distract both author and reader from the fact that knowledge and textuality are altogether rooted in the singularity of subjective concerns. Beyond its epistemological destinations, the characteristic Nietzschean interrogation ('Who is speaking? And why speaking thus?') also opens the space of a stringent ethical critique by retracing a text first to its author and thence to the ethical drives which motivated that text or system. Only by opening the text to its author in such fashion was Nietzsche able to uncover a fundamental will-to-power behind the façade of disinterested will-to-knowledge.

Following upon Nietzsche, the most radical alternatives to transcen-dental subjectivity have sought to situate rather than detach the subject from its work and world. For Freud, impersonality is a defence against an inescapable, almost unbearable situatedness in terms of personal desire, memory, biography. Within the Freudian model, every attempt at disinterestedness or transcendence is fated to collapse as the uncon-scious resituates and returns author to text, subject to discourse, and the traumatically personal to the defensive will-to-impersonality. Marx's opposition to the subject as 'the merest vapourings of idealism' likewise set out not to convert implicit into explicit absence but to demystify discourse via the author: as he and Engels made clear, one can only 'enthuse over the miracle-working of the pen' by divorcing the text from the 'living historical human subject' by whom it was produced.[25] In Heidegger, as in the other grand precursors of theory, contemporary receptions have similarly scored the deconstruction of the 'view from outside' over its corollary replacement by a situated subject, a historically full 'I' in contradistinction to the ontologically void 'I' of the Kantian analytic. As with Nietzsche and Freud, Heidegger's thought would be taken up with altogether more fidelity as a return of subject to world, author to text and one which is quite in defiance of not only the objective overseer of science, the omniscient subject of representation or the impersonal artificer of high modernist aesthetics, but also of the authorless discourse to whose elaboration his name is so often summoned. What in fact occurs in many theoretical appropriations of these discourses is that modernity's disengaged subject is challenged only through proposing a further locus of disengagement which neglects the fact that Nietzsche and Heidegger more or less explicitly opposed the Author through the author, the Subject through the subject. Jacques Derrida, in a recent interview, draws attention to these two aspects of this critique but does so under the signs of their discrepancy rather than their complicity:

> At the very moment in which they marked . . . their mistrust for substantialist or subjectivist metaphysics, Heidegger and Nietzsche, whatever serious differences there may be between the two, continued to endorse the question 'Who?' and subtracted the 'who' from the deconstruction of the subject. But we might still ask ourselves just how legitimate this is.[26]

The move – to my mind – is entirely legitimate since Nietzsche and Heidegger did not subtract the 'who' from the deconstruction of the subject but protracted their deconstruction precisely on its basis. The question 'who' ('is writing?'; 'is reading?') was destined to challenge generic subjectivity via the perspectivism of the situated subject so as to unmask the personal drives behind the abstract system. One can see that so many of the problems that bedevil the author-debate arise from the failure to realise that the notion of the author has been falsely analogised with the transcendent/impersonal subject and that the only way to deconstruct this latter subject is not to replace it with theories of language, *différance*, anonymity, *écriture féminine* and so on, but to reposition authorship as a situated activity present not so much to itself as to culture, ideology, language, difference, influence, biography.

Contemporary deconstructions of the subject themselves imply and yet recoil from such an undertaking. The deconstructive dismantling of .the stable subject of romantic irony provides the opening for a repositioning of authorship even as it declares the concept of the author to be overrun by textual indeterminacy. As David Simpson and others have astutely demonstrated, the romantic conception of a transcendental subjectivity which holds in place all of a text's contradictions, while ironically commenting on their play, affirms a paradigm of metacommentary which is untenable even in its own terms.[27] Given the impossibility of transcending romantic oppositions such as eternal/temporal, art/impermanence, the metacommenting position must in its turn be ironically disrupted by textual forces which exceed and elude its assumed mastery. Ironic metacomment is therefore collapsed into comment in such manner that neither formal closure nor aesthetic completion is any longer possible upon this ironic trumping of the ironising subject. However, thus to collapse the authorial metacomment back into comment does not necessarily remove the romantic subject from the overdetermined scene of his or her text. Faced with the toppling of the transcendental position into this 'irony of irony', one might equally infer the consequent embedding or situating of the authorial subject *within* rather than *outwith* the ironic competitions of the text. Such a relocation would move from impersonal detachment to personal engagement within a textual scene whose undecidability admits neither of authorial mastery nor of authorial disappearance. A view of subjectivity thus arises which is neither a limit nor a limiting concept but one which enables reading to pass beyond the constraining play of transcendence and disappearance.

Deconstruction is by no means unique in simultaneously suggesting and forestalling openings for a reconsideration of authorial subjectivity. Foucault's movement from an archaeological to a genealogical approach was dictated in part by the recognition that theoretical impersonalities reinvoke the transcendental presuppositions of modernity: such a reorientation implied the turn towards a model of situated authorial subjectivity which his discourse never quite explicitly takes. Similarly, the concerted return to context which we have recently witnessed in the discourses of New Historicism, Cultural Materialism and Postcolonialism suggest the restoration of a working concept of authorship if only to provide a point of access to historical, cultural and colonial contexts. Quite often, in fact, these discourses proceed covertly through the author while disclaiming the author with an embarrassment which presumably stems from too heavy and reactive an investment in modernity's characterisation of authorship as autonomous agency. The current contextualisation of political criticism would itself seem to beseech a restoration of situated agency and one which may not indefinitely bypass authorship if only because resistance and agency so often proclaim themselves in the form of written texts.

It is indeed no less difficult to see the renewal of context in ideological criticism as anything other than a legitimate and long-awaited response to the disarming effects of linguistic determinism than it is to envisage a future of effective political criticism without the vigorous rehabilitation of the referent. Similarly, the scission of sign and referent – and further that of signifier and signified – cannot but be related to the altogether more disabling than disabusing separation of author and text. Depriving discourse of authorship and agency has been gravely debilitating within Marxist and feminist criticism, and ironically so since feminism in particular offers such potentially productive resources for redefining subjectivity outwith and against the model of autonomy. As Nancy K. Miller writes:

> Because women have not had the same historical relation of identity, to origin, institution, production that men have had, they have not, I think, (collectively) felt burdened by *too much* self, ego, cogito, etc. Because the female subject has juridically been excluded from the polis, hence decentred, 'disoriginated', de-institutionalised, etc., her relation to integrity and textuality, desire and authority, displays structurally important differences from that universal position.[28]

What is true for feminism in this context would also apply to the postcolonial challenge to the 'universal position' which has reified its own European preoccupations into a global model of subjectivity. Furthermore, the second-order post-colonial critique of a hypostasised colonial subject would imply as its positive counter a defence of the specificity of the subject, the grounding of the text in the irreducible personal and cultural experiences of its author. In each case, a rigorous rejection of the universal subject must imply a reassertion of the subject in his/her particularity.[29]

The need to (re)situate subjectivity is prime among the many callings facing political theories as well as those facing the cluster of discourses we refer to as the postmodern. To refuse totalising histories or accounts of human nature should be itself to refuse the impersonalising consciousness that purportedly enables such stories to be told. The challenge to truth or truth effects must likewise be a challenge to the disengaged subjectivity which generates such a discursive effect in the first place, whether that effect arises through the neutrality of scientific observation, the panoramic consciousness of realism, or the grand philosophical narratives of history and thought.

Conversely, and by the same token, postmodern emphases on 'islands of discourse', on little narratives, language games, the locality of discourse, should acknowledge the situated author as principle of locality *par excellence*. When we consider that the war on totalities must be a war waged on the transcendental/impersonal subject through whose putative construction totalities emerge, it becomes clear that the great crises of postmodernism are crises of authorship even if they still disdain to announce themselves as such. The difficulties of envisaging how and where contemporary thought might relocate the authorship that is everywhere in its midst may only be outweighed by the necessity of the calling and should in no wise deter us from the attempt. In any eventuality, and as postmodernity slouches towards the millennium, it is clear that this project – glimpsed by Nietzsche more than a century ago – still lies before us.

NOTES

Epigraph Quoted in Zhang, Longxi, *The Tao and the Logos: Literary Hermeneutics, East and West* (Durham and London: Duke University Press, 1992), p. 150.

1. Harold Bloom, *A Map of Misreading* (New York and London: Oxford University Press, 1975), p. 62.
2. Roland Barthes, 'The Death of the Author', *Image – Music – Text*, trans. and ed. Stephen Heath (London: Fontana, 1977), pp. 142–8: p. 143.
3. Nicholas of Lyre, quoted in A. J. Minnis, *Medieval Theory of Authorship: Scholastic Literary Attitudes in the Later Middle Ages* (London: Scolar Press, 1984), p. 91.
4. Michel Foucault, *The Order of Things: An Archaeology of the Human Sciences*, trans. Alan Sheridan (London: Tavistock, 1970), p. 306.
5. Roland Barthes, 'The Death of the Author', op. cit., pp. 145–6.
6. See, for example, the etymo-critical account of authorship and authority in Edward Said, *Beginnings: Intention and Method* (Baltimore, MD: Johns Hopkins University Press, 1975), p. 83. The relevant passage is quoted below by Gilbert and Gubar in Part 2, Section 1.
7. As the seminal work in the cultural rise of the notion of genius, see Giorgio Vasari, *The Lives of the Artists* [1550 and 1568], trans. and ed. George Bull (Harmondsworth: Penguin, 1965).
8. Percy Bysshe Shelley, 'A Defence of Poetry', in *The Norton Anthology of English Literature*, 5th edn, vol. 2, pp. 778–92: p. 790.
9. William Wordsworth, *The Prelude*, ed. E. de Selincourt (Oxford, 1926), XIII, ll. 375–6. See also Charles Taylor's excellent work for a detailed account of the Romantic notion that imagination epiphanically completes nature: Charles Taylor, *Sources of the Self: The Making of the Modern Identity* (Cambridge: Cambridge University Press, 1989), pp. 368–90.
10. William Wordsworth, 'Preface to *The Excursion*', in *The Poetical Works*, ed. E. de Selincourt and Helen Darbishire (Oxford: Clarendon Press, 1949), V, ll. 63–71.
11. Ibid., ll. 35–41.
12. Samuel Taylor Coleridge, *Biographia Literaria I*, ed. James Engell and W. Jackson Bate, Bollingen Series LXXV (Princeton, NJ : Princeton University Press, 1983), p. 304.

13. Johann Gottfried Herder, quoted in Tzvetan Todorov, *Theorie du Symbole* (Paris: Editions du Seuil, 1977), p. 175.

14. Friedrich Schiller, 'On Naïve and Sentimental Poetry', trans. Julius A. Elias, in David Simpson, *The Origins of Modern Critical Thought: German Aesthetic and Literary Criticism from Lessing to Hegel* (Cambridge and New York: Cambridge University Press, 1988), pp. 148–73: p. 156.

15. See M. H. Abrams, *The Mirror and the Lamp: Romantic Theory and the Critical Tradition* (London: Oxford University Press, 1953), pp. 239–41.

16. Samuel Taylor Coleridge, *The Philosophical Lectures*, ed. Kathleen Coburn (London, 1949), p. 179.

17. On K. W. F. Solger's impersonal aesthetic, see David Simpson, *The Origins of Modern Critical Thought: German Aesthetic and Literary Criticism from Lessing to Hegel* (Cambridge and New York: Cambridge University Press, 1988), pp. 319–28; and René Wellek, *A History of Modern Criticism 1750–1950, 2. The Romantic Age* (London: Jonathan Cape, 1955), pp. 298–303.

18. Immanuel Kant, *The Critique of Judgement*, trans. James Creed Meredith (Oxford: Oxford University Press, 1952), pp. 50–1.

19. Cf. Gustave Flaubert, *Correspondence II*, ed. Eugene Fasquelle (Paris, 1900), p. 155.

20. T. S. Eliot, 'Tradition and the Individual Talent', in *The Sacred Wood: Essays on Poetry and Criticism* (London: Methuen, 1920), pp. 47–59: p. 58.

21. Ibid., p. 54.

22. Samuel Taylor Coleridge, *Biographia Literaria II*, op. cit., p. 22.

23. The New Criticism was in fact a rather more complex cluster of discources than either its general reception or its theoretical reconstitution would suggest – the latter usually serving merely as summary prologue to its rejection.

24. Michel Foucault, 'What is an Author?', in Michel Foucault, *Language, Counter-Memory Practice: Selected Essays and Interviews*, ed. Donald Bouchard, trans. Donald Bouchard and Sherry Simon (Ithaca, NY: Cornell University Press, 1977), pp. 113–38: pp. 119–20.

25. Karl Marx, *The German Ideology I* (London: Lawrence and Wishart, 1970), pp. 84–5. For a comprehensive selection of the aesthetic observations of Marx and Engels, see Karl Marx and Friedrich Engels, *On Literature and Art: A Selection of Writings*, ed. Lee Baxandall and Stefan Morawski (New York: International General, 1973).

26. Jacques Derrida, ' "Eating Well": An Interview', in *Who Comes after the Subject?*, ed. Eduardo Cadava, Peter Connor and Jean-Luc Nancy (New York and London: Routledge, 1991), p. 101.

27. In following here David Simpson's excellent work in this field, I do not mean to dispute his demonstration, merely to show how it could nudged towards the median conception of subjectivity which I recommend in general. See David Simpson, *Irony and Authority in Romantic Poetry* (Totowa, NJ: Rowman and Littlefield, 1979).

28. Nancy K. Miller, *Subject to Change: Reading Feminist Writing* (Ithaca, NY: Cornell University Press, 1988), p. 106.

29. See, for example, Gayatri Chakravorty Spivak, 'Can the Subaltern Speak?', in *Colonial Discourse and Post-Colonial Theory: A Reader*, ed. and introduced by Patrick Williams and Laura Chrisman (Hemel Hempstead: Harvester, 1993), pp. 66–111.

Part 1

The Aesthetic and Textual Debate

Section 1

Changing Conceptions of Authorship

Changing Conceptions of Authorship

The oldest conceptions of authorship view literature as either an imitative or an inspirational discourse. The inspirational tradition can be retraced at least as far back as the practices of the South American shamans whose psychic voyages mediated between the spiritual and material worlds. In a similar vein, Hellenic culture saw the origins of poetry in the Muse to whom the poet was merely messenger, avatar or mouthpiece. The inspirational source of literature has maintained a strong hold upon thought partly because it accords with the stated experience of writers themselves who have felt moved by a remote or otherworldly power to compose discourses of which they had no prior conception. Such a view of discourse at once elevates the poet or author as an elect figure – set apart from the rest of humanity via the gift of a divine afflatus – but deprives the author of the role of originating force. In the nineteenth and twentieth centuries, this notion of alterity or 'otherness' has persisted but in a manner often transplanted from its sacred or idealist sources. While aspects of romantic and symbolist thought have attempted to preserve this hieratic view of poetic origins, twentieth-century theory has relocated the source of otherness in the unconscious or language itself.

The imitative model generally sees the artist as a copyist of reality but also can refer to the author's place within a literary tradition. Imitation in classical thought was broadly conceived according to these two basic modalities. Plato and Aristotle advanced theories of mimesis: the former negatively in terms of the artist copying a natural world which was itself a copy of the higher realm of Ideas; the latter positively as a representation of a significant action. In either case, the mimetic picture accords very little significance to authorial inventiveness. On this view, the author renders reality objectively as an entirely receptive subject through whom impersonal truth is registered. A similar ethos has been affirmed in traditional Marxist criticism of the Lukácsian variety wherein it is not the responsibility of the author to represent his or her inner feelings but to allow the truth of a historical moment to unfold within the text.

The second way in which imitation was registered related to pre-established systems, rules or conventions of the kind which Aristotle's *Poetics* laid down for poets and tragedians. Within a technical description of the literary work, the author becomes an adept within the tradition rather than the elect of an inspirational calling. Medieval views of the artist as a copyist working within long-established conventions also reflect this designation of the authorial role, as do Russian Formalist notions of the author as craftsperson and the Structuralist picture of the writer as an impersonal assembler and arranger of literary codes.

The tension between the imitative and inspirational can be discerned in Plato's seemingly antithetical statements on poetry. In *The Republic*, Plato takes up the imitative model but does so to argue for the banishment of poets from his ideal city-state. Plato views literature as both morally and epistemologically defective in its attempt to represent the world given to the senses which is itself only a shadowy reflection of the Eternal Forms. On the other hand, in *Ion* he seems to bestow upon poetic discourse a semi-divine status. In this early dialogue, Plato tells the eponymous rhapsode (reciter of poetry) that a divine power strips the poet of any conscious or rational faculty so as to declaim its own script through the passive agency of the chosen individual. Many commentators have suggested that the Socratic speech is intended as ironic, and certainly it needs to be contextualised in terms of the perceived loss of balance in the late Periclean Age between intellect and emotion. If the speech is heard with an ear for irony, it says little to contradict Plato's banishment of poets from a republic which was to be established on purely rational grounds: the argument of *Ion* that poets do not achieve true knowledge but are fleetingly inspired to mystic vision is itself central to *The Republic*'s exclusion of the poets from its rationally controlled society. Until recent times, however, it has been the literal rather than the ironic reading of *Ion* which has proved the most influential: Sidney and Shelley seem to take the Socratic claim at face value, while from the Renaissance onwards celebrations of poetic irrationality have invoked *Ion* as a literal precedent. The exuberant reading was also assisted by the second-century BC writer known as 'Longinus' who believed that a quasi-divine poetic frenzy opened the poet's soul to the sublime.

The reservations which Plato expresses about poetry stem in part from his conviction that the higher truth of the Forms is only attainable through disinterested rational enquiry. The realm of truth Plato believed to be autonomous, independent of human agency and quite distinct from the frenzies of poetic inspiration which substitute temporary aesthetic pleasure for the arduous acquisition of philosophical knowledge. Plato thus sharply demarcated between the modes of philosophical and literary authorship so as to banish the latter in favour of the former. Within an emergent Christian culture, however, the notion of inspiration was reconciled with that of autonomous truth via the notion of *auctoritas* or authority derived from God. Inspiration thus shed its Bacchic and irrationalist connotations to be seen as the direct revelation of Scriptural truth from God to the Evangelists through to the Church Fathers who assembled the Biblical canon. The Scriptural authors or *auctores* were thus granted the charisma of divinely-revealed truth which at the same time prescribed against any sense of individual originality.

A. J. Minnis's *Medieval Theory of Authorship* analyses the influence of Early Church theology on the textual theory of scholars in the late Middle Ages for whom the name of the author designated less an empirical self than a seal of religious authority. Minnis traces the tension between a growth of interest in the human *auctores* and the theological tenet that since God is the author of life the personality of the human author of Scripture should properly be a matter of indifference. Minnis provides compelling evidence against the assumption that the author is a relatively modern category of thought and locates its emergence in the thirteenth-century shift from an allegorical to a literal interpretation of the Bible. Where the allegorical (i.e. divinely-authored) view admitted of no literary or theoretical description, the shift to a literal (i.e. humanly-authored) exegesis focused attention on the moral and literary status of the individual author. Intriguingly, where contemporary thought has seen the author as a theoretical obstacle, Minnis demonstrates that only through the question of authorship did the Medieval age develop a sophisticated theory of the text.

Though Sir Philip Sidney in his 'An Apology for Poetry' (also known as 'The Defence of Poesy') insists that he 'speak[s] of the art, and not of the artificer', his essay clearly reflects both the influence of Renaissance humanism and the emergence of the human author which Minnis traces back to the thirteenth century. Indeed, Sidney's claim that the psalms of David are poetry – thus making the Scriptural author in some sense a poet – clearly marks Renaissance ideas of authorship not as a break with but as development from the late-Medieval humanisation of authorial roles. Sidney's essay is composed in dialogue with his more puritanical contemporaries and in particular with the writer and clergyman Stephen Gosson. The prime antagonism of the work, though, is with Plato's banishment of the poets in *The Republic*. In assigning the greater didactic worth to poetry over philosophy and history, Sidney invokes Aristotle so as to trump Plato's central objection to literature. He also reads Socrates' eulogisation of poetry in literal contradiction with the *Republic*'s gesture of exclusion. Sidney himself distinguishes his own view of poetry from the inspirational model while making the most profound claims for poetry in moral, supra-mimetic and didactic terms. Coming too late for a strictly theological account of poetic origins and too early for the opening of creative imagination, Sidney's text is understandably silent on the origins of this sublime poetic authority.

While Edward Young's monograph 'Conjectures on Original Composition' is often seen as an aberration within mid-eighteenth-century aesthetics, it culminates a neo-Longinian emphasis on poetic genius which ran almost subterraneanly through the neo-Classical age. Young's essay overtly constructs itself against the neo-Classical emphasis on imitation understood in both mimetic and technical terms. Seeking to preserve the former while completely evacuating the latter, Young contended that contemporary classics could only be achieved through the negation or transcendence of technical models: in this sense, his work powerfully prefigures the insistent and often anxious romantic will towards poetic precedence. In the 'Conjectures', Young proceeds more though a series of striking and slippery metaphors than by strict argument, but he does attempt to make account of the source of poetic genius. For Young, genius works at a level below consciousness and derives from the 'stranger within', a kind of 'inner God' who dictates to the imagination from a darkling region of the poetic self. Young thus begins the movement towards locating the inspirational impulse in a subjective rather than theological construction of the self. At the same time, he distantly prefigures the tenebrous interiorities of Freud and Jung, who were – respectively – to explain creativity as emanating from a libidinal unconscious and shadow self.

In his classic work 'A Defence of Poetry', Percy Bysshe Shelley reconciles the inspirational explanation of poetic genesis with the newly-emerged category of the creative imagination. Rather than see inspiration in conflict with the originality of the work, Shelley affirmed a model of the poetic self generous enough to bound not only that which is given to it in consciousness but also those intuitions which arise unbidden from the unconscious. A retort in the first instance to Thomas Love Peacock's witty attack on the Lake Poets in his 'Four Ages of Poetry', Shelley's essay recalls Plato's *Ion* and echoes the defence made by Sidney in more than title. Like Sidney, Shelley accords the highest didactic worth to poetry, but diverges radically in asserting that this worth is independent of any external authority and derives from the fecundity of the creative imagination itself. Indeed, so far does Shelley extend the demesne of imagination that he subsumes even the cognitive under the sign of the poetic, thus decisively reversing Plato's privileging of the philosopher over the poet. Indeed, 'poet' in Shelley's 'Defence' is to be read not in conventional terms but as denoting a privileged class of authors to which belong visual artists, seers and legislators whose imaginative vision soars above the confines of the episteme. Shelley's justly famous closing sentence dramatically registers the status newly conferred upon poetic imagination and reflects the disappearance of patronage: so far from being subordinated to monarchical will, the poet is now lauded as the constructive force in the political as well as the aesthetic realm.

In 'Crisis in Verse', the French symbolist poet and critic, Stephane Mallarmé, affirms the sacred and idealist view of poetic alterity while pointing to its twentieth-century theorisation. Defining the poetic function in terms of the separation rather than union of author and work, Mallarmé refuses to locate poetic origins in either imagination or the poetic unconscious, but rather attributes the austere beauty of the ideal work to the word itself understood as a pure and hollow logos. Mallarmé thus affirms a negative logocentrism by equating the word with a mysterious and thrilling absence or nothingness. For this reason, Mallarmé's influence has been as divergent as it is potent in the twentieth century. On the one hand, his work has been admired by idealist aestheticians concerned to distance poetry from the material referent; on the other, Mallarmé's adumbrations of intertextuality, the disappearance of the author and the generative power of language itself have made him the elect precursor of French theories of *écriture*.

The psychoanalytic theories of Sigmund Freud provided the twentieth century with its dominant mode and metaphor for negotiating the idea of literature as constituted through radical alterity. Hitherto registered outside the author in theological or inspirational terms, or somewhat nebulously as the expression of an 'inner voice', Freud affirmed that the voice of the other is that of an individual unconscious built from buried childhood memories and repressed drives of a sexual and destructive nature. Representing the darkest font discovered in modernity's will towards interiority, Freud's theory also wished to restore conscious control through its aim that 'where id was, there ego shall be'. The influence of Freudian theory has, however, been less in this messianic attempt to restore the disengaged reason of the Enlightenment subject than in its diagnosis of the chthonic forces that seem to make any such return inconceivable.

'Creative Writers and Daydreaming' sees Freud attempting to link his theory of human behaviour to literary creation. For Freud, writing can be psychoanalytically perceived as an adult renegotiation of the childhood urge to discharge socially unacceptable wishes in the form of fantasy. Such a view of literary origins leads to a curious paradigm in terms of critical practice. At once heavily biographicist, Freud's theory is yet anti-intentionalist since the details of an author's life are used to turn the text against the grain of authorial purpose (read as aesthetically analogous to the repressive mechanism in general). Though by no means anti-authorial in Freud's formulation, his theory of the unconscious has been revised in linguistic terms by subsequent psychoanalysts such as Jacques Lacan and used in this textualist version to promote pivotal arguments against the involvement of the authorial psyche in the reading of literature.

SUGGESTED FURTHER READINGS

Abrams, M. H., *The Mirror and the Lamp: Romantic Theory and the Critical Tradition* (London: Oxford University Press, 1953).

Auerbach, Erich, *Mimesis: The Representation of Reality in Western Literature* (Princeton, NJ: Princeton University Press, 1953).

Bakhtin, Mikhail, *Problems of Dostoyevsky's Poetics* (Ann Arbor, MI: University of Michigan Press, 1973).

Battersby, Christine, *Gender and Genius: Towards a Feminist Aesthetics* (London: The Women's Press, 1989).

Coleridge, Samuel Taylor, *Biographia Literaria*, ed. James Engell and W. Jackson Bate (Princeton, NJ: Princeton University Press, 1983).

Collins, A. S., *Authorship in the Days of Johnson* (New York: Dutton, 1929).

Duff, William, *An Essay on Original Genius* (Gainsville, FL: Scholars' Facsimiles, 1964).

Geertz, Clifford, *Works and Lives: The Anthropologist as Author* (Cambridge: Polity Press, 1988).

Johnson, Samuel, *Lives of the English Poets*, 2 vols (London, 1952).

Miller, Karl, *Authors* (Oxford: Clarendon Press, 1989).

Nitzsche, Jane Chance, *The Genius Figure in Antiquity and the Middle Ages* (New York: Columbia University Press, 1975).

Quaint, David, *Origin and Originality in Renaissance Literature* (New Haven, CT: Yale University Press, 1983).

Rose, Mark, *Authors and Owners* (Cambridge, MA: Harvard University Press, 1993).

Simpson, David, *Irony and Authority in Romantic Poetry* (Totowa, NY: Rowman and Littlefeld, 1979).

—— *The Origins of Modern Critical Thought* (Cambridge and New York: Cambridge University Press, 1988).

Taylor, Charles, *Sources of the Self: The Making of the Modern Identity* (Cambridge: Cambridge University Press, 1989).

Vasari, Giorgio, *The Lives of the Artists* (Harmondsworth: Penguin, 1965).

1

PLATO

from *Ion*

. . .

SOCRATES: We may therefore generalize, and say: When several persons are discussing a given subject, the man who can distinguish the one who is talking well on it, and the one who is talking badly, will always be the same. Or, if he does not recognize the one who is talking badly, then, clearly, neither will he recognize the one who is talking well, granted that the subject is the same.

ION: That is so.

SOCRATES: Then the same man will be skilled with respect to both?

ION: Yes.

SOCRATES: Now you assert that Homer and the other poets, among them Hesiod and Archilochus, all treat of the same subjects, yet not all in the same fashion, but the one speaks well, and the rest of them speak worse.

ION: And what I say is true.

SOCRATES: Then you, if you can recognize the poet who speaks well, could also recognize the poets who speak worse, and see that they speak worse.

ION: So it seems.

SOCRATES: Well then, my best of friends, when we say that Ion has equal skill in Homer and all other poets, we shall not be mistaken. It must be so, since you yourself admit that the same man will be competent to judge of all who speak of the same matters, and that the poets virtually all deal with the same subjects.

ION: Then what can be the reason, Socrates, for my behavior?

When anyone discusses any other poet, I pay no attention, and can offer no remark of any value. I frankly doze. But whenever anyone mentions Homer, immediately I am awake, attentive, and full of things to say.

SOCRATES: The riddle is not hard to solve, my friend. No, it is plain to everyone that not from art and knowledge comes your power to speak concerning Homer. If it were art that gave you power, then you could speak about all the other poets as well. There is an art of poetry as a whole? Am I not right?

ION: Yes.

SOCRATES: And is not the case the same with any other art you please, when you take it as a whole? The same method of inquiry holds for all the arts? Do you want some explanation, Ion, of what I mean by that?

ION: Yes, Socrates, upon my word I do. It gives me joy to listen to you wise men.

SOCRATES: I only wish you were right in saying that, Ion. But 'wise men'! That means you, the rhapsodists and actors, and the men whose poems you chant, while I have nothing else to tell besides the truth, after the fashion of the ordinary man. For example, take the question I just now asked you. Observe what a trivial and commonplace remark it was that I uttered, something anyone might know, when I said that the inquiry is the same whenever one takes an art in its entirety. Let us reason the matter out. There is an art of painting taken as a whole?

ION: Yes.

SOCRATES: And there are and have been many painters, good and bad?

ION: Yes indeed.

SOCRATES: Now, take Polygnotus, son of Aglaophon. Have you ever seen a man with the skill to point out what is good and what is not in the works of Polygnotus, but without the power to do so in the works of other painters? A man who, when anybody shows the works of other painters, dozes off, is at a loss, has nothing to suggest, but when he has to express a judgement on one particular painter, say Polygnotus or anyone else you choose, wakes up, and is attentive, and is full of things to say?

ION: No, on my oath, I never saw the like.

SOCRATES: Or, again, take sculpture. Have you ever seen a man with the skill to judge the finer works of Daedalus, son of Metion, or of Epeus, son of Panopeus, or of Theodorus of Samos, or the works of any other single sculptor, but, confronted by the works of other sculptors, is at a loss, and dozes off, without a thing to say?

ION: No, on my oath, I never saw one.

SOCRATES: Yet further, as I think, the same is true of playing on the flute, and on the harp, and singing to the harp, and rhapsody. You never saw a man with the skill to judge of Olympus, of Thamyras, or of Orpheus, or of Phemius, the rhapsodist at Ithaca, but is at a loss, has no remark to make concerning Ion the Ephesian, and his success or failure in reciting.

ION: On that I cannot contradict you, Socrates. But of this thing I am conscious, that I excel all men in speaking about Homer, and on him have much to say, and that everybody else avers I do it well, but on the other poets I do not. Well then, see what that means.

SOCRATES: I do see, Ion, and in fact will proceed to show you what to my mind it betokens. As I just now said, this gift you have of speaking well on Homer is not an art; it is a power divine, impelling you like the power in the stone Euripides called the magnet, which most call 'stone of Heraclea.' This stone does not simply attract the iron rings, just by themselves; it also imparts to the rings a force enabling them to do the same thing as the stone itself, that is, to attract another ring, so that sometimes a chain is formed, quite a long one, of iron rings, suspended from one another. For all of them, however, their power depends upon that loadstone. Just so the Muse. She first makes men inspired, and then through these inspired ones others share in the enthusiasm, and a chain is formed, for the epic poets, all the good ones, have their excellence, not from art, but are inspired, possessed, and thus they utter all these admirable poems. So is it also with the good lyric poets; as the worshiping Corybantes are not in their senses when they dance, so the lyric poets are not in their senses when they make these lovely lyric poems. No, when once they launch into harmony and rhythm, they are seized with the Bacchic transport, and are possessed – as the bacchants, when possessed, draw milk and honey from the rivers, but not when in their senses. So the spirit of the lyric poet works, according to their own report. For the poets tell us, don't they, that the melodies they bring us are gathered from rills that run with honey, out of glens and gardens of the Muses, and they bring them as the bees do honey, flying like the bees? And what they say is true, for a poet is a light and winged thing, and holy, and never able to compose until he has become inspired, and is beside himself, and reason is no longer in him. So long as he has this in his possession, no man is able to make poetry or to chant in prophecy. Therefore, since their making is not by art, when they utter many things and fine about the deeds of men, just as you do about Homer, but is by lot divine – therefore each is able to do well only that to which the Muse has impelled him – one to make dithyrambs, another panegyric odes, another choral songs, another epic poems, another iambs. In all the rest, each one of them is poor, for not by art do they utter these, but by power divine, since if it were by art that they knew how to treat one subject finely, they would know how to deal with all the others too. Herein lies the reason why the deity has bereft them of their senses, and uses them as ministers, along with soothsayers and godly seers; it is in order that we listeners may know that it is not they who utter these precious revelations while their mind is not within them, but that it is the god himself who speaks, and through them becomes articulate to us. The most convincing evidence of this statement is offered by Tynnichus of Chalcis. He never composed a single poem worth recalling, save the song of praise which everyone repeats, wellnigh the finest of all lyrical poems, and absolutely what he called it, an 'Invention of the Muses.' By this example above all, it seems to me, the god would show us, lest we doubt, that these lovely poems are not of man or human workmanship, but are divine and from the gods, and that the poets are nothing but interpreters of the gods, each one possessed by the divinity to whom he is in bondage. And to prove this, the deity on purpose sang the loveliest of all lyrics through the most miserable poet. Isn't it so, Ion? Don't you think that I am right?

ION: You are indeed, I vow! Socrates, your words in some way touch my very soul, and it does seem to me that by dispensation from above good poets convey to us these utterances of the gods.

SOCRATES: Well, and you rhapsodists, again, interpret the utterances of the poets?

ION: There also you are right.

SOCRATES: Accordingly, you are interpreters of interpreters?

ION: Undeniably.

SOCRATES: Wait now, Ion; tell me this. And answer frankly what I ask you. Suppose you are reciting epic poetry well, and thrill the spectators most deeply. You are chanting, say, the story of Odysseus as he leaped up to the dais, unmasked himself to the suitors, and poured the arrows out before his feet, or of Achilles rushing upon Hector, or one of the pitiful passages, about Andromache, or Hecuba, or Priam. When you chant these, are you in your senses? Or are you carried out of yourself, and does not your soul in an ecstasy conceive herself to be engaged in the actions you relate, whether they are in Ithaca, or Troy, or wherever the story puts them?

ION: How vivid, Socrates, you make your proof for me! I will tell you frankly that whenever I recite a tale of pity, my eyes are filled with tears, and when it is one of horror or dismay, my hair stands up on end with fear, and my heart goes leaping.

SOCRATES: Well now, Ion, what are we to say of a man like that? There he is, at a sacrifice or festival, got up in holiday attire, adorned with golden chaplets, and he weeps, though he has lost nothing of his finery. Or he recoils with fear, standing in the presence of more than twenty thousand friendly people, though nobody is stripping him or doing him damage. Shall we say that the man is in his senses?

ION: Never, Socrates, upon my word. That is strictly true.

SOCRATES: Now then, are you aware that you produce the same effects in most of the spectators too?

ION: Yes, indeed, I know it very well. As I look down at them from the stage above, I see them, every time, weeping, casting terrible glances, stricken with amazement at the deeds recounted. In fact, I have to give them very close attention, for if I set them weeping, I myself shall laugh when I get my money, but if they laugh, it is I who have to weep at losing it.

SOCRATES: Well, do you see that the spectator is the last of the rings I spoke of, which receive their force from one another by virtue of the loadstone? You, the rhapsodist and actor, are the middle ring, and the first one is the poet himself. But it is the deity who, through all the series, draws the spirit of men wherever he desires, transmitting the attractive force from one into another. And so, as from the loadstone, a mighty chain hangs down, of choric dancers, masters of the chorus, undermasters, obliquely fastened to the rings which are suspended from the Muse. One poet is suspended from one Muse, another from another; we call it being 'possessed,' but the fact is much the same, since he is *held*. And from these primary rings, the poets, others are in turn suspended, some attached to this one, some to that, and are filled with inspiration, some by Orpheus, others by Musaeus. But the majority are possessed and held by Homer, and Ion, you are one of these, and are possessed by Homer. And whenever anyone chants the work of any other poet, you fall asleep, and haven't a thing to say, but when anybody gives tongue to a strain of this one, you are awake at once, your spirit dances, and you have much to say, for not by art or science do you say of Homer what you say, but by dispensation from above and by divine possession. So the worshipping Corybantes have a lively feeling for that strain alone which is of the deity by whom they are possessed, and for that melody are well supplied with attitudes and utterances, and heed no others. And so it is with you, Ion. When anyone mentions Homer, you are ready, but about the other poets you are at a loss. You ask me why you are ready about Homer and not about the rest. Because it is not by art but by lot divine that you are eloquent in praise of Homer.

    . . .

2

PLATO

from *The Republic*

. . .

But we have not yet brought our chief accusation against it. Its power to corrupt, with rare exceptions, even the better sort is surely the chief cause for alarm.

How could it be otherwise, if it really does that?

Listen and reflect. I think you know that the very best of us, when we hear Homer or some other of the makers of tragedy imitating one of the heroes who is in grief, and is delivering a long tirade in his lamentations or chanting and beating his breast, feel pleasure, and abandon ourselves and accompany the representation with sympathy and eagerness, and we praise as an excellent poet the one who most strongly affects us in this way.

I do know it, of course.

But when in our own lives some affliction comes to us, you are also aware that we plume ourselves upon the opposite, on our ability to remain calm and endure, in the belief that this is the conduct of a man, and what we were praising in the theater that of a woman.

I do note that.

Do you think, then, said I, that this praise is rightfully bestowed when, contemplating a character that we would not accept but would be ashamed of in ourselves, we do not abominate it but take pleasure and approve?

No, by Zeus, he said, it does not seem reasonable.

Oh yes, said I, if you would consider it in this way.

In what way?

If you would reflect that the part of the soul that in the former case, in our own misfortunes, was forcibly restrained, and that has hungered for tears and a good cry and satisfaction, because it is its nature to desire these things, is the element in us that the poets satisfy and delight, and that the best element in our nature, since it has never been properly educated by reason or even by habit, then relaxes its guard over the plaintive part, inasmuch as this is contemplating the woes of others and it is no shame to it to praise and pity another who, claiming to be a good man, abandons himself to excess in his grief, but it thinks this vicarious pleasure is so much clear gain, and would not consent to forfeit it by disdaining the poem altogether. That is, I think, because few are capable of reflecting that what we enjoy in others will inevitably react upon ourselves. For after feeding fat the emotion of pity there, it is not easy to restrain it in our own sufferings.

Most true, he said.

Does not the same principle apply to the laughable, namely, that if in comic representations, or for that matter in private talk, you take intense pleasure in buffooneries that you would blush to practice yourself, and do not detest them as base, you are doing the same thing as in the case of the pathetic? For here again what your reason, for fear of the reputation of buffoonery, restrained in yourself when it fain would play the clown, you release in turn, and so, fostering its youthful impudence, let yourself go so far that often ere you are aware you become yourself a comedian in private.

Yes, indeed, he said.

And so in regard to the emotions of sex and anger, and all the appetites and pains and pleasures of the soul which we say accompany all our actions, the effect of poetic imitation is the same. For it waters and fosters these feelings when what we ought to do is to dry them up, and it establishes them as our rulers when they ought to be ruled, to the end that we may be better and happier men instead of worse and more miserable.

I cannot deny it, said he.

Then, Glaucon, said I, when you meet encomiasts of Homer who tell us that this poet has been the educator of Hellas, and that for the conduct and refinement of human life he is worthy of our study and devotion, and that we should order our entire lives by the guidance of this poet, we must love and salute them as doing the best they can, and concede to them that Homer is the most poetic of poets and the first of tragedians, but we must know the truth, that we can admit no poetry into our city save only hymns to the gods and the praises of good men.

For if you grant admission to the honeyed Muse in lyric or epic, pleasure and pain will be lords of your city instead of law and that which shall from time to time have approved itself to the general reason as the best.

Most true, he said.

Let us, then, conclude our return to the topic of poetry and our apology, and affirm that we really had good grounds then for dismissing her from our city, since such was her character. For reason constrained us. And let us further say to her, lest she condemn us for harshness and rusticity, that there is from of old a quarrel between philosophy and poetry. For such expressions as 'the yelping hound barking at her master and mighty in the idle babble of fools,' and 'the mob that masters those who are too wise for their own good,' and the subtle thinkers who reason that after all they are poor, and countless others are tokens of this ancient enmity. But nevertheless let it be declared that, if the mimetic and dulcet poetry can show any reason for her existence in a well-governed state, we would gladly admit her, since we ourselves are very conscious of her spell. But all the same it would be impious to betray what we believe to be the truth. Is not that so, friend? Do not you yourself feel her magic and especially when Homer is her interpreter?

Greatly.

Then may she not justly return from this exile after she has pleaded her defense, whether in lyric or other measure?

By all means.

And we would allow her advocates who are not poets but lovers of poetry to plead her cause in prose without meter, and show that she is not only delightful but beneficial to orderly government and all the life of man. And we shall listen benevolently, for it will be clear gain for us if it can be shown that she bestows not only pleasure but benefit.

How could we help being the gainers? said he.

But if not, my friend, even as men who have fallen in love, if they think that the love is not good for them, hard though it be, nevertheless refrain, so we, owing to the love of this kind of poetry inbred in us by our education in these fine polities of ours, will gladly have the best possible case made out for her goodness and truth, but so long as she is unable to make good her defense we shall chant over to ourselves as we listen to the reasons that we have given as a countercharm to her spell, to preserve us from slipping back into the childish loves of the multitude, for we have come to see that we must not take such poetry seriously as a serious thing that lays hold on truth, but that he who lends an ear to it must be on his guard fearing for the polity in his soul and must believe what we have said about poetry.

By all means, he said, I concur.

Yes, for great is the struggle, I said, dear Glaucon, a far greater contest than we think it, that determines whether a man prove good or bad, so that not the lure of honor or wealth or any office, no, nor of poetry either, should incite us to be careless of righteousness and all excellence.

I agree with you, he replied, in view of what we have set forth, and I think that anyone else would do so too.

. . .

3

A. J. MINNIS

'The Significance of the Medieval Theory of Authorship'

In recent years, in discussions of late-medieval literature, it has become fashionable to employ a number of critical terms which derive their meaning from modern, not medieval, literary theory.[1] This practice can to some extent be interpreted as a tacit admission of defeat. There are many major aspects of medieval texts which cannot be discussed adequately in the terminology and framework of those sources of medieval rhetoric and poetic which have to date enjoyed full scholarly attention. For example, the arts of preaching are very specialised, while the arts of poetry offer practical instruction in the use of tropes, figures and other poetic devices. Neither type of source has much to say about the usual preoccupations of literary theory, namely 'the principles of literature, its categories, criteria, and the like'.[2] Faced with such apparent limitations, naturally the scholar is inclined to adopt concepts from modern literary theory, concepts which have no historical validity as far as medieval literature is concerned. Is it not better to search again, in a different range of medieval writings, for a conceptual equipment which is at once historically valid and theoretically adequate?[3]

I suggest that such a range of writings is provided by the glosses and commentaries on the authoritative Latin writers, or *auctores*, studied in the schools and universities of the later Middle Ages (by which I mean the period extending roughly from 1100 to 1400). In particular, the prologues to these commentaries are valuable repositories of medieval theory of authorship, i.e. the literary theory centered on the concepts of *auctor* and *auctoritas*.

A medieval lecture-course on an *auctor* usually began with an introductory discourse in which the text would be considered as a whole, and an outline provided of those literary and doctrinal principles and criteria supposed to be appropriate to it. When the series of lectures was written down by pupils, or prepared for publication by the teacher himself, the opening lecture became the prologue to the commentary on the text. Thanks to the extensive research on the educational contexts of this textual explication carried out by such scholars as H. Marrou and P. Riché (for the late classical and early medieval periods) and P. Glorieux and M.-D. Chenu (for the later medieval period) I am able to concentrate on the way in which its terminology was developed by successive generations of medieval teachers into a precise and comprehensive 'critical idiom'. Thereby the academic prologue became an important vehicle for the advancement of literary theory relating to *auctores* and *auctoritas*.

It is possible to speak of 'theory' of authorship rather than 'theories' because of the high degree of consistency with which medieval scholars treated the subject and employed its characteristic vocabulary. This is hardly surprising in an age which was obsessed with classification, valuing the universal over the particular and the typical over the individual. Yet medieval theory of authorship was not homogeneous in the sense of being uncomplicated and narrowly monolithic: there was a rich abundance of kinds, degrees, properties and aspects of authorship to describe and relate to not one but several systems of classification. Neither was the theory static: it is best defined in terms of basic literary assumptions, approaches and methods of analysis which altered, sometimes considerably, over the centuries and were applied to many types of writing for many different purposes.

This book is not offered as a comprehensive 'history' of medieval theory of authorship. To attempt such a book would be premature in the present state of our knowledge. My aim has been to illuminate one area of the subject which has largely been ignored, namely the contribution made by several generations of schoolmen who, in the main, were connected with the schools and universities of late-medieval France and England. The Italian contribution is so singular and complex that it merits a study all of its own, and therefore I have confined myself to a brief mention of Petrarch and Boccaccio. Neither has an attempt been made to assess the extent to which the theory of authorship discussed below meets the demands of modern literary critics and theorists. Full historical description of the literary theory produced in the later Middle Ages naturally precedes the comparative analysis of medieval and modern literary theory.

The study of late medieval literary theory is still in its infancy. It is most unfortunate that research on it has been hindered by what I regard as an anachronistic and highly misleading notion, namely the distinction between twelfth-century 'humanism' and thirteenth-century 'scholasticism'. According to a common exposé, by the end of the twelfth century grammar had lost the battle of the seven liberal arts and Dame Logic held the field.[4] Rhetoric and poetic gave way to logic and dialectic; humanism retreated before scholasticism. Orléans, where the songs of the muses had been guarded zealously, became a law school. The pagan *Fasti* (by Ovid) was replaced by a blatantly Christian one, the *Ecclesiale* of Alexander of Villa Dei;[5] the study of grammar – and therefore of 'literature' – was generally impoverished. In such unfavourable conditions, literary theory died or at least went underground.

This view is untenable, as the evidence presented below will attest. It is impossible to square with, for example, the sophisticated literary analyses of texts – particularly Scriptural texts – produced by commentators of the thirteenth and fourteenth centuries. At a time when the study of grammar had moved a long way from explication of classical *auctores* to speculative analysis of the theoretical structures of language, theologians and Bible-scholars were elaborating a comprehensive and flexible interpretative model for the diverse literary styles and structures supposed to be present in sacred Scripture, and for the diverse roles or functions – both literary and moral – believed to be performed by the human *auctores* of the Bible.

Some recent writers have countered the facile distinction between twelfth-century humanism and thirteenth-century scholasticism with the suggestion that, in many major respects, thirteenth-century scholasticism was a natural growth out of twelfth-century scholasticism. Hence, Sir Richard Southern can speak of 'a process of accumulation and increasingly refined analysis of the deposit of the past' from the twelfth century into the thirteenth century.[6] The scholastic literary theory formulated in the thirteenth and fourteenth centuries is quite clearly a product of this process of accumulation and refinement. In the twelfth century, certain scholars – notably Peter Abelard and Gilbert of Poitiers – had in their Bible-commentaries applied the conventions and categories of secular literary theory to sacred literature. Later scholars built on this by, for example, producing an intricate framework for discussion of each and every 'form of literary treatment' (*forma tractandi*) found in Scripture.

Another consequence of the emphasis on accumulation and refinement is that the so-called 'School of Chartres' is not afforded undue
prominence on the twelfth-century intellectual landscape. The typical
rather than the supposedly unique qualities of this 'school' are emphasised in my chapter on 'Academic Prologues to *Auctores*'. Hence, the
standard techniques of Latin literary scholarship current in the twelfth
century can emerge clearly, as can, in subsequent chapters, the ways in
which these techniques were developed, adapted, and altered in later
centuries.

Chapters 2–4 are chronological, tracing the development of this
scholarship from the twelfth century to the fourteenth century, with
special reference to commentaries on the Bible. As the authoritative
text *par excellence*, the 'Book of Life' and the book of books, the Bible
was for medieval scholars the most difficult text to describe accurately
and adequately. Medieval theologians were eminently aware of both
the comparisons and the contrasts which could be made between the
Bible and secular texts. On the one hand, they stressed the unique
status of the Bible; on the other, they believed that the budding exegete
had to be trained in the liberal arts before he could begin to understand
the infinitely more complex 'sacred page'. Consequently, in theologians' prologues academic literary theory is at its most elaborate and
sophisticated.

The literary analysis in academic prologues was conducted in an
orderly fashion, each and every text being discussed under a series of
headings. The most popular series of headings employed in twelfth-
century commentaries on *auctores* was as follows: the title of the work,
the name of the author, the intention of the author, the material or
subject-matter of the work, its mode of literary procedure, its order or
arrangement, its usefulness, and the branch of learning to which it
belonged. This system of textual explication is discussed in Chapter 2
with illustrations from commentaries on classical *auctores*, especially
Ovid, and on the various books of the Bible, especially the Song of
Solomon and the Psalter.

In the early thirteenth century a different series of prologue-headings
came into use as a result of the new methods of thinking and techniques
of study which scholars derived from Aristotle. The 'Aristotelian
prologue' was based on the four major causes which, according to
Aristotle, governed all activity and change in the universe. Hence, the
auctor would be discussed as the 'efficient cause' or motivating agent of
the text, his materials would be discussed as the 'material cause', his

literary style and structure would be considered as twin aspects of the 'formal cause', while his ultimate end or objective in writing would be considered as the 'final cause'. In Chapters 3 and 4 this system of textual explication is illustrated with examples from major schoolmen of the thirteenth and fourteenth centuries, including Hugh of St Cher, Albert the Great, Alexander of Hales, Robert Kilwardby, Thomas Aquinas, Bonaventure, Giles of Rome, Henry of Ghent, Nicholas of Lyre, Nicholas Trevet, and Robert Holcot.

As applied in literary analysis, the 'four causes' may seem to us a contrived and highly artificial framework, but in the later Middle Ages they brought commentators considerably closer to their *auctores*. The *auctor* remained an authority, someone to be believed and imitated, but his human qualities began to receive more attention. This crucial development is writ large in the prologues to commentaries on the Bible. In twelfth-century exegesis, the primacy of allegorical interpretation had hindered the emergence of viable literary theory: God was believed to have inspired the human writers of Scripture in a way which defied literary description. Twelfth-century exegetes were interested in the *auctor* mainly as a source of authority. But in the thirteenth century, a new type of exegesis emerged, in which the focus had shifted from the divine *auctor* to the human *auctor* of Scripture. It became fashionable to emphasise the literal sense of the Bible, and the intention of the human *auctor* was believed to be expressed by the literal sense. As a result, the exegetes' interest in their texts became more literary.

Two of the most important concerns which this new interest produced are considered in detail, namely the commentators' preoccupation with authorial role and literary form. The concern with authorial role or function – sometimes termed the author's 'office' (*officium*) – is manifest by two facets of the author's individuality which the exegete sought to describe, his individual literary activity and his individual moral activity. For example, in the prologue to his commentary on Lamentations,[7] the Franciscan John Lathbury (whose Oxford regency must have occurred soon after 1350) pieced together a life-story of the sacred poet in which all his authorial roles are considered: Jeremiah was a prophet, writer, priest, virgin, and martyr. I have paid special attention to medieval depictions of King David in his many, and apparently contradictory, roles – *auctor* and adulterer, saint and sinner. On the other hand, the preoccupation with literary form is manifest by the two facets of a text's formal cause which the commentators were describing, namely form considered as style and form considered as structure.

The medieval theory of authorship presented in these chapters calls for a qualification of the commonly-held notion that scholasticism was not interested in art in general or poetry in particular. In fact, the influence of Aristotle, far from destroying academic literary theory, enabled it to acquire a new prestige. Such theory was not dead or even decadent, merely different, and this essential difference is the proper object of scholarly inquiry. Thirteenth-century schoolmen produced a critical vocabulary which enabled the literary features of Scriptural texts to be analysed thoroughly, and which encouraged the emergence in the fourteenth century of a more liberal attitude to classical poetry. Something of the new status which had been afforded to Scriptural poetry in particular and to the poetic and rhetorical modes employed throughout Scripture in general, seems to have 'rubbed off' on secular poetry. Scriptural *auctores* were being read literally, with close attention being paid to those poetic methods believed to be part of the literal sense; pagan poets were being read allegorically or 'moralised' – and thus the twain could meet.

Scholastic idioms of literary theory, which received their fullest development at the hands of theologians, became widely disseminated, appearing in works written both in Latin and in the European vernaculars. They influenced the attitudes which many major writers – including Petrarch, Boccaccio, Chaucer and Gower – had towards the moral and aesthetic value of their creativity, the literary roles and forms they had adopted, and the ultimate functions which they envisaged their works as performing.

This is illustrated in the final chapter, entitled 'Literary Theory and Literary Practice', which concentrates on the ways in which two practising poets of fourteenth-century England, Chaucer and Gower, exploited a few aspects of the vast corpus of literary theory indicated in the previous chapters. Then, in a short Epilogue, by way of contrast we turn to attitudes concerning authorship which are associated with the Italian Renaissance. Certain aspects of the literary theory advocated by Petrarch and Boccaccio can be regarded as imaginative extensions of ideas which had developed in scholastic literary theory. Yet along with these continuities there are new beginnings. The *auctor* is becoming the reader's respected friend.

The tacit assumption behind all these chapters is that medieval theory of authorship provides us moderns with a window on the medieval world of books. To our gaze this window may seem small and its glass unclear and distorting, but these, after all, are characteristic features of a medieval window, indications that it is genuine and historically right.

Our standards must change if we are to appreciate what it has to offer. To make the same point in a different way, while we cannot re-·experience the past, we can recognise the integrity of past experience and apply the resultant information in evaluating our present experience of the past. In this process of recognition and application, knowledge of late medieval literary theory must play a crucial part: it will help us to understand how major writings of the same period entered into the culture of their time, and it will provide criteria for the acceptance or rejection of those modern concepts and terms which seem to have some bearing on medieval literature.

Of course, I am not suggesting that knowledge of late medieval literary theory is the unique key to definitive understanding of late medieval literature. Literature is not rigidly determined by the literary theory contemporaneous with it. To take the case of one extraordinary writer, Chaucer often reacted against the literary theory of his day, or exploited it in a very unusual way; sometimes his narrators talk like the schoolmaster Holofernes in Shakespeare's *Love's Labour Lost*, trotting out learned literary cliché which has little apparent relevance to the matter in hand. My point is rather that the strangeness (what some would call the 'alterity') of late medieval literary theory will to some extent free us from that 'blind modernism' which obscures our view of the past.[8] We cannot understand how Chaucer exploited or reacted against the literary theory of his day until we understand what that literary theory was; his extensive 'defamiliarization' (notably of literary convention and of genre) cannot be appreciated until we know what was normal to him and what was not.[9] How valuable would be Holofernes' reading of Shakespeare? At the very least, it would provide a register with which to measure Shakespeare's originality. More optimistically, it would focus attention on those areas of literary discourse important to him as a man of his age, and illuminate the categories and concepts which informed his thinking about literature in general and his own works in particular. If used with discretion, with what Matthew Arnold called 'tact', late medieval literary theory can serve as a stimulus and a corrective in modern speculation about authorial intention and audience expectancy in the late Middle Ages.

NOTES

1. Cf. P. Dronke, *Fabula: Explorations into the Uses of Myth in Medieval Platonism*, Mittellateinische Studien und Texte, ix (Leiden, 1974), p. 13.
2. R. Wellek and A. Warren, *Theory of Literature*, 3 ed. (Harmondsworth, 1963), p. 39. For this reason such treatises on the art of poetry as Geoffrey of Vinsauf's *Poetria Nova* and John of Garland's *Poetria Parisiana* fall outside the scope of this study – they represent a tradition of

'writing about writing' which is different in kind from the commentary-tradition discussed here. Arts of preaching are mentioned only to the extent that some of them contain literary theory derived from commentary-tradition.

3. Dronke, *Fabula*, p. 13.

4. The oft-repeated comments summarised here are conveniently brought together in the introduction to *Arnulfi Aurelianensis Glosule super Lucanum*, ed. B. Marti, Papers and Monographs of the American Academy in Rome, xviii (Rome, 1958).

5. This particular cliché has been refuted convincingly by L. R. Lind in the introduction to his edition of *The Ecclesiale of Alexander of Villa Dei* (Lawrence, Kansas, 1958), p. 3.

6. *Platonism, Scholastic Method, and the School of Chartres*, the 1979 Stenton Lecture (University of Reading, 1979). The work of R. H. and M. A. Rouse offers a similar conclusion: see especially their 'Florilegia and Latin Classical Authors in Twelfth- and Thirteenth-Century Orléans', *Viator*, x (1979), pp. 131–60.

7. *Lattehurius in threnos Ieremiae* (Oxford, 1482), unfol.

8. In a paper entitled 'Chaucer and Comparative Literary Theory' which I gave at the Second International Congress of the New Chaucer Society, I emphasised the 'alterity' or 'surprising otherness' of scholastic literary theory and advocated the comparative study of late medieval literary theory and modern literary theory. This usage of the term 'alterity' is derived from H. R. Jauss, who has defined the 'alterity' of medieval literature in terms of the essential differences between the world which it opens up and the world in which we live, the extent to which old texts make us aware of the 'otherness' of a departed past. See his *Alterität und Modernität der mittelalterlichen Literatur* (Munich, 1977), and 'The Alterity and Modernity of Medieval Literature', *New Literary History*, x (1979), pp. 385–90. Paul Zumthor defines 'blind modernism' as the unthinking imposition of modern principles of literature on medieval writings: 'Comments on H. R. Jauss's Article', *ibid.*, pp. 367–76 (p. 371).

9. For a succinct account of 'defamiliarization', which in a literary context involves deliberate deviation from the norms of writing and of audience expectancy, see R. H. Stacy, *Defamiliarization in Language and Literature* (Syracuse University Press, 1977).

4

SIR PHILIP SIDNEY

from *An Apology for Poetry*

. . .

Among the Romans a poet was called *vates*, which is as much as a diviner, foreseer, or prophet, as by his conjoined words *vaticinium* and *vaticinari* is manifest: so heavenly a title did that excellent people bestow upon this heart-ravishing knowledge. And so far were they carried into the admiration thereof, that they thought in the chanceable hitting upon any such verses great foretokens of their following fortunes were placed. Whereupon grew the word of *Sortes Virgilianae*, when by sudden opening Virgil's book they lighted upon any verse of his making as it is reported by many: whereof the Histories of the Emperors' Lives are full, as of Albinus, the governor of our island, who in his childhood met with this verse,

Arma amens capio nec sat rationis in armis;

and in his age performed it: which, although it were a very vain and godless superstition, as also it was to think that spirits were commanded by such verses – whereupon this word charms, derived of *carmina*, cometh – so yet serveth it to show the great reverence those wits were held in. And altogether not without ground, since both the oracles of Delphos and Sibylla's prophecies were wholly delivered in verses. For that same exquisite observing of number and measure in words, and that high flying liberty of conceit proper to the poet, did seem to have some divine force in it.

And may not I presume a little further, to show the reasonableness of this word *vates*, and say that the holy David's Psalms are a divine poem?

If I do, I shall not do it without the testimony of great learned men, both ancient and modern. But even the name psalms will speak for me, which being interpreted, is nothing but songs; then, that it is fully written in metre, as all learned hebricians agree, although the rules be not yet fully found; lastly and principally, his handling his prophecy, which is merely poetical. For what else is the awaking his musical instruments, the often and free changing of persons, his notable *prosopopeias*, when he maketh you, as it were, see God coming in His majesty, his telling of the beasts' joyfulness, and hills leaping, but a heavenly poesy, wherein almost he showeth himself a passionate lover of that unspeakable and everlasting beauty to be seen by the eyes of the mind, only cleared by faith? But truly now having named him, I fear me I seem to profane that holy name, applying it to Poetry, which is among us thrown down to so ridiculous an estimation. But they that with quiet judgements will look a little deeper into it, shall find the end and working of it such as, being rightly applied, deserveth not to be scourged out of the Church of God.

But now let us see how the Greeks named it, and how they deemed of it. The Greeks called him 'a poet', which name hath, as the most excellent, gone through other languages. It cometh of this word *poiein*, which is 'to make': wherein I know not whether by luck or wisdom, we Englishmen have met with the Greeks in calling him 'a maker': which name, how high and incomparable a title it is, I had rather were known by marking the scope of other sciences than by my partial allegation.

There is no art delivered to mankind that hath not the works of Nature for his principal object, without which they could not consist, and on which they so depend, as they become actors and players, as it were, of what Nature will have set forth. So doth the astronomer look upon the stars, and, by that he seeth, setteth down what order Nature hath taken therein. So do the geometrician and arithmetician in their diverse sorts of quantities. So doth the musician in times tell you which by nature agree, which not. The natural philosopher thereon hath his name, and the moral philosopher standeth upon the natural virtues, vices, and passions of man; and 'follow Nature' (saith he) 'therein, and thou shalt not err'. The lawyer saith what men have determined; the historian what men have done. The grammarian speaketh only of the rules of speech; and the rhetorician and logician, considering what in Nature will soonest prove and persuade, thereon give artificial rules, which still are compassed within the circle of a question according to the proposed matter. The physician weigheth the nature of a man's body, and the nature of things helpful or hurtful unto it. And the metaphysic, though it be in the second and abstract notions, and therefore be counted supernatural, yet doth he indeed build upon the depth of Nature.

Only the poet, disdaining to be tied to any such subjection, lifted up with the vigour of his own invention, doth grow in effect into another nature, in making things either better than Nature bringeth forth, or, quite anew, forms such as never were in Nature, as the Heroes, Demigods, Cyclops, Chimeras, Furies, and such like: so as he goeth hand in hand with Nature, not enclosed within the narrow warrant of her gifts, but freely ranging only within the zodiac of his own wit.

Nature never set forth the earth in so rich tapestry as divers poets have done; neither with pleasant rivers, fruitful trees, sweet-smelling flowers, nor whatsoever else may make the too much loved earth more lovely. Her world is brazen, the poets only deliver a golden.

. . .

The philosopher therefore and the historian are they which would win the goal, the one by precept, the other by example. But both, not having both, do both halt. For the philosopher, setting down with thorny argument the bare rule, is so hard of utterance and so misty to be conceived, that one that hath no other guide but him shall wade in him till he be old before he shall find sufficient cause to be honest. For his knowledge standeth so upon the abstract and general, that happy is that man who may understand him, and more happy that can apply what he doth understand. On the other side, the historian, wanting the precept, is so tied, not to what should be but to what is, to the particular truth of things and not to the general reason of things, that his example draweth no necessary consequence, and therefore a less fruitful doctrine.

Now doth the peerless poet perform both: for whatsoever the philosopher saith should be done, he giveth a perfect picture of it in some one by whom he presupposeth it was done, so as he coupleth the general notion with the particular example. A perfect picture I say, for he yieldeth to the powers of the mind an image of that whereof the philosopher bestoweth but a wordish description, which doth neither strike, pierce, nor possess the sight of the soul so much as that other doth.

. . .

Since then Poetry is of all human learning the most ancient and of most fatherly antiquity, as from whence other learnings have taken their beginnings; since it is so universal that no learned nation doth despise it, nor no barbarous nation is without it; since both Roman and Greek gave divine names unto it, the one of 'prophesying', the other of 'making', and that indeed that name of 'making' is fit for him, considering that whereas other arts retain themselves within their subject, and receive, as it were, their being from it, the poet only bringeth his own stuff, and doth not learn a conceit out of a matter, but maketh matter for a conceit; since neither his description nor his end containeth any evil, the thing described cannot be evil; since his effects be so good as to teach goodness and to delight the learners; since therein (namely in moral doctrine, the chief of all knowledges) he doth not only far pass the historian, but, for instructing, is well nigh comparable to the philosopher, and, for moving, leaves him behind him; since the Holy Scripture (wherein there is no uncleanness) hath whole parts in it poetical, and that even our Saviour Christ vouchsafed to use the flowers of it; since all his kinds are not only in their united forms but in their severed dissections fully commendable; I think (and think I rightly) the laurel crown appointed for triumphing captains doth worthily (of all other learnings) honour the poet's triumph.

. . .

Now then go we to the most important imputations laid to the poor poets. For aught I can yet learn, they are these. First, that there being many other more fruitful knowledges, a man might better spend his time in them than in this. Secondly, that it is the mother of lies. Thirdly, that it is the nurse of abuse, infecting us with many pestilent desires, with a siren's sweetness drawing the mind to the serpent's tale of sinful fancy – and herein, especially, comedies give the largest field to ear (as Chaucer saith); how both in other nations and in ours, before poets did soften us, we were full of courage, given to martial exercises, the pillars of manlike liberty, and not lulled asleep in shady idleness with poets' pastimes. And lastly, and chiefly, they cry out with an open mouth as if they outshot Robin Hood, that Plato banished them out of his commonwealth. Truly, this is much, if there be much truth in it.

. . .

But now indeed my burden is great; now Plato's name is laid upon me, whom, I must confess, of all philosophers I have ever esteemed most worthy of reverence, and with great reason: since of all philosophers he is the most poetical. Yet if he will defile the fountain out of which his flowing streams have proceeded, let us boldly examine with what reasons he did it. First, truly a man might maliciously object that Plato, being a philosopher, was a natural enemy of poets. For indeed, after the philosophers had picked out of the sweet mysteries of Poetry the right discerning true points of knowledge, they forthwith, putting it in method, and making a school-art of that which the poets did only teach by a divine delightfulness, beginning to spurn at their guides, like ungrateful prentices, were not content to set up shops for themselves, but sought by all means to discredit their masters; which by the force of delight being barred them, the less they could overthrow them, the more they hated them. For indeed, they found for Homer seven cities strave who should have him for their citizen; where many cities banished philosophers as not fit members to live among them. For only repeating certain of Euripides' verses, many Athenians had their lives saved of the Syracusans, when the Athenians themselves thought many philosophers unworthy to live. Certain poets, as Simonides and Pindar, had so prevailed with Hiero the First, that of a tyrant they made him a just king; where Plato could do so little with Dionysius, that he himself of a philosopher was made a slave. But who should do thus, I confess, should requite the objections made against poets with like cavillation against philosophers; as likewise one should do that should bid one read *Phaedrus* or *Symposium* in Plato, or the discourse of love in Plutarch, and see whether any poet do authorize abominable filthiness, as they do. Again, a man might ask out of what commonwealth Plato did banish them. In sooth, thence where he himself alloweth community of women. So as belike this banishment grew not for effeminate wantonness, since little should poetical sonnets be hurtful when a man might have what woman he listed. But I honour philosophical instructions, and bless the wits which bred them: so as they be not abused, which is likewise stretched to Poetry.

St Paul himself (who yet, for the credit of poets, allegeth twice two poets, and one of them by the name of a prophet), setteth a watchword upon Philosophy, – indeed upon the abuse. So doth Plato upon the abuse, not upon Poetry. Plato found fault that the poets of his time filled the world with wrong opinions of the gods, making light tales of that unspotted essence, and therefore would not have the youth depraved with such opinions. Herein may much be said; let this suffice: the poets did not induce such opinions, but did imitate those opinions already induced. For all the Greek stories can well testify that the very religion of that time stood upon many and many-fashioned gods, not taught so by the poets, but followed according to their nature of imitation. Who list may read in Plutarch the discourses of Isis and Osiris, of the cause why oracles ceased, of the divine providence, and see whether the theology of that nation stood not upon such dreams which the poets indeed superstitiously observed and truly (since they had not the light of Christ) did much better in it than the philosophers, who, shaking off superstition, brought in atheism. Plato therefore (whose authority I had much rather justly construe than unjustly resist) meant not in general of poets, in those words of which Julius Scaliger saith, *Qua authoritate barbari quidam atque hispidi abuti velint ad poetas e republica exigendos*; but only meant to drive out those wrong opinions of the Deity (whereof now, without further law, Christianity hath taken away all the hurtful belief), perchance (as he thought) nourished by the then esteemed poets. And a man need go no further than to Plato himself to know his meaning: who, in his dialogue called *Ion*, giveth high and rightly divine commendation to Poetry. So as Plato, banishing the abuse, not the thing – not banishing it, but giving due honour unto it – shall be our patron and not our adversary. For indeed I had much rather (since truly I may do it) show their mistaking of Plato (under whose lion's skin they would make an ass-like braying against Poesy) than go about to overthrow his authority; whom, the wiser a man is, the more just cause he shall find to have in admiration; especially since he attributeth unto Poesy more than myself do, namely, to be a very inspiring of a divine force, far above man's wit, as in the afore-named dialogue is apparent.

    . . .

5

EDWARD YOUNG

from 'Conjectures on Original Composition'

. . . The mind of a man of genius is a fertile and pleasant field, pleasant as Elysium, and fertile as Tempe; it enjoys a perpetual spring. Of that spring, originals are the fairest flowers: imitations are of quicker growth, but fainter bloom. Imitations are of two kinds: one of nature, one of authors. The first we call originals, and confine the term imitation to the second. I shall not enter into the curious inquiry of what is, or is not, strictly speaking, original, content with what all must allow, that some compositions are more so than others; and the more they are so, I say, the better. Originals are, and ought to be, great favourites, for they are great benefactors; they extend the republic of letters, and add a new province to its dominion. Imitators only give us a sort of duplicates of what we had, possibly much better, before; increasing the mere drug of books, while all that makes them valuable, knowledge and genius, are at a stand. The pen of an original writer, like Armida's wand, out of a barren waste calls a blooming spring. Out of that blooming spring an imitator is a transplanter of laurels, which sometimes die on removal, always languish in a foreign soil.

But suppose an imitator to be most excellent (and such there are), yet still he but nobly builds on another's foundation; his debt is, at least, equal to his glory; which, therefore, on the balance, cannot be very great. On the contrary, an original, though but indifferent (its originality being set aside), yet has something to boast; it is something to say with him in *Horace*,

Meo sum Pauper in aere;

and to share ambition with no less than Caesar, who declared he had rather be the first in a village than the second at Rome.

Still farther: an imitator shares his crown, if he has one, with the chosen object of his imitation; an original enjoys an undivided applause. An original may be said to be of a vegetable nature; it rises spontaneously from the vital root of genius; it grows, it is not made. Imitations are often a sort of manufacture wrought up by those mechanics, art and labour, out of pre-existent materials not their own.

Again: we read imitation with somewhat of his languor, who listens to a twice-told tale. Our spirits rouse at an original; that is a perfect stranger, and all throng to learn what news from a foreign land: and though it comes, like an Indian prince, adorned with feathers only, having little of weight; yet of our attention it will rob the more solid, if not equally new. Thus every telescope is lifted at a new-discovered star; it makes a hundred astronomers in a moment, and denies equal notice to the sun. But if an original, by being as excellent as new, adds admiration to surprise, then are we at the writer's mercy; on the strong wing of his imagination, we are snatched from Britain to Italy, from climate to climate, from pleasure to pleasure; we have no home, no thought, of our own; till the magician drops his pen. And then falling down into ourselves, we awake to flat realities, lamenting the change, like the beggar who dreamt himself a prince.

It is with thoughts as it is with words; and with both as with men; they may grow old and die. Words tarnished, by passing through the mouths of the vulgar, are laid aside as inelegant and obsolete. So thoughts, when become too common, should lose their currency; and we should send new metal to the mint, that is, new meaning to the press. The division of tongues at Babel did not more effectually debar men from making themselves a name (as the Scripture speaks), than the too great concurrence, or union of tongues will do for ever. We may as well grow good by another's virtue, or fat by another's food, as famous by another's thought. The world will pay its debt of praise but once; and instead of applauding, explode a second demand, as a cheat.

If it is said, that most of the Latin classics, and all the Greek, except, perhaps, Homer, Pindar, and Anacreon, are in the number of imitators, yet receive our highest applause; our answer is, That they, though not real, are accidental originals; the works they imitated, few excepted, are lost; they, on their father's decease, enter as lawful heirs, on their estates in fame. The fathers of our copyists are still in possession; and secured in it, in spite of Goths, and flames, by the perpetuating power of the Press. Very late must a modern imitator's fame arrive, if it waits for their decease.

An original enters early on reputation: Fame, fond of new glories, sounds her trumpet in triumph at its birth; and yet how few are awakened by it into the noble ambition of like attempts! Ambition is sometimes no vice in life; it is always a virtue in composition. High in the towering Alps is the fountain of the Po; high in fame and in antiquity is the fountain of an imitator's undertaking; but the river, and the imitation, humbly creep along the vale. So few are our originals, that, if all other books were to be burnt, the lettered world would resemble some metropolis in flames, where a few incombustible buildings, a fortress, temple, or tower, lift their heads, in melancholy grandeur, amid the mighty ruin. Compared with this conflagration, old Omar lighted up but a small bonfire, when he heated the baths of the barbarians, for eight months together, with the famed Alexandrian library's inestimable spoils, that no profane book might obstruct the triumphant progress of his holy Alcoran round the globe.

But why are originals so few? not because the writer's harvest is over, the great reapers of antiquity having left nothing to be gleaned after them; nor because the human mind's teeming time is past, or because it is incapable of putting forth unprecedented births; but because illustrious examples engross, prejudice, and intimidate. They engross our attention, and so prevent a due inspection of ourselves; they prejudice our judgement in favour of their abilities, and so lessen the sense of our own; and they intimidate us with the splendour of their renown, and thus under diffidence bury our strength. Nature's imposs-ibilities, and those of diffidence lie wide asunder.

Let it not be suspected, that I would weakly insinuate anything in favour of the moderns, as compared with ancient authors; no, I am lamenting their great inferiority. But I think it is no necessary inferiority; that it is not from divine destination, but from some cause far beneath the moon: I think that human souls, through all periods, are equal; that due care and exertion would set us nearer our immortal predecessors than we are at present; and he who questions and confutes this, will show abilities not a little tending towards a proof of that equality which he denies.

After all, the first ancients had no merit in being originals: they could not be imitators. Modern writers have a choice to make; and therefore have a merit in their power. They may soar in the regions of liberty, or move in the soft fetters of easy imitation; and imitation has as many plausible reasons to urge, as pleasure had to offer to Hercules. Hercules made the choice of an hero, and so became immortal.

Yet let not assertors of classic excellence imagine, that I deny the tribute it so well deserves. He that admires not ancient authors, betrays a secret he would conceal, and tells the world that he does not understand them. Let us be as far from neglecting, as from copying, their admirable compositions: sacred be their rights, and inviolable their fame. Let our understanding feed on theirs; they afford the noblest nourishment; but let them nourish, not annihilate, our own. When we read, let our imagination kindle at their charms; when we write, let our judgement shut them out of our thoughts; treat even Homer himself as his royal admirer was treated by the cynic; bid him stand aside, nor shade our composition from the beams of our own genius; for nothing original can rise, nothing immortal can ripen, in any other sun.

Must we then, you say, not imitate ancient authors? Imitate them by all means; but imitate aright. He that imitates the divine *Iliad* does not imitate Homer; but he who takes the same method, which Homer took, for arriving at a capacity of accomplishing a work so great. Tread in his steps to the sole fountain of immortality; drink where he drank, at the true Helicon, that is, at the breast of Nature: imitate; but imitate not the composition, but the man. For may not this paradox pass into a maxim? viz. 'The less we copy the renowned ancients, we shall resemble them the more.'

But possibly you may reply, that you must either imitate Homer, or depart from Nature. Not so: for suppose you was to change place, in time, with Homer; then, if you write naturally, you might as well charge Homer with an imitation of you. Can you be said to imitate Homer for writing so, as you would have written, if Homer had never been? As far as a regard to Nature, and sound sense, will permit a departure from your great predecessors; so far, ambitiously, depart from them; the farther from them in similitude, the nearer are you to them in excellence; you rise by it into an original; become a noble collateral, not an humble descendant from them. Let us build our compositions with the spirit, and in the taste, of the ancients; but not with their materials: thus will they resemble the structures of Pericles at Athens, which Plutarch commends for having had an air of antiquity as soon as they were built. All eminence, and distinction, lies out of the beaten road; excursion and deviation are necessary to find it; and the more remote your path from the highway, the more reputable; if, like poor Gulliver (of whom anon), you fall not into a ditch, in your way to glory.

What glory to come near, what glory to reach, what glory (presumptuous thought!) to surpass our predecessors! And is that then in Nature absolutely impossible? Or is it not, rather, contrary to Nature to fail in it? Nature herself sets the ladder, all wanting is our ambition to climb. For by the bounty of Nature we are as strong as our predecessors; and by the favour of time (which is but another round in Nature's scale) we stand on higher ground. As to the first, were they more than men? Or are we less? Are not our minds cast in the same mould with those before the flood? The flood affected matter; mind escaped. As to the second; though we are moderns, the world is an ancient; more ancient far, than when they, whom we most admire, filled it with their fame. Have we not their beauties, as stars, to guide; their defects, as rocks, to be shunned; the judgement of ages on both, as a chart to conduct, and a sure helm to steer us in our passage to greater perfection than theirs? And shall we be stopped in our rival pretensions to fame by this just reproof?

> *Stat contra, dicitque tibi tua pagina, fur es.*
> Mart.

It is by a sort of noble contagion, from a general familiarity with their writings, and not by any particular sordid theft, that we can be the better for those who went before us. Hope we, from plagiarism, any dominion in literature; as that of Rome arose from a nest of thieves?

Rome was a powerful ally to many states; ancient authors are our powerful allies; but we must take heed, that they do not succour till they enslave, after the manner of Rome. Too formidable an idea of their superiority, like a spectre, would fright us out of a proper use of our wits; and dwarf our understanding, by making a giant of theirs. Too great awe for them lays genius under restraint, and denies it that free scope, that full elbow-room, which is requisite for striking its most masterly strokes. Genius is a master-workman, learning is but an instrument; and an instrument, though most valuable, yet not always indispensable. Heaven will not admit of a partner in the accomplishment of some favourite spirits; but rejecting all human means, assumes the whole glory to itself. Have not some, though not famed for erudition, so written, as almost to persuade us, that they shone brighter, and soared higher, for escaping the boasted aid of that proud ally?

Nor is it strange; for what, for the most part, mean we by genius, but the power of accomplishing great things without the means generally reputed necessary to that end? A genius differs from a good under-standing, as a magician from a good architect: that raises his structure by means invisible; this by the skilful use of common tools. Hence genius has ever been supposed to partake of something divine. . . .

6

PERCY BYSSHE SHELLEY

from 'A Defence of Poetry'

. . .

It is difficult to define pleasure in its highest sense; the definition involving a number of apparent paradoxes. For, from an inexplicable defect of harmony in the constitution of human nature, the pain of the inferior is frequently connected with the pleasures of the superior portions of our being. Sorrow, terror, anguish, despair itself are often the chosen expressions of an approximation to the highest good. Our sympathy in tragic fiction depends on this principle; tragedy delights by affording a shadow of the pleasure which exists in pain. This is the source also of the melancholy which is inseparable from the sweetest melody. The pleasure that is in sorrow is sweeter than the pleasure of pleasure itself. And hence the saying, 'It is better to go to the house of mourning, than to the house of mirth.'[1] Not that this highest species of pleasure is necessarily linked with pain. The delight of love and friendship, the ecstasy of the admiration of nature, the joy of the perception and still more of the creation of poetry is often wholly unalloyed.

The production and assurance of pleasure in this highest sense is true utility. Those who produce and preserve this pleasure are Poets or poetical philosophers.

The exertions of Locke, Hume, Gibbon, Voltaire, Rousseau,[2] and their disciples, in favour of oppressed and deluded humanity, are entitled to the gratitude of mankind. Yet it is easy to calculate the degree of moral and intellectual improvement which the world would have exhibited, had they never lived. A little more nonsense would have been talked for a century or two; and perhaps a few more men, women, and children, burnt as heretics. We might not at this moment have been congratulating each other on the abolition of the Inquisition in Spain.[3] But it exceeds all imagination to conceive what would have been the moral condition of the world if neither Dante, Petrarch, Boccaccio, Chaucer, Shakespeare, Calderon, Lord Bacon, nor Milton, had ever existed; if Raphael and Michael Angelo had never been born; if the Hebrew poetry had never been translated; if a revival of the study of Greek literature had never taken place; if no monuments of ancient sculpture had been handed down to us; and if the poetry of the religion of the antient world had been extinguished together with its belief. The human mind could never, except by the intervention of these excitements, have been awakened to the invention of the grosser sciences, and that application of analytical reasoning to the aberrations of society, which it is now attempted to exalt over the direct expression of the inventive and creative faculty itself.

We have more moral, political and historical wisdom, than we know how to reduce into practice; we have more scientific and economical knowledge than can be accommodated to the just distribution of the produce which it multiplies. The poetry in these systems of thought, is concealed by the accumulation of facts and calculating processes. There is no want of knowledge respecting what is wisest and best in morals, government, and political economy, or at least, what is wiser and better than what men now practise and endure. But we let '*I dare not wait upon I would*, like the poor cat i' the adage.'[4] We want the creative faculty to imagine that which we know; we want the generous impulse to act that which we imagine; we want the poetry of life: our calculations have outrun conception; we have eaten more than we can digest. The cultivation of those sciences which have enlarged the limits of the empire of man over the external world, has, for want of the poetical faculty, proportionally circumscribed those of the internal world; and man, having enslaved the elements, remains himself a slave. To what but a cultivation of the mechanical arts in a degree disproportioned to the presence of the creative faculty, which is the basis of all knowledge, is to be attributed the abuse of all invention for abridging and combining labour, to the exasperation of the inequality of mankind? From what other cause has it arisen that these inventions which should have lightened, have added a weight to the curse imposed on Adam? Poetry, and the principle of Self, of which money is the visible incarnation, are the God and Mammon of the world.[5]

The functions of the poetical faculty are two-fold; by one it creates new materials of knowledge, and power and pleasure; by the other it engenders in the mind a desire to reproduce and arrange them according to a certain rhythm and order which may be called the beautiful and the good. The cultivation of poetry is never more to be desired than at periods when, from an excess of the selfish and calculating principle, the accumulation of the materials of external life exceed the quantity of the power of assimilating them to the internal laws of human nature. The body has then become too unwieldy for that which animates it.

Poetry is indeed something divine. It is at once the centre and circumference of knowledge; it is that which comprehends all science, and that to which all science must be referred. It is at the same time the root and blossom of all other systems of thought; it is that from which all spring, and that which adorns all; and that which, if blighted, denies the fruit and the seed, and withholds from the barren world the nourishment and the succession of the scions of the tree of life. It is the perfect and consummate surface and bloom of things; it is as the odour and the colour of the rose to the texture of the elements which compose it, as the form and the splendour of unfaded beauty to the secrets of anatomy and corruption. What were Virtue, Love, Patriotism, Friendship etc. – what were the scenery of this beautiful Universe which we inhabit – what were our consolations on this side of the grave – and what were our aspirations beyond it – if Poetry did not ascend to bring light and fire from those eternal regions where the owl-winged faculty of calculation dare not ever soar? Poetry is not like reasoning, a power to be exerted according to the determination of the will. A man cannot say, 'I will compose poetry.' The greatest poet even cannot say it: for the mind in creation is as a fading coal which some invisible influence, like an inconstant wind, awakens to transitory brightness: this power arises from within, like the colour of a flower which fades and changes as it is developed, and the conscious portions of our natures are unprophetic either of its approach or its departure.[6] Could this influence be durable in its original purity and force, it is impossible to predict the greatness of the results; but when composition begins, inspiration is already on the decline, and the most glorious poetry that has ever been communicated to the world is probably a feeble shadow of the original conception of the poet. I appeal to the greatest Poets of the present day, whether it be not an error to assert that the finest passages of poetry are produced by labour and study. The toil and the delay recommended by critics can be justly interpreted to mean no more than a careful observation of the inspired moments, and an artificial connexion of the spaces between their suggestions by the intertexture of conventional expressions; a necessity only imposed by the limitedness of the poetical faculty itself. For Milton conceived the Paradise Lost as a whole before he executed it in portions. We have his own authority also for the Muse having 'dictated' to him the 'unpremeditated song,'[7] and let this be an answer to those who would allege the fifty-six various readings of the first line of the Orlando Furioso.[8] Compositions so produced are to poetry what mosaic is to painting. This instinct and intuition of the poetical faculty is still more observable in the plastic and pictorial arts: a great statue or picture grows under the power of the artist as a child in the mother's womb; and the very mind which directs the hands in formation is incapable of accounting to itself for the origin, the gradations, or the media of the process.

Poetry is the record of the best and happiest[9] moments of the happiest and best minds. We are aware of evanescent visitations of thought and feeling sometimes associated with place or person, sometimes regarding our own mind alone, and always arising unforeseen and departing unbidden, but elevating and delightful beyond all expression: so that even in the desire and the regret they leave, there cannot but be pleasure, participating as it does in the nature of its object. It is as it were the interpenetration of a diviner nature through our own; but its footsteps are like those of a wind over a sea, where the coming calm erases, and whose traces remain only as on the wrinkled sand which paves it. These and corresponding conditions of being are experienced principally by those of the most delicate sensibility and the most enlarged imagination; and the state of mind produced by them is at war with every base desire. The enthusiasm of virtue, love, patriotism, and friendship is essentially linked with these emotions; and while they last, self appears as what it is, an atom to a Universe. Poets are not only subject to these experiences as spirits of the most refined organization, but they can colour all that they combine with the evanescent hues of this etherial world; a word, or a trait in the representation of a scene or a passion, will touch the enchanted chord, and reanimate, in those who have ever experienced these emotions, the sleeping, the cold, the buried image of the past. Poetry thus makes immortal all that is best and most beautiful in the world; it arrests the vanishing apparitions which haunt the interlunations[10] of life, and veiling them or in language or in form sends them forth among mankind, bearing sweet news of kindred joy to those with whom their sisters abide – abide, because there is no portal of expression from the caverns of the spirit which they inhabit into the universe of things. Poetry redeems from decay the visitations of the divinity in man.

Poetry turns all things to loveliness; it exalts the beauty of that which is most beautiful, and it adds beauty to that which is most deformed; it marries exultation and horror, grief and pleasure, eternity and change; it subdues to union under its light yoke all irreconcilable things. It transmutes all that it touches, and every form moving within the radiance of its presence is changed by wondrous sympathy to an incarnation of the spirit which it breathes; its secret alchemy turns to potable gold[11] the poisonous waters which flow from death through life; it strips the veil of familiarity from the world, and lays bare the naked and sleeping beauty which is the spirit of its forms.

All things exist as they are perceived: at least in relation to the percipient. 'The mind is its own place, and of itself can make a heaven of hell, a hell of heaven.'[12] But poetry defeats the curse which binds us to be subjected to the accident of surrounding impressions. And whether it spreads its own figured curtain or withdraws life's dark veil from before the scene of things, it equally creates for us a being within our being. It makes us the inhabitants of a world to which the familiar world is a chaos. It reproduces the common universe of which we are portions and percipients, and it purges from our inward sight the film of familiarity which obscures from us the wonder of our being. It compels us to feel that which we perceive, and to imagine that which we know. It creates anew the universe after it has been annihilated in our minds by the recurrence of impressions blunted by reiteration.[13] It justifies that bold and true word of Tasso: *Non merita nome di creatore, se non Iddio ed il Poeta.*[14]

A Poet, as he is the author to others of the highest wisdom, pleasure, virtue and glory, so he ought personally to be the happiest, the best, the wisest, and the most illustrious of men. As to his glory, let Time be challenged to declare whether the fame of any other institutor of human life be comparable to that of a poet. That he is the wisest, the happiest, and the best, inasmuch as he is a poet, is equally incontrovertible: the greatest poets have been men of the most spotless virtue, of the most consummate prudence, and, if we could look into the interior of their lives, the most fortunate of men: and the exceptions, as they regard those who possessed the poetic faculty in a high yet inferior degree, will be found on consideration to confirm rather than destroy the rule. Let us for a moment stoop to the arbitration of popular breath, and usurping and uniting in our own persons the incompatible characters of accuser, witness, judge and executioner, let us decide without trial, testimony, or form that certain motives of those who are 'there sitting where we dare not soar'[15] are reprehensible. Let us assume that Homer was a drunkard, that Virgil was a flatterer, that Horace was a coward, that Tasso was a madman, that Lord Bacon was a peculator, that Raphael was a libertine, that Spenser was a poet laureate.[16] It is inconsistent with this division of our subject to cite living poets, but Posterity has done ample justice to the great names now referred to. Their errors have been weighed and found to have been dust in the balance; if their sins 'were as scarlet, they are now white as snow';[17] they have been washed in the blood of the mediator and the redeemer Time. Observe in what a ludicrous chaos the imputations of real or fictitious crime have been confused in the contemporary calumnies against poetry and poets;[18] consider how little is, as it appears – or appears, as it is; look to your own motives, and judge not, lest ye be judged.

Poetry, as has been said, in this respect differs from logic, that it is not subject to the controul of the active powers of the mind, and that its birth and recurrence has no necessary connexion with consciousness or will. It is presumptuous to determine that these[19] are the necessary conditions of all mental causation, when mental effects are experienced insusceptible of being referred to them. The frequent recurrence of the poetical power, it is obvious to suppose, may produce in the mind an habit of order and harmony correlative with its own nature and with its effects upon other minds. But in the intervals of inspiration, and they may be frequent without being durable, a poet becomes a man, and is abandoned to the sudden reflux of the influences under which others habitually live. But as he is more delicately organized than other men, and sensible to pain and pleasure, both his own and that of others, in a degree unknown to them, he will avoid the one and pursue the other with an ardour proportioned to this difference. And he renders himself obnoxious to calumny,[20] when he neglects to observe the circumstances under which these objects of universal pursuit and flight have disguised themselves in one another's garments.

But there is nothing necessarily evil in this error, and thus cruelty, envy, revenge, avarice, and the passions purely evil, have never formed any portion of the popular imputations on the lives of poets.

I have thought it most favourable to the cause of truth to set down these remarks according to the order in which they were suggested to my mind, by a consideration of the subject itself, instead of following that of the treatise that excited me to make them public.[21] Thus although devoid of the formality of a polemical reply; if the view they contain be just, they will be found to involve a refutation of the doctrines of the Four Ages of Poetry, so far at least as regards the first division of the subject. I can readily conjecture what should have moved the gall of the learned and intelligent author of that paper; I confess myself, like him, unwilling to be stunned by the Theseids of the hoarse Codri of the day. Bavius and Mævius[22] undoubtedly are, as they ever were, insufferable persons. But it belongs to a philosophical critic to distinguish rather than confound.

The first part of these remarks has related to Poetry in its elements and principles; and it has been shewn, as well as the narrow limits assigned them would permit, that what is called poetry, in a restricted sense, has a common source with all other forms of order and of beauty according to which the materials of human life are susceptible of being arranged, and which is poetry in an universal sense.

The second part[23] will have for its object an application of these principles to the present state of the cultivation of Poetry, and a defence of the attempt to idealize the modern forms of manners and opinions, and compel them into a subordination to the imaginative and creative faculty. For the literature of England, an energetic developement of which has ever preceded or accompanied a great and free developement of the national will, has arisen as it were from a new birth. In spite of the low-thoughted envy which would undervalue contemporary merit, our own will be a memorable age in intellectual achievements, and we live among such philosophers and poets as surpass beyond comparison any who have appeared since the last national struggle for civil and religious liberty.[24] The most unfailing herald, companion, and follower of the awakening of a great people to work a beneficial change in opinion or institution, is Poetry. At such periods there is an accumulation of the power of communicating and receiving intense and impassioned conceptions respecting man and nature. The persons in whom this power resides, may often, as far as regards many portions of their nature, have little apparent correspondence with that spirit of good of which they are the ministers. But even while they deny and abjure, they are yet compelled to serve, the Power which is seated upon the throne of their own soul. It is impossible to read the compositions of the most celebrated writers of the present day without being startled with the electric life which burns within their words. They measure the circumference and sound the depths of human nature with a comprehensive and all-penetrating spirit, and they are themselves perhaps the most sincerely astonished at its manifestations, for it is less their spirit than the spirit of the age.[25] Poets are the hierophants[26] of an unapprehended inspiration, the mirrors of the gigantic shadows which futurity casts upon the present, the words which express what they understand not; the trumpets which sing to battle, and feel not what they inspire: the influence which is moved not, but moves.[27] Poets are the unacknowledged legislators of the World.

NOTES

1. Ecclesiastes 7.2.
2. In a note Shelley says that although Peacock had classified Rousseau with these other thinkers of the 17th and 18th centuries, 'he was essentially a poet. The others, even Voltaire, were mere reasoners.'
3. The Inquisition had been suspended in 1820, the year before Shelley wrote this essay; it was not abolished permanently until 1834.
4. *Macbeth* 1.7 44–45.
5. 'Ye cannot serve God and Mammon' (Matthew 6.24).
6. This passage reiterates the ancient belief that the highest poetry is 'inspired,' and therefore occurs independently of the intention, effort, or consciousness of the poet. Unlike earlier critics, however, Shelley attributes such poetry not to a god or muse but to the unconscious depths of the poet's own mind.
7. *Paradise Lost* 9:21–24.
8. The epic poem by the 16th-century Italian poet Ariosto, noted for his care in composition.
9. In the double sense of 'most joyous' and 'most apt or felicitous in invention.'
10. The dark intervals between the old and new moons.
11. Alchemists aimed to produce a drinkable form of gold that would be an elixir of life, curing all diseases.
12. Satan's speech, *Paradise Lost* 1.254–55.
13. Shelley's version of a widespread Romantic doctrine that the poetic imagination transforms the familiar into the miraculous and recreates the old world into a new world. . . .
14. 'No one merits the name of Creator except God and the Poet.' Quoted by Pierantonio Serassi in his *Life of Torquato Tasso* (1785).
15. *Paradise Lost* 4.829.
16. Charges, some of them valid, which had in fact been made against these men. 'Peculator': a misappropriator of public money. Raphael is the 16th-century Italian painter. The use of 'poet laureate' as a derogatory term was a dig at Robert Southey, who held that honor at the time of Shelley's writing.
17. Isaiah 1.18.
18. Shelley alludes especially to the charges of immorality by contemporary reviewers against Lord Byron and himself.
19. I.e., consciousness or will. Shelley again proposes that some mental processes are unconscious – outside our control or awareness.
20. Exposed to slander.
21. Thomas Love Peacock's *The Four Ages of Poetry* (1820).
22. Would-be poets satirized by Virgil and Horace. 'Thesecids': epic poems about Theseus. Codrus (plural 'Codri') was the Roman author of a long, dull *Theseid* attacked by Juvenal and others.
23. Shelley, however, completed only the first part of his *Defence*.
24. In the age of Milton and the English Civil War.
25. By 'the spirit of the age' Shelley identifies what was later to be called 'the Romantic movement' in contemporary literature and philosophy; he recognized its greatness, as well as its relation to the ferment of ideas and aspirations effected by the French Revolution. . . .
26. Priests who are expositors of sacred mysteries.
27. Aristotle had said that God is the 'Unmoved Mover' of the universe.

7

STÉPHANE MALLARMÉ

from 'Crisis in Verse'

. . .

Speech has only a commercial interest in the reality of things. In literature, allusion is enough; the essence is distilled and embodied in some idea.

And song, when it becomes a joy freed of material constraint, arises in the same manner.

I call this goal Transposition – Structure is a different one.

The pure work implies the disappearance of the poet-speaker who yields the initiative to words animated by the inequality revealed in their collision with one another; they illuminate one another and pass like a trail of fire over precious stones, replacing the audible breathing of earlier lyrical verse or the exalted personality which directed the phrase.

The structure of a book of verse must arise throughout from internal necessity – in this way both chance and the author will be excluded; a subject will imply inevitably the harmony of the parts brought together and, since every sound has an echo, their corresponding locations in the volume. Thus similarly constructed motifs will move in space till there is equilibrium. There will be neither the sublime incoherence of the Romantic page-settings nor the artificial unity imposed upon the book by a compositor's calculations: everything will be fluid, the arrangement of parts, their alternation and interruption by blank spaces, and will yield a total rhythmic movement, the silent poem itself, translated in its own way by each unit of the structure. The instinct for such a work seems to be hinted at in a number of recent publications where

some young poets seem disposed towards a goal similar and complementary to our own. They stress the perfect and stunning structure of a
poem and mumble about the magic concept of the ultimate Work.
Likewise some symmetry, which will arise from the relation of lines
within the poem and poems within the volume, will reach out beyond
the volume to other poets who will themselves inscribe on spiritual
space the expanding paraph of genius, anonymous and perfect like a
work of art.

Thought alone of a chimera reveals – by the reflection from its scales
– how much the present phase of poetry, the last quarter of the century,
owes to some absolute flash of lightning. The ensuing downpour has
washed away the indeterminate rivulets of the older poetry from my
window panes and brought forth a new light, revealing that virtually
all books contain versions of certain well-known themes and that there
might be only one book on earth, the Bible of all the world's bibles; and
the only difference between the various works might merely be the
interpretations proposed by all those ages we call civilized or literary
for the one authentic text.

Certainly I never sit in the tiers of a concert hall without perceiving,
in the sublime darkness, some primitive version of a poem which
dwells deep in human nature, and which can be understood because the
composer knows that in order to convey its vast contour he must resist
the temptation to explain. And so I imagine, no doubt heeding a
writer's ineradicable instinct, that nothing endures if it is not uttered;
and since the great rhythms of literature are being broken down, as I
have said, and dispersed in fragmentary rhythmic units or orchestrated
vocables, we need just now to investigate the art of transposing the
symphony to the book: this would be nothing more than a realization
of our own wealth. For Music must undeniably result from the full
power of the intellectual word, not from the elemental sounds of
strings, brass and woodwind: it must be a full, manifest totality of
relationships.

One of the undeniable desires of my age is to separate the functions
of words, with the result that there is a crude and immediate language
on the one hand and an essential language on the other.

The former use of language in narration, instruction and description
– necessary of course, though one could get by with a silent language of
coins – is reflected by the ubiquitous *journalism* which attracts all forms
of contemporary writing except literature.

What purpose, ask those who use the latter language, is served by the
miracle which transposes a natural phenomenon into a disappearing

aural one by the device of written language – if it is not to allow the pure idea to arise from it, divorced of its direct and material associations?

And so when I make the sound – a flower – out of the oblivion to which my voice relegates all contours, something other than the visible petals arises musically, the fragrant idea itself, the absent flower of all bouquets.

Whereas, in the hands of the mob, language functions as a collection of meaningful coins, in those of the Poet it reaches its full potential, as an art dedicated to fiction, above all in dream and in song.

With several words the line of verse constructs a completely new word, foreign to the language and a part, it seems, of an incantation; and thus it perfects the separation of the word: denying, in a sovereign gesture, any chance – any descriptive sense which may have lingered in spite of the artful renewal both in meaning and sonority; and so you feel the surprise of never having heard any such fragment of speech, while, at the same time, your recollection of the object named bathes in a new atmosphere.

8

SIGMUND FREUD

'Creative Writers and Day-Dreaming'

We laymen have always been intensely curious to know – like the Cardinal who put a similar question to Ariosto[1] – from what sources that strange being, the creative writer, draws his material, and how he manages to make such an impression on us with it and to arouse in us emotions of which, perhaps, we had not even thought ourselves capable. Our interest is only heightened the more by the fact that, if we ask him, the writer himself gives us no explanation, or none that is satisfactory; and it is not at all weakened by our knowledge that not even the clearest insight into the determinants of his choice of material and into the nature of the art of creating imaginative form will ever help to make creative writers of *us*.

If we could at least discover in ourselves or in people like ourselves an activity which was in some way akin to creative writing! An examination of it would then give us a hope of obtaining the beginnings of an explanation of the creative work of writers. And, indeed, there is some prospect of this being possible. After all, creative writers themselves like to lessen the distance between their kind and the common run of humanity; they so often assure us that every man is a poet at heart and that the last poet will not perish till the last man does.

Should we not look for the first traces of imaginative activity as early as in childhood? The child's best-loved and most intense occupation is with his play or games. Might we not say that every child at play behaves like a creative writer, in that he creates a world of his own, or, rather, re-arranges the things of his world in a new way which pleases him? It would be wrong to think he does not take that world seriously;

on the contrary, he takes his play very seriously and he expends large amounts of emotion on it. The opposite of play is not what is serious but what is real. In spite of all the emotion with which he cathects his world of play, the child distinguishes it quite well from reality; and he likes to link his imagined objects and situations to the tangible and visible things of the real world. This linking is all that differentiates the child's 'play' from 'phantasying'.

The creative writer does the same as the child at play. He creates a world of phantasy which he takes very seriously – that is, which he invests with large amounts of emotion – while separating it sharply from reality. Language has preserved this relationship between children's play and poetic creation. It gives [in German] the name of '*Spiel*' ['play'] to those forms of imaginative writing which require to be linked to tangible objects and which are capable of representation. It speaks of a '*Lustspiel*' or '*Trauerspiel*' ['comedy' or 'tragedy': literally, 'pleasure play' or 'mourning play'] and describes those who carry out the representation as '*Schauspieler*' ['players': literally 'show-players']. The unreality of the writer's imaginative world, however, has very important consequences for the technique of his art; for many things which, if they were real, could give no enjoyment, can do so in the play of phantasy, and many excitements which, in themselves, are actually distressing, can become a source of pleasure for the hearers and spectators at the performance of a writer's work.

There is another consideration for the sake of which we will dwell a moment longer on this contrast between reality and play. When the child has grown up and has ceased to play, and after he has been labouring for decades to envisage the realities of life with proper seriousness, he may one day find himself in a mental situation which once more undoes the contrast between play and reality. As an adult he can look back on the intense seriousness with which he once carried on his games in childhood; and, by equating his ostensibly serious occupations of to-day with his childhood games, he can throw off the too heavy burden imposed on him by life and win the high yield of pleasure afforded by *humour*.[2]

As people grow up, then, they cease to play, and they seem to give up the yield of pleasure which they gained from playing. But whoever understands the human mind knows that hardly anything is harder for a man than to give up a pleasure which he has once experienced. Actually, we can never give anything up; we only exchange one thing for another. What appears to be a renunciation is really the formation of a substitute or surrogate. In the same way, the growing child, when he stops playing, gives up nothing but the link with real objects; instead of *playing*, he now *phantasies*. He builds castles in the air and creates what are called *daydreams*. I believe that most people construct phantasies at times in their lives. This is a fact which has long been overlooked and whose importance has therefore not been sufficiently appreciated.

People's phantasies are less easy to observe than the play of children. The child, it is true, plays by himself or forms a closed psychical system with other children for the purposes of a game; but even though he may not play his game in front of the grown-ups, he does not, on the other hand, conceal it from them. The adult, on the contrary, is ashamed of his phantasies and hides them from other people. He cherishes his phantasies as his most intimate possessions, and as a rule he would rather confess his misdeeds than tell anyone his phantasies. It may come about that for that reason he believes he is the only person who invents such phantasies and has no idea that creations of this kind are widespread among other people. This difference in the behaviour of a person who plays and a person who phantasies is accounted for by the motives of these two activities, which are nevertheless adjuncts to each other.

A child's play is determined by wishes: in point of fact by a single wish – one that helps in his upbringing – the wish to be big and grown up. He is always playing at being 'grown up', and in his games he imitates what he knows about the lives of his elders. He has no reason to conceal this wish. With the adult, the case is different. On the one hand, he knows that he is expected not to go on playing or phantasying any longer, but to act in the real world; on the other hand, some of the wishes which give rise to his phantasies are of a kind which it is essential to conceal. Thus he is ashamed of his phantasies as being childish and as being unpermissible.

But, you will ask, if people make such a mystery of their phantasying, how is it that we know such a lot about it? Well, there is a class of human beings upon whom, not a god, indeed, but a stern goddess – Necessity – has allotted the task of telling what they suffer and what things give them happiness.[3] These are the victims of nervous illness, who are obliged to tell their phantasies, among other things, to the doctor by whom they expect to be cured by mental treatment. This is our best source of knowledge, and we have since found good reason to suppose that our patients tell us nothing that we might not also hear from healthy people.

Let us now make ourselves acquainted with a few of the characteristics of phantasying. We may lay it down that a happy person never phantasies, only an unsatisfied one. The motive forces of phantasies are unsatisfied wishes, and every single phantasy is the fulfilment of a wish, a correction of unsatisfying reality. These motivating wishes vary according to the sex, character and circumstances of the person who is having the phantasy; but they fall naturally into two main groups. They are either ambitious wishes, which serve to elevate the subject's personality; or they are erotic ones. In young women the erotic wishes predominate almost exclusively, for their ambition is as a rule absorbed by erotic trends. In young men egoistic and ambitious wishes come to the fore clearly enough alongside of erotic ones. But we will not lay stress on the opposition between the two trends; we would rather emphasize the fact that they are often united. Just as, in many altar-pieces, the portrait of the donor is to be seen in a corner of the picture, so, in the majority of ambitious phantasies, we can discover in some corner or other the lady for whom the creator of the phantasy performs all his heroic deeds and at whose feet all his triumphs are laid. Here, as you see, there are strong enough motives for concealment; the well-brought-up young woman is only allowed a minimum of erotic desire, and the young man has to learn to suppress the excess of self-regard which he brings with him from the spoilt days of his childhood, so that he may find his place in a society which is full of other individuals making equally strong demands.

We must not suppose that the products of this imaginative activity – the various phantasies, castles in the air and day-dreams – are stereotyped or unalterable. On the contrary, they fit themselves in to the subject's shifting impressions of life, change with every change in his situation, and receive from every fresh active impression what might be called a 'date-mark'. The relation of a phantasy to time is in general very important. We may say that it hovers, as it were, between three times – the three moments of time which our ideation involves. Mental work is linked to some current impression, some provoking occasion in the present which has been able to arouse one of the subject's major wishes. From there it harks back to a memory of an earlier experience (usually an infantile one) in which this wish was fulfilled; and it now creates a situation relating to the future which represents a fulfilment of the wish. What it thus creates is a day-dream or phantasy, which carries about it traces of its origin from the occasion which provoked it and from the memory. Thus past, present and future are strung together, as it were, on the thread of the wish that runs through them.

A very ordinary example may serve to make what I have said clear. Let us take the case of a poor orphan boy to whom you have given the address of some employer where he may perhaps find a job. On his way there he may indulge in a day-dream appropriate to the situation from which it arises. The content of his phantasy will perhaps be something like this. He is given a job, finds favour with his new employer, makes himself indispensable in the business, is taken into his employer's family, marries the charming young daughter of the house, and then himself becomes a director of the business, first as his employer's partner and then as his successor. In this phantasy, the dreamer has regained what he possessed in his happy childhood – the protecting house, the loving parents and the first objects of his affectionate feelings. You will see from this example the way in which the wish makes use of an occasion in the present to construct, on the pattern of the past, a picture of the future.

There is a great deal more that could be said about phantasies; but I will only allude as briefly as possible to certain points. If phantasies become over-luxuriant and over-powerful, the conditions are laid for an onset of neurosis or psychosis. Phantasies, moreover, are the immediate mental precursors of the distressing symptoms complained of by our patients. Here a broad by-path branches off into pathology.

I cannot pass over the relation of phantasies to dreams. Our dreams at night are nothing else than phantasies like these, as we can demonstrate from the interpretation of dreams.[4] Language, in its unrivalled wisdom, long ago decided the question of the essential nature of dreams by giving the name of 'day-dreams' to the airy creations of phantasy. If the meaning of our dreams usually remains obscure to us in spite of this pointer, it is because of the circumstance that at night there also arise in us wishes of which we are ashamed; these we must conceal from ourselves, and they have consequently been repressed, pushed into the unconscious. Repressed wishes of this sort and their derivatives are only allowed to come to expression in a very distorted form. When scientific work had succeeded in elucidating this factor of *dream-distortion*, it was no longer difficult to recognize that night-dreams are wish-fulfilments in just the same way as day-dreams – the phantasies which we all know so well.

So much for phantasies. And now for the creative writer. May we really attempt to compare the imaginative writer with the 'dreamer in broad daylight',[5] and his creations with day-dreams? Here we must begin by making an initial distinction. We must separate writers who, like the ancient authors of epics and tragedies, take over their material ready-made, from writers who seem to originate their own material.

We will keep to the latter kind, and, for the purposes of our comparison, we will choose not the writers most highly esteemed by the critics, but the less pretentious authors of novels, romances and short stories, who nevertheless have the widest and most eager circle of readers of both sexes. One feature above all cannot fail to strike us about the creations of these story-writers: each of them has a hero who is the centre of interest, for whom the writer tries to win our sympathy by every possible means and whom he seems to place under the protection of a special Providence. If, at the end of one chapter of my story, I leave the hero unconscious and bleeding from severe wounds, I am sure to find him at the beginning of the next being carefully nursed and on the way to recovery; and if the first volume closes with the ship he is in going down in a storm at sea, I am certain, at the opening of the second volume, to read of his miraculous rescue – a rescue without which the story could not proceed. The feeling of security with which I follow the hero through his perilous adventures is the same as the feeling with which a hero in real life throws himself into the water to save a drowning man or exposes himself to the enemy's fire in order to storm a battery. It is the true heroic feeling, which one of our best writers has expressed in an inimitable phrase: 'Nothing can happen to *me*!'[6] It seems to me, however, that through this revealing characteristic of invulnerability we can immediately recognize His Majesty the Ego, the hero alike of every day-dream and of every story.[7]

Other typical features of these egocentric stories point to the same kinship. The fact that all the women in the novel invariably fall in love with the hero can hardly be looked on as a portrayal of reality, but it is easily understood as a necessary constituent of a day-dream. The same is true of the fact that the other characters in the story are sharply divided into good and bad, in defiance of the variety of human characters that are to be observed in real life. The 'good' ones are the helpers, while the 'bad' ones are the enemies and rivals, of the ego which has become the hero of the story.

We are perfectly aware that very many imaginative writings are far removed from the model of the naïve day-dream; and yet I cannot suppress the suspicion that even the most extreme deviations from that model could be linked with it through an uninterrupted series of transitional cases. It has struck me that in many of what are known as 'psychological' novels only one person – once again the hero – is described from within. The author sits inside his mind, as it were, and looks at the other characters from outside. The psychological novel in general no doubt owes its special nature to the inclination of the modern writer to split up his ego, by self-observation, into many part-egos, and, in consequence, to personify the conflicting currents of his own mental life in several heroes. Certain novels, which might be described as 'eccentric', seem to stand in quite special contrast to the type of the day-dream. In these, the person who is introduced as the hero plays only a very small active part; he sees the actions and sufferings of other people pass before him like a spectator. Many of Zola's later works belong to this category. But I must point out that the psychological analysis of individuals who are not creative writers, and who diverge in some respects from the so-called norm, has shown us analogous variations of the day-dream, in which the ego contents itself with the role of spectator.

If our comparison of the imaginative writer with the day dreamer, and of poetical creation with the day-dream, is to be of any value, it must, above all, show itself in some way or other fruitful. Let us, for instance, try to apply to these authors' works the thesis we laid down earlier concerning the relation between phantasy and the three periods of time and the wish which runs through them; and, with its help, let us try to study the connections that exist between the life of the writer and his works. No one has known, as a rule, what expectations to frame in approaching this problem; and often the connection has been thought of in much too simple terms. In the light of the insight we have gained from phantasies, we ought to expect the following state of affairs. A strong experience in the present awakens in the creative writer a memory of an earlier experience (usually belonging to his childhood) from which there now proceeds a wish which finds its fulfilment in the creative work. The work itself exhibits elements of the recent provoking occasion as well as of the old memory.[8]

Do not be alarmed at the complexity of this formula. I suspect that in fact it will prove to be too exiguous a pattern. Nevertheless, it may contain a first approach to the true state of affairs; and, from some experiments I have made, I am inclined to think that this way of looking at creative writings may turn out not unfruitful. You will not forget that the stress it lays on childhood memories in the writer's life – a stress which may perhaps seem puzzling – is ultimately derived from the assumption that a piece of creative writing, like a day-dream, is a continuation of, and a substitute for, what was once the play of childhood.

We must not neglect, however, to go back to the kind of imaginative works which we have to recognize, not as original creations, but as the re-fashioning of ready-made and familiar material [pp. 58–9 below].

Even here, the writer keeps a certain amount of independence, which can express itself in the choice of material and in changes in it which are .often quite extensive. In so far as the material is already at hand, however, it is derived from the popular treasure-house of myths, legends and fairy tales. The study of constructions of folk-psychology such as these is far from being complete, but it is extremely probable that myths, for instance, are distorted vestiges of the wishful phantasies of whole nations, the *secular dreams* of youthful humanity.

You will say that, although I have put the creative writer first in the title of my paper, I have told you far less about him than about phantasies. I am aware of that, and I must try to excuse it by pointing to the present state of our knowledge. All I have been able to do is to throw out some encouragements and suggestions which, starting from the study of phantasies, lead on to the problem of the writer's choice of his literary material. As for the other problem – by what means the creative writer achieves the emotional effects in us that are aroused by his creations – we have as yet not touched on it at all. But I should like at least to point out to you the path that leads from our discussion of phantasies to the problems of poetical effects.

You will remember how I have said [p. 56 below] that the day-dreamer carefully conceals his phantasies from other people because he feels he has reasons for being ashamed of them. I should now add that even if he were to communicate them to us he could give us no pleasure by his disclosures. Such phantasies, when we learn them, repel us or at least leave us cold. But when a creative writer presents his plays to us or tells us what we are inclined to take to be his personal day-dreams, we experience a great pleasure, and one which probably arises from the confluence of many sources. How the writer accomplishes this is his innermost secret; the essential *ars poetica* lies in the technique of overcoming the feeling of repulsion in us which is undoubtedly connected with the barriers that rise between each single ego and the others. We can guess two of the methods used by this technique. The writer softens the character of his egoistic day-dreams by altering and disguising it, and he bribes us by the purely formal – that is, aesthetic – yield of pleasure which he offers us in the presentation of his phantasies. We give the name of an *incentive bonus*, or a *fore-pleasure*, to a yield of pleasure such as this, which is offered to us so as to make possible the release of still greater pleasure arising from deeper psychical sources. In my opinion, all the aesthetic pleasure which a creative writer affords us has the character of a fore-pleasure of this kind, and our actual enjoyment of an imaginative work proceeds from a liberation of tensions in our minds. It may even be that not a little of this effect is due to the writer's enabling us thenceforward to enjoy our own day-dreams without self-reproach or shame. This brings us to the threshold of new, interesting and complicated enquiries; but also, at least for the moment, to the end of our discussion.

NOTES

1. Cardinal Ippolito d'Este was Ariosto's first patron, to whom he dedicated the *Orlando Furioso*. The poet's only reward was the question: 'Where did you find so many stories, Lodovico?'
2. See Section 7 of Chapter VII of Freud's book on jokes: *Jokes and their Relation to the Unconscious* (1905*c*), *The Standard Edition of the Complete Psychological Works of Sigmund Freud*, vol. VIII (London: Hogarth Press, 1953).
3. This is an allusion to some well-known lines spoken by the poet-hero in the final scene of Goethe's *Torquato Tasso*:

> 'Und wenn der Mensch in seiner Qual verstummt,
> Gab mir ein Gott, zu sagen, wie ich leide.'

'And when mankind is dumb in its torment, a god granted me to tell how I suffer.'
4. Cf. Freud, *The Interpretation of Dreams* (1900*a*).
5. '*Der Träumer am hellichten Tag.*'
6. 'Es kann dir nix g'schehen!' This phrase from Anzengruber, the Viennese dramatist, was a favourite one of Freud's. Cf. 'Thoughts on War and Death' (1915*b*), *Standard Ed.*, 14, 296.
7. Cf. 'On Narcissism' (1914*c*), *Standard Ed.*, 14, 91.
8. A similar view had already been suggested by Freud in a letter to Fliess of July 7, 1898, on the subject of one of C. F. Meyer's short stories (Freud, 1950*a*, Letter 92).
9. This theory of 'fore-pleasure' and the 'incentive bonus' had been applied by Freud to jokes in the last paragraphs of Chapter IV of his book on that subject (1905*c*). The nature of 'fore-pleasure' was also discussed in the *Three Essays* (1905*d*). See especially *Standard Ed.*, 7, 208 ff.

Section 2

The Twentieth-century Controversy

The Twentieth-century Controversy

Though the question of authorship has been disputed with considerable intensity during the twentieth century, the debate has been conducted within a largely technical lexicon and has focused on conceptual rather than humanist issues. Even those who have sought to defend personality do so in the largely impersonal mode of theoretical analysis and focus on the principles rather than practices by which the relation of author and text might be assessed. Leaving aside the political issues which are represented in Part 2, we might isolate four cardinal intersections which appear and reappear in this debate:

1. the relation of the writer to tradition understood as literary history, literary language, conventions, genres, textual systems, etc.;
2. a suspicion of expressivist notions of literature combined with a general rejection of biographicist criticism;
3. concern with the relevance or irrelevance of intention to evaluation and/or interpretation;
4. a subordination of the question of authorship to that of reading in such a way that the former is refracted through the latter.

The assumption underlying these developments is that the determination of authorial roles resides with the critic rather than the author. Although T. S. Eliot – whose work begins this section – spoke more from the authorial rather than the critical perspective, his reflections of poetry were to provide the early momentum for this shift from creative aesthetic to critical theory.

In 'Tradition and the Individual Talent', Eliot provided the classic statement of modernist impersonality through weaving together two ostensibly anti-romantic arguments. Eliot's insistence that poetry involved the emptying-out of personal feeling rather than its expression is formulated in opposition to the Wordsworthian 'egotistical sublime'. While Eliot's argument is here valid in terms of the expressivist turn in romanticism and decadent forms of nineteenth-century criticism, it nonetheless displays close affinities with the arguments for artistic disinterestedness propounded in the more austere aesthetics of Schiller, Coleridge and others. The corollary claim that an author's work derives its identity purely in terms of its relation to tradition is more telling in its anti-romantic rejection of originality. Eliot argues that authors are least original where they would be most so: the distinctive cast of a work can be most clearly discerned in those places where the voices of classical precursors make themselves heard beneath the striving for precedence. For Eliot, then, the individual author is constituted, to some extent, within a network of textual relations which the most talented of modern writers will come to realign retrospectively. Eliot here prefigures the revisionist theory of Harold Bloom as well as the theory of intertextuality which moves from the subjective paradigm of influence to a model of synchronic discursive constellations. Eliot's poetic also coincides suggestively in this regard with his literary practice, particularly in 'The Waste Land' which consistently locates itself in relation to a synchronic sense of tradition.

Boris Tomaševskij's 'Literature and Biography' is similarly concerned with distancing the writer's life and work but according to requirements of critical methodology rather than those of artistic achievement. Tomaševskij's essay was written during the latter stages of the Russian Formalist movement – a circle of young writers who pioneered a more rigorous approach to literary studies against the psychologistic, biographical and historicist speculation of late nineteenth- and early twentieth-century criticism. Earlier Formalist statements had tended to deny any relevance of the author to the reading of his or her text so as to focus exclusively on the 'literariness' of literature: its devices, genres and general rules of formation. Between the radical Formalist emphasis on the autonomy of the literary object and the biographicist impulse there would seem scant possibility of productive commerce or compromise. Tomaševskij manages, however, to devise an intricate path between the two by allowing relevance to biographical information which bears upon the author's literary themes. Advocating a limited and judicious use of those biographical facts which seem to be pre-programmed by the author according to aesthetic aims, Tomaševskij thereby maintains the principle of literariness while expanding the category to incorporate aesthetically-conceived biographical 'legends': the biographical is thus bounded by literary rather than positivist criteria, while the connection of life and work is maintained but reversed in terms of priority. Somewhat prefigured in the aestheticism of Wilde and Pater, this median ground was to be lost in structuralism but reappears in the later Barthes and in Foucault's view of personal identity as aesthetic self-creation.

W. K. Wimsatt and Monroe C. Beardsley were influenced by modernist theories of impersonality, though they transferred the demands of objectivity from author to critic. In their landmark essay 'The Intentional Fallacy', they argue that the author's intentions in writing are neither recoverable nor pertinent to the judgement of the work. Such a position prescribes the irrelevance of intention not to a work's composition but to its reception. Intention may well govern the scene of writing but not that of reading, since, once the work journeys from the private to the public sphere, the author's statement of what (s)he meant can at best take its unprivileged place alongside any other aesthetic judgement. This removal of authorial involvement in the work's evaluation reflects the growing professionalisation of literary studies and might also be taken (against the customary reading) as an ethical defence of the author against the attribution of spurious or calumniating intentions. It is also important to note that 'The Intentional Fallacy' is more concerned with forbidding intention as a standard in the evaluation rather than the interpretation of the work. Ironically, it is this latter and largely 'unintended' claim that has proved most influential and has served to justify an interpretative freedom quite at odds with the claims of 'The Intentional Fallacy' and its companion essay 'The Affective Fallacy'.

Georges Poulet's work is associated with the Geneva school of critics which took up Husserlian phenomenology during the 1950s to argue that the critical act consists in a total receptivity to authorial consciousness as it unfolds in the structure of a work. In 'Criticism and the Experience of Interiority', Poulet recommends an ideal intersubjectivity which involves the negation of the readerly 'I' in order that critical consciousness be filled entirely by the authorial *cogito*. The work is seen as a near-perfect expression of the structures of the author's mind so that the responsibility of the critic becomes not so much that of thinking through the work as allowing the author to think through the critic. Poulet's thesis largely evades the intentional debate by identifying the whole range of linguistic effects with the consciousness of the author. Such a position, however, raises the difficulty of distinguishing author and work: if the author is identified with the entirety of the text, how does the phenomenological view differ from its ostensible anti-thesis, namely the removal of the author in the apprehension of the pure work?

The work of E. D. Hirsch also has its roots in Husserlian phenom-enology but takes up the question of authorial consciousness specific-ally in terms of intention. Hirsch conducts a defence of the author against modernist impersonality and New Critical anti-intentionalism which he sees as two sides of a common will to depersonalise literature. Hirsch accepts the limited gains made by the stricture of textual autonomy but resists the growth of relativism and interpretative pluralism concomitant upon abandoning any determining standard of critical validation. In arguing for authorial intention as such a standard, Hirsch distinguishes between meaning (the original and fixed intentions of the author) and significance (the relative and historically variable interpretations which given periods impose upon a work) in such a way as to establish the former as valid and objective, the latter as relative and subjective. Hirsch's thesis draws on Husserl's claim that a text can only mean what a writer meant it to mean in the act of composition, but it fails to establish sound principles whereby the critic could verify his or her knowledge of the writer's mental state. Furthermore, Hirsch's principle of validation cannot guard against the possibility of subjective impositions on the part of the critic who might well assert as meaning what Hirsch reduces to significance. There is also a potential circularity in Hirsch's position, since authorial intention guarantees the text's determinate meaning and vice versa. Here again, the phenomenological view of authorship ends up asserting a model of interpretation not dissimilar to the formalist ethos which it disputes: one no more establishes the *relation* between author and textual meaning by collaps-ing one into the other than by radically dissociating the two terms.

Often misconstrued as radically anti-intentionalist, Jacques Derrida's work actually resists the polarities of the debate. Derrida affirms that intention is a cardinally relevant category of both writing and reading but insists that it cannot encompass the full range of textual significa-tion. What is meant by a text is therefore a subset of what is written in a text: intention will generate its own area of significance but will also confront moments of contradiction whereby the text will open itself to a reading which legitimately eludes or evades the conscious purposes of its author. For Derrida, this interplay of design and deconstruction arises from the very constitution of writing which cannot be composed into unilateral patterns of meaning. Critical production therefore consists in a redoubling of the intentional structure and the warring play of signification by which intention is destabilised.

In the case of Rousseau – the 'subject' of Derrida's reading in Book II of *Of Grammatology* – the figure of writing as the supplement of speech opens one such moment of generative crisis and allows Derrida to unfurl his fascinating reading of the Rousseauian text as an enquiry into the origins of language which at every crucial turn undoes its own attempts to establish the priority of speech. While Derrida's position steers an ingenious and persuasive path between the impasses of transcendent and formalist/textualist descriptions, the problem of establishing precisely where intention ends and inadvertent significance begins – the moment itself of deconstruction – is always vulnerable to challenge in terms of reappropriation for the author.

Roland Barthes's 'The Death of the Author' short-circuits the intention-debate by positing writing as the origin of meaning-effects and the reader as the sufficient principle of the text's unity. In what was to become the central point of reference for an era of theory, Barthes reaches the zero-degree of the impersonalising tradition through negatively maintaining the analogy of Author and Divinity to argue that the death of the latter implies the removal of the former. Barthes enlists further analogies with bourgeois individualism and arguments drawn from linguistics so as to conflate the grammar and ontology of the 'I' – the suggestion being that the hollow linguistic function necessitates the emptiness of the subject writing. This empty subject position is then filled by the Reader, though it remains unclear that Barthes's Reader is any less mystifying than the author (s)he (it?) would replace. Certainly, this move goes no way towards the political in that the 'Reader' is not presented in collective or situated terms but as a hollow subject function. Given however that Barthes was deftly to revise this position, and that he initially penned 'The Death of the Author' with an avant-garde rather than academic audience in mind, it is not certain that he would have countenanced the literal reception that proved to be his essay's fate in Anglo-American theoretical schools. Indeed, with scrupulous attention to the curious play of capitalisation and decapitalisation which Barthes studs into his text, it might be possible to rescue some sense of the author from this declaration of the author's demise.

Though Barthes was to return with grace and guile to a modified conception of authorship which maintained his commitment to a language-centred conception of the text, it is only with Harold Bloom that a rhetorical criticism is *theorised* in relation to strong authorial categories. At once poststructuralist rhetor and priestly champion of poetic genius, Bloom affirms author over language while privileging trope over meaning. His paradigm of literary influence is humanist but darkly so, author-centred but largely non-biographicist and insistent on division within the creative authorial psyche between the consciousness of the poet and the unconscious influence of the precursor. Bloom's theory of revisionism is broadly Freudian in that influence is conceived in Oedipal terms as a psychic war for precedence between precursor and ephebe. The latecoming ephebe carves out a space of expression via a series of desperate misreadings of the precursor's text and thereby comes to poetic adulthood. The model or map of misreading is focused almost exclusively on romantic poetry in which the psychodynamic denial of influence was most marked upon the decline of an aesthetic of technical imitation.

Bloom reverses commonsensical assumptions in asserting that influence is most surely expressed in the mode of denial. The culmination of the revisionary process consists in the ephebe revising the precursor's work with such intensity that priority is seemingly reversed, with the influential text coming to seem as though it were influenced by the latecomer's (along such lines, the question 'Discuss the influence of Yeats on Keats' would not contain a typographical error). Bloom's theory itself perhaps invites revision, however, in its resolute and exclusive concentration on a male-centred Oedipality, and rewarded Sandra Gilbert and Susan Gubar's feminist transposition of authorial anxiety in their resonant account of nineteenth-century female authorship.

SUGGESTED FURTHER READINGS

Beardsley, Monroe C., 'Intentions and Interpretations', in Beardsley, *The Aesthetic Point of View* (Ithaca, NY: Cornell University Press, 1982).

Burke, Seán, *The Death and Return of the Author* (Edinburgh: Edinburgh University Press, 1992).

Cadava, Eduardo (ed.), *Who Comes after the Subject?* (New York and London: Routledge, 1991).

Caughie, John (ed.), *Theories of Authorship: A Reader* (London: Routledge and Kegan Paul, 1981).

Coomaraswamy, Ananda K., 'Intention', *American Bookman* 1:1 (1944), pp. 41–8.

Ellmann, Maud, *The Poetics of Impersonality: T. S. Eliot and Ezra Pound* (Brighton: Harvester, 1987).

Erlich, Victor, *Russian Formalism: History-Doctrine* (The Hague: Mouton, 1980).

Fish, Stanley, *Is There a Text in This Class?* (Cambridge, MA Harvard University Press, 1980).

Huyssen, Andreas, 'Mapping the Postmodern', in Linda J. Nicholson (ed.), *Feminism/Postmodernism* (New York and London: Routledge, 1990).

Lacan, Jacques, *Écrits: A Selection* (London: Tavistock, 1977).

Lentricchia, Frank, *After the New Criticism* (Chicago, IL: University of Chicago Press, 1980).

Lyotard, Jean-François, *The Postmodern Condition* (Manchester: Manchester University Press, 1985).

Man, Paul de, *Blindness and Insight* (London: Methuen, 1983).

Patterson, Annabel, 'Intention', in Frank Lentricchia and Thomas McLaughlin (eds), *Critical Terms for Literary Study* (Chicago and London: University of Chicago Press, 1990), pp. 135–46.

Said, Edward, *Beginnings: Intention and Method* (Baltimore, MD: Johns Hopkins University Press, 1975).

Siebers, Tobin, *The Ethics of Criticism* (Ithaca, NY: Cornell University Press, 1988).

Waugh, Patricia, *Practicing Postmodernism/Reading Modernism* (London: Edward Arnold, 1992).

Wimsatt, W. K., 'Genesis: A Fallacy Revisited', in Gregory T. Polletta (ed.), *Issues in Contemporary Criticism* (Boston, MA Little Brown, 1973), pp. 255–76.

9

T. S. ELIOT

'Tradition and the Individual Talent'

I

In English writing we seldom speak of tradition, though we occasionally apply its name in deploring its absence. We cannot refer to 'the tradition' or to 'a tradition'; at most, we employ the adjective in saying that the poetry of So-and-so is 'traditional' or even 'too traditional'. Seldom, perhaps, does the word appear except in a phrase of censure. If otherwise, it is vaguely approbative, with the implication, as to the work approved, of some pleasing archaeological reconstruction. You can hardly make the word agreeable to English ears without this comfortable reference to the reassuring science of archaeology.

Certainly the word is not likely to appear in our appreciations of living or dead writers. Every nation, every race, has not only its own creative, but its own critical turn of mind; and is even more oblivious of the shortcomings and limitations of its critical habits than of those of its creative genius. We know, or think we know, from the enormous mass of critical writing that has appeared in the French language the critical method or habit of the French; we only conclude (we are such unconscious people) that the French are 'more critical' than we, and sometimes even plume ourselves a little with the fact, as if the French were the less spontaneous. Perhaps they are; but we might remind ourselves that criticism is as inevitable as breathing, and that we should be none the worse for articulating what passes in our minds when we read a book and feel an emotion about it, for criticizing our own minds in their work of criticism. One of the facts that might come to light in this process is our tendency to insist, when we praise a poet, upon those aspects of his work in which he least resembles anyone else. In these aspects or parts of his work we pretend to find what is individual, what is the peculiar essence of the man. We dwell with satisfaction upon the poet's difference from his predecessors, especially his immediate predecessors; we endeavour to find something that can be isolated in order to be enjoyed. Whereas if we approach a poet without this prejudice we shall often find that not only the best, but the most individual parts of his work may be those in which the dead poets, his ancestors, assert their immortality most vigorously. And I do not mean the impressionable period of adolescence, but the period of full maturity.

Yet if the only form of tradition, of handing down, consisted in following the ways of the immediate generation before us in a blind or timid adherence to its successes, 'tradition' should positively be discouraged. We have seen many such simple currents soon lost in the sand; and novelty is better than repetition. Tradition is a matter of much wider significance. It cannot be inherited, and if you want it you must obtain it by great labour. It involves, in the first place, the historical sense, which we may call nearly indispensable to anyone who would continue to be a poet beyond his twenty-fifth year; and the historical sense involves a perception, not only of the pastness of the past, but of its presence; the historical sense compels a man to write not merely with his own generation in his bones, but with a feeling that the whole of the literature of Europe from Homer and within it the whole of the literature of his own country has a simultaneous existence and composes a simultaneous order. This historical sense, which is a sense of the timeless as well as of the temporal and of the timeless and of the temporal together, is what makes a writer traditional. And it is at the same time what makes a writer most acutely conscious of his place in time, of his own contemporaneity.

No poet, no artist of any art, has his complete meaning alone. His significance, his appreciation is the appreciation of his relation to the dead poets and artists. You cannot value him alone; you must set him, for contrast and comparison, among the dead. I mean this as a principle of aesthetic, not merely historical, criticism. The necessity that he shall conform, that he shall cohere, is not onesided; what happens when a new work of art is created is something that happens simultaneously to all the works of art which preceded it. The existing monuments form an ideal order among themselves, which is modified by the introduction of the new (the really new) work of art among them. The existing order is complete before the new work arrives; for order to persist after the supervention of novelty, the *whole* existing order must be, if ever so slightly, altered; and so the relations, proportions, values of each work of art towards the whole are readjusted; and this is conformity between the old and the new. Whoever has approved this idea of order, of the form of European, of English literature will not find it preposterous that the past should be altered by the present as much as the present is directed by the past. And the poet who is aware of this will be aware of great difficulties and responsibilities.

In a peculiar sense he will be aware also that he must inevitably be judged by the standards of the past. I say judged not amputated, by them; not judged to be as good as, or worse or better than, the dead; and certainly not judged by the canons of dead critics. It is a judgement, a comparison, in which two things are measured by each other. To conform merely would be for the new work not really to conform at all; it would not be new, and would therefore not be a work of art. And we do not quite say that the new is more valuable because it fits in; but its fitting in is a test of its value – a test, it is true, which can only be slowly and cautiously applied, for we are none of us infallible judges of conformity. We say: it appears to conform, and is perhaps individual, or it appears individual, and may conform; but we are hardly likely to find that it is one and not the other.

To proceed to a more intelligible exposition of the relation of the poet to the past: he can neither take the past as a lump, an indiscriminate bolus, nor can he form himself wholly on one or two private admirations, nor can he form himself wholly upon one preferred period. The first course is inadmissible, the second is an important experience of youth, and the third is a pleasant and highly desirable supplement. The poet must be very conscious of the main current, which does not at all flow invariably through the most distinguished reputations. He must be quite aware of the obvious fact that art never improves, but that the material of art is never quite the same. He must be aware that the mind of Europe – the mind of his own country – a mind which he learns in time to be much more important than his own private mind – is a mind which changes, and that this change is a development which abandons nothing *en route*, which does not super-annuate either Shakespeare, or Homer, or the rock drawing of the Magdalenian draughtsmen. That this development, refinement perhaps, complication certainly, is not, from the point of view of the artist, any improvement. Perhaps not even an improvement from the point of view of the psychologist or not to the extent which we imagine; perhaps only in the end based upon a complication in economics and machinery. But the difference between the present and the past is that the conscious present is an awareness of the past in a way and to an extent which the past's awareness of itself cannot show.

Someone said: 'The dead writers are remote from us because we *know* so much more than they did'. Precisely, and they are that which we know.

I am alive to a usual objection to what is clearly part of my programme for the *métier* of poetry. The objection is that the doctrine requires a ridiculous amount of erudition (pedantry), a claim which can be rejected by appeal to the lives of poets in any pantheon. It will even be affirmed that much learning deadens or perverts poetic sensibility. While, however, we persist in believing that a poet ought to know as much as will not encroach upon his necessary receptivity and necessary laziness, it is not desirable to confine knowledge to whatever can be put into a useful shape for examinations, drawing-rooms, or the still more pretentious modes of publicity. Some can absorb knowledge, the more tardy must sweat for it. Shakespeare acquired more essential history from Plutarch than most men could from the whole British Museum. What is to be insisted upon is that the poet must develop or procure the consciousness of the past and that he should continue to develop this consciousness throughout his career.

What happens is a continual surrender of himself as he is at the moment to something which is more valuable. The progress of an artist is a continual self-sacrifice, a continual extinction of personality.

There remains to define this process of depersonalization and its relation to the sense of tradition. It is in this depersonalization that art may be said to approach the condition of science. I therefore invite you to consider, as a suggestive analogy, the action which takes place when a bit of finely filiated platinum is introduced into a chamber containing oxygen and sulphur dioxide.

II

Honest criticism and sensitive appreciation is directed not upon the poet but upon the poetry. If we attend to the confused cries of the newspaper critics and the susurrus of popular repetition that follows, we shall hear the names of poets in great numbers; if we seek not Blue-book knowledge but the enjoyment of poetry, and ask for a poem, we shall seldom find it. I have tried to point out the importance of the relation of the poem to other poems by other authors, and suggested the conception of poetry as a living whole of all the poetry that has ever been written. The other aspect of this Impersonal theory of poetry is the relation of the poem to its author. And I hinted, by an analogy, that the mind of the mature poet differs from that of the immature one not precisely in any valuation of 'personality', not being necessarily more interesting, or having 'more to say', but rather by being a more finely perfected medium in which special, or very varied, feelings are at liberty to enter into new combinations.

The analogy was that of the catalyst. When the two gases previously mentioned are mixed in the presence of a filament of platinum, they form sulphurous acid. This combination takes place only if the platinum is present; nevertheless the newly formed acid contains no trace of platinum, and the platinum itself is apparently unaffected: has remained inert, neutral, and unchanged. The mind of the poet is the shred of platinum. It may partly or exclusively operate upon the experience of the man himself; but, the more perfect the artist, the more completely separate in him will be the man who suffers and the mind which creates; the more perfectly will the mind digest and transmute the passions which are its material.

The experience, you will notice, the elements which enter the presence of the transforming catalyst, are of two kinds: emotions and feelings. The effect of a work of art upon the person who enjoys it is an experience different in kind from any experience not of art. It may be formed out of one emotion, or may be a combination of several; and various feelings, inhering for the writer in particular words or phrases or images, may be added to compose the final result. Or great poetry may be made without the direct use of any emotion whatever: composed out of feelings solely. Canto XV of the *Inferno* (Brunetto Latini) is a working up of the emotion evident in the situation; but the effect, though single as that of any work of art, is obtained by considerable complexity of detail. The last quatrain gives an image, a feeling attaching to an image, which 'came', which did not develop simply out of what precedes, but which was probably in suspension in the poet's mind until the proper combination arrived for it to add itself to. The poet's mind is in fact a receptacle for seizing and storing up numberless feelings, phrases, images, which remain there until all the particles which can unite to form a new compound are present together.

If you compare several representative passages of the greatest poetry you see how great is the variety of types of combination, and also how completely any semi-ethical criterion of 'sublimity' misses the mark. For it is not the 'greatness', the intensity, of the emotions, the components, but the intensity of the artistic process, the pressure, so to speak, under which the fusion takes place, that counts. The episode of Paolo and Francesca employs a definite emotion, but the intensity of the poetry is something quite different from whatever intensity in the supposed experience it may give the impression of. It is no more intense, furthermore, than Canto XXVI, the voyage of Ulysses, which has not the direct dependence upon an emotion. Great variety is possible in the process of transmutation of emotion: the murder of Agamemnon, or the agony of Othello, gives an artistic effect apparently closer to a possible original than the scenes from Dante. In the *Agamemnon*, the artistic emotion approximates to the emotion of an actual spectator; in *Othello* to the emotion of the protagonist himself. But the difference between art and the event is always absolute; the combination which is the murder of Agamemnon is probably as complex as that which is the voyage of Ulysses. In either case there has been a fusion of elements. The ode of Keats contains a number of feelings which have nothing particular to do with the nightingale, but which the nightingale, partly perhaps because of its attractive name, and partly because of its reputation, served to bring together.

The point of view which I am struggling to attack is perhaps related to the metaphysical theory of the substantial unity of the soul: for my meaning is, that the poet has, not a 'personality' to express, but a particular medium, which is only a medium and not a personality, in which impressions and experiences combine in peculiar and unexpected ways. Impressions and experiences which are important for the man may take no place in the poetry, and those which become important in the poetry may play quite a negligible part in the man, the personality.

I will quote a passage which is unfamiliar enough to be regarded with fresh attention in the light – or darkness – of these observations:

> *And now methinks I could e'en chide myself*
> *For doating on her beauty, though her death*
> *Shall be revenged after no common action.*
> *Does the silkworm expend her yellow labours*
> *For thee? For thee does she undo herself?*
> *Are lordships sold to maintain ladyships*
> *For the poor benefit of a bewildering minute?*

> *Why does yon fellow falsify highways,*
> *And put his life between the judge's lips,*
> *To refine such a thing – keeps horse and men*
> *To beat their valours for her? . . .*

In this passage (as is evident if it is taken in its context) there is a combination of positive and negative emotions: an intensely strong attraction towards beauty and an equally intense fascination by the ugliness which is contrasted with it and which destroys it. This balance of contrasted emotion is in the dramatic situation to which the speech is pertinent, but that situation alone is inadequate to it. This is, so to speak, the structural emotion, provided by the drama. But the whole effect, the dominant tone, is due to the fact that a number of floating feelings, having an affinity to this emotion by no means superficially evident, have combined with it to give us a new art emotion.

It is not in his personal emotions, the emotions provoked by particular events in his life, that the poet is in any way remarkable or interesting. His particular emotions may be simple, or crude, or flat. The emotion in his poetry will be a very complex thing, but not with the complexity of the emotions of people who have very complex or unusual emotions in life. One error, in fact, of eccentricity in poetry is to seek for new human emotions to express; and in this search for novelty in the wrong place it discovers the perverse. The business of the poet is not to find new emotions, but to use the ordinary ones and, in working them up into poetry, to express feelings which are not in actual emotions at all. And emotions which he has never experienced will serve his turn as well as those familiar to him. Consequently, we must believe that 'emotion recollected in tranquillity' is an inexact formula. For it is neither emotion, nor recollection, nor, without distortion of meaning, tranquillity. It is a concentration, and a new thing resulting from the concentration, of a very great number of experiences which to the practical and active person would not seem to be experiences at all; it is a concentration which does not happen consciously or of deliberation. These experiences are not 'recollected', and they finally unite in an atmosphere which is 'tranquil' only in that it is a passive attending upon the event. Of course this is not quite the whole story. There is a great deal, in the writing of poetry, which must be conscious and deliberate. In fact, the bad poet is usually unconscious where he ought to be conscious, and conscious where he ought to be unconscious. Both errors tend to make him 'personal'. Poetry is not a turning loose of emotion, but an escape from emotion; it is not the expression of personality, but an escape from personality. But, of course, only those who have personality and emotions know what it means to want to escape from these things.

III

ὁ δὲ νοῦς ἴσως θειότερόν τι καὶ ἀπαθές ἐστιν.

This essay proposes to halt at the frontier of metaphysics or mysticism, and confine itself to such practical conclusions as can be applied by the responsible person interested in poetry. To divert interest from the poet to the poetry is a laudable aim: for it would conduce to a juster estimation of actual poetry, good and bad. There are many people who appreciate the expression of sincere emotion in verse, and there is a smaller number of people who can appreciate technical excellence. But very few know when there is an expression of *significant* emotion, emotion which has its life in the poem and not in the history of the poet. The emotion of art is impersonal. And the poet cannot reach this impersonality without surrendering himself wholly to the work to be done. And he is not likely to know what is to be done unless he lives in what is not merely the present, but the present moment of the past, unless he is conscious, not of what is dead, but of what is already living.

10

BORIS TOMAŠEVSKIJ

'Literature and Biography'

Diaries as well as curiosity about unpublished documents and bio-graphical 'findings' mark an unhealthy sharpening of interest in documentary literary history, that is, history that is concerned with mores, personalities, and with the interrelationship between writers and their milieu. Most of the 'documents' are relevant, not to literature or its history, but rather to the study of the author as a man (if not to the study of his brothers and aunts).

In contrast to these biographical studies, there is a concurrent development of critical literature concentrating on the specific poetic elements in verbal art (the contributions of the *Opojaz* and other branches of 'Formalism'). Thus at first glance there would appear to be a profound split among literary scholars. These two currents seem to have diverged in a definitive way, and no reconciliation seems possible. To a certain extent this is true: many biographers cannot be made to comprehend an artistic work as anything but a fact of the author's biography; on the other hand, there are those for whom any kind of biographical analysis is unscientific contraband, a 'back-door' approach.

Consider Puškin's poem, *Ja pomnju čudnoe mgnoven'e* [I Recall a Wondrous Instant]. Is this an artistic reference to the personal relation of Puškin to A. Kern? Or is it a free lyrical composition which uses the image of Kern as an indifferent 'emblem,' as structural material having no relationship to biography? Is it possible to take a neutral position on this question? Or would this be sitting down between two chairs? The question itself is very clear: do we need the poet's biography in order to understand his work, or do we not?

Before we can answer this question, however, we must remember that creative literature exists, not for literary historians, but for readers, and we must consider how the poet's biography operates in the reader's consciousness. Here we shall not regard 'biography' as a self-sufficient class of historical writing (from this point of view Puškin's biography is no different from the biographies of generals and engineers); instead, we shall consider the 'literary functions' of biography as the traditional concomitant of artistic work.

There have been eras during which the personality of the artist was of no interest at all to the audience. Paintings were signed with the donor's name, not the artist's; literary works bore the name of the customer or the printer. There was a great tendency toward anonymity, thus leaving a wide field of investigation for present-day archaeologists and textologists. The name of the master had as much significance as the trademark of a company has today. Thus Rembrandt had no qualms about signing the paintings of his pupil, Maas.

However, during the individualization of creativity – an epoch which cultivated subjectivism in the artistic process – the name and personality of the author came to the forefront. The reader's interest reached beyond the work to its creator. This new relationship towards creativity began with the great writers of the eighteenth century. Before that time the personality of the author was hidden. Bits of gossip and anecdotes about authors did penetrate society, but these anecdotes were not combined into biographical images and considered equally along with authors and personages not connected with literature. In fact, the less gifted the writer, the more numerous the anecdotes about him. Thus anecdotes have come down to us concerning, for example, the Abbé Cotin, a minor eighteenth-century poet – but no one knows his works. At the same time, our information about Molière or about Shakespeare is quite meager, though it is true that nineteenth-century biographers later 'created' the biographies of these writers and even projected their plays onto these imagined biographies. However, such biographies did not prevent others from just as successfully attributing the tragedies of Shakespeare to Bacon, Rutland, or others. From a biographical standpoint, Shakespeare remains the 'iron mask' of literature.

On the other hand, eighteenth-century writers, especially Voltaire, were not only writers but also public figures. Voltaire made his artistic work a tool for propaganda, and his life, bold and provocative, served this same end. The years of exile, the years of reigning at Ferney, were used as weapons for the ideological battle and for preaching. Voltaire's works were inseparably linked with his life. His audience not only read his work but even went on pilgrimages to him. Those who admired his writings were worshipers of his personality; the adversaries of his writings were his personal enemies. Voltaire's personality linked his literary works together. When his name was mentioned, his literary works were not what first came to mind. Even today, when most of his tragedies and poems have been completely forgotten, the image of Voltaire is still alive; those forgotten works shine with reflected light in his unforgettable biography. Equally unforgettable is the biography of his contemporary, Rousseau, who left his *Confessions* and thus bequeathed to posterity the history of his life.

Voltaire and Rousseau, like many of their contemporaries, were prolific in many genres, from musical comedies to novels and philosophical treatises, from epigrams and epitaphs to theoretical articles on physics and music. Only their lives could have united these various forms of verbal creation into a system. This is why their biographies, their letters and memoirs, have become such an integral part of their literary heritage. In fact, the knowledge that their biographies were a constant background for their works compelled Voltaire and Rousseau to dramatize certain epic motifs in their own lives and, furthermore, to create for themselves an artificial legendary biography composed of intentionally selected real and imaginary events. The biographies of such authors require a Ferney or a Jasnaja Poljana: they require pilgrimages by admirers and condemnations from Sorbonnes or Holy Synods.

Following in the footsteps of these eighteenth-century writers, Byron, the poet of sharp-tempered characters, created the canonical biography for a lyrical poet. A biography of a Romantic poet was more than a biography of an author and public figure. The Romantic poet *was* his own hero. His *life* was poetry, and soon there developed a canonical set of actions to be carried out by the poet. Here, the traditions of the eighteenth century served as a model. The end of that century had produced the stereotype of the 'dying poet': young, unable to overcome the adversities of life, perishing in poverty, the fame he merited coming too late. Such were the legendary biographies of two poets, Malfilâtre and Gilbert, later popularized by the Romantics (for example, Alfred de Vigny). The late eighteenth-century poets Parny and Bertin wrote their elegies with a definite orientation toward autobiography. They arranged those elegies in such a way as to convince the reader that their poems were fragments of a real romance, that their Eleonoras and Eucharidas were actual people. Delille in France and our own Xvostov appended footnotes to the feminine names they used, such as 'the poet's name for his wife.'

The necessity for such 'real' commentary was dictated by the style of the period. Readers demanded the complete illusion of life. They made pilgrimages to the final resting places of the heroes of even the most unbelievable novels. For example, near Moscow one can still visit 'Liza's Pond,' in which Karamzin's sugary heroine drowned herself. They say that at Lermontov's house in Pjatigorsk artifacts which belonged to Princess Mary are exhibited.

The readers' demand for a living hero results in the perennial question: from whom is the character drawn? This is the question which Lermontov contemptuously brushed aside in the introduction to *A Hero of Our Time*. In this connection we should consider the usual commentary to Griboedov's *Gore ot uma* [Woe from Wit]; the Moscow 'old-timers' assigned all of Griboedov's heroes to actual people – as is typical of old-timers.

Once the question of copying characters from life has arisen, writers actually *do* begin to copy from life – or at least they pretend to do so. The author becomes a witness to and a living participant in his novels, a living hero. A double transformation takes place: heroes are taken for living personages, and poets become living heroes – their biographies become poems.

In the Puškin era, when the genre of 'friendly epistles' flourished, poets paraded before their audience as characters. Now Puškin writes to Baratynskij from Bessarabia, now Jazykov writes to Puškin. And then all three of them become the themes of lyrical poems.

The lyricism of Puškin's long poems is clearly the result of an orientation towards autobiography. The reader had to feel that he was reading, not the words of an abstract author, but those of a living person whose biographical data were at his disposal. Thus the author had to make literary use of his own biography. So Puškin used his southern exile as a poetic banishment. Motifs of exile, of wanderings, run throughout his poetry in many variations. We must assume that Puškin poetically fostered certain facts of his life. For example, he jealously expunged references to *deva junaja* [the young maid] from poems already completed and well-known in print, and from those widely circulated in manuscript. At the same time, he wrote to his friends in an ambiguous and enigmatic tone about unrequited love. In conversation, he became prone to mysteriously incoherent outpourings. And behold, the poetic legend of a 'concealed love' was created with its ostentatious devices used for concealing love, when it would have been much simpler to keep silent. However, Puškin was concerned about his 'biography,' and the image of a young exile with a hidden and unrequited love, set against the background of Crimean nature, fascinated him. He needed this image as a frame for his southern poems. Nonetheless, present-day biographers have dealt mercilessly with this stylish legend. They have been determined to learn at any cost the identity of the woman whom Puškin so hopelessly loved (or pretended to love). Thus they have destroyed the very core of the legend – the unknown. In place of 'young maids,' they have proposed various respectable society women.

The interrelationships of life and literature became confused during the Romantic era. Romanticism and its mores constitute a problem to which careful investigations have been devoted. It is sometimes difficult to decide whether literature recreates phenomena from life or whether the opposite is in fact the case: that the phenomena of life are the result of the penetration of literary clichés into reality. Such motifs as the duel, the Caucasus, etc., were invariant components both of literature and of the poet's biography.

The poets used their lives to realize a literary purpose, and these literary biographies were necessary for the readers. The readers cried: 'Author! author!' – but they were actually calling for the slender youth in a cloak, with a lyre in his hands and an enigmatic expression on his face. This demand for a potentially existing author, whether real or not, gave rise to a special kind of anonymous literature: literature with an invented author, whose biography was appended to the work. We find a literary precedent for this genre in Voltaire's mystifications. He published stories under the name of Guillaume Vadé and appended a letter written by Catherine Vadé (the imaginary first cousin of the imagined author) describing the last days of her cousin Guillaume.

In this connection, we should also consider the stories of Belkin and Rudyj Pan'ko. At the basis of these mystifications lies the very same demand of the public: 'Give us a living author!' If the author wanted to hide, then he had to send forth an invented narrator. Biography became an element of literature.

The biographies of real authors, for example of Puškin and Lermontov, were cultivated as oral legends. How many interesting anecdotes the old-timers 'knew' about Puškin! Read the reminiscences of the Kišenev inhabitants about the poet. You will find tales that even Puškin

wouldn't have dreamt of. In these tales, a tragic love and an exotic lover
(a gypsy or a Greek) are absolutely necessary. As fiction, however, all
this is far more superior to the recently published anecdote in the notes
of Naščokin-Bartenevskij concerning Puškin and the Countess Finkel-
'mon.

Thus, legends about poets were created, and it was extremely
important for the literary historian to occupy himself with the restoration of these legends, i.e., with the removal of later layers and the
reduction of the legend to its pure 'canonical' form. These biographical
legends are the literary conception of the poet's life, and this conception
was necessary as a perceptible background for the poet's literary works.
The legends are a premise which the author himself took into account
during the creative process.

The biographical commentary to a literary work often consists of the
curriculum vitae, the genealogy, of the characters mentioned in the
work. However, in referring to a given character, the author did not
assume that the reader knew the curriculum vitae of that character.
However, he did assume that the reader knew the character's anecdotal
representation, consisting of actual and invented material, created in the
reader's milieu. When Puškin was writing *Mozart and Salieri*, what was
important was not the actual historical relationship between these two
composers (and here their biographies, based on documents and
investigations, would not help anyway), but the fact that there existed a
legend about the poisoning of Mozart by Salieri, and that rumors were
current that Beaumarchais had poisoned his wives. The question of
whether these rumors and legends had any foundation in fact was
irrelevant to their function.

In exactly the same way, the poet considers as a premise to his
creations not his actual curriculum vitae, but his ideal biographical
legend. Therefore, only this biographical legend should be important
to the literary historian in his attempt to reconstruct the psychological
milieu surrounding a literary work. Furthermore, the biographical
legend is necessary only to the extent that the literary work includes
references to 'biographical' facts (real or legendary) of the author's life.

However, the poet did not always have a biography. Toward the
middle of the nineteenth century, the poet-hero was replaced by the
professional poet, the businessman-journalist. The writer wrote down
his manuscript and gave it to a publisher; he did not allow any glimpses
of his personal life. The human face of the author peered out only in
pasquinades, in satirical pamphlets, or in monetary squabbles which
burst out noisily in public whenever contributors were not satisfied

with their royalties. Thus the phenomenon of writers without biographies appeared. All attempts to invent biographies for these writers and to project their work onto these biographies have consistently ended in farce. Nekrasov, for example, appears on the literary scene without a biography, as do Ostrovskij and Fet. Their works are self-contained units. There are no biographical features shedding light on the meaning of their works. Nevertheless, there are scholars who want to imagine literary biographies even for these authors.

It is, of course, obvious that these authors do have *actual* biographies, and that their literary work enters into these biographies as a fact of their lives. Such actual biographies of private individuals may be interesting for cultural history, but not for the history of literature. (I say nothing of those literary historians who classify literary phenomena on the basis of the circumstances of the writer's birth.) No poetic image of the author – except perhaps as a deliberately invented narrator who is introduced into the story itself (like Puškin's Belkin) – can be found in this period. Works did not depend on the presence of a biographical background.

This 'cold' nineteenth-century writer, however, did not represent an exclusive type which was to replace 'biographically oriented' literature forever. At the very end of the century interest in the author began to arise once again, and this interest has continued to grow to the present day. First, there appeared a timid interest in 'good people.' We suffered through a period when the writer was necessarily considered 'a good person'; we suffered through images of wretched victims, images of oppressed consumptive poets. We suffered through them to the point of nausea.

In the twentieth century there appeared a special type of writer with a demonstrative biography, one which shouted out: 'Look at how bad and how impudent I am! Look! And don't turn your head away, because all of you are just as bad, only you are faint-hearted and hide yourselves. But I am bold; I strip myself stark naked and walk around in public without feeling ashamed.' This was the reaction to the 'sweetness' of the 'good man.'

Fifteen years ago someone came out with a 'calendar of writers,' in which the autobiographies of the men of letters fashionable at that time were collected. These writers all vied with one another in crying out that they had no formal education because they had been expelled from high school and from trade school, that they had only torn trousers and a few buttons – and all this because they absolutely didn't care about anything.

However, alongside this petty naughtiness in literature, there emerged a new intimate style. Many writers, of course, still persisted in concealing their private lives from the public. Sologub, for one, systematically refused to provide any information whatsoever about himself. But other and rather different trends were also present in literature. Vasilij Rozanov created a distinctive intimate style. The pages of his books were like 'falling leaves,' and he strolled through them uncombed, whole, completely himself. He produced a special literature of intimate conversations and confidential confessions. We know, by his own admission, that he was a mystifier. It is the business of cultural historians to judge to what extent the face he carefully drew in his fragments and aphorisms was his own. As a literary legend, Rozanov's image has been drawn, by him, definitively and with complete consistency. This image shows little resemblance either to the 'heroic poets' of the beginning of the nineteenth century or to the 'good persons' with progressive convictions of the end of the century. However, it is impossible to deny that this image was viable and artistically functional during the years of Rozanov's literary work. Furthermore, the autobiographical devices of Rozanov's literary manner have survived him and are still present today in novelistic or fragmentary memoirs.

Parallel to this prosaic element in the Symbolist movement, there also developed a biographical lyricism. Blok was certainly a poet with a lyrical biography. The numerous memoirs and biographical works on Blok which appeared within a year of his death testify to the fact that his biography was a living and necessary commentary to his works. His poems are lyrical episodes about himself, and his readers always informed themselves (perhaps at third-hand) about the principal events of his life. It would be inaccurate to say that Blok put his life on display. Nonetheless, his poems did arouse an insurmountable desire to know about the author, and they made his readers avidly follow the various twists and turns of his life. Blok's legend is an inescapable concomitant to his poetry. The elements of intimate confession and biographical allusion in his poetry must be taken into account.

Symbolism was superseded by Futurism, which intensified to a hyperbolic clarity those features which had previously appeared only in hidden, mystically masked forms of Symbolism. Intimate confessions and allusions were transformed into demonstrative declarations delivered in a monumental style. Whereas Blok's biography appeared only as a legendary concomitant to his poetry, the Futurist legendary biographies were boldly inserted into the works themselves.

Futurism took the Romantic orientation towards autobiography to its ultimate conclusions. The author really became the hero of his works. We need mention here only the construction of Majakovskij's books: they are an open diary in which intimate feelings are recorded. This type of construction, in fact, intersects the path of the future biographer, who will have to try to construct a different, extraliterary, biography. Today the writer shows his readers his own life and writes his own biography, tightly binding it to the literary cycles of his work. If, for example, Gor'kij drives away importunate idlers, then he does this knowingly, as a demonstration: he knows that this very fact will be taken into account in his biography. Just consider how many of today's poets reminisce about themselves and their friends, how many of them produce memoir literature – memoirs transformed into artistic structures.

Obviously, the question of the role of biography in literary history cannot be solved uniformly for all literatures. There are writers with biographies and writers without biographies. To attempt to compose biographies for the latter is to write satires or denunciations on the alive or the dead as well. On the other hand, for a writer with a biography, the facts of the author's life must be taken into consideration. Indeed, in the works themselves the juxtaposition of the texts and the author's biography plays a structural role. The literary work plays on the potential reality of the author's subjective outpourings and confessions. Thus the biography that is useful to the literary historian is not the author's curriculum vitae or the investigator's account of his life. What the literary historian really needs is the biographical legend created by the author himself. Only such a legend is a *literary fact*.

As far as 'documentary biographies' are concerned, these belong to the domain of cultural history, on a par with the biographies of generals and inventors. With regard to literature and its history, these biographies may be considered only as external (even if necessary) reference material of an auxiliary nature.

NOTE

This essay was originally published as 'Literatura i biografija,' *Kniga i revoljucija*, 4 (1923), pp. 6–9. Translated by Herbert Eagle.

11

W. K. WIMSATT JR
and MONROE C. BEARDSLEY

from 'The Intentional Fallacy'

The claim of the author's 'intention' upon the critic's judgement has been challenged in a number of recent discussions, notably in the debate entitled *The Personal Heresy*, between Professors Lewis and Tillyard. But it seems doubtful if this claim and most of its romantic corollaries are as yet subject to any widespread questioning. The present writers, in a short article entitled 'Intention' for a *Dictionary*[1] of literary criticism, raised the issue but were unable to pursue its implications at any length. We argued that the design or intention of the author is neither available nor desirable as a standard for judging the success of a work of literary art, and it seems to us that this is a principle which goes deep into some differences in the history of critical attitudes. It is a principle which accepted or rejected points to the polar opposites of classical 'imitation' and romantic expression. It entails many specific truths about inspiration, authenticity, biography, literary history and scholarship, and about some trends of contemporary poetry, especially its allusiveness. There is hardly a problem of literary criticism in which the critic's approach will not be qualified by his view of 'intention.'

'Intention,' as we shall use the term, corresponds to *what he intended* in a formula which more or less explicitly has had wide acceptance. 'In order to judge the poet's performance, we must know *what he intended.*' Intention is design or plan in the author's mind. Intention has obvious affinities for the author's attitude towards his work, the way he felt, what made him write.

We begin our discussion with a series of propositions summarized and abstracted to a degree where they seem to us axiomatic.

1. A poem does not come into existence by accident. The words of a poem, as Professor Stoll has remarked, come out of a head, not out of a hat. Yet to insist on the designing intellect as a *cause* of a poem is not to grant the design or intention as a *standard* by which the critic is to judge the worth of the poet's performance.

2. One must ask how a critic expects to get an answer to the question about intention. How is he to find out what the poet tried to do? If the poet succeeded in doing it, then the poem itself shows what he was trying to do. And if the poet did not succeed, then the poem is not adequate evidence, and the critic must go outside the poem – for evidence of an intention that did not become effective in the poem. 'Only one *caveat* must be borne in mind,' says an eminent intentional-ist[2] in a moment when his theory repudiates itself; 'the poet's aim must be judged at the moment of the creative act, that is to say, by the art of the poem itself.'

3. Judging a poem is like judging a pudding or a machine. One demands that it work. It is only because an artifact works that we infer the intention of an artificer. 'A poem should not mean but be.' A poem can *be* only through its *meaning* – since its medium is words – yet it *is*, simply *is*, in the sense that we have no excuse for inquiring what part is intended or meant. Poetry is a feat of style by which a complex of meaning is handled all at once. Poetry succeeds because all or most of what is said or implied is relevant; what is irrelevant has been excluded, like lumps from pudding and 'bugs' from machinery. In this respect poetry differs from practical messages, which are successful if and only if we correctly infer the intention. They are more abstract than poetry.

4. The meaning of a poem may certainly be a personal one, in the sense that a poem expresses a personality or state of soul rather than a physical object like an apple. But even a short lyric poem is dramatic, the response of a speaker (no matter how abstractly conceived) to a situation (no matter how universalized). We ought to impute the thoughts and attitudes of the poem immediately to the dramatic *speaker*, and if to the author at all, only by an act of biographical inference.

5. There is a sense in which an author, by revision, may better achieve his original intention. But it is a very abstract sense. He intended to write a better work, or a better work of a certain kind, and now has done it. But it follows that his former concrete intention was not his intention. 'He's the man we were in search of, that's true,' says Hardy's rustic constable, 'and yet he's not the man we were in search of. For the man we were in search of was not the man we wanted.'

'Is not a critic,' asks Professor Stoll, 'a judge, who does not explore his own consciousness, but determines the author's meaning or intention, as if the poem were a will, a contract, or the constitution? The poem is not the critic's own.' He has accurately diagnosed two forms of irresponsibility, one of which he prefers. Our view is yet different. The poem is not the critic's own and not the author's (it is detached from the author at birth and goes about the world beyond his power to intend about it or control it). The poem belongs to the public. It is embodied in language, the peculiar possession of the public, and it is about the human being, an object of public knowledge. What is said about the poem is subject to the same scrutiny as any statement in linguistics or in the general science of psychology.

A critic of our *Dictionary* article, Ananda K. Coomaraswamy, has argued[3] that there are two kinds of inquiry about a work of art: (1) whether the artist achieved his intentions; (2) whether the work of art 'ought ever to have been undertaken at all' and so 'whether it is worth preserving.' Number (2), Coomaraswamy maintains, is not 'criticism of any work of art *qua* work of art,' but is rather moral criticism; number (1) is artistic criticism. But we maintain that (2) need not be moral criticism: that there is another way of deciding whether works of art are worth preserving and whether, in a sense, they 'ought' to have been undertaken, and this is the way of objective criticism of works of art as such, the way which enables us to distinguish between a skillful murder and a skillful poem. A skillful murder is an example which Coomaraswamy uses, and in his system the difference between the murder and the poem is simply a 'moral' one, not an 'artistic' one, since each if carried out according to plan is 'artistically' successful. We maintain that (2) is an inquiry of more worth than (1), and since (2) and not (1) is capable of distinguishing poetry from murder, the name 'artistic criticism' is properly given to (2).

II

It is not so much a historical statement as a definition to say that the intentional fallacy is a romantic one. When a rhetorician of the first century A.D. writes: 'Sublimity is the echo of a great soul,' or when he tells us that 'Homer enters into the sublime actions of his heroes' and 'shares the full inspiration of the combat,' we shall not be surprised to find this rhetorician considered as a distant harbinger of romanticism and greeted in the warmest terms by Saintsbury. One may wish to argue whether Longinus should be called romantic, but there can hardly be a doubt that in one important way he is.

Goethe's three questions for 'constructive criticism' are 'What did the author set out to do? Was his plan reasonable and sensible, and how far did he succeed in carrying it out?' If one leaves out the middle question, one has in effect the system of Croce – the culmination and crowning philosophic expression of romanticism. The beautiful is the successful intuition-expression, and the ugly is the unsuccessful; the intuition or private part of art is *the* aesthetic fact, and the medium or public part is not the subject of aesthetic at all.

> The Madonna of Cimabue is still in the Church of Santa Maria Novella; but does she speak to the visitor of to-day as to the Florentines of the thirteenth century?
>
> *Historical interpretation* labours . . . to reintegrate in us the psychological conditions which have changed in the course of history. It . . . enables us to see a work of art (a physical object) as its *author saw it* in the moment of production.[4]

The first italics are Croce's, the second ours. The upshot of Croce's system is an ambiguous emphasis on history. With such passages as a point of departure a critic may write a nice analysis of the meaning or 'spirit' of a play by Shakespeare or Corneille – a process that involves close historical study but remains aesthetic criticism – or he may, with equal plausibility, produce an essay in sociology, biography, or other kinds of non-aesthetic history.

III

> I went to the poets; tragic, dithyrambic, and all sorts . . . I took them some of the most elaborate passages in their own writings, and asked what was the meaning of them . . . Will you believe me? . . . there is hardly a person present who would not have talked better about their poetry than they did themselves. Then I knew that not by wisdom do poets write poetry, but by a sort of genius and inspiration.

That reiterated mistrust of the poets which we hear from Socrates may have been part of a rigorously ascetic view in which we hardly wish to participate, yet Plato's Socrates saw a truth about the poetic mind which the world no longer commonly sees – so much criticism, and that the most inspirational and most affectionately remembered, has proceeded from the poets themselves.

Certainly the poets have had something to say that the critic and professor could not say; their message has been more exciting: that poetry should come as naturally as leaves to a tree, that poetry is the lava of the imagination, or that it is emotion recollected in tranquillity. But it is necessary that we realize the character and authority of such testimony. There is only a fine shade of difference between such expressions and a kind of earnest advice that authors often give. Thus Edward Young, Carlyle, Walter Pater:

> I know two golden rules from *ethics*, which are no less golden in *Composition*, than in life. 1. *Know thyself*, 2dly, *Reverence thyself.*

> This is the grand secret for finding readers and retaining them: let him who would move and convince others, be first moved and convinced himself. Horace's rule, *Si vis me flere*, is applicable in a wider sense than the literal one. To every poet, to every writer, we might say: Be true, if you would be believed.

> Truth! there can be no merit, no craft at all, without that. And further, all beauty is in the long run only *fineness* of truth, or what we call expression, the finer accommodation of speech to that vision within.

And Housman's little handbook to the poetic mind yields this illustration:

> Having drunk a pint of beer at luncheon – beer is a sedative to the brain, and my afternoons are the least intellectual portion of my life – I would go out for a walk of two or three hours. As I went along, thinking of nothing in particular, only looking at things around me and following the progress of the seasons, there would flow into my mind, with sudden and unaccountable emotion, sometimes a line or two of verse, sometimes a whole stanza at once.

This is the logical terminus of the series already quoted. Here is a confession of how poems were written which would do as a definition of poetry just as well as 'emotion recollected in tranquillity' – and which the young poet might equally well take to heart as a practical rule. Drink a pint of beer, relax, go walking, think on nothing in particular, look at things, surrender yourself to yourself, search for the truth in your own soul, listen to the sound of your own inside voice, discover and express the *vraie vérité*.

It is probably true that all this is excellent advice for poets. The young imagination fired by Wordsworth and Carlyle is probably closer to the verge of producing a poem than the mind of the student who has been sobered by Aristotle or Richards. The art of inspiring poets, or at least of inciting something like poetry in young persons, has probably .gone further in our day than ever before. Books of creative writing such as those issued from the Lincoln School are interesting evidence of what a child can do.[5] All this, however, would appear to belong to an art separate from criticism – to a psychological discipline, a system of self-development, a yoga, which the young poet perhaps does well to notice, but which is something different from the public art of evaluating poems.

Coleridge and Arnold were better critics than most poets have been, and if the critical tendency dried up the poetry in Arnold and perhaps in Coleridge, it is not inconsistent with our argument, which is that judgement of poems is different from the art of producing them. Coleridge has given us the classic 'anodyne' story, and tells what he can about the genesis of a poem which he calls a 'psychological curiosity,' but his definitions of poetry and of the poetic quality 'imagination' are to be found elsewhere and in quite other terms.

It would be convenient if the passwords of the intentional school, 'sincerity,' 'fidelity,' 'spontaneity,' 'authenticity,' 'genuineness,' 'originality,' could be equated with terms such as 'integrity,' 'relevance,' 'unity,' 'function,' 'maturity,' 'subtlety,' 'adequacy,' and other more precise terms of evaluation – in short, if 'expression' always meant aesthetic achievement. But this is not so.

'Aesthetic' art, says Professor Curt Ducasse, an ingenious theorist of expression, is the conscious objectification of feelings, in which an intrinsic part is the critical moment. The artist corrects the objectification when it is not adequate. But this may mean that the earlier attempt was not successful in objectifying the self, or 'it may also mean that it was a successful objectification of a self which, when it confronted us clearly, we disowned and repudiated in favor of another.'[6] What is the standard by which we disown or accept the self? Professor Ducasse does not say. Whatever it may be, however, this standard is an element in the definition of art which will not reduce to terms of objectification. The evaluation of the work of art remains public; the work is measured against something outside the author.

. . .

v

If the distinction between kinds of evidence has implications for the historical critic, it has them no less for the contemporary poet and his critic. Or, since every rule for a poet is but another side of a judgement by a critic, and since the past is the realm of the scholar and critic, and the future and present that of the poet and the critical leaders of taste, we may say that the problems arising in literary scholarship from the intentional fallacy are matched by others which arise in the world of progressive experiment.

The question of 'allusiveness,' for example, as acutely posed by the poetry of Eliot, is certainly one where a false judgement is likely to involve the intentional fallacy. The frequency and depth of literary allusion in the poetry of Eliot and others has driven so many in pursuit of full meanings to the *Golden Bough* and the Elizabethan drama that it has become a kind of commonplace to suppose that we do not know what a poet means unless we have traced him in his reading – a supposition redolent with intentional implications. The stand taken by F. O. Matthiessen is a sound one and partially forestalls the difficulty.

> If one reads these lines with an attentive ear and is sensitive to their sudden shifts in movement, the contrast between the actual Thames and the idealized vision of it during an age before it flowed through a megalopolis is sharply conveyed by that movement itself, whether or not one recognizes the refrain to be from Spenser.

Eliot's allusions work when we know them – and to a great extent even when we do not know them, through their suggestive power.

But sometimes we find allusions supported by notes, and it is a nice question whether the notes function more as guides to send us where we may be educated, or more as indications in themselves about the character of the allusions. 'Nearly everything of importance . . . that is apposite to an appreciation of "The Waste Land," ' writes Matthiessen of Miss Weston's book, 'has been incorporated into the structure of the poem itself, or into Eliot's Notes.' And with such an admission it may begin to appear that it would not much matter if Eliot invented his sources (as Sir Walter Scott invented chapter epigraphs from 'old plays' and 'anonymous' authors, or as Coleridge wrote marginal glosses for *The Ancient Mariner*). Allusions to Dante, Webster, Marvell, or Baudelaire doubtless gain something because these writers existed, but it is doubtful whether the same can be said for an allusion to an obscure Elizabethan:

> The sound of horns and motors, which shall bring
> Sweeney to Mrs. Porter in the spring.

'Cf. Day, *Parliament of Bees:*' says Eliot,

> When of a sudden, listening, you shall hear,
> A noise of horns and hunting, which shall bring
> Actaeon to Diana in the spring,
> Where all shall see her naked skin.

The irony is completed by the quotation itself; had Eliot, as is quite conceivable, composed these lines to furnish his own background, there would be no loss of validity. The conviction may grow as one reads Eliot's next note: 'I do not know the origin of the ballad from which these lines are taken: it was reported to me from Sydney, Australia.' The important word in this note – on Mrs. Porter and her daughter who washed their feet in soda water – is 'ballad.' And if one should feel from the lines themselves their 'ballad' quality, there would be little need for the note. Ultimately, the inquiry must focus on the integrity of such notes as parts of the poem, for where they constitute special information about the meaning of phrases in the poem, they ought to be subject to the same scrutiny as any of the other words in which it is written. Matthiessen believes the notes were the price Eliot 'had to pay in order to avoid what he would have considered muffling the energy of his poem by extended connecting links in the text itself.' But it may be questioned whether the notes and the need for them are not equally muffling. F. W. Bateson has plausibly argued that Tennyson's 'The Sailor Boy' would be better if half the stanzas were omitted, and the best versions of ballads like 'Sir Patrick Spens' owe their power to the very audacity with which the minstrel has taken for granted the story upon which he comments. What then if a poet finds he cannot take so much for granted in a more recondite context and rather than write informatively, supplies notes? It can be said in favor of this plan that at least the notes do not pretend to be dramatic, as they would if written in verse. On the other hand, the notes may look like unassimilated material lying loose beside the poem, necessary for the meaning of the verbal symbol, but not integrated, so that the symbol stands incomplete.

We mean to suggest by the above analysis that whereas notes tend to seem to justify themselves as external indexes to the author's *intention*, yet they ought to be judged like any other parts of a composition (verbal arrangement special to a particular context), and when so judged their reality as parts of the poem, or their imaginative integration with the rest of the poem, may come into question. Mathiessen, for instance, sees that Eliot's titles for poems and his epigraphs are informative apparatus, like the notes. But while he is worried by some of the notes and thinks that Eliot 'appears to be mocking himself for writing the note at the same time that he wants to convey something by it,' Matthiessen believes that the 'device' of epigraphs 'is not at all open to the objection of not being sufficiently structural.' 'The *intention*,' he says, 'is to enable the poet to secure a condensed expression in the poem itself.' 'In each case the epigraph is *designed* to form an integral part of the effect of the poem.' And Eliot himself, in his notes, has justified his poetic practice in terms of intention.

> The Hanged Man, a member of the traditional pack, fits my purpose in two ways: because he is associated in my mind with the Hanged God of Frazer, and because I associate him with the hooded figure in the passage of the disciples to Emmaus in Part V . . . The man with Three Staves (an authentic member of the Tarot pack) I associate, quite arbitrarily, with the Fisher King himself.

And perhaps he is to be taken more seriously here, when off guard in a note, than when in his Norton Lectures he comments on the difficulty of saying what a poem means and adds playfully that he thinks of prefixing to a second edition of *Ash Wednesday* some lines from *Don Juan*:

> I don't pretend that I quite understand
> My own meaning when I would be *very* fine;
> But the fact is that I have nothing planned
> Unless it were to be a moment merry.

If Eliot and other contemporary poets have any characteristic fault, it may be in *planning* too much.

Allusiveness in poetry is one of several critical issues by which we have illustrated the more abstract issue of intentionalism, but it may be for today the most important illustration. As a poetic practice allusiveness would appear to be in some recent poems an extreme corollary of the romantic intentionalist assumption, and as a critical issue it challenges and brings to light in a special way the basic premise of intentionalism. The following instance from the poetry of Eliot may serve to epitomize the practical implications of what we have been saying. In Eliot's 'Love Song of J. Alfred Prufrock,' toward the end, occurs the line: 'I have heard the mermaids singing, each to each,' and this bears a certain resemblance to a line in a Song by John Donne, 'Teach me to heare Mermaides singing,' so that for the reader acquainted to a certain degree with Donne's poetry, the critical question arises: Is Eliot's line an allusion to Donne's? Is Prufrock thinking about Donne? Is Eliot thinking about Donne? We suggest that there are two radically different ways of looking for an answer to this question. There is (1) the way of poetic analysis and exegesis, which inquires whether it makes any sense if Eliot-Prufrock *is* thinking about Donne. In an earlier part of the poem, when Prufrock asks, 'Would it have been worth while, . . . To have squeezed the universe into a ball,' his words take half their sadness and irony from certain energetic and passionate lines of Marvel 'To His Coy Mistress.' But the exegetical inquirer may wonder whether mermaids considered as 'strange sights' (to hear them is in Donne's poem analogous to getting with child a mandrake root) have much to do with Prufrock's mermaids, which seem to be symbols of romance and dynamism, and which incidentally have literary authentication, if they need it, in a line of a sonnet by Gérard de Nerval. This method of inquiry may lead to the conclusion that the given resemblance between Eliot and Donne is without significance and is better not thought of, or the method may have the disadvantage of providing no certain conclusion. Nevertheless, we submit that this is the true and objective way of criticism, as contrasted to what the very uncertainty of exegesis might tempt a second kind of critic to undertake: (2) the way of biographical or genetic inquiry, in which, taking advantage of the fact that Eliot is still alive, and in the spirit of a man who would settle a bet, the critic writes to Eliot and asks what he meant, or if he had Donne in mind. We shall not here weigh the probabilities – whether Eliot would answer that he meant nothing at all, had nothing at all in mind – a sufficiently good answer to such a question – or in an unguarded moment might furnish a clear and, within its limit, irrefutable answer. Our point is that such an answer to such an inquiry would have nothing to do with the poem 'Prufrock'; it would not be a critical inquiry. Critical inquiries, unlike bets, are not settled in this way. Critical inquiries are not settled by consulting the oracle.

NOTES

1. *Dictionary of World Literature*, Joseph T. Shipley, ed. (New York, 1942), 326–9.
2. J. E. Spingarn, 'The new criticism', in Criticism in America (New York, 1924), 24–5.
3. Ananda K. Coomaraswamy, 'Intention', in American Bookman, i (1944), 41–8.
4. It is true that Croce himself in his *Ariosto, Shakespeare, and Corneille* (London, 1920), chap. vii, 'The Practical Personality and the Poetical Personality', and in his *Defence of Poetry* (Oxford, 1933), 24, and elsewhere, early and late, has delivered telling attacks on emotive geneticism, but the main drive of the *Aesthetic* is surely towards a kind of cognitive intentionalism.
5. See Hughes Mearns, *Creative Youth* (Garden City, 1925), esp. 10, 27–9. The technique of inspiring poems has apparently been outdone more recently by the study of inspiration in

successful poets and other artists. See, for instance, Rosamond E. M. Harding, *An Anatomy of Inspiration* (Cambridge, 1940); Julius Portnoy, *A Psychology of Art Creation* (Philadelphia, 1942); Rudolf Arnheim and others, *Poets at Work* (New York, 1947); Phyllis Bartlett, *Poems in Process* (New York, 1951); Brewster Ghiselin, ed., *The Creative Process: a symposium* (Berkeley and Los Angeles, 1952).

6. Curt Ducasse, *The Philosophy of Art* (New York, 1929), 116.

12

GEORGES POULET

from 'Criticism and the Experience of Interiority'

At the beginning of Mallarmé's unfinished story *Igitur* there is the description of an empty room, in the middle of which, on a table, there is an open book. This seems to me the situation of every book, until someone comes and begins to read it. Books are objects. On a table, on shelves, in store windows, they wait for someone to come and deliver them from their materiality, from their immobility. When I see them on display, I look at them as I would at animals for sale, kept in little cages, and so obviously hoping for a buyer. For – there is no doubting it – animals do know that their fate depends on a human intervention, thanks to which they will be delivered from the shame of being treated as objects. Isn't the same true of books? Made of paper and ink, they lie where they are put until the moment someone shows an interest in them. They wait. Are they aware that an act of man might suddenly transform their existence? They appear to be lit up with that hope. Read me, they seem to say. I find it hard to resist their appeal. No, books are not just objects among others.

This feeling they give me – I sometimes have it with other objects. I have it, for example, with vases and statues. It would never occur to me to walk around a sewing machine or to look at the under side of a plate. I am quite satisfied with the face they present to me. But statues make me want to circle around them, vases make me want to turn them in my hands. I wonder why. Isn't it because they give me the illusion that there is something in them which, from a different angle, I might be able to see? Neither vase nor statue seems fully revealed by the unbroken perimeter of its surfaces. In addition to its surfaces it must have an interior. What this interior might be, that is what intrigues me and makes me circle around them, as though looking for the entrance to a secret chamber. But there is no such entrance (save for the mouth of the vase, which is not a true entrance since it gives access only to a little space to put flowers in). So the vase and the statue are closed. They oblige me to remain outside. We can have no true rapport – whence my sense of uneasiness.

So much for statues and vases. I hope books are not like them. Buy a vase, take it home, put it on your table or your mantel, and, after a while, it will allow itself to be made a part of your household. But it will be no less a vase, for that. On the other hand, take a book, and you will find it offering, opening itself. It is this openness of the book which I find so moving. A book is not shut in by its contours, is not walled-up as in a fortress. It asks nothing better than to exist outside itself, or to let you exist in it. In short, the extraordinary fact in the case of a book is the falling away of the barriers between you and it. You are inside it; it is inside you; there is no longer either outside or inside.

Such is the initial phenomenon produced whenever I take up a book, and begin to read it. At the precise moment that I see, surging out of the object I hold open before me, a quantity of significations which my mind grasps, I realize that what I hold in my hands is no longer just an object, or even simply a living thing. I am aware of a rational being, of a consciousness; the consciousness of another, no different from the one I automatically assume in every human being I encounter, except that in this case the consciousness is open to me, welcomes me, lets me look deep inside itself, and even allows me, with unheard-of license, to think what it thinks and feel what it feels.

Unheard of, I say. Unheard of, first, is the disappearance of the 'object.' Where is the book I held in my hands? It is still there, and at the same time it is there no longer, it is nowhere. That object wholly object, that thing made of paper, as there are things made of metal or porcelaine, that object is no more, or at least it is as if it no longer existed, as long as I read the book. For the book is no longer a material reality. It has become a series of words, of images, of ideas which in their turn begin to exist. And where is this new existence? Surely not in the paper object. Nor, surely, in external space. There is only one place left for this new existence: my innermost self.

How has this come about? By what means, through whose intercession? How can I have opened my own mind so completely to what is usually shut out of it? I do not know. I know only that, while reading, I perceive in my mind a number of significations which have made themselves at home there. Doubtless they are still objects: images, ideas, words, objects of my thought. And yet, from this point of view, there is an enormous difference. For the book, like the vase, like the statue, like the table, was an object among others, residing in the external world: the world which objects ordinarily inhabit exclusively in their own society or each on its own, in no need of being thought by my thought; whereas, in this interior world where, like fish in an aquarium, words, images, and ideas disport themselves, these mental entities, in order to exist, need the shelter which I provide; they are dependent on my consciousness.

This dependence is at once a disadvantage and an advantage. As I have just observed, it is the privilege of exterior objects to dispense with any interference from the mind. All they ask is to be let alone. They manage by themselves. But the same is surely not true of interior objects. By definition they are condemned to change their very nature, condemned to lose their materiality. They become images, ideas, words, that is to say purely mental entities. In sum, in order to exist as mental objects they must relinquish their existence as real objects. On the one hand, this is cause for regret. As soon as I replace my direct perception of reality by the words of a book, I deliver myself, bound hand and foot, to the omnipotence of fiction. I say farewell to what is, in order to feign belief in what is not. I surround myself with fictitious beings; I become the prey of language. There is no escaping this takeover. Language surrounds me with its unreality. On the other hand, the transmutation through language of reality into a fictional equivalent, has undeniable advantages. The universe of fiction is infinitely more elastic than the world of objective reality. It lends itself to any use: it yields with little resistance to the importunities of the mind. Moreover – and of all its benefits I find this the most appealing – this interior universe constituted by language does not seem radically opposed to the *me* who thinks it. Doubtless what I glimpse through the words, are mental forms not divested of an appearance of objectivity. But they do not seem to be of another nature than my mind which thinks them. They are objects, but subjectified objects. In short, since everything has become part of my mind thanks to the intervention of language, the opposition between the subject and its objects has been considerably attenuated. And thus the greatest advantage of literature is that I am persuaded by it that I am free from my usual sense of incompatibility between my consciousness and its objects.

This is the remarkable transformation wrought in me through the act of reading. Not only does it cause the physical objects around me to disappear, including the very book I am reading, but it replaces those external objects with a congeries of mental objects in close *rapport* with my own consciousness. And yet the very intimacy in which I now live with my objects is going to present me with new problems. The most curious of these is the following: I am someone who happens to have as objects of his own thought, thoughts which are part of a book I am reading, and which are therefore the cogitations of another. They are the thoughts of another, and yet it is I who am their subject. The situation is even more astonishing than the one noted above. I am thinking the thoughts of another. Of course, there would be no cause for astonishment if I were thinking it as the thought of another. But I think it as my very own. Ordinarily there is the *I* which thinks, which recognizes itself (when it takes its bearings) in thoughts which may have come from elsewhere but which it takes upon itself as its own in the moment it thinks them. This is how we must take Diderot's declaration 'Mes pensées sont *mes* catins' ('My thoughts are *my* whores'). That is, they sleep with everybody without ceasing to belong to their author. Now, in the present case things are quite different. Because of the strange invasion of my person by the thoughts of another, I am a self who is granted the experience of thinking thoughts foreign to him. I am the subject of thoughts other than my own. My consciousness behaves as though it were the consciousness of another.

This merits reflection. In a certain sense I must recognize that no idea really belongs to me. Ideas belong to no one. They pass from one mind to another as coins pass from hand to hand. Consequently, nothing could be more misleading than the attempt to define a consciousness by the ideas which it utters or entertains. But whatever these ideas may be, however strong the tie which binds them to their source, however transitory may be their sojourn in my own mind, so long as I entertain them I assert myself as subject of these ideas; I am the subjective principle for whom the ideas serve for the time being as the predications. Furthermore, this subjective principle can in no wise be conceived as a predication, as something which is discussed, referred to. It is I who think, who contemplate, who am engaged in speaking. In short it is never a *he* but an *I*.

Now what happens when I read a book? Am I then the subject of a series of predications which are not *my* predications? That is impossible, perhaps even a contradiction in terms. I feel sure that as soon as I think something, that something becomes in some indefinable way my own. Whatever I think is a part of *my* mental world. And yet here I am thinking a thought which manifestly belongs to another mental world, which is being thought in me just as though I did not exist. Already the notion is inconceivable and seems even more so if I reflect that, since every thought must have a subject to think it, this *thought* which is alien to me and yet in me, must also have in me a *subject* which is alien to me. It all happens, then, as though reading were the act by which a thought managed to bestow itself within me with a subject not myself. Whenever I read, I mentally pronounce an *I*, and yet the *I* which I pronouce is not myself. This is true even when the hero of a novel is presented in the third person, and even when there is no hero and nothing but reflections or propositions: for as soon as something is presented as *thought*, there has to be a thinking subject with whom, at least for the time being, I identify, forgetting myself, alienated from myself. 'Je est un autre,' said Rimbaud. Another *I*, who has replaced my own, and who will continue to do so as long as I read. Reading is just that: a way of giving way not only to a host of alien words, images, ideas, but also to the very alien principle which utters them and shelters them.

The phenomenon is indeed hard to explain, even to conceive, and yet, once admitted, it explains to me what might otherwise seem even more inexplicable. For how could I explain, without such take-over of my innermost subjective being, the astonishing facility with which I not only understand but even *feel* what I read. When I read as I ought – that is without mental reservation, without any desire to preserve my independence of judgement, and with the total commitment required of any reader – my comprehension becomes intuitive and any feeling proposed to me is immediately assumed by me. In other words, the kind of comprehension in question here is not a movement from the unknown to the known, from the strange to the familiar, from outside to inside. It might rather be called a phenomenon by which mental objects rise up from the depths of consciousness into the light of recognition. On the other hand – and without contradiction – reading implies something resembling the apperception I have of myself, the action by which I grasp straightway what I think as being thought by a subject (who, in this case, is not I). Whatever sort of alienation I may endure, reading does not interrupt my activity as subject.

Reading, then, is the act in which the subjective principle which I call *I*, is modified in such a way that I no longer have the right, strictly speaking, to consider it as my *I*. I am on loan to another, and this other thinks, feels, suffers, and acts within me. The phenomenon appears in its most obvious and even naïvest form in the sort of spell brought about by certain cheap kinds of reading, such as thrillers, of which I say, 'It gripped me.' Now it is important to note that this possession of myself by another takes place not only on the level of objective thought, that is with regard to images, sensations, ideas which reading affords me, but also on the level of my very subjectivity.

When I am absorbed in reading, a second self takes over, a self which thinks and feels for me. Withdrawn in some recess of myself, do I then silently witness this dispossession? Do I derive from it some comfort, or, on the contrary, a kind of anguish? However that may be, someone else holds the center of the stage, and the question which imposes itself, which I am absolutely obliged to ask myself, is this: 'Who is the usurper who occupies the forefront? Who is this mind who alone all by himself fills my consciousness and who, when I say *I*, is indeed that *I*?'

There is an immediate answer to this question, perhaps too easy an answer. This *I* who 'thinks in me' when I read a book, is the *I* of the one who writes the book. When I read Baudelaire or Racine, it is really Baudelaire or Racine who thinks, feels, allows himself to be read within me. Thus a book is not only a book, it is the means by which an author actually preserves his ideas, his feelings, his modes of dreaming and living. It is his means of saving his identity from death. Such an interpretation of reading is not false. It seems to justify what is commonly called the biographical explication of literary texts. Indeed every word of literature is impregnated with the mind of the one who wrote it. As he makes us read it, he awakens in us the analogue of what he thought or felt. To understand a literary work, then, is to let the individual who wrote it reveal himself to us *in* us. It is not the biography which explicates the work, but rather the work which sometimes enables us to understand the biography.

But biographical interpretation is in part false and misleading. It is true that there is an analogy between the works of an author and the experiences of his life. The works may be seen as an incomplete translation of the life. And further, there is an even more significant analogy among all the works of a single author. Each of the works, however, while I am reading it, lives in me its own life. The subject who is revealed to me through my reading of it is not the author, either in the disordered totality of his outer experiences, or in the aggregate, better organized, and concentrated totality, which is the one of his writings. Yet the subject which presides over the work can exist only in the work. To be sure, nothing is unimportant for understanding the work, and a mass of biographical, bibliographical, textual, and general critical information is indispensable to me. And yet this knowledge does not coincide with the internal knowledge of the work. Whatever may be the sum of the information I acquire on Baudelaire or Racine, in whatever degree of intimacy I may live with their genius, I am aware that this contribution does not suffice to illuminate for me in its own inner meaning, in its formal perfection, and in the subjective principle which animates it, the particular work of Baudelaire or of Racine the reading of which now absorbs me. At this moment what matters to me is to live, from the inside, in a certain identity with the work and the work alone. It could hardly be otherwise. Nothing external to the work could possibly share the extraordinary claim which the work now exerts on me. It is there within me, not to send me back, outside itself, to its author, nor to his other writings, but on the contrary to keep my attention riveted on itself. It is the work which traces in me the very boundaries within which this consciousness will define itself. It is the work which forces on me a series of mental objects and creates in me a network of words, beyond which, for the time being, there will be no room for other mental objects or for other words. And it is the work, finally, which, not satisfied thus with defining the content of my consciousness, takes hold of it, appropriates it, and makes of it that *I* which, from one end of my reading to the other, presides over the unfolding of the work, of the single work which I am reading.

And so the work forms the temporary mental substance which fills my consciousness; and it is moreover that consciousness, the *I*-subject, the continued consciousness of what is, revealing itelf within the interior of the work. Such is the characteristic condition of every work which I summon back into existence by placing my own consciousness at its disposal. I give it not only existence, but awareness of existence. And so I ought not to hesitate to recognize that so long as it is animated by this vital inbreathing inspired by the act of reading, a work of literature becomes at the expense of the reader whose own life it suspends a sort of human being, that it is a mind conscious of itself and constituting itself in me as the subject of its own objects.

. . .

13

E. D. HIRSCH JR

from *Validity in Interpretation*

BANISHMENT OF THE AUTHOR

It is a task for the historian of culture to explain why there has been in the past four decades a heavy and largely victorious assault on the sensible belief that a text means what its author meant. In the earliest and most decisive wave of the attack (launched by Eliot, Pound, and their associates) the battleground was literary: the proposition that textual meaning is independent of the author's control was associated with the literary doctrine that the best poetry is impersonal, objective and autonomous; that it leads an afterlife of its own, totally cut off from the life of its author.[1] This programmatic notion of what poetry should be became subtly identified with a notion of what all poetry and indeed all forms of literature necessarily must be. It was not simply desirable that literature should detach itself from the subjective realm of the author's personal thoughts and feelings; it was, rather, an indubitable fact that all written language remains independent of that subjective realm. At a slightly later period, and for different reasons, this same notion of semantic autonomy was advanced by Heidegger and his followers.[2] The idea also has been advocated by writers who believe with Jung that individual expressions may quite unwittingly express archetypal, communal meanings. In some branches of linguistics, particularly in so-called information theory, the semantic autonomy of language has been a working assumption. The theory has found another home in the work of non-Jungians who have interested themselves (as Eliot did earlier) in symbolism, though Cassirer, whose name is sometimes invoked by such writers, did not believe in the semantic autonomy of language.[3] As I said, it is the job of the cultural historian to explain why this doctrine should have gained currency in recent times, but it is the theorist's job to determine how far the theory of semantic autonomy deserves acceptance.

Literary scholars have often contended that the theory of authorial irrelevance was entirely beneficial to literary criticism and scholarship because it shifted the focus of discussion from the author to his work. Made confident by the theory, the modern critic has faithfully and closely examined the text to ferret out its independent meaning instead of its supposed significance to the author's life. That this shift towards exegesis has been desirable most critics would agree, whether or not they adhere to the theory of semantic autonomy. But the theory accompanied the exegetical movement for historical not logical reasons, since no logical necessity compels a critic to banish an author in order to analyze his text. Nevertheless, through its historical association with close exegesis, the theory has liberated much subtlety and intelligence. Unfortunately, it has also frequently encouraged willful arbitrariness and extravagance in academic criticism and has been one very important cause of the prevailing skepticism which calls into doubt the possibility of objectively valid interpretation. These disadvantages would be tolerable, of course, if the theory were true. In intellectual affairs skepticism is preferable to illusion.

The disadvantages of the theory could not have been easily predicted in the exciting days when the old order of academic criticism was being overthrown. At that time such naïvetés as the positivistic biases of literary history, the casting about for influences and other causal patterns, and the post-romantic fascination with the habits, feelings, and experiences surrounding the act of composition were very justly brought under attack. It became increasingly obvious that the theoretical foundations of the old criticism were weak and inadequate. It cannot be said, therefore, that the theory of authorial irrelevance was inferior to the theories or quasi-theories it replaced, nor can it be doubted that the immediate effect of banishing the author was wholly beneficial and invigorating. Now, at a distance of several decades, the difficulties that attend the theory of semantic autonomy have clearly emerged and are responsible for that uneasiness which persists in the academies, although the theory has long been victorious.

That this state of academic skepticism and disarray results largely from the theory of authorial irrelevance is, I think, a fact of our recent intellectual history. For, once the author had been ruthlessly banished as the determiner of his text's meaning, it very gradually appeared that no adequate principle existed for judging the validity of an interpretation. By an inner necessity the study of 'what a text says' became the study of what it says to an individual critic. It became fashionable to talk about a critic's 'reading' of a text, and this word began to appear in the titles of scholarly works. The word seemed to imply that if the author had been banished, the critic still remained, and his new, original, urbane, ingenious, or relevant 'reading' carried its own interest.

What had not been noticed in the earliest enthusiasm for going back to 'what the text says' was that the text had to represent *somebody's* meaning – if not the author's, then the critic's. It is true that a theory was erected under which the meaning of the text was equated with everything it could plausibly be taken to mean. [. . .] The theory of semantic autonomy forced itself into such unsatisfactory, ad hoc formulations because in its zeal to banish the author it ignored the fact that meaning is an affair of consciousness not of words. Almost any word sequence can, under the conventions of language, legitimately represent more than one complex of meaning. A word sequence means nothing in particular until somebody either means something by it or understands something from it. There is no magic land of meanings outside human consciousness. Whenever meaning is connected to words, a person is making the connection, and the particular meanings he lends to them are never the only legitimate ones under the norms and conventions of his language.

One proof that the conventions of language can sponsor different meanings from the same sequence of words resides in the fact that interpreters can and do disagree. When these disagreements occur, how are they to be resolved? Under the theory of semantic autonomy they cannot be resolved, since the meaning is not what the author meant, but 'what the poem means to different sensitive readers'.[4] One interpretation is as valid as another, so long as it is 'sensitive' or 'plausible.' Yet the teacher of literature who adheres to Eliot's theory is also by profession the preserver of a heritage and the conveyor of knowledge. On what ground does he claim that his 'reading' is more valid than that of any pupil? On no very firm ground. This impasse is a principal cause of the loss of bearings sometimes felt though not often confessed by academic critics.

One ad hoc theory that has been advanced to circumvent this chaotic democracy of 'readings' deserves special mention here because it involves the problem of value, a problem that preoccupies some modern literary theorists. The most valid reading of a text is the 'best' reading.[5] But even if we assumed that a critic did have access to the divine criteria by which he could determine the best reading, he would still be left with two equally compelling normative ideals – the best meaning and the author's meaning. Moreover, if the best meaning were not the author's, then it would have to be the critic's – in which case the critic would be the author of the best meaning. Whenever meaning is attached to a sequence of words it is impossible to escape an author.

Thus, when critics deliberately banished the original author, they themselves usurped his place, and this led unerringly to some of our present-day theoretical confusions. Where before there had been but one author, there now arose a multiplicity of them, each carrying as much authority as the next. To banish the original author as the determiner of meaning was to reject the only compelling normative principle that could lend validity to an interpretation. On the other hand, it might be the case that there does not really exist a viable normative ideal that governs the interpretation of texts. This would follow if any of the various arguments brought against the author were to hold. For if the meaning of a text is not the author's, then no interpretation can possibly correspond to *the* meaning of the text, since the text can have no determinate or determinable meaning. My demonstration of this point will be found in [. . .] the sections on determinacy in Chapter 2.[6] If a theorist wants to save the ideal of validity he has to save the author as well, and, in the present-day context, his first task will be to show that the prevailing arguments against the author are questionable and vulnerable.

. . .

DETERMINACY: VERBAL, MEANING AND TYPIFICATION

Reproducibility is a quality of verbal meaning that makes interpretation possible: if meaning were not reproducible, it could not be actualized by someone else and therefore could not be understood or interpreted. Determinacy, on the other hand, is a quality of meaning required in order that there *be* something to reproduce. Determinacy is a necessary attribute of any sharable meaning, since an indeterminacy cannot be shared: if a meaning were indeterminate, it would have no boundaries, no self-identity, and therefore could have no identity with a meaning entertained by someone else. But determinacy does not mean definiteness or precision. Undoubtedly, most verbal meanings are imprecise and ambiguous, and to call them such is to acknowledge their determinacy: they are what they are – namely ambiguous and imprecise – and they are not univocal and precise. This is another way of saying that an ambiguous meaning has a boundary like any other verbal meaning, and that one of the frontiers on this boundary is that between ambiguity and univocality. Some parts of the boundary might, of course, be thick; that is, there might at some points be a good many submeanings that belonged equally to the meaning and not to it – borderline meanings. However, such ambiguities would, on another level, simply serve to define the character of the meaning so that any overly precise construing of it would constitute a misunderstanding. Determinacy, then, first of all means self-identity. This is the minimum requirement for sharability. Without it neither communication nor validity in interpretation would be possible.

But by determinacy I also mean something more. Verbal meaning would be determinate in one sense even if it were merely a locus of possibilities – as some theorists have considered it. However, this is a kind of determinacy that cannot be shared in any act of understanding or interpretation. An array of *possible* meanings is no doubt a determinate entity in the sense that it is not an array of *actual* meanings; thus, it too has a boundary. But the human mind cannot entertain a possible meaning; as soon as the meaning is entertained it is actual. 'In that case, then,' the proponent of such a view might argue, 'let us consider the text to represent an array of different, *actual* meanings, corresponding to different actual interpretations.' But this escape from the frying pan leads right into the amorphous fire of indeterminacy. Such a conception really denies the self-identity of verbal meaning by suggesting that the meaning of the text can be one thing, and also another, different thing, and also another; and this conception (which has nothing to do with the ambiguity of meaning) is simply a denial that the text means anything in particular. I have already shown that such an indeterminate meaning is not sharable. Whatever it may be, it is not verbal meaning nor anything that could be validly interpreted.

'Then,' says the advocate of rich variousness, 'let us be more precise. What I really mean is that verbal meaning is historical or temporal. It is something in particular for a span of time, but it is something different in a different period of time.' Certainly the proponent of such a view cannot be reproached with the accusation that he makes verbal meaning indeterminate. On the contrary, he insists on the self-identity of meaning at any moment of time. But [. . .] this remarkable, quantum-leap theory of meaning has no foundation in the nature of linguistic acts nor does it provide any criterion of validity in interpretation. If a meaning can change its identity and in fact does, then we have no norm for judging whether we are encountering the real meaning in a changed form or some spurious meaning that is pretending to be the one we seek. Once it is admitted that a meaning can change its characteristics, then there is no way of finding the true Cinderella among all the contenders. There is no dependable glass slipper we can use as a test, since the old slipper will no longer fit the new Cinderella. To the interpreter this lack of a stable normative principle is equivalent to the indeterminacy of meaning. As far as his interests go, the meaning could have been defined as indeterminate from the start and his predicament would have been precisely the same.

When, therefore, I say that a verbal meaning is determinate I mean that it is an entity which is self-identical. Furthermore, I also mean that it is an entity which always remains the same from one moment to the next – that it is changeless. Indeed, these criteria were already implied in the requirement that verbal meaning be reproducible, that it be always the same in different acts of construing. Verbal meaning, then, is what it is and not something else, and it is always the same. That is what I mean by determinacy.

A determinate verbal meaning requires a determining will. Meaning is not made determinate simply by virtue of its being represented by a determinate sequence of words. Obviously, any brief word sequence could represent quite different complexes of verbal meaning, and the same is true of long word sequences, though it is less obvious. If that were not so, competent and intelligent speakers of a language would not disagree as they do about the meaning of texts. But if a determinate word sequence does not in itself necessarily represent one, particular, self-identical, unchanging complex of meaning, then the determinacy of its verbal meaning must be accounted for by some other discriminating force which causes the meaning to be *this* instead of *that* or *that* or *that*, all of which it could be. That discriminating force must involve an act of will, since unless one particular complex of meaning is *willed* (no matter how 'rich' and 'various' it might be), there would be no distinction between what an author does mean by a word sequence and what he could mean by it. Determinacy of verbal meaning requires an act of will.

It is sometimes said that 'meaning is determined by context,' but this is a very loose way of speaking. It is true that the surrounding text or the situation in which a problematical word sequence is found tends to narrow the meaning probabilities for that particular word sequence;

otherwise, interpretation would be hopeless. And it is a measure of stylistic excellence in an author that he should have managed to formulate a decisive context for any particular word sequence within his text. But this is certainly not to say that context determines verbal meaning. At best a context determines the guess of an interpreter (though his construction of the context may be wrong, and his guess correspondingly so). To speak of context as a determinant is to confuse an exigency of interpretation with an author's determining acts. An author's verbal meaning is limited by linguistic possibilities but is determined by his actualizing and specifying some of those possibilities. Correspondingly, the verbal meaning that an interpreter construes is determined by *his* act of will, limited by those same possibilities. The fact that a particular context has led the interpreter to a particular choice does not change the fact that the determination is a choice, even when it is unthinking and automatic. Furthermore, a context is something that has been determined – first by an author and then, through a construction, by an interpreter. It is not something that is simply there without anybody having to make any determinations.

While the author's will is a formal requirement for any determinate verbal meaning, it is quite evident that will is not the same as meaning. On the other hand, it is equally evident that verbal meaning is not the same as the 'content' of which an author is conscious. [. . .] An author almost always means more than he is aware of meaning, since he cannot explicitly pay attention to all the aspects of his meaning. Yet I have insisted that meaning is an affair of consciousness. In what sense is a meaning an object of consciousness even when one is not aware of it? Consider the example given in the earlier passage just referred to, in which a speaker admits he meant something he was not aware of meaning. Such an admission is possible because he conceived his meaning as a whole, and on reflection later perceived that the unattended meaning properly falls within that whole. That is, in fact, the only way the speaker's admission could be true.

What kind of whole is it that could contain a meaning even though the meaning was not explicitly there? And how can such a generous sort of entity still have very stern barriers which exclude other meanings that the author might actually have been attending to, as well as countless others that he was not? Clearly this remarkable characteristic of verbal meaning is the crucial one to examine.

Suppose I say, in a casual talk with a friend. 'Nothing pleases me so much as the Third Symphony of Beethoven.' And my friend asks me, 'Does it please you more than a swim in the sea on a hot day?' And I reply, 'You take me too literally. I meant that no *work of art* pleases me more than Beethoven's Third.' How was my answer possible? How did I know that 'a swim in the sea' did not fall under what I meant by 'things that please me'? (The hyperbolic use of 'nothing' to stand for 'no work of art' is a common sort of linguistic extension and can constitute verbal meaning in any context where it is communicable. My friend could have understood me. He misunderstands for the sake of the example.) Since I was not thinking either of 'a swim in the sea' or 'Brueghel's *Hay Gathering*,' some principle in my meaning must cause it to exclude the first and include the second. This is possible because I meant a certain *type* of 'thing that pleases me' and willed all possible members belonging to that type, even though very few of those possible members could have been attended to by me. Thus, it is possible to will an et cetera without in the least being aware of all the individual members that belong to it. The acceptability of any given candidate applying for membership in the et cetera depends entirely on the type of whole meaning that I willed. That is to say, the acceptability of a submeaning depends upon the *author's* notion of the subsuming type whenever this notion is sharable in the particular linguistic circumstances.

The definition of verbal meaning given earlier in this chapter can now be expanded and made more descriptive. I said before that verbal meaning is whatever an author wills to convey by his use of linguistic symbols and which can be so conveyed. Now verbal meaning can be defined more particularly as a *willed type* which an author expresses by linguistic symbols and which can be understood by another through those symbols. It is essential to emphasize the concept of type since it is only through this concept that verbal meaning can be (as it is) a determinate object of consciousness and yet transcend (as it does) the actual contents of consciousness.

A type is an entity with two decisive characteristics. First, it is an entity that has a boundary by virtue of which something belongs to it or does not. In this respect it is like a class, though it has the advantage of being a more unitary concept: a type can be entirely represented in a single instance, while a class is usually thought of as an array of instances. The second decisive characteristic of a type is that it can always be represented by more than one instance. When we say that two instances are of the same type, we perceive common (identical) traits in the instances and allot these common traits to the type. Thus a type is an entity that has a boundary by virtue of which something belongs to it or does not, and it is also an entity which can be

represented by different instances or different contents of consciousness. It follows that a verbal meaning is always a type since otherwise it
could not be sharable: If it lacked a boundary, there would be nothing
in particular to share; and if a given instance could not be accepted or
rejected as an instance of the meaning (the representational character of
a type), the interpreter would have no way of knowing what the
boundary was. In order that a meaning be determinate for another it
must be a type. For this reason, verbal meanings, i.e. shared meanings,
are always types and can never relinquish their type character.

Thus verbal meaning can never be limited to a unique, concrete
content. It can, of course, refer to unique entities, but only by means
that transcend unique entities, and this transcendence always has the
character of a typification. This is so even when a verbal meaning has
reference to something that is obviously unique, like 'the death of
Buonaparte.' 'Death,' 'the,' and 'of' all retain their type character even
though their combination might effect a particular new type. The same
is true of 'Buonaparte,' for a name is a type, and the particular name
'Buonaparte' could not relinquish its type character without thereby
ceasing to be a name, in which case it would be incomprehensible and
unsharable. No doubt this particular name in a particular use would not
have a meaning identical to 'Buonaparte' in another usage. But that
would simply mean that they are different types as well as, on another
level, instances of the same type. However, they could never be merely
concrete instances. The determinacy and sharability of verbal meaning
resides in its being a type. The particular type that it is resides in the
author's determining will. *A verbal meaning is a willed type.*

. . .

NOTES

1. The classic statement is in T. S. Eliot, 'Tradition and the Individual Talent,' *Selected Essays*
   (New York, 1932).
2. See, for example, Martin Heidegger, *Unterwegs zur Sprache* (Pfullingen, 1959).
3. See Ernst Cassirer, *The Philosophy of Symbolic Forms*: Vol. 1, *Language*, trans. R. Manheim
   (New Haven, 1953), particularly pp. 69, 178, 213, 249–50, and passim.
4. The phrase is from T. S. Eliot, *On Poetry and Poets* (New York, 1957), p. 126.
5. It would be invidious to name any individual critic as the begetter of this widespread and
   imprecise notion. By the 'best' reading, of course, some critics mean the most valid reading,
   but the idea of bestness is widely used to embrace indiscriminately both the idea of validity and
   of such aesthetic values as richness, inclusiveness, tension or complexity – as though validity
   and aesthetic excellence must somehow be identical.
6. See pp. 111–14 below.

14

JACQUES DERRIDA

'The Exorbitant. Question of Method'

'For me there has never been an intermediary between everything or nothing.' The intermediary is the mid-point and the mediation, the middle term between total absence and the absolute plenitude of presence. It is clear that mediacy is the name of all that Rousseau wanted opinionatedly to efface. This wish is expressed in a deliberate, sharp, thematic way. It does not have to be deciphered. Jean-Jacques recalls it here at the very moment when he is spelling out the supplements that are linked together to replace a mother or a Nature. And here the supplement occupies the middle point between total absence and total presence. The play of substitution fills and marks a determined lack. But Rousseau argues as if the recourse to the supplement – here to Thérèse – was going to appease his impatience when confronted with the intermediary: 'From that moment I was alone; for me there has never been an intermediary between everything and nothing. I found in Thérèse the substitute that I needed.' The virulence of this concept is thus appeased, as if one were able to *arrest it*, domesticate it, tame it.

This brings up the question of the usage of the word 'supplement': of Rousseau's situation within the language and the logic that assures to this word or this concept sufficiently *surprising* resources so that the presumed subject of the sentence might always say, through using the 'supplement,' more, less, or something other than what he *would mean* [*voudrait dire*]. This question is therefore not only of Rousseau's writing but also of our reading. We should begin by taking rigorous account of this *being held within* [*prise*] or this *surprise*: the writer writes *in a* language and *in* a logic whose proper system, laws, and life his discourse by definition cannot dominate absolutely. He uses them only by letting himself, after a fashion and up to a point, be governed by the system. And the reading must always aim at a certain relationship, unperceived by the writer, between what he commands and what he does not command of the patterns of the language that he uses. This relationship is not a certain quantitative distribution of shadow and light, of weakness or of force, but a signifying structure that critical reading should *produce*.

What does produce mean here? In my attempt to explain that, I would initiate a justification of my principles of reading. A justification, as we shall see, entirely negative, outlining by exclusion a space of reading that I shall not fill here: a task of reading.

To produce this signifying structure obviously cannot consist of reproducing, by the effaced and respectful doubling of commentary, the conscious, voluntary, intentional relationship that the writer institutes in his exchanges with the history to which he belongs thanks to the element of language. This moment of doubling commentary should no doubt have its place in a critical reading. To recognize and respect all its classical exigencies is not easy and requires all the instruments of traditional criticism. Without this recognition and this respect, critical production would risk developing in any direction at all and authorize itself to say almost anything. But this indispensable guardrail has always only *protected*, it has never *opened*, a reading.

Yet if reading must not be content with doubling the text, it cannot legitimately transgress the text towards something other than it, towards a referent (a reality that is metaphysical, historical, psycho-biographical, etc.) or towards a signified outside the text whose content could take place, could have taken place outside of language, that is to say, in the sense that we give here to that word, outside of writing in general. That is why the methodological considerations that we risk applying here to an example are closely dependent on general propositions that we have elaborated above; as regards the absence of the referent or the transcendental signified. *There is nothing outside of the text* [there is no outside-text; *il n'y a pas de hors-texte*]. And that is neither because Jean-Jacques' life, or the existence of Mamma or Thérèse *themselves*, is not of prime interest to us, nor because we have access to their so-called 'real' existence only in the text and we have neither any means of altering this, nor any right to neglect this limitation. All reasons of this type would already be sufficient, to be sure, but there are more radical reasons. What we have tried to show by following the guiding line of the 'dangerous supplement,' is that in what one calls the real life of these existences 'of flesh and bone,' beyond and behind what one believes can be circumscribed as Rousseau's text, there has never been anything but writing; there have never been anything but supplements, substitutive significations which could only come forth in a chain of differential references, the 'real' supervening, and being added only while taking on meaning from a trace and from an invocation of the supplement, etc. And thus to infinity, for we have read, *in the text*, that the absolute present, Nature, that which words like 'real mother' name, [has] always already escaped, [has] never existed; that what opens meaning and language is writing as the disappearance of natural presence.

Although it is not commentary, our reading must be intrinsic and remain within the text. That is why, in spite of certain appearances, the locating of the word *supplement* is here not at all psychoanalytical, if by that we understand an interpretation that takes us outside of the writing towards a psychobiographical signified, or even towards a general psychological structure that could rightly be separated from the signifier. This method has occasionally been opposed to the traditional doubling commentary; it could be shown that it actually comes to terms with it quite easily. *The security with which the commentary considers the self-identity of the text, the confidence with which it carves out its contour, goes hand in hand with the tranquil assurance that leaps over the text towards its presumed content, in the direction of the pure signified.* And in effect, in Rousseau's case, psychoanalytical studies like those of Dr. Laforgue transgress the text only after having read it according to the most current methods. The reading of the literary 'symptom' is most banal, most academic, most naive. And once one has thus blinded oneself to the very tissue of the 'symptom,' to its proper texture, one cheerfully exceeds it towards a psychobiographical signified whose link with the literary signifier then becomes perfectly extrinsic and contingent. One recognizes the other aspect of the same gesture when, in general works on Rousseau, in a package of classical shape that gives itself out to be a synthesis that faithfully restores, through commentary and compilation of themes, the totality of the work and the thought, one encounters a chapter of biographical and psychoanalytical cast on the 'problem of sexuality in Rousseau,' with a reference in an Appendix to the author's medical case-history.

If it seems to us in principle impossible to separate, through interpretation or commentary, the signified from the signifier, and thus to destroy writing by the writing that is yet reading, we nevertheless believe that this impossibility is historically articulated. It does not limit attempts at deciphering in the same way, to the same degree, and according to the same rules. Here we must take into account the history of the text in general. When we speak of the writer and of the encompassing power of the language to which he is subject, we are not only thinking of the writer in literature. The philosopher, the chronicler, the theoretician in general, and at the limit everyone writing, is thus taken by surprise. But, in each case, the person writing is inscribed in a determined textual system. Even if there is never a pure signified, there are different relationships as to that which, from the signifier, *is presented* as the irreducible stratum of the signified. For example, the philosophical text, although it is in fact always written, includes, precisely as its philosophical specificity, the project of effacing itself in the face of the signified content which it transports and in general teaches. Reading should be aware of this project, even if, in the last analysis, it intends to expose the project's failure. The entire history of texts, and within it the history of literary forms in the West, should be studied from this point of view. With the exception of a thrust or a point of resistance which has only been very lately recognized as such, literary writing has, almost always and almost everywhere, according to some fashions and across very diverse ages, lent itself to this *transcendent* reading, in that search for the signified which we here put in question, not to annul it but to understand it within a system to which such a reading is blind. Philosophical literature is only one example within this history but it is among the most significant. And it interests us particularly in Rousseau's case. Who at the same time and for profound reasons produced a philosophical literature to which belong *The Social Contract* and *La nouvelle Héloise,* and chose to live by literary writing; by a writing which would not be exhausted by the message – philosophical or otherwise – which it could, so to speak, deliver. And what Rousseau has said, as philosopher or as psychologist, of writing in general, cannot be separated from the system of his own writing. We should be aware of this.

This poses formidable problems. Problems of outlining in particular. Let me give three examples.

1. If the course I have followed in the reading of the 'supplement' is not merely psychoanalytical, it is undoubtedly because the habitual psychoanalysis of literature begins by putting the literary signifier as such within parentheses. It is no doubt also because psychoanalytic theory itself is for me a collection of texts belonging to my history and my culture. To that extent, if it marks my reading and the writing of

my interpretation, it does not do so as a principle or a truth that one could abstract from the textual system that I inhabit in order to illuminate it with complete neutrality. In a certain way, I am *within* the history of psychoanalysis as I am *within* Rousseau's text. Just as Rousseau drew upon a language that was already there – and which is found to be somewhat our own, thus assuring us a certain minimal readability of French literature – in the same way we operate today within a certain network of significations marked by psychoanalytic theory, even if we do not master it and even if we are assured of never being able to master it perfectly.

But it is for another reason that this is not even a somewhat inarticulate psychoanalysis of Jean-Jacques Rousseau. Such a psycho-analysis is already obliged to have located all the structures of appurtenance within Rousseau's text, all that is not unique to it – by reason of the encompassing power and the already-thereness of the language or of the culture – all that could be inhabited rather than produced by writing. Around the irreducible point of originality of this writing an immense series of structures, of historical totalities of all orders, are organized, enveloped, and blended. Supposing that psy-choanalysis can by rights succeed in outlining them and their interpre-tations, supposing that it takes into account the entire history of metaphysics – the history of that Western metaphysics that entertains relationships of cohabitation with Rousseau's text, it would still be necessary for this psychoanalysis to elucidate the law of its own appurtenance to metaphysics and Western culture. Let us not pursue this any further. We have already measured the difficulty of the task and the element of frustration in our interpretation of the supplement. We are sure that something irreducibly Rousseauist is captured there but we have carried off, at the same time, a yet quite unformed mass of roots, soil, and sediments of all sorts.

2. Even supposing that Rousseau's text can be rigorously isolated and articulated within history in general, and then within the history of the sign 'supplement,' one must still take into consideration many other possibilities. Following the appearances of the word 'supplement' and of the corresponding concept or concepts, we traverse a certain path within Rousseau's text. To be sure, this particular path will assure us the economy of a synopsis. But are other paths not possible? And as long as the totality of paths is not effectively exhausted, how shall we justify this one?

3. In Rousseau's text, after having indicated – by anticipation and as a prelude – the function of the sign 'supplement,' I now prepare myself

to give special privilege, in a manner that some might consider exorbitant, to certain texts like the *Essay on the Origin of Languages* and other fragments on the theory of language and writing. By what right? And why these short texts, published for the most part after the author's death, difficult to classify, of uncertain date and inspiration?

To all these questions and within the logic of their system, there is no satisfying response. In a certain measure and in spite of the theoretical precautions that I formulate, my choice is in fact *exorbitant*.

But what is the exorbitant?

I wished to reach the point of a certain exteriority in relation to the totality of the age of logocentrism. Starting from this point of exteriority, a certain deconstruction of that totality which is also a traced path, of that orb (*orbis*) which is also orbitary (*orbita*), might be broached. The first gesture of this departure and this deconstruction, although subject to a certain historical necessity, cannot be given methodological or logical intra-orbitary assurances. Within the closure, one can only judge its style in terms of the accepted oppositions. It may be said that this style is empiricist and in a certain way that would be correct. The *departure* is radically empiricist. It proceeds like a wandering thought on the possibility of itinerary and of method. It is affected by nonknowledge as by its future and it *ventures out* deliberately. I have myself defined the form and the vulnerability of this empiricism. But here the very concept of empiricism destroys itself. To *exceed* the metaphysical orb is an attempt to get out of the orbit (*orbita*), to think the entirety of the classical conceptual oppositions, particularly the one within which the value of empiricism is held: the opposition of philosophy and nonphilosophy, another name for empiricism, for this incapability to sustain on one's own and to the limit the coherence of one's own discourse, for being produced as truth at the moment when the value of truth is shattered, for escaping the internal contradictions of skepticism, etc. *The thought of this historical opposition between philosophy and empiricism is not simply empirical and it cannot be thus qualified without abuse and misunderstanding.*

Let us make the diagram more specific. What is exorbitant in the reading of Rousseau? No doubt Rousseau, as I have already suggested, has only a very relative privilege in the history that interests us. If we merely wished to situate him within this history, the attention that we accord him would be clearly disproportionate. But that is not our intention. We wish to identify a decisive articulation of the logocentric epoch. For purposes of this identification Rousseau seems to us to be most revealing. That obviously supposes that we have already prepared the exit, determined the repression of writing as the fundamental operation of the epoch, read a certain number of texts but not all of them, a certain number of Rousseau's texts but not all of them. This avowal of empiricism can sustain itself only by the strength of the question. The opening of the question, the departure from the closure of a self-evidence, the putting into doubt of a system of oppositions, all these movements necessarily have the form of empiricism and of errancy. At any rate, they cannot be described, *as to past norms*, except in this form. No other trace is available, and as these errant questions are not absolute beginnings in every way, they allow themselves to be effectively reached, on one entire surface, by this description which is also a criticism. We must begin *wherever we are* and the thought of the trace, which cannot not take the scent into account, has already taught us that it was impossible to justify a point of departure absolutely. *Wherever we are*: in a text where we already believe ourselves to be.

Let us narrow the arguments down further. In certain respects, the theme of supplementarity is certainly no more than one theme among others. It is in a chain, carried by it. Perhaps one could substitute something else for it. *But it happens that this theme describes the chain itself, the being-chain of a textual chain, the structure of substitution, the articulation of desire and of language, the logic of all conceptual oppositions taken over by Rousseau*, and particularly the role and the function, in his system, of the concept of Nature. It tells us in a text what a text is, it tells us in writing what writing it, in Rousseau's writing it tells us Jean-Jacques' desire, etc. If we consider, according to the axial proposition of this essay, that there is nothing outside the text, our ultimate justification would be the following: the concept of the supplement and the theory of writing designate textuality itself in Rousseau's text in an indefinitely multiplied structure – en *abyme* [in an abyss] – to employ the current phrase. And we shall see that this abyss is not a happy or unhappy accident. An entire theory of the structural necessity of the abyss will be gradually constituted in our reading; the indefinite process of supplementarity has always already *infiltrated* presence, always already inscribed there the space of repetition and the splitting of the self. Representation *in the abyss* of presence is not an accident of presence; the desire of presence is, on the contrary, born from the abyss (the indefinite multiplication) of representation, from the representation of representation, etc. The supplement itself is quite exorbitant, in every sense of the word.

Thus Rousseau inscribes textuality in the text. But its operation is not simple. It tricks with a gesture of effacement, and strategic relations like the relationships of force among the two movements form a complex design. This design seems to us to be represented in the handling of the concept of the supplement. Rousseau cannot utilize it at the same time in all the virtualities of its meaning. The way in which he determines the concept and, in so doing, lets himself be determined by that very thing that he excludes from it, the direction in which he bends it, here as addition, there as substitute, now as the positivity and exteriority of evil, now as a happy auxiliary, all this conveys neither a passivity nor an activity, neither an unconsciousness nor a lucidity on the part of the author. Reading should not only abandon these categories – which are also, let us recall in passing, the founding categories of metaphysics – but should produce the law of this relationship to the concept of the supplement. It it certainly a production, because I do not simply duplicate what Rousseau thought of this relationship. The concept of the supplement is a sort of blind spot in Rousseau's text, the not-seen that opens and limits visibility. But the production, if it attempts to make the not-seen accessible to sight, does not leave the text. It has moreover only believed it was doing so by illusion. It is contained in the transformation of the language it designates, in the regulated exchanges between Rousseau and history. We know that these exchanges only take place by way of the language and the text, in the infrastructural sense that we now give to that word. And *what we call production is necessarily a text, the system of a writing and of a reading which we know is ordered around its own blind spot.* We know this *a priori,* but only now and with a knowledge that is not a knowledge at all.

15

ROLAND BARTHES

'The Death of the Author'

In his story *Sarrasine* Balzac, describing a castrato disguised as a woman, writes the following sentence: '*This was woman herself, with her sudden fears, her irrational whims, her instinctive worries, her impetuous boldness, her fussings, and her delicious sensibility.*' Who is speaking thus? Is it the hero of the story bent on remaining ignorant of the castrato hidden beneath the woman? Is it Balzac the individual, furnished by his personal experience with a philosophy of Woman? Is it Balzac the author professing 'literary' ideas on femininity? Is it universal wisdom? Romantic psychology? We shall never know, for the good reason that writing is the destruction of every voice, of every point of origin. Writing is that neutral, composite, oblique space where our subject slips away, the negative where all identity is lost, starting with the very identity of the body writing.

No doubt it has always been that way. As soon as a fact is *narrated* no longer with a view to acting directly on reality but intransitively, that is to say, finally outside of any function other than that of the very practice of the symbol itself, this disconnection occurs, the voice loses its origin, the author enters into his own death, writing begins. The sense of this phenomenon, however, has varied; in ethnographic societies the responsibility for a narrative is never assumed by a person but by a mediator, shaman or relator whose 'performance' – the mastery of the narrative code – may possibly be admired but never his 'genius'. The author is a modern figure, a product of our society insofar as, emerging from the Middle Ages with English empiricism, French rationalism and the personal faith of the Reformation, it discovered the prestige of the individual, of, as it is more nobly put, the 'human person'. It is thus logical that in literature it should be this positivism, the epitome and culmination of capitalist ideology, which has attached the greatest importance to the 'person' of the author. The *author* still reigns in histories of literature, biographies of writers, interviews, magazines, as in the very consciousness of men of letters anxious to unite their person and their work through diaries and memoirs. The image of literature to be found in ordinary culture is tyrannically centred on the author, his person, his life, his tastes, his passions, while criticism still consists for the most part in saying that Baudelaire's work is the failure of Baudelaire the man, Van Gogh's his madness, Tchaikovsky's his vice. The *explanation* of a work is always sought in the man or woman who produced it, as if it were always in the end, through the more or less transparent allegory of the fiction, the voice of a single person, the *author* 'confiding' in us.

Though the sway of the Author remains powerful (the new criticism has often done no more than consolidate it), it goes without saying that certain writers have long since attempted to loosen it. In France, Mallarmé was doubtless the first to see and to foresee in its full extent the necessity to substitute language itself for the person who until then had been supposed to be its owner. For him, for us too, it is language which speaks, not the author; to write is, through a prerequisite impersonality (not at all to be confused with the castrating objectivity of the realist novelist), to reach that point where only language acts, 'performs', and not 'me'. Mallarmé's entire poetics consists in suppressing the author in the interests of writing (which is, as will be seen, to restore the place of the reader). Valéry, encumbered by a psychology of the Ego, considerably diluted Mallarmé's theory but, his taste for classicism leading him to turn to the lessons of rhetoric, he never stopped calling into question and deriding the Author; he stressed the linguistic and, as it were, 'hazardous' nature of his activity, and throughout his prose works he militated in favour of the essentially verbal condition of literature, in the face of which all recourse to the writer's interiority seemed to him pure superstition. Proust himself, despite the apparently psychological character of what are called his *analyses*, was visibly concerned with the task of inexorably blurring, by an extreme subtilization, the relation between the writer and his characters; by making of the narrator not he who has seen and felt nor even he who is writing, but he who *is going to write* (the young man in the novel – but, in fact, how old is he and who is he? – wants to write but cannot; the novel ends when writing at last becomes possible),

Proust gave modern writing its epic. By a radical reversal, instead of putting his life into his novel, as is so often maintained, he made of his very life a work for which his own book was the model; so that it is clear to us that Charlus does not imitate Montesquieu but that Montesquieu – in his anecdotal, historical reality – is no more than a secondary fragment, derived from Charlus. Lastly, to go no further than this prehistory of modernity, Surrealism, though unable to accord language a supreme place (language being system and the aim of the movement being, romantically, a direct subversion of codes – itself moreover illusory: a code cannot be destroyed, only 'played off'), contributed to the desacrilization of the image of the Author by ceaselessly recommending the abrupt disappointment of expectations of meaning (the famous surrealist 'jolt'), by entrusting the hand with the task of writing as quickly as possible what the head itself is unaware of (automatic writing), by accepting the principle and the experience of several people writing together. Leaving aside literature itself (such distinctions really becoming invalid), linguistics has recently provided the destruction of the Author with a valuable analytical tool by showing that the whole of the enunciation is an empty process, functioning perfectly without there being any need for it to be filled with the person of the interlocutors. Linguistically, the author is never more than the instance writing, just as *I* is nothing other than the instance saying *I*: language knows a 'subject', not a 'person', and this subject, empty outside of the very enunciation which defines it, suffices to make language 'hold together', suffices, that is to say, to exhaust it.

The removal of the Author (one could talk here with Brecht of a veritable 'distancing', the Author diminishing like a figurine at the far end of the literary stage) is not merely an historical fact or an act of writing; it utterly transforms the modern text (or – which is the same thing – the text is henceforth made and read in such a way that at all its levels the author is absent). The temporality is different. The Author, when believed in, is always conceived of as the past of his own book: book and author stand automatically on a single line divided into a *before* and an *after*. The Author is thought to *nourish* the book, which is to say that he exists before it, thinks, suffers, lives for it, is in the same relation of antecedence to his work as a father to his child. In complete contrast, the modern scriptor is born simultaneously with the text, is in no way equipped with a being preceding or exceeding the writing, is not the subject with the book as predicate; there is no other time than that of the enunciation and every text is eternally written *here and now*. The fact is (or, it follows) that *writing* can no longer designate an operation of recording, notation, representation, 'depiction' (as the Classics would say); rather, it designates exactly what linguists, referring to Oxford philosophy, call a performative, a rare verbal form (exclusively given in the first person and in the present tense) in which the enunciation has no other content (contains no other proposition) than the act by which it is uttered – something like the *I declare* of kings or the *I sing* of very ancient poets. Having buried the Author, the modern scriptor can thus no longer believe, as according to the pathetic view of his predecessors, that this hand is too slow for his thought or passion and that consequently, making a law of necessity, he must emphasize this delay and indefinitely 'polish' his form. For him, on the contrary, the hand, cut off from any voice, borne by a pure gesture of inscription (and not of expression), traces a field without origin – or which, at least, has no other origin than language itself, language which ceaselessly calls into question all origins.

We know now that a text is not a line of words releasing a single 'theological' meaning (the 'message' of the Author-God) but a multi-dimensional space in which a variety of writings, none of them original, blend and clash. The text is a tissue of quotations drawn from the innumerable centres of culture. Similar to Bouvard and Pécuchet, those eternal copyists, at once sublime and comic and whose profound ridiculousness indicates precisely the truth of writing, the writer can only imitate a gesture that is always anterior, never original. His only power is to mix writings, to counter the ones with the others, in such a way as never to rest on any one of them. Did he wish to *express himself*, he ought at least to know that the inner 'thing' he thinks to 'translate' is itself only a ready-formed dictionary, its words only explainable through other words, and so on indefinitely; something experienced in exemplary fashion by the young Thomas de Quincey, he who was so good at Greek that in order to translate absolutely modern ideas and images into that dead language, he had, so Baudelaire tells us (in *Paradis Artificiels*), 'created for himself an unfailing dictionary, vastly more extensive and complex than those resulting from the ordinary patience of purely literary themes'. Succeeding the Author, the scriptor no longer bears within him passions, humours, feelings, impressions, but rather this immense dictionary from which he draws a writing that can know no halt: life never does more than imitate the book, and the book itself is only a tissue of signs, an imitation that is lost, infinitely deferred.

Once the Author is removed, the claim to decipher a text becomes quite futile. To give a text an Author is to impose a limit on that text, to furnish it with a final signified, to close the writing. Such a conception suits criticism very well, the latter then allotting itself the important task of discovering the Author (or its hypostases: society, history psyché, liberty) beneath the work: when the Author has been found, the text is 'explained' – victory to the critic. Hence there is no surprise in the fact that, historically, the reign of the Author has also been that of the Critic, nor again in the fact that criticism (be it new) is today undermined along with the Author. In the multiplicity of writing, everything is to be *disentangled*, nothing *deciphered*; the structure can be followed, 'run' (like the thread of a stocking) at every point and at every level, but there is nothing beneath: the space of writing is to be ranged over, not pierced; writing ceaselessly posits meaning ceaselessly to evaporate it, carrying out a systematic exemption of meaning. In precisely this way literature (it would be better from now on to say *writing*), by refusing to assign a 'secret', an ultimate meaning, to the text (and to the world as text), liberates what may be called an anti-theological activity, an activity that is truly revolutionary since to refuse to fix meaning is, in the end, to refuse God and his hypostases – reason, science, law.

Let us come back to the Balzac sentence. No one, no 'person', says it: its source, its voice, is not the true place of the writing, which is reading. Another – very precise – example will help to make this clear: recent research (J.-P. Vernant[1]) has demonstrated the constitutively ambiguous nature of Greek tragedy, its texts being woven from words with double meanings that each character understands unilaterally (this perpetual misunderstanding is exactly the 'tragic'); there is, however, someone who understands each word in its duplicity and who, in addition, hears the very deafness of the characters speaking in front of him – this someone being precisely the reader (or here, the listener). Thus is revealed the total existence of writing: a text is made of multiple writings, drawn from many cultures and entering into mutual relations of dialogue, parody, contestation, but there is one place where this multiplicity is focused and that place is the reader, not, as was hitherto said, the author. The reader is the space on which all the quotations that make up a writing are inscribed without any of them being lost; a text's unity lies not in its origin but in its destination. Yet this destination cannot any longer be personal: the reader is without history, bio-graphy, psychology; he is simply that *someone* who holds together in a single field all the traces by which the written text is constituted. Which is why it is derisory to condemn the new writing in the name of a humanism hypocritically turned champion of the reader's rights.

Classic criticism has never paid any attention to the reader; for it, the writer is the only person in literature. We are now beginning to let ourselves be fooled no longer by the arrogant antiphrastical recriminations of good society in favour of the very thing it sets aside, ignores, smothers, or destroys; we know that to give writing its future, it is necessary to overthrow the myth: the birth of the reader must be at the cost of the death of the Author.

NOTE

1. Cf. Jean-Pierre Vernant (with Pierre Vidal–Naquet), *Mythe et tragédie en Grèce ancienne*, Paris 1972, esp. pp. 19–40, 99–131.

16

HAROLD BLOOM

'A Meditation upon Priority, and a Synopsis'

This short book offers a theory of poetry by way of a description of poetic influence, or the story of intra-poetic relationships. One aim of this theory is corrective: to de-idealize our accepted accounts of how one poet helps to form another. Another aim, also corrective, is to try to provide a poetics that will foster a more adequate practical criticism.

Poetic history, in this book's argument, is held to be indistinguishable from poetic influence, since strong poets make that history by misreading one another, so as to clear imaginative space for themselves.

My concern is only with strong poets, major figures with the persistence to wrestle with their strong precursors, even to the death. Weaker talents idealize; figures of capable imagination appropriate for themselves. But nothing is got for nothing, and self-appropriation involves the immense anxieties of indebtedness, for what strong maker desires the realization that he has failed to create himself? Oscar Wilde, who knew he had failed as a poet because he lacked strength to overcome his anxiety of influence, knew also the darker truths concerning influence. *The Ballad of Reading Gaol* becomes an embarrassment to read, directly one recognizes that every lustre it exhibits is reflected from *The Rime of the Ancient Mariner*; and Wilde's lyrics anthologize the whole of English High Romanticism. Knowing this, and armed with his customary intelligence, Wilde bitterly remarks in *The Portrait of Mr. W. H.* that: 'Influence is simply a transference of personality, a mode of giving away what is most precious to one's self, and its exercise produces a sense, and, it may be, a reality of loss. Every disciple takes away something from his master.' This is the anxiety of influencing, yet no reversal in this area is a true reversal. Two years later, Wilde refined this bitterness in one of Lord Henry Wotton's elegant observations in *The Picture of Dorian Gray*, where he tells Dorian that all influence is immoral:

> Because to influence a person is to give him one's own soul. He does not think his natural thoughts, or burn with his natural passions. His virtues are not real to him. His sins, if there are such things as sins, are borrowed. He becomes an echo of someone else's music, an actor of a part that has not been written for him.

To apply Lord Henry's insight to Wilde, we need only read Wilde's review of Pater's *Appreciations*, with its splendidly self-deceptive closing observation that Pater 'has escaped disciples.' Every major aesthetic consciousness seems peculiarly more gifted at denying obligation as the hungry generations go on treading one another down. Stevens, a stronger heir of Pater than even Wilde was, is revealingly vehement in his letters:

> While, of course, I come down from the past, the past is my own and not something marked Coleridge, Wordsworth, etc. I know of no one who has been particularly important to me. My reality-imagination complex is entirely my own even though I see it in others.

He might have said: 'particularly because I see it in others,' but poetic influence was hardly a subject where Stevens' insights could center. Towards the end, his denials became rather violent, and oddly humored. Writing to the poet Richard Eberhart, he extends a sympathy all the stronger for being self-sympathy:

> I sympathize with your denial of any influence on my part. This sort of thing always jars me because, in my own case, I am not conscious of having been influenced by anybody and have purposely held off from reading highly mannered people like Eliot and Pound so that I should not absorb anything, even unconsciously. But there is a kind of critic who spends his time dissecting what he reads for echoes, imitations, influences, as if no one was ever simply himself but is always compounded of a lot of other people. As for W. Blake, I think that this means Wilhelm Blake.

This view, that poetic influence scarcely exists, except in furiously active pedants, is itself an illustration of one way in which poetic influence is a variety of melancholy or an anxiety-principle. Stevens was, as he insisted, a highly individual poet, as much an American original as Whitman or Dickinson, or his own contemporaries: Pound, Williams, Moore. But poetic influence need not make poets less original; as often it makes them more original, though not therefore necessarily better. The profundities of poetic influence cannot be reduced to source-study, to the history of ideas, to the patterning of images. Poetic influence, or as I shall more frequently term it, poetic misprision, is necessarily the study of the life-cycle of the poet-as-poet. When such study considers the context in which that life-cycle is enacted, it will be compelled to examine simultaneously the relations between poets as cases akin to what Freud called the family romance, and as chapters in the history of modern revisionism, 'modern' meaning here post-Enlightenment. The modern poet, as W. J. Bate shows in *The Burden of the Past and the English Poet*, is the inheritor of a melancholy engendered in the mind of the Enlightenment by its skepticism of its own double heritage of imaginative wealth, from the ancients and from the Renaissance masters. In this book I largely neglect the area Bate has explored with great skill, in order to center upon intra-poetic relationships as parallels of family romance. Though I employ these parallels, I do so as a deliberate revisionist of some of the Freudian emphases.

Nietzsche and Freud are, so far as I can tell, the prime influences upon the theory of influence presented in this book. Nietzsche is the prophet of the antithetical, and his *Genealogy of Morals* is the profoundest study available to me of the revisionary and ascetic strains in the aesthetic temperament. Freud's investigations of the mechanisms of defense and their ambivalent functionings provide the clearest analogues I have found for the revisionary ratios that govern intra-poetic relations. Yet, the theory of influence expounded here is un-Nietzschean in its deliberate literalism, and in its Viconian insistence that priority in divination is crucial for every strong poet, lest he dwindle merely into a latecomer. My theory rejects also the qualified Freudian optimism that happy substitution is possible, that a second chance can save us from the repetitive quest for our earliest attachments. Poets as poets cannot accept substitutions, and fight to the end to have their initial chance alone. Both Nietzsche and Freud underestimated poets and poetry, yet each yielded more power to phantasmagoria than it truly possesses. They too, despite their moral realism, over-idealized the imagination. Nietzsche's disciple, Yeats, and Freud's disciple, Otto Rank, show a greater awareness of the artist's fight against art, and of the relation of this struggle to the artist's antithetical battle against nature.

Freud recognized sublimation as the highest human achievement, a recognition that allies him to Plato and to the entire moral traditions of both Judaism and Christianity. Freudian sublimation involves the yielding-up of more primordial for more refined modes of pleasure, which is to exalt the second chance above the first. Freud's poem, in the view of this book, is not severe enough, unlike the severe poems written by the creative lives of the strong poets. To equate emotional maturation with the discovery of acceptable substitutes may be pragmatic wisdom, particularly in the realm of Eros, but this is not the wisdom of the strong poets. The surrendered dream is not merely a phantasmogoria of endless gratification, but is the greatest of all human illusions, the vision of immortality. If Wordsworth's *Ode: Intimations of Immortality from Recollections of Earliest Childhood* possessed only the wisdom found also in Freud, then we could cease calling it 'the Great Ode.' Wordsworth too saw repetition or second chance as essential for development, and his ode admits that we can redirect our needs by substitution or sublimation. But the ode plangently also awakens into failure, and into the creative mind's protest against time's tyranny. A Wordsworthian critic, even one as loyal to Wordsworth as Geoffrey Hartman, can insist upon clearly distinguishing between *priority*, as a concept from the natural order, and *authority*, from the spiritual order, but Wordsworth's ode declines to make this distinction. 'By seeking to overcome priority,' Hartman wisely says, 'art fights nature on nature's own ground, and is bound to lose.' The argument of this book is that strong poets are condemned to just this unwisdom; Wordsworth's Great Ode fights nature on nature's own ground, and suffers a great defeat, even as it retains its greater dream. That dream, in Wordsworth's ode, is shadowed by the anxiety of influence, due to the greatness of the precursor-poem, Milton's *Lycidas*, where the human refusal wholly to sublimate is even more rugged, despite the ostensible yielding to Christian teachings of sublimation.

For every poet begins (however 'unconsciously') by rebelling more strongly against the consciousness of death's necessity than all other men and women do. The young citizen of poetry, or ephebe as Athens would have called him, is already the anti-natural or antithetical man, and from his start as a poet he quests for an impossible object, as his precursor quested before him. That this quest encompasses necessarily the diminishment of poetry seems to me an inevitable realization, one that accurate literary history must sustain. The great poets of the

English Renaissance are not matched by their Enlightened descendants, and the whole tradition of the post-Enlightenment, which is Romanticism, shows a further decline in its Modernist and post-Modernist heirs. The death of poetry will not be hastened by any reader's broodings, yet it seems just to assume that poetry in our tradition, when it dies, will be self-slain, murdered by its own past strength. An implied anguish throughout this book is that Romanticism, for all its glories, may have been a vast visionary tragedy, the self-baffled enterprise not of Prometheus but of blinded Oedipus, who did not know that the Sphinx was his Muse.

Oedipus, blind, was on the path to oracular godhood, and the strong poets have followed him by transforming their blindness towards their precursors into the revisionary insights of their own work. The six revisionary movements that I will trace in the strong poet's life-cycle could as well be more, and could take quite different names than those I have employed. I have kept them to six, because these seem to be minimal and essential to my understanding of how one poet deviates from another. The names, though arbitrary, carry on from various traditions that have been central in Western imaginative life, and I hope can be useful.

The greatest poet in our language is excluded from the argument of this book for several reasons. One is necessarily historical; Shakespeare belongs to the giant age before the flood, before the anxiety of influence became central to poetic consciousness. Another has to do with the contrast between dramatic and lyric form. As poetry has become more subjective, the shadow cast by the precursors has become more dominant. The main cause, though, is that Shakespeare's prime precursor was Marlowe, a poet very much smaller than his inheritor. Milton, with all his strength, yet had to struggle, subtly and crucially, with a major precursor in Spenser, and this struggle both formed and malformed Milton. Coleridge, ephebe of Milton and later of Wordsworth, would have been glad to find his Marlowe in Cowper (or in the much weaker Bowles), but influence cannot be willed. Shakespeare is the largest instance in the language of a phenomenon that stands outside the concern of this book: the absolute absorption of the precursor. Battle between strong equals, father and son as mighty opposites, Laius and Oedipus at the crossroads; only this is my subject here, though some of the fathers, as will be seen, are composite figures. That even the strongest poets are subject to influences not poetical is obvious even to me, but again my concern is only with *the poet in a poet*, or the aboriginal poetic self.

A change like the one I propose in our ideas of influence should help us read more accurately any group of past poets who were contemporary with one another. To give one example, as misinterpreters of Keats, *in their poems*, the Victorian disciples of Keats most notably include Tennyson, Arnold, Hopkins, and Rossetti. That Tennyson triumphed in his long, hidden contest with Keats, no one can assert absolutely, but his clear superiority over Arnold, Hopkins, and Rossetti is due to his relative victory or at least holding of his own in contrast to their partial defeats. Arnold's elegiac poetry uneasily blends Keatsian style with anti-Romantic sentiment, while Hopkins' strained intensities and convolutions of diction and Rossetti's densely inlaid art are also at variance with the burdens they seek to alleviate in their own poetic selves. Similarly, in our time we need to look again at Pound's unending match with Browning, as at Stevens' long and largely hidden civil war with the major poets of English and American Romanticism – Wordsworth, Keats, Shelley, Emerson, and Whitman. As with the Victorian Keatsians, these are instances among many, if a more accurate story is to be told about poetic history.

This book's main purpose is necessarily to present one reader's critical vision, in the context both of the criticism and poetry of his own generation, where their current crises most touch him, and in the context of his own anxieties of influence. In the contemporary poems that most move me, like the *Corsons Inlet* and *Saliences* of A. R. Ammons and the *Fragment* and *Soonest Mended* of John Ashbery, I can recognize a strength that battles against the death of poetry, yet also the exhaustions of being a latecomer. Similarly, in the contemporary criticism that clarifies for me my own evasions, in books like *Allegory* by Angus Fletcher, *Beyond Formalism* by Geoffrey Hartman, and *Blindness and Insight* by Paul de Man, I am made aware of the mind's effort to overcome the impasse of Formalist criticism, the barren moralizing that Archetypal criticism has come to be, and the anti-humanistic plain dreariness of all those developments in European criticism that have yet to demonstrate that they can aid in reading any one poem by any poet whatsoever. My Interchapter, proposing a more antithetical practical criticism than any we now have, is my response in this area of the contemporary.

A theory of poetry that presents itself as a severe poem, reliant upon aphorism, apothegm, and a quite personal (though thoroughly traditional) mythic pattern, still may be judged, and may ask to be judged, as argument. Everything that makes up this book – parables, definitions, the working-through of the revisionary ratios as mechanisms of defense – intends to be part of a unified meditation on the melancholy of the creative mind's desperate insistence upon priority. Vico, who read all creation as a severe poem, understood that priority in the natural order and authority in the spiritual order had been one and had to remain one, *for poets*, because only this harshness constituted Poetic Wisdom. Vico reduced both natural priority and spiritual authority to property, a Hermetic reduction that I recognize as the *Ananke*, the dreadful necessity still governing the Western imagination.

Valentinus, second-century Gnostic speculator, came out of Alexandria to teach the Pleroma, the Fullness of thirty Aeons, manifold of Divinity: 'It was a great marvel that they were in the Father without knowing Him.' To search for where you already are is the most benighted of quests, and the most fated. Each strong poet's Muse, his Sophia, leaps as far out and down as can be, in a solipsistic passion of quest. Valentinus posited a Limit, at which quest ends, but no quest ends, if its context is Unconditioned Mind, the cosmos of the greatest post-Miltonic poets. The Sophia of Valentinus recovered, wed again within the Pleroma, and only her Passion or Dark Intention was separated out into our world, beyond the Limit. Into this Passion, the Dark Intention that Valentinus called 'strengthless and female fruit,' the ephebe must fall. If he emerges from it, however crippled and blinded, he will be among the strong poets.

SYNOPSIS: SIX REVISIONARY RATIOS

1. *Clinamen*, which is poetic misreading or misprision proper; I take the word from Lucretius, where it means a 'swerve' of the atoms so as to make change possible in the universe. A poet swerves away from his precursor, by so reading his precursor's poem as to execute a *clinamen* in relation to it. This appears as a corrective movement in his own poem, which implies that the precursor poem went accurately up to a certain point, but then should have swerved, precisely in the direction that the new poem moves.

2. *Tessera*, which is completion and antithesis; I take the word not from mosaic-making, where it is still used, but from the ancient mystery cults, where it meant a token of recognition, the fragment say of a small pot which with the other fragments would re-constitute the vessel. A poet antithetically 'completes' his precursor, by so reading the

parent-poem as to retain its terms but to mean them in another sense, as though the precursor had failed to go far enough.

3. *Kenosis*, which is a breaking-device similar to the defense mechanisms our psyches employ against repetition compulsions; *kenosis* then is a movement towards discontinuity with the precursor. I take the word from St. Paul, where it means the humbling or emptying-out of Jesus by himself, when he accepts reduction from divine to human status. The later poet, apparently emptying himself of his own afflatus, his imaginative goodhood, seems to humble himself as though he were ceasing to be a poet, but this ebbing is so performed in relation to a precursor's poem-of-ebbing that the precursor is emptied out also, and so the later poem of deflation is not as absolute as it seems.

4. *Daemonization*, or a movement towards a personalized Counter-Sublime, in reaction to the precursor's Sublime; I take the term from general Neo-Platonic usage, where an intermediary being, neither divine nor human, enters into the adept to aid him. The later poet opens himself to what he believes to be a power in the parent-poem that does not belong to the parent proper, but to a range of being just beyond that precursor. He does this, in his poem, by so stationing its relation to the parent-poem as to generalize away the uniqueness of the earlier work.

5. *Askesis*, or a movement of self-purgation which intends the attainment of a state of solitude; I take the term, general as it is, particularly from the practice of pre-Socratic shamans like Empedocles. The later poet does not, as in *kenosis*, undergo a revisionary movement of emptying, but of curtailing; he yields up part of his own human and imaginative endowment, so as to separate himself from others, including the precursor, and he does this in his poem by so stationing it in regard to the parent-poem as to make that poem undergo an *askesis* too; the precursor's endowment is also truncated.

6. *Apophrades*, or the return of the dead; I take the word from the Athenian dismal or unlucky days upon which the dead returned to reinhabit the houses in which they had lived. The later poet, in his own final phase, already burdened by an imaginative solitude that is almost a solipsism, holds his own poem so open again to the precursor's work that at first we might believe the wheel has come full circle, and that we are back in the later poet's flooded apprenticeship, before his strength

began to assert itself in the revisionary ratios. But the poem is now *held* open to the precursor, where once it *was* open, and the uncanny effect is that the new poem's achievement makes it seem to us, not as though the precursor were writing it, but as though the later poet himself had written the precursor's characteristic work.

Part 2

The Politics of Authorship

Section 1

Feminism and the Authorial Subject

Feminism and the Authorial Subject

It would scarcely be an exaggeration to say that the struggles of feminism have been primarily a struggle for authorship – understood in the widest sense as the arena in which culture attempts to define itself. Feminist ideas on authorship will be inevitably political since authorship involves the appropriation of cultural space and serves to underpin the principle of the literary canon which – on feminist thought – has been defined in terms of patriarchal prejudice. The very idea of the canon enables patriarchy to police the border between authorship and writing in hierarchical terms which have traditionally placed women 'writers' in the second and devalued category. Feminist ideas on authorship thereby serve to characterise three phases of the movement which are – respectively – sponsorial, revisionist and theoretical in regard of the author-question:

1. the assertion by the female author of the right of belonging to the state and estate of authorship;
2. the attempt to redefine authorship over and against the patriarchal model and to promote a counter-canon of female authors;
3. the recognition that authorship and canonicity are inherently and inalienably patriarchal institutions which feminist thought should pass beyond.

Jane Austen's remark that she wished to be considered not as a woman but as an author characterises the earliest phase in claiming the place of women within the canonical realm without challenging the principles upon which that realm was founded. The use of male pseudonyms by nineteenth-century women novelists provides a dramatic illustration of both the force of exclusion and the desperate strategies forced upon women in their attempt to circumvent patriarchal prejudice: authorship had to be denied so as to be attained. Indeed, the prejudicial foundations of the canon were made shockingly apparent when the proper name (and thereby sex of the writer) declared itself from behind the pseudonymous mask: the text concerned was often downgraded, trivialised and forbidden access to a canon by which it had previously been accepted on intrinsic merits.

Furthermore, as became apparent to feminists in the twentieth century, the authorial canon was actively exclusive in conceptual as well as constituent terms: the very mode in which the idea of authorship was conceived rested on a phallocentric picture of the autonomous creator consolidated in turn by criteria of aesthetic merit which were inadequate to the diversities of female experience. Such recognition required a reconstruction of the nature of authorship and of the male-objectivist criteria of canon formation in terms appropriate to women's creativity. With the development of theoretical feminism in the 1980s, the notion of a realm of authentic female experience was dismissed as essentialist and mystificatory, while the attempt to establish a female authorial canon was seen to do little more than recuperate women's writing for a moribund humanist aesthetics.

The revisionist or 'gynocritical' phase of feminist criticism flourished in Britain and the USA during the 1970s and sought to rediscover what Elaine Showalter called 'the lost continent of women's writing'. Taking the nineteenth century as the continent of its exploration, Sandra Gilbert and Susan Gubar's monumental *The Madwoman in the Attic* remains one of the most impressive attempts to establish a canon of women's authorship. Gilbert and Gubar do not so much strive to sponsor the achievements of the feminist tradition against its male counterpart but instead redefine feminist authorship itself over and against male theologies of creativity. Harold Bloom's Oedipal model of literary tradition is for them an acute diagnosis of the anxious and aggressive dynamics of influence by which the patriarchal canon is formed. For Gilbert and Gubar the female author's anxieties extend beyond those generated by the influence of the precursor to form a general anxiety of authorship. While the male newcomer is anxiously striving after originality so as to claim his canonical place, the female author perceives that very tradition as being constructed precisely in terms of her exclusion.

The effects of such exclusion are for Gilbert and Gubar double-edged. Negatively, it produces feelings of unworthiness in the woman writer which are unconsciously projected in the form of a textual 'mad double' via what Gilbert and Gubar call 'the female schizophrenia of authorship': it then becomes the task of the feminist critic to reconstruct the authorial psyche from this specular image of feminist rage and imprisonment within a hostile tradition. Positively, where the male writer is overwhelmed by the already-written, the female author has all too few precursors and is therefore involved in the creation rather than the misreading of precedents: hence for Gilbert and Gubar the greater exhilaration of contemporary women's writing as it seeks to build rather than trope a tradition. Gilbert and Gubar's work points to decisive psychodynamic and modal differences between male and female authorship, but is vulnerable to criticism on the grounds that the autobiographical inscription of the author remains a fundamentally unexamined category. Furthermore, theoretically sophisticated as much of the reading is, they are often charged with the naïve error of moving with unqualified assurance from character to writer – from the 'mad double' to authorial psyche – as too with promoting a feminist politics on the basis of an aesthetics no less patriarchal for being reversely gendered.

The language-centred challenge from French theory in the 1980s problematised the notions of gendered subjectivity and female authorship. Both the subject who represents (the author) and the subject of representation (the female subject) were called into question by a psychoanalytic feminism which shifted attention from the sex of the writer to the sex of writing. Lacan's distinction between the imaginary and symbolic orders of language served to distinguish between a 'feminine' mode of signification, characterised by the use of words for their sound, pulsion and music, and a 'masculine' use of language, which stressed the rational, linear and logical. The manner in which the child enters into language – its inclination towards one or other of these orders – is held to determine the gender of its writing over and above the sex of the writer.

The French theorist and author, Hélène Cixous, stresses that feminine writing (*écriture féminine*) is accessible to both men and women, since in avant-garde writing it is woman who speaks regardless of whether the text is signed in the name of 'woman' or 'man'. Quite against the tenets of Anglo-American feminism, the canon that Cixous establishes is actually dominated by male avant-gardists such as Joyce, Kafka, Kleist and others through whom the feminine most vitally inscribes itself. 'Castration and Decapitation' – written in an anti-authoritarian, ludic and elliptical style reflective of Cixous's desire to perform as *écriture féminine* what her text describes – thus ingeniously overturns commonsensical gender assumptions through its assertion of a libidinal femininity that cuts across biological identity. As Cixous further argues, the binarism 'male/female' is the engendering opposition of patriarchal metaphysics, and to promote the woman over the man in a counter-hegemonic reversal is simply to perpetuate the very logocentric assumptions from which feminist criticism should liberate itself. Absorbing and plangent as it is, Cixous's theory of *écriture féminine* raises certain difficulties: first, in assigning a generative power to an 'unlocalisable' feminine principle, the argument would seem to betray a fundamental kinship with the metaphysical strategy of locating the origins of discourse in a supersensible realm; and second, neither the specificity nor the ethical status of women's authorship would seem to be at issue within a generalised feminine writing.

Alice Jardine's 'Feminist Tracks' clearly marks the destabilising influence of French thought on Anglophone feminism. Her term *gynesis* – 'the putting into discourse of "woman"' – marks the inscription of the radically feminine within the gynocritical space mapped out by Gilbert and Gubar, Showalter and others. Following on from Cixous, Jardine recommends that woman be henceforth reconceived as 'a woman-in-effect that is never stable and has no identity'. The project of gynocriticism is thereby seen as the exaltation of an illusory female 'subject' generated by metaphysical assumptions. *Gynesis*, on the other hand, proposes an *écriture féminine* as the ground of all discourse and – as its prospect – a sexually and textually plural heterotopia in which man, woman and metaphysics will finally disappear. Woman as writer is replaced by writing as woman, just as woman as subject is replaced by woman as sign. Though Jardine acknowledges the tensions between the postmodern fragmentation of subjectivity and the ethical and canonical imperatives of more traditional feminist politics, the intersections which she proposes are more clearly weighted towards the vertiginous exploration of French textualism. For this reason, Jardine's text perhaps attests less cogently to meeting-places between French and Anglo–American thought than to the continuingly fraught exchange between radical textualism and radical politics.

Not surprisingly, the removal of woman-as-woman and woman-as-author has caused considerable consternation among feminists committed to the subjective, ethical and political issues of feminism as articulated in the Anglo–American tradition. Gender difference is not likely to disappear because a few texts will it so, and even if the opposition man/woman is itself a metaphysical illusion, it remains an illusion with a considerable claim on the reality of women's lives and their writing. The fractured dialogue between textual radicalism and ethical reaction repeats the deadlocked polarisation common to debates about the author in contemporary literary studies. Critics committed to the centrality of woman's experience have often refused the revisionary challenge offered by French theorists, whereas the latter have tended to consign auteurist feminism to a pretheoretical wilderness.

Nancy K. Miller signals a positive move beyond this deadlock and one which preserves the political force of earlier feminism while acknowledging the linguistic resources of French theory. On her argument, female authorship should be rethought outwith the alternatives of patriarchal humanism and theoretical anti-subjectivism. By affirming a model of situated feminist subjectivity, Miller's 'Changing the Subject' is able to counter the twin monoliths of universal subjectivity and anonymous textuality via a conception of authorship as open to difference and change. Miller alerts the reader to the ironic situation whereby no sooner did feminism excavate the space of women's authorship than it consorted with a (largely male-inspired) attempt to close off the space of authorship altogether. She also argues that the most effective challenge to patriarchy consists in developing the structural difference in female subjectivity against the notion of a unified subject. This 'rematerialisation' of female authorship and subjectivity in opposition to the transcendent subject of patriarchal aesthetics could also be extended to other marginalised subject groups whose difference to the 'universal position' is marked – questions of ethnicity and postcolonialism being of especial urgency here. Miller's bold argument shows with clarity how a return to the author is necessary if feminist politics and theory are not to become terms of a reciprocal hostility. As she stresses, this reshaping of the subject exists as a prospect and process no less compelling for the uncertainty of its resolution, or its status as becoming. One might in fact see the current feminist celebration of the 'body' over patriarchal abstraction as a synecdochic movement towards the situatedness which Miller recommends.

SUGGESTED FURTHER READINGS

Beauvoir, Simone de, *The Ethics of Ambiguity* (New York: Philosophical Library, 1948).
—— *The Second Sex* (Harmondsworth: Penguin Books, 1972).
Friedman, Susan Stanford, 'Creativity and the Childbirth Metaphor', *Feminist Studies* 13:1 (Spring 1987), pp. 49–82.
Irigaray, Luce, *Speculum of the Other Woman* (Ithaca, NY: Cornell University Press, 1985).
Jones, Ann Rosalind, 'Writing the Body', *Feminist Studies* 7:2 (Summer 1981), pp. 247–63.
Kristeva, Julia, *Desire in Language* (Oxford: Basil Blackwell, 1980).
Laurentis, Teresa de, *Alice Doesn't: Feminism, Semiotics and Cinema* (Bloomington, IN: Indiana University Press, 1984).
Lovibond, Sabina, 'Feminism and Postmodernism', in R. Boyne and A. Rattansi (eds), *Postmodernism and Society* (Basingstoke, Macmillan Education; New York: St Martin's Press, 1990).
Moi, Toril, *Sexual/Textual Politics* (London: Methuen, 1985).
Nicholson, Linda J. (ed.), *Feminism/Postmodernism* (New York and London: Routledge, 1990).
Nye, Andrea, *Feminist Theory and the Philosophies of Man* (New York: Croom Helm, 1988).
Patemen, Carole and Elizabeth Grosz (eds), *Feminist Challenges* (Boston, MA: Northeastern University Press, 1986), pp. 125–43.
Showalter, Elaine, *A Literature of Their Own* (Princeton, NJ: Princeton University Press, 1977).
—— (ed.), *The New Feminist Criticism: Essays on Women, Literature and Theory* (New York: Pantheon Press, 1985)..
Warhol, Robyn R. and Diane Price Herndl, *Feminisms: An Anthology of Literary Theory and Criticism* (New Brunswick, NJ: Rutgers University Press, 1991).
Woolf, Virginia, *A Room of One's Own* (Harmondsworth: Penguin, 1975).
Wollstonecraft, Mary, *A Vindication of the Rights of Women* (New York: Norton, 1967).

17

SANDRA M. GILBERT and SUSAN GUBAR

from *The Madwoman in the Attic*

. . .

Is a pen a metaphorical penis? Gerard Manley Hopkins seems to have thought so. In a letter to his friend R. W. Dixon in 1886 he confided a crucial feature of his theory of poetry. The artist's 'most essential quality,' he declared, is 'masterly execution, which is a kind of male gift, and especially marks off men from women, the begetting of one's thought on paper, on verse, or whatever the matter is.' In addition, he noted that 'on better consideration it strikes me that the mastery I speak of is not so much in the mind as a puberty in the life of that quality. The male quality is the creative gift.'[1] Male sexuality, in other words, is not just analogically but actually the essence of literary power. The poet's pen is in some sense (even more than figuratively) a penis.

Eccentric and obscure though he was, Hopkins was articulating a concept central to that Victorian culture of which he was in this case a representative male citizen. But of course the patriarchal notion that the writer 'fathers' his text just as God fathered the world is and has been all-pervasive in Western literary civilization, so much so that, as Edward Said has shown, the metaphor is built into the very word, *author*, with which writer, deity, and *pater familias* are identified. Said's miniature meditation on the word *authority* is worth quoting in full because it summarizes so much that is relevant here:

> *Authority* suggests to me a constellation of linked meanings: not only, as the OED tells us, 'a power to enforce obedience,' or 'a derived or delegated power,' or 'a power to influence action,' or

'a power to inspire belief,' or 'a person whose opinion is accepted'; not only those, but a connection as well with *author* – that is, a person who originates or gives existence to something, a begetter, beginner, father, or ancestor, a person also who sets forth written statements. There is still another cluster of meanings: *author* is tied to the past participle *auctus* of the verb *augere*; therefore *auctor*, according to Eric Partridge, is literally an increaser and thus a founder. *Auctoritas* is production, invention, cause, in addition to meaning a right of possession. Finally, it means continuance, or a causing to continue. Taken together these meanings are all grounded in the following notions: (1) that of the power of an individual to initiate, institute, establish – in short, to begin; (2) that this power and its product are an increase over what had been there previously; (3) that the individual wielding this power controls its issue and what is derived therefrom; (4) that authority maintains the continuity of its course.[2]

In conclusion, Said, who is discussing 'The Novel as Beginning Intention,' remarks that 'All four of these [last] abstractions can be used to describe the way in which narrative fiction asserts itself psychologically and aesthetically through the technical efforts of the novelist.' But they can also, of course, be used to describe both the author and the authority of any literary text, a point Hopkins's sexual/aesthetic theory seems to have been designed to elaborate. Indeed, Said himself later observes that a convention of most literary texts is 'that the unity or integrity of the text is maintained by a series of genealogical connections: author–text, beginning–middle–end, text–meaning, reader–interpretation, and so on. *Underneath all these is the imagery of succession, of paternity, or hierarchy*' (italics ours).[3]

There is a sense in which the very notion of paternity is itself, as Stephen Dedalus puts it in *Ulysses*, a 'legal fiction,'[4] a story requiring imagination if not faith. A man cannot verify his fatherhood by either sense or reason, after all; that his child is *his* is in a sense a tale he tells himself to explain the infant's existence. Obviously, the anxiety implicit in such storytelling urgently needs not only the reassurances of male superiority that patriarchal misogyny implies, but also such compensatory fictions of the Word as those embodied in the genealogical imagery Said describes. Thus it is possible to trace the history of this compensatory, sometimes frankly stated and sometimes submerged imagery that elaborates upon what Stephen Dedalus calls the 'mystical estate' of paternity[5] through the works of many literary theoreticians besides Hopkins and Said. Defining poetry as a mirror held up to nature, the mimetic aesthetic that begins with Aristotle and descends through Sidney, Shakespeare, and Johnson implies that the poet, like a lesser God, has made or engendered an alternative, mirror-universe in which he actually seems to enclose or trap shadows of reality. Similarly, Coleridge's Romantic concept of the human 'imagination or esemplastic power' is of a virile, generative force which echoes 'the eternal act of creation in the infinite I AM,' while Ruskin's phallic-sounding 'Penetrative Imagination' is a 'possession-taking faculty' and a 'piercing . . . mind's tongue' that seizes, cuts down, and gets at the root of experience in order 'to throw up what new shoots it will.'[6] In all these aesthetics the poet, like God the Father, is a paternalistic ruler of the fictive world he has created. Shelley called him a 'legislator.' Keats noted, speaking of writers, that 'the antients [*sic*] were Emperors of vast Provinces' though 'each of the moderns' is merely an 'Elector of Hanover.'[7]

In medieval philosophy, the network of connections among sexual, literary, and theological metaphors is equally complex: God the Father both engenders the cosmos and, as Ernst Robert Curtius notes, writes the Book of Nature: both tropes describe a single act of creation.[8] In addition, the Heavenly Author's ultimate eschatological power is made manifest when, as the *Liber Scriptus* of the traditional requiem mass indicates, He writes the Book of Judgement. More recently, male artists like the Earl of Rochester in the seventeenth century and Auguste Renoir in the nineteenth, have frankly defined aesthetics based on male sexual delight. 'I . . . never Rhym'd, but for my Pintle's [penis's] sake,' declares Rochester's witty Timon,[9] and (according to the painter Bridget Riley) Renoir 'is supposed to have said that he painted his paintings with his prick.'[10] Clearly, both these artists believe, with Norman O. Brown, that 'the penis is the head of the body,' and they might both agree, too, with John Irwin's suggestion that the relationship 'of the masculine self with the feminine-masculine work is also an autoerotic act . . . a kind of creative onanism in which through the use of the phallic pen on the 'pure space' of the virgin page . . . the self is continually spent and wasted . . .'[11] No doubt it is for all these reasons, moreover, that poets have traditionally used a vocabulary derived from the patriarchal 'family romance' to describe their relations with each other. As Harold Bloom has pointed out, 'from the sons of Homer to the sons of Ben Jonson, poetic influence [has] been described as a filial relationship,' a relationship of '*sonship*.' The fierce struggle at the heart of literary history, says Bloom, is a 'battle between strong equals, father and son as mighty opposites, Laius and Oedipus at the cross-roads.'[12]

Though many of these writers use the metaphor of literary paternity in different ways and for different purposes, all seem overwhelmingly to agree that a literary text is not only speech quite literally embodied, but also power mysteriously made manifest, made flesh. In patriarchal Western culture, therefore, the text's author is a father, a progenitor, a procreator, an aesthetic patriarch whose pen is an instrument of generative power like his penis. More, his pen's power, like his penis's power, is not just the ability to generate life but the power to create a posterity to which he lays claim, as, in Said's paraphrase of Partridge, 'an increaser and thus a founder.' In this respect, the pen is truly mightier than its phallic counterpart the sword, and in patriarchy more resonantly sexual. Not only does the writer respond to his muse's quasi-sexual excitation with an outpouring of the aesthetic energy Hopkins called 'the fine delight that fathers thought' – a delight poured seminally from pen to page – but as the author of an enduring text the writer engages the attention of the future in exactly the same way that a king (or father) 'owns' the homage of the present. No sword-wielding general could rule so long or possess so vast a kingdom.

Finally, that such a notion of 'ownership' or possession is embedded in the metaphor of paternity leads to yet another implication of this complex metaphor. For if the author/father is owner of his text and of his reader's attention, he is also, of course, owner/possessor of the subjects of his text, that is to say of those figures, scenes, and events – those brain children – he has both incarnated in black and white and 'bound' in cloth or leather. Thus, because he is an *author*, a 'man of letters' is simultaneously, like his divine counterpart, a father, a master or ruler, and an owner: the spiritual type of a patriarch, as we understand that term in Western society.

. . .

What does it mean to be a woman writer in a culture whose fundamental definitions of literary authority are, as we have seen, both overtly and covertly patriarchal? If the vexed and vexing polarities of angel and monster, sweet dumb Snow White and fierce mad Queen, are major images literary tradition offers women, how does such imagery influence the ways in which women attempt the pen? If the Queen's looking glass speaks with the King's voice, how do its perpetual kingly admonitions affect the Queen's own voice? Since his is the chief voice she hears, does the Queen try to sound like the King, imitating his tone, his inflections, his phrasing, his point of view? Or does she 'talk back' to him in her own vocabulary, her own timbre, insisting on her own viewpoint? We believe these are basic questions feminist literary criticism – both theoretical and practical – must answer, and consequently they are questions to which we shall turn again and again, not only in this chapter but in all our readings of nineteenth-century literature by women.

That writers assimilate and then consciously or unconsciously affirm or deny the achievements of their predecessors is, of course, a central fact of literary history, a fact whose aesthetic and metaphysical implications have been discussed in detail by theorists as diverse as T. S. Eliot, M. H. Abrams, Erich Auerbach, and Frank Kermode.[13] More recently, some literary theorists have begun to explore what we might call the psychology of literary history – the tensions and anxieties, hostilities and inadequacies writers feel when they confront not only the achievements of their predecessors but the traditions of genre, style, and metaphor that they inherit from such 'forefathers.' Increasingly, these critics study the ways in which, as J. Hillis Miller has put it, a literary text 'is inhabited . . . by a long chain of parasitical presences, echoes, allusions, guests, ghosts of previous texts.'[14]

As Miller himself also notes, the first and foremost student of such literary psychohistory has been Harold Bloom. Applying Freudian structures to literary genealogies, Bloom has postulated that the dynamics of literary history arise from the artist's 'anxiety of influence,' his fear that he is not his own creator and that the works of his predecessors, existing before and beyond him, assume essential priority over his own writings. In fact, as we pointed out in our discussion of the metaphor of literary paternity, Bloom's paradigm of the sequential historical relationship between literary artists is the relationship of father and son, specifically that relationship as it was defined by Freud. Thus Bloom explains that a 'strong poet' must engage in heroic warfare with his 'precursor,' for, involved as he is in a literary Oedipal struggle, a man can only become a poet by somehow invalidating his poetic father.

Bloom's model of literary history is intensely (even exclusively) male, and necessarily patriarchal. For this reason it has seemed, and no doubt will continue to seem, offensively sexist to some feminist critics. Not only, after all, does Bloom describe literary history as the crucial warfare of fathers and sons, he sees Milton's fiercely masculine fallen Satan as *the* type of the poet in our culture, and he metaphorically defines the poetic process as a sexual encounter between a male poet and his female muse. Where, then, does the female poet fit in? Does she want to annihilate a 'forefather' or a 'foremother'? What if she can find no models, no precursors? Does she have a muse, and what is its sex? Such questions are inevitable in any female consideration of Bloomian poetics.[15] And yet, from a feminist perspective, their inevitability may be just the point; it may, that is, call our attention not to what is wrong about Bloom's conceptualization of the dynamics of Western literary history, but to what is right (or at least suggestive) about his theory.

For Western literary history *is* overwhelmingly male – or, more accurately, patriarchal – and Bloom analyzes and explains this fact, while other theorist have ignored it, precisely, one supposes, because they assumed literature had to be male. Like Freud, whose psychoanalytic postulates permeate Bloom's literary psychoanalyses of the 'anxiety of influence,' Bloom has defined processes of interaction that his predecessors did not bother to consider because, among other reasons, they were themselves so caught up in such processes. Like Freud, too, Bloom has insisted on bringing to consciousness assumptions readers and writers do not ordinarily examine. In doing so, he has clarified the implications of the psychosexual and sociosexual con-texts by which every literary text is surrounded, and thus the meanings of the 'guests' and 'ghosts' which inhabit texts themselves. Speaking of Freud, the feminist theorist Juliet Mitchell has remarked that 'psychoanalysis is not a recommendation *for* a patriarchal society, but an analysis of one.'[16] The same sort of statement could be made about Bloom's model of literary history, which is not a recommendation for but an analysis of the patriarchal poetics (and attendant anxieties) which underlie our culture's chief literary movements.

For our purposes here, however, Bloom's historical construct is useful not only because it helps identify and define the patriarchal psychosexual context in which so much Western literature was authored, but also because it can help us distinguish the anxieties and achievements of female writers from those of male writers. If we return to the question we asked earlier – where does a woman writer 'fit in' to the overwhelmingly and essentially male literary history Bloom describes? – we find we have to answer that a woman writer does *not* 'fit in.' At first glance, indeed, she seems to be anomalous, indefinable, alienated, a freakish outsider. Just as in Freud's theories of male and female psychosexual development there is no symmetry between a boy's growth and a girl's (with, say, the male 'Oedipus complex' balanced by a female 'Electra complex') so Bloom's male-oriented theory of the 'anxiety of influence' cannot be simply reversed or inverted in order to account for the situation of the woman writer.

. Certainly if we acquiesce in the patriarchal Bloomian model, we can be sure that the female poet does not experience the 'anxiety of influence' in the same way that her male counterpart would, for the simple reason that she must confront precursors who are almost exclusively male, and therefore significantly different from her. Not only do these precursors incarnate patriarchal authority (as our discussion of the metaphor of literary paternity argued), they attempt to enclose her in definitions of her person and her potential which, by reducing her to extreme stereotypes (angel, monster) drastically conflict with her own sense of her self – that is, of her subjectivity, her autonomy, her creativity. On the one hand, therefore, the woman writer's male precursors symbolize authority; on the other hand, despite their authority, they fail to define the ways in which she experiences her own identity as a writer. More, the masculine authority with which they construct their literary personae, as well as the fierce power struggles in which they engage in their efforts of self-creation, seem to the woman writer directly to contradict the terms of her own gender definition. Thus the 'anxiety of influence' that a male poet experiences is felt by a female poet as an even more primary 'anxiety of authorship' – a radical fear that she cannot create, that because she can never become a 'precursor' the act of writing will isolate or destroy her.

This anxiety is, of course, exacerbated by her fear that not only can she not fight a male precursor on 'his' terms and win, she cannot 'beget' art upon the (female) body of the muse. As Juliet Mitchell notes, in a concise summary of the implications Freud's theory of psychosexual development has for women, both a boy and a girl, 'as they learn to speak and live within society, want to take the father's [in Bloom's terminology the precursor's] place, and *only the boy will one day be allowed to do so*. Furthermore both sexes are born into the desire of the mother, and as, through cultural heritage, what the mother desires is the phallus-turned-baby, *both* children desire to be the phallus for the mother. Again, *only the boy can fully recognize himself in his mother's desire*. Thus *both* sexes repudiate the implications of femininity,' but the girl learns (in relation to her father) 'that her subjugation to the law of the father entails her becoming the representative of 'nature' and 'sexuality,' a chaos of spontaneous, intuitive creativity.'[17]

Unlike her male counterpart, then, the female artist must first struggle against the effects of a socialization which makes conflict with the will of her (male) precursors seem inexpressibly absurd, futile, or even – as in the case of the Queen in 'Little Snow White' – self-annihilating. And just as the male artist's struggle against his precursor takes the form of what Bloom calls revisionary swerves, flights, misreadings, so the female writer's battle for self-creation involves her in a revisionary process. Her battle, however, is not against her (male) precursor's reading of the world but against his reading of *her*. In order to define herself as an author she must redefine the terms of her socialization. Her revisionary struggle, therefore, often becomes a struggle for what Adrienne Rich has called 'Revision – the act of looking back, of seeing with fresh eyes, of entering an old text from a new critical direction . . . an act of survival.'[18] Frequently, moreover, she can begin such a struggle only by actively seeking a *female* precursor who, far from representing a threatening force to be denied or killed, proves by example that a revolt against patriarchal literary authority is possible.

For this reason, as well as for the sound psychoanalytic reasons Mitchell and others give, it would be foolish to lock the woman artist into an Electra pattern matching the Oedipal structure Bloom proposes for male writers. The woman writer – and we shall see women doing this over and over again – searches for a female model not because she wants dutifully to comply with male definitions of her 'femininity' but because she must legitimize her own rebellious endeavors. At the same time, like most women in patriarchal society, the woman writer does experience her gender as a painful obstacle, or even a debilitating inadequacy; like most patriarchally conditioned women, in other words, she is victimized by what Mitchell calls 'the inferiorized and 'alternative' (second sex) psychology of women under patriarchy.'[19] Thus the loneliness of the female artist, her feelings of alienation from male predecessors coupled with her need for sisterly precursors and successors, her urgent sense of her need for a female audience together with her fear of the antagonism of male readers, her culturally conditioned timidity about self-dramatization, her dread of the patriarchal authority of art, her anxiety about the impropriety of female invention – all these phenomena of 'inferiorization' mark the woman writer's struggle for artistic self-definition and differentiate her efforts at self-creation from those of her male counterpart.

As we shall see, such sociosexual differentiation means that, as Elaine Showalter has suggested, women writers participate in a quite different literary subculture from that inhabited by male writers, a subculture which has its own distinctive literary traditions, even – though it defines itself *in relation to* the 'main,' male-dominated, literary culture –

a distinctive history.[20] At best, the separateness of this female subculture has been exhilarating for women. In recent years, for instance, while male writers seem increasingly to have felt exhausted by the need for revisionism which Bloom's theory of the 'anxiety of influence' accurately describes, women writers have seen themselves as pioneers in a creativity so intense that their male counterparts have probably not experienced its analog since the Renaissance, or at least since the Romantic era. The son of many fathers, today's male writer feels hopelessly belated; the daughter of too few mothers, today's female writer feels that she is helping to create a viable tradition which is at last definitively emerging.

There is a darker side of this female literary subculture, however, especially when women's struggles for literary self-creation are seen in the psychosexual context described by Bloom's Freudian theories of patrilineal literary inheritance. As we noted above, for an 'anxiety of influence' the woman writer substitutes what we have called an 'anxiety of authorship,' an anxiety built from complex and often only barely conscious fears of that authority which seems to the female artist to be by definition inappropriate to her sex. Because it is based on the woman's socially determined sense of her own biology, this anxiety of authorship is quite distinct from the anxiety about creativity that could be traced in such male writers as Hawthorne or Dostoevsky. Indeed, to the extent that it forms one of the unique bonds that link women in what we might call the secret sisterhood of their literary subculture, such anxiety, in itself constitutes a crucial mark of that subculture.

In comparison to the 'male' tradition of strong, father-son combat, however, this female anxiety of authorship is profoundly debilitating. Handed down not from one woman to another but from the stern literary 'fathers' of patriarchy to all their 'inferiorized' female descendants, it is in many ways the germ of a dis-ease or, at any rate, a disaffection, a disturbance, a distrust, that spreads like a stain throughout the style and structure of much literature by women especially . . . throughout literature by women before the twentieth century. For if contemporary women do now attempt the pen with energy and authority, they are able to do so only because their eighteenth- and nineteenth-century foremothers struggled in isolation that felt like illness, alienation that felt like madness, obscurity that felt like paralysis to overcome the anxiety of authorship that was endemic to their literary subculture. Thus, while the recent feminist emphasis on positive role models has undoubtedly helped many women, it should not keep us from realizing the terrible odds against which a creative female subculture was established. Far from reinforcing socially oppressive sexual stereotyping, only a full consideration of such problems can reveal the extraordinary strength of women's literary accomplishments in the eighteenth and nineteenth centuries.

. . .

NOTES

1. *The Correspondence of Gerard Manley Hopkins and Richard Watson Dixon*, ed. C. C. Abbott (London: Oxford University Press, 1935), p. 133.
2. Edward W. Said, *Beginnings: Intention and Method* (New York: Basic Books, 1975), p. 83.
3. Ibid., p. 162. For an analogous use of such imagery of paternity, see Gayatri Chakravorty Spivak's 'Translator's Preface' to Jacques Derrida, *Of Grammatology* (Baltimore: Johns Hopkins University Press, 1976), p. xi: 'to use one of Derrida's structural metaphors, [a preface is] the son or seed . . . caused or engendered by the father (text or meaning).' Also see her discussion of Nietzsche where she considers the 'masculine style of possession' in terms of 'the stylus, the stiletto, the spurs,' p. xxxvi.
4. James Joyce, *Ulysses* (New York: Modern Library, 1934), p. 205.
5. Ibid. The whole of this extraordinarily relevant passage develops this notion further: 'Fatherhood, in the sense of conscious begetting, is unknown to man,' Stephen notes. 'It is a mystical estate, an apostolic succession, from only begetter to only begotten. On that mystery and not on the madonna which the cunning Italian intellect flung to the mob of Europe the church is founded and founded irremovably because founded, like the world, macro- and microcosm, upon the void. Upon incertitude, upon unlikelihood. *Amor matris*, subjective and objective genitive, may be the only true thing in life. Paternity may be a legal fiction' (pp. 204–5).
6. Coleridge, *Biographia Literaria*, chapter 13. John Ruskin, *Modern Painters*, vol. 2, *The Works of John Ruskin*, ed. E. T. Cook and Alexander Wedderburn (London: George Allen, 1903), pp. 250–51. Although Virginia Woolf noted in *A Room of One's Own* that Coleridge thought 'a great mind is androgynous' she added dryly that 'Coleridge certainly did not mean . . . that it is a mind that has any special sympathy with women' (*A Room of One's Own* [New York: Harcourt Brace, 1929], p. 102). Certainly the imaginative power Coleridge describes does not sound 'man-womanly' in Woolf's sense.
7. Shelley, 'A Defense of Poetry.' Keats to John Hamilton Reynolds, 3 February 1818; *The Selected Letters of John Keats*, ed. Lionel Trilling (New York: Doubleday, 1956), p. 121.
8. See E. R. Curtius, *European Literature and the Latin Middle Ages* (New York: Harper Torchbooks, 1963), pp. 305, 306. For further commentary on both Curtius's 'The Symbolism of the Book' and the "Book of Nature' metaphor itself, see Derrida, *Of Grammatology*, pp. 15–17.
9. 'Timon, A Satyr,' in *Poems by John Wilmot Earl of Rochester*, ed. Vivian de Sola Pinto (London: Routledge and Kegan Paul, 1953), p. 99.
10. Bridget Riley, 'The Hermaphrodite,' *Art and Sexual Politics*, ed. Thomas B. Hass and Elizabeth C. Baker (London: Collier Books, 1973), p. 82. Riley comments that she herself would 'interpret this remark as expressing his attitude to his work as a celebration of life.'
11. Norman O. Brown, *Love's Body* (New York: Vintage Books, 1968), p. 134.; John, T. Irwin, *Doubling and Incest, Repetition and Revenge* (Baltimore: Johns Hopkins University Press, 1975), p. 163. Irwin also speaks of 'the phallic generative power of the creative imagination' (p. 159).
12. Harold Bloom, *The Anxiety of Influence* (New York: Oxford University Press, 1973), pp. 11, 26.
13. In 'Tradition and the Individual Talent,' Eliot of course considers these matters; in *Mimesis* Auerbach traces the ways in which the realist includes what has been previously excluded from art; and in *The Sense of an Ending* Frank Kermode shows how poets and novelists lay bare the literariness of their predecessors' forms in order to explore the dissonance between fiction and reality.

14. J. Hillis Miller, 'The Limits of Pluralism, III: The Critic as Host,' *Critical Inquiry* (Spring 1977): 446.

15. For a discussion of the woman writer and her place in Bloomian literary history, see Joanne Feit Diehl, ' "Come Slowly – Eden": An Exploration of Women Poets and their Muse,' *Signs* 3, no. 3 (Spring 1978): 572–87. See also the responses to Diehl in *Signs* 4, no. 1 (Autumn 1978): 188–96.

16. Juliet Mitchell, *Psychoanalysis and Feminism* (New York: Vintage, 1975), p. xiii.

17. Ibid., pp. 404–5.

18. Adrienne Rich, 'When We Dead Awaken: Writing as Re-Vision,' in *Adrienne Rich's Poetry*, ed. Barbara Charlesworth Gelpi and Albert Gelpi (New York: Norton, 1975), p. 90.

19. Mitchell, *Psychoanalysis and Feminism*, p. 402.

20. See Elaine Showalter, *A Literature of Their Own* (Princeton: Princeton University Press, 1977).

18

HÉLÈNE CIXOUS

'Castration or Decapitation?'

On sexual difference: Let's start with these small points. One day Zeus and Hera, the ultimate couple, in the course of one of their intermittent and thoroughgoing disagreements – which today would be of the greatest interest to psychoanalysts – called on Tiresias to arbitrate. Tiresias, the blind seer who had enjoyed the uncommon fortune of having lived seven years as a woman and seven years as a man.

He was gifted with second sight. Second sight in a sense other than we might usually understand it: it isn't simply that as a prophet he could see into the future. He could also see it from both side: from the side of the male and from the side of the female.

The subject of the disagreement was the question of sexual pleasure: 'Of man and woman, who enjoys the greater pleasure?' Obviously neither Zeus nor Hera could answer this without giving their *own* answer, which they saw would be inadequate, since the ancients made fewer assumptions than we do about the possibility of making such identifications. So it came about that Tiresias was sought, as the only person who could know 'which of the two.' And Tiresias answered: 'If sexual pleasure could be divided up into ten parts, nine of them would be the woman's.' Nine. It's no councidence that Tiresias makes another appearance in none other than the oedipal scene. It was Tiresias who, at Oedipus's command, reminded Oedipus that blindness was his master, and Tiresias who, so they say, 'made the scales fall from his eyes' and showed Oedipus who he really was. We should note that these things are all linked together and bear some relation to the question 'What is woman for man?'

It reminds me of a little Chinese story. Every detail of this story counts. I've borrowed it from a very serious text, Sun Tse's manual of strategy, which is a kind of handbook for the warrior. This is the anecdote. The king commanded General Sun Tse: 'You who are a great strategist and claim to be able to train anybody in the arts of war . . . take my wives (all one hundred and eighty of them!) and make soldiers out of them.' We don't know why the king conceived this desire – it's the one thing we don't know . . . it remains precisely 'un(re)countable' or unaccountable in the story. But it is a king's wish, after all.

So Sun Tse had the women arranged in two rows, each headed by one of the two favorite wives, and then taught them the language of the drumbeat. It was very simple: two beats – right, three beats – left, four beats – about turn or backward march. But instead of learning the code very quickly, the ladies started laughing and chattering and paying no attention to the lesson, and Sun Tse, the master, repeated the lesson several times over. But the more he spoke, the more the women fell about laughing, upon which Sun Tse put his code to the test. It is said in this code that should women fall about laughing instead of becoming soldiers, their actions might be deemed mutinous, and the code has ordained that cases of mutiny call for the death penalty. So the women were condemned to death. This bothered the king somewhat: a hundred and eighty wives are a lot to lose! He didn't want his wives put to death. But Sun Tse replied that since he was put in charge of making soldiers out of the women, he would carry out the order: Sun Tse was a man of absolute principle. And in any case there's an order even more 'royal' than that of the king himself: the Absolute Law . . . One does not go back on an order. He therefore acted according to the code and with his saber beheaded the two women commanders. They were replaced and the exercise started again, and as if they had never done anything except practice the art of war, the women turned right, left, and about in silence and with never a single mistake.

It's hard to imagine a more perfect example of a particular relationship between two economies: a masculine economy and a feminine economy, in which the masculine is governed by a rule that keeps time with two beats, three beats, four beats, with pipe and drum, exactly as it should be. An order that works by inculcation, by education: it's always a question of education. An education that consists of trying to make a soldier of the feminine by force, the force history keeps reserved for woman, the 'capital' force that is effectively decapitation. Women have no choice other than to be decapitated, and in any case the moral is that if they don't actually lose their heads by the sword, *they only keep them on condition that they lose them* – lose them, that is, to complete silence, turned into automatons.

It's a question of submitting feminine disorder, its laughter, its inability to take the drumbeats seriously, to the threat of decapitation. If man operates under the threat of castration, if masculinity is culturally ordered by the castration complex, it might be said that the backlash, the return, on women of this castration anxiety is its displacement as decapitation, execution, of woman, as loss of her head.

We are led to pose the woman question to history in quite elementary forms like, 'Where is she? Is there any such thing as woman?' At worst, many women wonder whether they even exist. They feel they don't exist and wonder if there has ever been a place for them. I am speaking of woman's place, *from* woman's place, if she takes (a) place.

In *La Jeune Née*[1] I made use of a story that seemed to me particularly expressive of woman's place: the story of Sleeping Beauty. Woman, if you look for her, has a strong chance of always being found in one position: in bed. In bed and asleep – 'laid (out).' She is always to be found on or in a bed: Sleeping Beauty is lifted from her bed by a man because, as we all know, women don't wake up by themselves: man has to intervene, you understand. She is lifted up by the man who will lay her in her next bed so that she may be confined to bed ever after, just as the fairy tales say.

And so her trajectory is from bed to bed: one bed to another, where she can dream all the more. There are some extraordinary analyses by Kierkegaard on women's 'existence' – or that part of it set aside for her by culture – in which he says he sees her as sleeper. She sleeps, he says, and first love dreams her and then she dreams of love. From dream to dream, and always in second position. In some stories, though, she can be found standing up, but not for long. Take Little Red Riding Hood as an example: it will not, I imagine, be lost on you that the 'red riding hood' in question is a little clitoris. Little Red Riding Hood basically gets up to some mischief: she's the little female sex that tries to play a bit and sets out with her little pot of butter and her little jar of honey. What is interesting is that it's her mother who gives them to her and sends her on an excursion that's tempting precisely because it's forbidden: Little Red Riding Hood leaves one house, mommy's house, not to go out into the big wide world but to go from one house to another by the shortest route possible: to make haste, in other words, from the mother to the other. The other in this case is grandmother, whom we might imagine as taking the place of the 'Great Mother,' because there are great men but no great women: there are Grand-

Mothers instead. And grandmothers are always wicked: she is the bad mother who always shuts the daughter in whenever the daughter might by chance want to live or take pleasure. So she'll always be carrying her little pot of butter and her little jar of honey to grandmother, who is there as jealousy . . . the jealousy of the woman who can't let her daughter go.

But in spite of all this Little Red Riding Hood makes her little detour, does what women should never do, travels through her own forest. She allows herself the forbidden . . . and pays dearly for it: she goes back to bed, in grandmother's stomach. The Wolf is grandmother; and all women recognize the Big Bad Wolf! We know that always lying in wait for us somewhere in some big bed is a Big Bad Wolf. The Big Bad Wolf represents, with his big teeth, his big eyes, and his grandmother's looks, that great Superego that threatens all the little female red riding hoods who try to go out and explore their forest without the psychoanalyst's permission. So, between two houses, between two beds, she is laid, ever caught in her chain of metaphors, metaphors that organize culture . . . ever her moon to the masculine sun, nature to culture, concavity to masculine convexity, matter to form, immobility/inertia to the march of progress, terrain trod by the masculine footstep, vessel . . . While man is obviously the active, the upright, the productive . . . and besides, that's how it happens in History.

This opposition to woman cuts endlessly across all the oppositions that order culture. It's the classic opposition, dualist and hierarchical. Man/Woman automatically means great/small, superior/inferior . . . means high or low, means Nature/History, means transformation/ inertia. In fact, every theory of culture, every theory of society, the whole conglomeration of symbolic systems – everything, that is, that's spoken, everything that's organized as discourse, art, religion, the family, language, everything that seizes us, everything that acts on us – it is all ordered around hierarchical oppositions that come back to the man/woman opposition, an opposition that can only be sustained by means of a difference posed by cultural discourse as 'natural,' the difference between activity and passivity. It always works this way, and the opposition is founded in the *couple*. A couple posed in opposition, in tension, in conflict . . . a couple engaged in a kind of war in which death is always at work – and I keep emphasizing the importance of the opposition as *couple*, because all this isn't just about one word; rather everything turns on the Word: everything is the Word and only the Word. To be aware of the couple, that it's the couple that makes it all work, is also to point to the fact that it's on the couple that we have to work if we are to deconstruct and transform culture. The couple as terrain, as space of cultural struggle, but also as terrain, as space demanding, insisting on, a complete transformation in the relation of one to the other. And so work still has to be done on the couple . . . on the question, for example, of what a completely different couple relationship would be like, what a love that was more than merely a cover for, a veil of, war would be like.

I said it turns on the Word: we must take culture at its word, as it takes us into its Word, into its tongue. You'll understand why I think that no political reflection can dispense with reflection on language, with work on language. For as soon as we exist, we are born into language and language speaks (to) us, dictates its law, a law of death: it lays down its familial model, lays down its conjugal model, and even at the moment of uttering a sentence, admitting a notion of 'being,' a question of being, an ontology, we are already seized by a certain kind of masculine desire, the desire that mobilizes philosophical discourse. As soon as the question 'What is it?' is posed, from the moment a question is put, as soon as a reply is sought, *we are already caught up in masculine interrogation*. I say 'masculine interrogation': as we say so-and-so was interrogated by the police. And this interrogation precisely involves the work of signification: 'What is it? Where is it?' A work of meaning, 'This means that,' the predicative distribution that always at the same time orders the constitution of meaning. And while meaning is being constituted, it only gets constituted in a movement in which one of the terms of the couple is destroyed in favor of the other.

'Look for the lady,' as they say in the stories . . . 'Cherchez la femme' – we always know that means: you'll find her in bed. Another question that's posed in History, rather a strange question, a typical male question, is: 'What do women want?' The Freudian question, of course. In his work on desire, Freud asks somewhere, or rather doesn't ask, leaves hanging in the air, the question 'What do women want?' Let's talk a bit about this desire and about why/how the question 'What do women want?' gets put, how it's both posed and left hanging in the air by philosophical discourse, by analytic discourse (analytic discourse being only one province of philosophical discourse), and how it is posed, let us say, by the Big Bad Wolf and the Grand-Mother.

'What does she want?' Little Red Riding Hood knew quite well what she wanted, but Freud's question is not what it seems: it's a rhetorical question. To pose the question 'What do women want?' is to pose it already as answer, as from a man who isn't expecting any answer, because the answer is 'She wants nothing.' . . . 'What does she want?

. . . Nothing! Nothing because she is passive. The only thing man can do is offer the question 'What could she want, she who wants nothing?' Or in other words: 'Without me, what could she want?'

Old Lacan takes up the slogan 'What does she want?' when he says, 'A woman cannot speak of her pleasure.' Most interesting! It's all there, a woman *cannot*, is unable, hasn't the power. Not to mention 'speaking': it's exactly this that she's forever deprived of. Unable to speak of pleasure = no pleasure, no desire: power, desire, speaking, pleasure, none of these is for woman. And as a quick reminder of how this works in theoretical discourse, one question: you are aware, of course, that for Freud/Lacan, woman is said to be 'outside the Symbolic': outside the Symbolic, that is outside language, the place of the Law, excluded from any possible relationship with culture and the cultural order. And she is outside the Symbolic because she lacks any relation to the phallus, because she does not enjoy what orders masculinity – the castration complex. Woman does not have the advantage of the castration complex – it's reserved solely for the little boy. The phallus, in Lacanian parlance also called the 'transcendental signifier,' transcendental precisely as primary organizer of the structure of subjectivity, is what, for psychoanalysis, inscribes its effects, its effects of castration and resistance to castration and hence the very organization of language, as unconscious relations, and so it is the phallus that is said to constitute the *a priori* condition of all symbolic functioning. This has important implications as far as the body is concerned: the body is not sexed, does not recognize itself as, say, female or male without having gone through the castration complex.

What psychoanalysis points to as defining woman is that she lacks lack. She lacks lack? Curious to put it in so contradictory, so extremely paradoxical, a manner: she lacks lack. To say she lacks lack is also, after all, to say she doesn't miss lack . . . since she doesn't miss the lack of lack. Yes, they say, but the point is 'she lacks The Lack,' The Lack, lack of the Phallus. And so, supposedly, she misses the great lack, so that without man she would be indefinite, indefinable, nonsexed, unable to recognize herself: outside the Symbolic. But fortunately there is man: he who comes . . . Prince Charming. And it's man who teaches woman (because man is always the Master as well), who teaches her to be aware of lack, to be aware of absence, aware of death. It's man who will finally order woman, 'set her to rights,' by teaching her that without man she could 'misrecognize.' He will teach her the Law of the Father. Something of the order of: 'Without me, without me – the Absolute – Father (the father is always that much more absolute the more he is improbable, dubious) – without me you wouldn't exist, I'll show you.' Without him she'd remain in a state of distressing and distressed undifferentiation, unbordered, unorganized, 'unpoliced' by the phallus . . . incoherent, chaotic, and embedded in the Imaginary in her ignorance of the Law of the Signifier. Without him she would in all probability not be contained by the threat of death, might even, perhaps, believe herself eternal, immortal. Without him she would be deprived of sexuality. And it might be said that man works very actively to produce 'his woman.' Take for example *Le Ravissement de Lol V. Stein*[2] and you will witness the moment when man can finally say 'his' woman, 'my' woman. It is that moment when he has taught her to be aware of Death. So man *makes*, he makes (up) his woman, not without being himself seized up and drawn into the dialectical move-ment that this sort of thing sets in play. We might say that the Absolute Woman, in culture, the woman who really reprents femininity most effectively . . . who is closest to femininity as *prey* to masculinity, is actually the hysteric . . . he makes her image for her!

The hysteric is a divine spirit that is always at the edge, the turning point, of making. She is one who does not make herself . . . she does not make herself but she does make the other. It is said that the hysteric 'makes-believe' the father, plays the father, 'makes-believe' the master. Plays, makes up, makes-believe: she makes-believe she is a woman, unmakes-believe too . . . plays at desire, plays the father . . . turns herself into him, unmakes him at the same time. Anyway, without the hysteric, there's no father . . . without the hysteric, no master, no analyst, no analysis! She's the *unorganizable* feminine construct, whose power of producing the other is a power that never returns to her. She is really a wellspring nourishing the other for eternity, yet not drawing back from the other . . . not recognizing herself in the images the other may or may not give her. She is given images that don't belong to her, and she forces herself, as we've all done, to resemble them.

And so in the face of this person who lacks lack, who does not miss lack of lack, we have the construct that is infinitely easier to analyze, to put in place – manhood, flaunting its metaphors like banners through history. You know those metaphors: they are most effective. It's always clearly a question of war, of battle. If there is no battle, it's replaced by the stake of battle: strategy. Man is strategy, is reckoning . . . 'how to win' with the least possible loss, at the lowest possible cost. Throughout literature masculine figures all say the same thing:

'I'm reckoning' what to do to win. Take Don Juan and you have the whole masculine economy getting together to 'give women just what it takes to keep them in bed' then swiftly taking back the investment, then reinvesting, etc., so that nothing ever gets given, everything gets taken back, while in the process the greatest possible dividend of pleasure is taken. Consumption without payment, of course.

Let's take an example other than Don Juan, one clearly pushed to the point of paroxysm . . . Kafka. It was Kafka who said there was one struggle that terrified him beyond all others (he was an embattled man, but his battle was with death – in this sense he was a man greater than the rest): but in matters concerning women his was a struggle that terrified him (death did not). He said the struggle with women ended up in bed: this was his greatest fear. If you know a little about Kafka's life you should know that in his complete integrity, his absolute honesty, he attempted to live through this awful anguish in his relationships with women, in the struggle whose only outcome is bed, by working . . . finally to produce a neurosis of quite extraordinary beauty and terror consisting of a life-and-death relationship with a woman, but at the greatest possible distance. As close as possible and as distanced as possible. He would be betrothed, passionately desire a marriage which he feared above all else, and keep putting off the wedding by endless unconscious maneuvers . . . by a pattern of repeated breakups that took him right to his deathbed, the very deathbed he'd always wanted – a bed, that is, in which he could finally be alone with death. This work of keeping women at a distance while at the same time drawing them to him shows up strikingly in his diary, again because Kafka was honest enough to reveal everything, to say everything. He wrote in little columns, putting debits on the left and credits on the right . . . all the reasons I absolutely must marry, all the reasons I absolutely must not. This tension points to the spirit of male/ female relationships in a way it isn't normally revealed, because what is normally revealed is actually a decoy . . . all those words about love, etc. All that is always just a cover for hatred nourished by the fear of death: woman, for man, is death. This is actually the castration complex at its most effective: giving is really dicing with death.

Giving: there you have a basic problem, which is that masculinity is always associated – in the unconscious, which is after all what makes the whole economy function – with debt. Freud, in deciphering the latent antagonisms between parents and children, shows very well the extent to which the family is founded, as far as the little boy is concerned, on a fearful debt. The child *owes* his parents his life and his problem is exactly to *repay* them: nothing is more dangerous than obligation. Obligation is submission to the enormous weight of the other's generosity, is being threatened by a blessing . . . and a blessing is always an evil when it comes from someone else. For the moment you receive something you are effectively 'open' to the other, and if you are a man you have only one wish, and that is hastily to return the gift, to break the circuit of an exchange that could have no end . . . to be nobody's child, to owe no one a thing.

And so debt, what is always expressed in religions by laws like 'a tooth for a tooth,' 'a gift for a gift,' 'an eye for an eye,' is a system of absolute equivalence . . . of no inequality, for inequality is always interpreted by the masculine as a difference of strength, and thus as a threat. This economy is ruled by price: there's a price to pay, life is dear, the price of life has to be paid. And here lies a difficulty in connection with love, in that, at coming, love starts escaping the system of equivalence in all sorts of ways. It's very hard to give back something you can't pin down. What's so frightening in relations between male and female at the moment of coming (*au niveau de la jouissance*) is the possibility that there might be more on one side than on the other and the Symbolic finds it really tough to know who wins and who loses, who gives more in a relationship of this sort. The memory of debt and the fear of having to recognize one's debt rise up straightaway. But the refusal to know is nonetheless ambivalent in its implications, for not knowing is threatening while at the same time (and this is where the castration complex comes in) it reinforces the desire to know. So in the end woman, in man's desire, stands in the place of not knowing, the place of mystery. In this sense she is no good, but at the same time she is good because it's this mystery that leads man to keep overcoming, dominating, subduing, putting his manhood to the test, against the mystery he has to keep forcing back.

And so they want to keep woman in the place of mystery, consign her to mystery, as they say 'keep her in her place,' keep her at a distance: she's always not quite there . . . but no one knows exactly where she is. She is kept in place in a quite characteristic way – coming back to Oedipus, the place of one who is too often forgotten,[3] the place of the sphinx . . . she's kept in the place of what we might call the 'watch-bitch' (*chienne chanteuse*). That is to say, she is outside the city, at the edge of the city – the city is man, ruled by masculine law – and there she is. In what way is she there? She is there not recognizing: the sphinx doesn't recognize herself, she it is who poses questions, just as it's man who holds the answer and furthermore, as you know, his answer is completely worthy of him: 'Man,' simple answer . . . but it says everything. 'Watch-bitch,' the sphinx was called: she's an animal and she sings out. She sings out because women do . . . they do utter a little, but they don't speak. Always keep in mind the distinction between speaking and talking. It is said, in philosophical texts, that women's weapon is the word, because they talk, talk endlessly, chatter, overflow with sound, mouth-sound: but they don't actually *speak*, they have nothing to say. They always inhabit the place of silence, or at most make it echo with their singing. And neither is to their benefit, for they remain outside knowledge.

Silence: silence is the mark of hysteria. The great hysterics have lost speech, they are aphonic, and at times have lost more than speech: they are pushed to the point of choking, nothing gets through. They are decapitated, their tongues are cut off and what talks isn't heard because it's the body that talks, and man doesn't hear the body. In the end, the woman pushed to hysteria is the woman who disturbs and is nothing but disturbance. The master dotes on disturbance right from the moment he can subdue it and call it up at his command. Conversely the hysteric is the woman who cannot not ask the master what he wants her to want: she wants nothing, truly she wants nothing. She wants . . . she wants to want. But what is it she wants to want? So she goes to school: she asks the master: 'What should I want?' and 'What do you want me to want, so that I might want it?' Which is what happens in analysis.

Let's imagine that all this functioned otherwise, that it could function otherwise. We'd first have to imagine resistance to masculine desire conducted by woman as hysteric, as distracted. We'd first have to imagine her ceasing to support with her body what I call the realm of the proper. The realm of the proper in the sense of the general cultural heterosocial establishment in which man's reign is held to be proper: proper may be the opposite of improper, and also of unfitting, just as black and white are opposites. Etymologically, the 'proper' is 'property,' that which is not separable from me. Property is proximity, nearness: we must love our neighbors, those close to us, as ourselves: we must draw close to the other so that we may love him/her, because we love ourselves most of all. The realm of the proper, culture, functions by the appropriation articulated, set into play, by man's classic fear of seeing himself expropriated, seeing himself deprived . . . by his refusal to be deprived, in a state of separation, by his fear of losing the prerogative, fear whose response is all of History. Everything must return to the masculine. 'Return': the economy is founded on a system of returns. If a man spends and is spent, it's on condition that his power returns. If a man should go out, if he should go out to the other, it's always done according to the Hegelian model, the model of the master–slave dialectic.

Woman would then have to start by resisting the movement of reappropriation that rules the whole economy, by being party no longer to the masculine return, but by proposing instead a desire no longer caught up in the death struggle, no longer implicated in the reservation and reckoning of the masculine economy, but breaking with the reckoning that 'I never lose anything except to win a bit more' . . . so as to put aside all negativeness and bring out a positiveness which might be called the living other, the rescued other, the other unthreatened by destruction. Women have it in them to organize this regeneration, this vitalization of the other, of otherness in its entirety. They have it in them to affirm the difference, *their* difference, such that nothing can destroy that difference, rather that it might be affirmed, affirmed to the point of strangeness. So much so that when sexual difference, when the preservation or dissolution of sexual difference, is touched on, the whole problem of destroying the strange, destroying all the forms of racism, all the exclusions, all those instances of outlaw and genocide that recur through History, is also touched on. If women were to set themselves to transform History, it can safely be said that every aspect of History would be completely altered. Instead of being made by man, History's task would be to make woman, to produce her. And it's at this point that work by women themselves on women might be brought into play, which would benefit not only women but all humanity.

But first she would have to *speak*, start speaking, stop saying that she has nothing to say! Stop learning in school that women are created to listen, to believe, to make no discoveries. Dare to speak her piece about giving, the possibility of a giving that doesn't take away, but *gives*. Speak of her pleasure and, God knows, she has something to say about that, so that she gets to unblock a sexuality that's just as much feminine as masculine, 'de-phallocentralize' the body, relieve man of his phallus, return him to an erogenous field and a libido that isn't stupidly organized round that monument, but appears shifting, diffused, taking on all the others of oneself. Very difficult: first we have to get rid of the systems of censorship that bear down on every attempt to speak in the feminine. We have to get rid of and also explain what all knowledge brings with it as its burden of power: to show in what ways, culturally, knowledge is the accomplice of power: that whoever stands in the place of knowledge is always getting a dividend of power: show that all thinking until now has been ruled by this dividend, this surplus value of power that comes back to him who knows. Take the philosophers, take their position of mastery, and you'll see that there is not a soul who dares to make an advance in thought, into the as-yet-unthought, without shuddering at the idea that he is under the surveillance of the ancestors, the grandfathers, the tyrants of the concept, without thinking that there behind your back is always the famous Name-of-the-Father, who knows whether or not you're writing whatever it is you have to write without any spelling mistakes.

Now, I think that what women will have to do and what they will do, right from the moment they venture to speak what they have to say, will of necessity bring about a shift in metalanguage. And I think we're completely crushed, especially in places like universities, by the highly repressive operations of metalanguage, the operations, that is, of the commentary on the commentary, the code, the operation that sees to it that the moment women open their mouths – women more often than men – they are immediately asked in whose name and from what theoretical standpoint they are speaking, who is their master and where they are coming from: they have, in short, to salute . . . and show their identity papers. There's work to be done against *class*, against categorization, against classification – classes. 'Doing classes' in France means doing military service. There's work to be done against military service, against all schools, against the pervasive masculine urge to judge, diagnose, digest, name . . . not so much in the sense of the loving precision of poetic naming as in that of the repressive censorship of philosophical nomination/conceptualization.

Women who write have for the most part until now considered themselves to be writing not as women but as writers. Such women may declare that sexual difference means nothing, that there's no attributable difference between masculine and feminine writing . . . What does it mean to 'take no position'? When someone says 'I'm not political' we all know what that means! It's just another way of saying: 'My politics are someone else's!' And it's exactly the case with writing! Most women are like this: they do someone else's – man's – writing, and in their innocence sustain it and give it voice, and end up producing writing that's in effect masculine. Great care must be taken in working on feminine writing not to get trapped by names: to be signed with a woman's name doesn't necessarily make a piece of writing feminine. It could quite well be masculine writing, and conversely, the fact that a piece of writing is signed with a man's name does not in itself exclude femininity. It's rare, but you can sometimes find femininity in writings signed by men: it does happen.

Which texts appear to be woman-texts and are recognized as such today, what can this mean, how might they be read?[4] In my opinion, the writing being done now that I see emerging around me won't only be of the kinds that exist in print today, though they will always be with us, but will be something else as well. In particular we ought to be prepared for what I call the 'affirmation of the difference,' not a kind of wake about the corpse of the mummified woman, nor a fantasy of woman's decapitation, but something different: a step forward, an adventure, an exploration of woman's powers: of her power, her potency, her ever-dreaded strength, of the regions of femininity. Things are starting to be written, things that will constitute a feminine Imaginary, the site, that is, of identifications of an ego no longer given over to an image defined by the masculine ('like the woman I love, I mean a dead woman'), but rather inventing forms for women on the march, or as I prefer to fantasize, 'in flight,' so that instead of lying down, women will go forward by leaps in search of themselves.

There is work to be done on female sexual pleasure and on the production of an unconscious that would no longer be the classic unconscious. The unconscious is always cultural and when it talks it tells you your old stories, it tells you the old stories you've heard before because it consists of the repressed of culture. But it's also always shaped by the forceful return of a libido that doesn't give up that easily, and also by what is strange, what is outside culture, by a language which is a savage tongue that can make itself understood quite well. This is why, I think, *political* and not just literary work is started as soon as writing gets done by women that goes beyond the bounds of censorship, reading, the gaze, the masculine command, in that cheeky risk taking women can get into when they set out into the unknown to look for themselves.

This is how I would define a feminine textual body: as a *female libidinal economy*, a regime, energies, a system of spending not necessarily carved out by culture. A feminine textual body is recognized by the fact that it is always endless, without ending: there's no closure, it doesn't stop, and it's this that very often makes the feminine text difficult to read. For we've learned to read books that basically pose the word 'end.' But this one doesn't finish, a feminine text goes on and on and at a certain moment the volume comes to an end but the writing continues and for the reader this means being thrust into the void.

These are texts that work on the beginning but not on the origin. The origin is a masculine myth: I always want to know where I come from. The question 'Where do children come from?' is basically a masculine, much more than a feminine, question. The quest for origins, illustrated by Oedipus, doesn't haunt a feminine unconscious. Rather it's the beginning, or beginning*s*, the manner of beginning, not promptly with the phallus in order to close with the phallus, but starting on all sides at once, that makes a feminine writing. A feminine text starts on all sides at once, starts twenty times, thirty times, over.

The question a woman's text asks is the question of giving – 'What does this writing give?' 'How does it give?' And talking about nonorigin and beginnings, you might say it 'gives a send-off' *(donne le départ)*. Let's take the expression, 'giving a send-off' in a metaphorical sense: giving a send-off is generally giving the *signal* to depart. I think it's more than giving the departure signal, it's really giving, making a *gift* of, departure, allowing departure, allowing breaks, 'parts,' partings, separations . . . from this we break with the return-to-self, with the specular relations ruling the coherence, the identification, of the individual. When a woman writes in nonrepression she passes on her others, her abundance of non-ego/s in a way that destroys the form of the family structure, so that it is defamilialized, can no longer be thought in terms of the attribution of roles within a social cell: what takes place is an endless circulation of desire from one body to another, above and across sexual difference, outside those relations of power and regeneration constituted by the family. I believe regeneration leaps, age leaps, time leaps . . . A woman-text gets across a detachment, a kind of disengagement, not the detachment that is immediately taken back, but a real capacity to lose hold and let go. This takes the metaphorical form of wandering, excess, risk of the unreckonable: no reckoning, a feminine text can't be predicted, isn't predictable, isn't knowable and is therefore very disturbing. It can't be anticipated, and I believe femininity is written outside anticipation: it really is the text of the unforeseeable.

Let's look not at syntax but at fantasy, at the unconscious: all the feminine texts I've read are very close to the voice, very close to the flesh of language, much more so than masculine texts . . . perhaps because there's something in them that's freely given, perhaps because they don't rush into meaning, but are straightway at the threshold of feeling. There's *tactility* in the feminine text, there's touch, and this touch passes through the ear. Writing in the feminine is passing on what is cut out by the Symbolic, the voice of the mother, passing on what is most archaic. The most archaic force that touches a body is one that enters by the ear and reaches the most intimate point. This innermost touch always echoes in a woman-text. So the movement, the movement of the text, doesn't trace a straight line. I see it as an outpouring . . . which can appear in primitive or elementary texts as a fantasy of blood, of menstrual flow, etc., but which I prefer to see as vomiting, as 'throwing up,' 'disgorging.' And I'd link this with a basic structure of property relations defined by mourning.

Man cannot live without resigning himself to loss. He has to mourn. It's his way of withstanding castration. He goes through castration, that is, and by sublimation incorporates the lost object. Mourning, resigning oneself to loss, means not losing. When you've lost something and the loss is a dangerous one, you refuse to admit that something of your self might be lost in the lost object. So you 'mourn,' you make haste to recover the investment made in the lost object. But I believe women *do not mourn*, and this is where their pain lies! When you've mourned, it's all over after a year, there's no more suffering. Woman, though, does not mourn, does not resign herself to loss. She basically *takes up the challenge of loss* in order to go on living: she lives it, gives it life, is capable of unsparing loss. She does not hold onto loss, she loses without holding onto loss. This makes her writing a body that overflows, disgorges, vomiting as opposed to masculine incorporation . . . She loses, and doubtless it would be to the death were it not for the intervention of those basic movements of a feminine unconscious (this is how I would define *feminine sublimation*) which provide the capacity of passing above it all by means of a form of oblivion which is not the oblivion of burial or interment but the oblivion of *acceptance*. This is taking loss, seizing it, living it. Leaping. This goes with not withholding: she does not withhold. She does not withhold, hence the impression of constant return evoked by this lack of withholding. It's like a kind of open memory that ceaselessly makes way. And in the end, she will write this not-withholding, this not-writing: she writes of not-writing, not-happening . . . She crosses limits: she is neither outside nor in, whereas the masculine would try to 'bring the outside in, if possible.'[5]

And finally this open and bewildering prospect goes hand in hand with a certain kind of laughter. Culturally speaking, women have wept a great deal, but once the tears are shed, there will be endless laughter instead. Laughter that breaks out, overflows, a humor no one would expect to find in women – which is nonetheless surely their greatest strength because it's a humor that sees man much further away than he has ever been seen. Laughter that shakes the last chapter of my text *LA*,[6] 'she who laughs last.' And her first laugh is at herself.

NOTES

This article, here translated by Annette Kuhn, first appeared as 'Le Sexe ou la tête?' in *Les Cahiers du GRIF*, no. 13 (1976), pp. 5–15. The text was transcribed from a conversation between Hélène Cixous and the editors of *Les Cahiers du GRIF* which took place in Brussels during 1975. The present translation follows the published transcript with two exceptions (signaled in nn. 4 and 5) and is published with the permission of Hélène Cixous. The approach and arguments are developed in Cixous's more recent work. See, e.g., *Vivre l'orange* (Paris: Editions des femmes, 1979), written in French and English, and *Illa* (Paris: Editions des femmes, 1980). Thanks are due to to Elaine Marks for suggesting this translation of the title, to Keith Cohen for advice on specific points of translation, and to Chris Holmlund for bibliographical assistance.

1. Hélène Cixous and Catherine Clément, *La Jeune Née* (Paris: 10/18, 1975) (translator's note).
2. Marguerite Duras, *Le Ravissement de Lol V. Stein* (Paris: Gallimard, 1964). There are two English translations of this work: *The Ravishing of Lol V. Stein*, trans. Richard Seaver (New York: Grove Press, 1966), and *The Rapture of Lol V. Stein*, trans Eileen Ellenbogen (London: Hamish Hamilton, 1967) (translator's note).
3. 'La place de celle qu'on oublie en français trop souvent parce qu'on dit "sphinx" au lieu de "sphinge"': That is, the French form of the word would suggest that the sphinx is male, whereas the sphinx of the oedipal myth is in fact female (translator's note).
4. There follows in the original a passage in which several categories of women's writing existing at the time (1975) are listed and discussed. These include: '"the little girl's story," where the little girl is getting even for a bad childhood,' 'texts of a return to a woman's own body,' and texts which were a critical success, 'ones about madwomen, deranged, sick women.' The passage is omitted here, at the author's request, on the grounds that such a categorization is outdated, and that the situation with regard to women's writing is very much different now than it was five or six years ago (translator's note).
5. The following passage, deleted from the main body of the text, is regarded by the author as expressing a position tangential to the central interest of her work, which has to do with homosexuality: 'And it's this being "neither out nor in," being "beyond the outside/inside opposition" that permits the play of "bisexuality." Female sexuality is always at some point bisexual. Bisexual doesn't mean, as many people think, that she can make love with both a man and a woman, it doesn't mean she has two partners, even if it can at times mean this. Bisexuality on an unconscious level is the possibility of extending into the other, of being in such a relation with the other that *I* move into the other without destroying the other: that I will look for the other where s/he is without trying to bring everything back to myself' (translator's note).
6. Hélène Cixous, *LA* (Paris: Gallimard, 1976) (translator's note).

19

ALICE JARDINE

'Feminist Tracks'

The words sung in the next room are unavoidable.
But their passionate intelligence will be studied in you.
John Ashbery, *Fragment*

In Walter Abish's short story 'Crossing the Great Void,'[1] Zachary – a deaf young man who, rather predictably, hates his uncle for having an affair with the mother he loves – feels compelled to search for his father, who was declared as missing, many years before, somewhere in the Great North African Desert. That Desert is described as empty and blank, as blank as a white sheet of paper – punctured only by the rhythm of Zachary's mother's high heel shoes clicking across the floor, '[framing] in his mind a succession of shots that puncture his eardrums, that puncture the blank piece of paper in his hand, that puncture the blankness, the vast blankness of all the deserts in the world' (p. 99). Zachary is fascinated by all those deserts – voided of any *image* (except that of his father, which exists only in his mind's eye) and heralding a *silence* to match only that of deafness (in his own ears), a deafness brought about, says the narrator, by 'hearing his mother recount the same story over and over again' (p. 103). It is only upon meeting Track – a modern young woman who knows the Dark Continent intimately – that his dream of searching for his lost father becomes 'real,' is named:

> Since you appear to be so intrigued by North Africa, you'll be interested to know that the map of Blitlu, an oasis in the center of the Great Desert, is tattooed on my back, Track said the next time she came by to pick up her car.

Your back?

She had taken him by complete surprise. He was dumbfounded. He was also unprepared for what was to follow that evening at her place. He had no prior experience, no knowledge upon which he could base an appropriate response when hours later, at her house, she unbuttoned her blouse and proceeded to take it off. With the lights off, it was too dark in her bedroom for him to see the map of Blitlu. In addition to your hearing aid you also seem to need glasses, she said matter-of-factly. He was convinced that her remark was devoid of malice. It was not an accusation, but merely a statement of fact. (p. 105)

Zachary proceeds to kill his uncle and set off for (the) Blitlu (on Track's back) to find his father – and to claim his uncle's property, which, he has just learned, is to be found in a place named 'Blitlu.' He leaves representation, mimesis, maps, and memory behind: 'For the first time he could peer into himself and see, so to speak, nothing that might make him feel uneasy [. . .] and, above all, no faces, absolutely no faces, except one that came and went without any prior warning – although he attempted to expunge it from his mind, eliminate all traces of it from his brain, but Track in all her nakedness kept embracing him' (pp. 109–110).

All that Zachary has upon which to base his quest for his missing father is an old book: a book on 'deserts,' written by a major general in the army, a book entitled *Crossing the Great Void*. But that is not quite all. There is also a small scrap of paper, slipped carefully between the pages of the book, on which Track had always written 'up until now correct' directions to Blitlu. There is no way of knowing how correct they are now. Nonetheless, from the last town on the outskirts of the desert, Zachary sets off for the emptiness of the oasis at the center of the desert. An old doorman with a whistle remains behind at the front of the hotel – a man and a whistle, a picture-soundtrack, frozen in the reader's memory as the only existent image of Zachary's father. It is, after all, Zachary's mother who has always possessed his father's image in the photograph, by her bed, of an old man with a whistle. Zachary's father has been framed.

Among all the pathways, roads, tracks, and spaces in Abish's short story, all crisscrossing their ways through false images, illusions, and misconnections, which direction might or should the feminist critic take? At the level of the narrative, she will recognize immediately the guilty mother and the woman introduced into the narrative only to provide an enigma, to keep the hermeneutic machine turning. She might also document a rather obviously acute case of Oedipal anxiety.

But rather than pursue an interpretation at this point, let this almost plot-summary stand simply as an allegory, a surface from which to re-depart. But let us now sharpen our focus, concentrate more specifically on literary criticism, rephrase some of the questions raised thus far with regard to possible new intersections for modernity and feminism through explorations in gynesis. *Gynesis*: a new kind of writing on the woman's body, a map of new spaces yet to be explored, with 'woman' supplying the only directions, the only images, upon which Post-modern Man feels he can rely.

Annette Kolodny wrote not too long ago that 'as yet, no one has formulated any exacting definition of the term "feminist criticism."'[2] Like Elaine Showalter . . ., she distinguishes between those women who write about 'men's books' and those women who write about 'women's books.'[3] Feminist criticism, within those parameters, is as multiple and heterogeneous as are the 'methodologies' available for use. She adds: '[These investigations] have allowed us to better define the portrayal of and attitudes towards female characters in a variety of authors and, where appropriate, helped us to expose the ways in which sexual bias and/or stereotyped formulations of women's roles in society become codified in literary texts.'[4] This short statement by Kolodny summarizes well, I think, feminist criticism in its most fundamental gesture: an analysis (and critique) of fictional representations of women (characters) in men's and women's writing.

If the 'author' is male, one finds that the female destiny (at least in the novel) rarely deviates from one or two seemingly irreversible, dualistic teleologies: monster and/or angel, she is condemned to death (or sexual mutilation or disappearance) or to happy-ever-after marriage. Her plot is not her own, and the classical feminist critic is at her best when drawing the painful analogies between those written plots and their mimetic counterparts in 'real life.'[5]

Increasingly, women feminist readers reach the point where they can no longer read 'the men.' That is, they begin to find the repetition unbearable. This is true of both kinds of male 'fictions' – 'fiction' and 'criticism.' This limit, when reached, is particularly relevant in the case of criticism, however, when one realizes that the majority of male critics (in all of their incarnations) seem not to have read (or taken seriously) what feminist criticism has produced. They continue either to ignore gender or else to incorporate it into an untransformed reading system, with an ironic wink of the eye, a guilty humanistic benevolence, or a bold stroke of 'male feminism.'[6]

This is perhaps one of the reasons why the focus on women writers (and critics) has given such fresh energy to feminist criticism. The analysis of female literary traditions, of the intersections between texts by women and prevailing literary conventions, and of female revisions of literary movements has changed the face of American literary criticism. Focusing on women writers, feminist critics can leave repetition behind, feel that they are charting an unknown territory which, at the same time, is strangely familiar. This mixture of unfamiliarity and intimate, identificatory reading seems, indeed, to be the key to a new creative feminist reading and writing style.

There is no doubt that this change in focus has produced some of the most important Anglo-American feminist criticism to date.[7] The movement towards defining a female tradition (as a female subculture, counterculture), and elaborating a feminist poetics (as hermeneutic) based on writing by women, has been a steady one. In fact, it may be the only way for feminist criticism *per se* to advance. For example, Kolodny, in the same article, first – *briefly* – refers to certain precautions that must be taken by the feminist critic looking for a uniquely 'feminine mode': the avoidance of the nature/culture aporia (as an 'unanswerable question'), the necessity of asking, first, whether women's writing *is* different from men's before asking *how* and so on. She then, nevertheless, continues *at length*: 'All of these precautions notwithstanding [. . .] I would be less than honest if I suggested that I had not already begun to be able to catalogue clearly demonstrable repetitions of particular thematic concerns, image patterns, and stylistic devices among these authors.'[8] The core and interest of the article is a survey of those concerns and of how we might begin to document them in women's texts.[9]

There are, however, at least two important questions that have been elided by this dual option on how to proceed – questions at the heart of what interests us here. Within the framework of these two options (produced by retaining the distinction between 'male' and 'female' authors), one question concerns what might be called the feminist posture towards our cultural canon. This is not a new question by any means, but it has not been adequately posed and its uncertain status seems to be at the center of some of the most radical disagreements – personal, political, professional – among feminist critical schools. Shulamith Firestone once wrote, 'It would take a denial of all cultural tradition for women to produce even a true 'female' art.'[10] Is this not so as well of feminist criticism, at least at its foundations? The feminist critic's 'material' is all of 'Man's History' or, at least, that of Western civilization. When working on 'the men,' feminists are involved, whether they like it or not, in an anti-culture project. From within this position, it is extremely difficult to avoid extremes: either that of methodically and completely rejecting what we may loosely call our patriarchal heritage (an endless and, sometimes, apolitical position) or that of deciding who are the 'good guys' and the 'bad guys.' When working on 'the women,' one must ultimately decide either that there is some mysterious transhistorical thread linking them all, or that 'some are okay' and 'others are not.' On the other hand, when the criteria are more largely political or ideological and the sex of the author is ignored (or bracketed), one can rarely avoid the dangers of what one critic has called 'the obligatory chapter on the 'woman novelist.'[11] This approach assumes that a woman writer is not writing as a woman but as a 'neuter' within a particular political and historical configuration, but that s(he) is just not ultimately as 'important' as the men. She remains in her separate chapter with subcategory status – where she has always been.

Further, to the extent that feminist criticism is confined for the most part to the academy, these variations, while certainly not mutually exclusive, do tend to generate a split between the 'radical' critic and the 'recuperative' critic. The former attempts to remain radically anti-cultural (a difficult posture to maintain in a literature department), while the latter (most often self-consciously) serves an integrative function, supplementing the 'core curriculum' with courses on women writers. One might argue that this split exists to the same extent between any politically radical critical stance and the academic norm. Feminist criticism's relationship to the dominant tradition is certainly not unlike that of, say, Marxist criticism. But it also resides strangely elsewhere in that it is unclear, *when gender is accounted for,* what part of that cultural tradition (including Marxism) one should attempt to use as a 'positive pole.' Only texts by women? Texts by the 'okay men'? Those lending themselves to a certain political reading whether written by men or women?

This conflict between feminist reading and the constantly renewed cultural canon operates most acutely, for the feminist critic, at a personal level. First, there is the woman who has chosen to assume a feminist discourse within the academy after having chosen her 'field of knowledge.' She would not be working in 'literature,' 'art,' etc. if it were not positively valorized in her life and, most often, in her class or social milieu. Her 'work' comes into conflict with her 'life.' Second, although clearly not a separate category, there are an increasing number of women, often younger women, who have developed their interest in 'literature' and 'feminist theory' coextensively. If they continue in their career, their work ('anti-canon') at some point comes into contradiction with their 'job' (teaching the canon). They find themselves in the position of the 'naughty daughter': tolerated if they can manage to separate their 'work' from their 'job' (or teach one course 'for women'); dismissed if they refuse to rescue patriarchal culture on a daily basis.

The implications of the feminist critic's relationship to men's writing, women's writings, the canon, the academy, etc. – problems deserving much more attention – become even more complex when the focus of one's energies is modernity or, more precisely, contemporary thought reflecting on the postmodern gesture. For a modernity presenting a new kind of discursivity on woman and women, a valorization and speaking of woman through gynesis, the feminist postures so briefly surveyed here become even more highly problematized.

The second question needing attention with regard to the dominant modes of Anglo-American feminist criticism is that of *address*. If it is more than annoying that men's question, addressed to each other, is still primarily 'But what do women want?' it sometimes appears that feminist literary critics have still not asked 'What do *we* want?' – and the answers to that question depend a great deal upon those with whom we are in dialogue. The question itself is already overdetermined culturally (woman as the suppliant); but the question remains alive, nonetheless, for the public feminist critic.

This question is related to the polemical or prescriptive problem that Kolodny speaks of in the article with which we began. While I strongly agree that one must not prescribe how or what someone should write, I cannot see how or why a feminist critic would want to or be able to 'separate political ideologies from aesthetic judgements' while '[continuing] for some time, to be avowedly "political"' (nor how she could evaluate Norman Mailer's *The Naked and the Dead* as 'probably the finest novel to come out of World War II').[12] However one feels about Mailer, what is troubling here is the separation of 'ideology' not only from 'politics,' but from something called 'aesthetic judgement' as well. If Kolodny is saying that feminist criticism must have a strategy of evaluation rooted in its own time and history in order to avoid idealization, I agree. But if she is implying that the kind of future

answers feminists want can be separated from the kind of questions
they ask now, I do not. And the answers will in part depend upon
whom we address the questions to. That is, to and for whom are
feminist critics writing? Is there a desire for men to start writing 'about'
woman in a 'feminist style'?[13] For them to stop writing about women
altogether? Do feminist critics want the male critics to read them? Or
do they want just women to do so? It is essential to ask these banal and
yet surprisingly unanswerable questions because feminist scholarship
has reached something of a double bind, raising numerous strategical
and political problems as well as contributing to the 'disagreements'
mentioned earlier. The style of any feminist criticism is radically
determined by its addressee. The radical feminist today tends to write
only to women; the so-called recuperative feminist may write to
women, but wants the male critics to overhear; and she needs for them
to like what they overhear. Not only does this raise several 'spectres of
separatism,' as Kolodny puts it,[14] but not thinking about whom one is
writing to – as men have always done while writing to themselves – is
to assume that one's reader is, once again, neuter or the same. One
feminist in France, sensitive to this problematic, has developed an
interesting strategy: explicitly writing to, addressing men, knowing
that women will overhear the men thinking they understand when they
do not. Her letter both does and does not reach its destination.[15] This
strategy recognizes, at the very least, that the one writing or reading is
always more than just one, writing or reading several texts which are
not simply pieces of an autonomous whole. And that brings us back to
modernity – and to France.

My reader will no doubt have noticed that the questions raised thus far,
within a labyrinth of 'men,' 'women,' and 'neuters' difficult to sort out,
have been based for the most part on Anglo-American feminist
concerns. While the translation of French theory into English has begun
to produce a promising, hybrid mode of feminist inquiry, especially in
film criticism, the distinctions between Anglo-American and French
critical modes remain remarkably tenacious. The sex of the author,
narrative destinies, images of women, and gender stereotypes continue
to be the touchstones of feminist literary criticism as it has developed,
most particularly, in the United States. When the feminist critic turns
to France, she learns that this bedrock of feminist inquiry has been
increasingly and rapidly dislodged: there, in step with what are seen as
the most important fictional texts of modernity, the 'author' (and his or
her intentionalities) has disappeared; the 'narrative' has no teleology;

'characters' are little more than proper name functions; the 'image' as icon must be rendered unrecognizable; and the framework of sexual identity, recognized as intrinsic to all of those structures, is to be dismantled.

We will be looking here at this new kind of inquiry where it intersects with what we are calling the fundamental feminist gesture. Of these intersections, three are particularly relevant.

The first concerns the word 'author,' and more generally the complex question of the speaking subject as evoked in Chapter 1. Lacanian psychoanalysis and Nietzschean and neo-Heideggerian philosophies in France have torn this concept apart. As Michel Foucault reminds us: 'None of this is recent; criticism and philosophy took note of the disappearance – or death – of the author some time ago. But the consequences of their discovery of it have not been sufficiently examined, nor has its impact been accurately measured.'[16] First, the 'I' and the 'we' have been utterly confused; the 'I' is several, psychoanalysis has shown; and, further, one of the major ruses of Western metaphysics' violence has been the appropriation of a 'we' by an imperialistic if imaginary 'I' (a whole individual with an interior and exterior, etc.). The notion of the 'self' – so intrinsic to Anglo–American thought – becomes absurd. It is not something called the self that speaks, but language, the unconscious, the textuality of the text. If nothing else, there is only a 'splendid unanimity,' or a plural and neuter 'they'. Contemporary fiction is cited as that which enacts this anonymity within a lottery of constantly shifting pronouns.

The assurance of an author's sex within this whirlpool of decentering is problematized beyond recognition. The policing of sexual identity is henceforth seen as complicitous with the appropriations of representation; gender (masculine, feminine) is separate from identity (male, female). The question of whether a 'man' or a 'woman' wrote a text (a game feminists know well at the level of literary history) becomes nonsensical. A man becomes a woman (*devient femme*) when he writes, or, if not, he does not 'write' (in the radical sense of *écriture*) what he writes, or, at least, does not *know* what he's writing. It is only a question of signature – of the name of the father – appropriating and reifying an unlocalizable process that is feminine in its essence . . . 'And behind all these questions, we would hear hardly anything but the stirring of an *indifference*: "What difference does it make who is speaking?" '[17] The feminist's initial incredulity faced with this complex 'beyonding' of sexual identity is largely based on common sense (after all, *someone* wrote it). But is it not that very sense (sense 'common to all,' that is, humanism) that the feminist is attempting to undermine? On the other hand, when you problematize 'Man' (as being at the foundations of Western notions of the self) to the extent that French thought has, you are bound to find 'woman' – no matter who is speaking – and that most definitely concerns feminist criticism.

The second major intersection of importance is the status and stakes of representation, where tools of representation (and of feminist criticism) – narrative, characters – are recognized as existing only at the level of the fantasies that have entrapped us. To analyze endlessly those fantasies is to ask for repetition. It is that process which moves beyond, behind, through these fantasies – the enunciation and disposition of *phantasies*[18] – which must be examined. That 'process' is attached to no self, no stable psychological entity, no content. And here again, 'theory' is presented in step with a certain kind of contemporary 'fiction': 'Classical narration camouflages the phantasy by the convention of characters, or by multiple logical justifications, which studies of actantial and narrative functions have examined. [Vladimir Propp, A. J. Greimas, etc.] By liberating itself from these conventions, the modern text lays bare the phantasy as produced by the conflictual state at the interior of the subject of the enunciation the modern text is even specifically destined to present this conflict as such.'[19]

This process, rendered tangible in modern works of art and music as well as in writing, in counterpart to form, melody, identity, has always existed, but has been localized (controlled and effaced) to a high degree in the West, within acceptably 'feminized' domains, especially 'religion' and 'literature.' Philosophy, as the traditional guardian of reason, has relegated it, most often pejoratively, to that which is 'oriental' or 'mystical' as opposed to the 'theological.' To focus exclusively on that process in the West may be only to valorize a kind of primary narcissism as it is located by modern psychoanalysis within the mother-infant dyad; hence the traditional link, for example, between modernist fiction and conservative politics. But to radically *rethink* that process and liberate it beyond fantasy and its static, predictable forms means rethinking and liberating that which has been relegated to Greek *physis* – allowing it to speak, perhaps even making it speak differently, in new spaces, within entirely new structural configurations. As suggested previously, this project has everything to do with woman and thus with women.

The third intersection, perhaps the most problematic of the three, is the radical requestioning of the status of *fiction* and (intrinsically) of *truth* in contemporary thought. One of the oldest of metaphysical problems, this is the newest and most fundamental problem for modernity. First, in what we have literally called fiction:

> The end of Beckett's *Molloy* is often given as an example of the status of truth in fiction: 'Then I went back into the house and wrote, It is midnight. The rain is beating on the windows. It was not midnight. It was not raining.' [(London: John Calder, 1959), p. 176]. These utterances are interpreted as typical examples of the unreality of fiction: *writing* would be the positive form ('It is midnight . . . etc.'), *reality*, the negative form ('It was not midnight . . .'). However, the negative form is neither more real nor more true than the positive form; both are discourses that mutually presuppose each other, and their reciprocal negation constitutes a single and same mode of language, that is, a *fiction* that is precisely this nonsynthetic reunion of 'is' and 'is not,' opposing and formulating each other all at the same time, and in this way adding to their dichotomy a third 'term,' undefined, where the subject in process searches for itself.[20]

Contemporary fiction, watching its own writing, has rendered this 'third term' particularly visible.

Of course, this heightened awareness of the fictional process is not limited to what is commonly called fiction; as process, it has infiltrated our daily lives in the West, provoking new kinds of crises in legitimation between discourse and reality. For example, through mass media, the fictions of others are lived as never before, and as the fictional process becomes more pervasive, the temptation to rescue written fiction from the immediately depressing multiple fictions of the modern world becomes stronger. While this represents an overall problem for the contemporary critic, I think it touches upon a particularly personal dilemma for feminists: the need felt to protect our written fictional heritage, now in danger of disappearance within a technological society, while at the same time laying bare the logical, ideological, and historical links between that heritage and patriarchal culture.

What does the foregrounding of the fictional process, the radical requestioning of the status of truth and fiction in theory (and fiction), imply for feminist criticism? As mentioned before, the feminist critic is traditionally concerned with the relationship between 'fiction' and 'reality' (the latter perceived, ultimately, as the truth) – with how the two intersect, mime each other, and reinforce cultural patterns. The 'theories' of that reality as written by men do not seem to conform to our own – so they must be fictions? And what then is feminist theory's difference? For example, to treat both the so-called theory and fiction under consideration in this study as fictions is to make a gesture assumed by contemporary thought and is also to conform to the feminist impulse.

What are the implications for feminist criticism – a criticism that points out the fictions of the male imagination as not conforming, or as conforming too painfully, to the *reality* of women's lives in the world – if 'truth' and 'reality' are, henceforth, radically and irrevocably problematized? Even more pointedly, we might ask: is all of this another male fiction, or is it a larger process that can begin to free women – and men – from Man's Truth?

More important, perhaps, what is it that so disarms (when it does not anger) traditional feminist criticism faced with these new directions in contemporary thought – beyond the Self, Representation, and Man's Truth? Why do these two modes of inquiry, feminism and post-modernism, prove so resistant to each other at these intersections when their projects are so irresistibly linked? If, as suggested in the last chapter, this contemporary thought finds its equal only in the most radical moments of feminist theory, why are these intersections so difficult to negotiate?

In terms of the work privileged in this study, principally that of Lacan, Derrida, and Deleuze, some possible reasons surface.[21] First, just at the historical moment when feminist criticism has found a clear and increasingly acceptable voice, it must confront and is confronted by a group of writers who, again, are thinking and writing in strange new ways. Radical changes in theoretical understanding have required radical changes in vocabulary and style as well as in conceptualization. Feminist theorists tend to see what is actually that understanding's most radical force – its emphasis on language – as mere rhetorical acrobatics, as a new ruse on the part of Reason.

Second, in the writings of those theorists participating in gynesis, woman may become intrinsic to entire conceptual systems without being 'about' women – much less 'about' feminism. First, this is the case literally, inasmuch as the texts in question are based almost entirely on *men's* writing and, most important, on fiction written by men. For example, a survey of such disparate but logically related writers as Lacan, Derrida, and Deleuze – or Cixous, Irigaray, and Kristeva – yields remarkably few references to women writers. (To women, yes; one even finds passing remarks on women theorists – Lou Andreas-Salomé, Marie Bonaparte, Melanie Klein – but to women writers, no.) Lacan has much advice for women analysts, but only focuses once on a woman writer (Marguerite Duras) – as having understood his theory (without him).[22] Derrida, to my knowledge, never explicity mentions ·a woman writer.[23] Deleuze and Guatarri refer to Virginia Woolf as having incorporated the process of what they call 'becoming woman' (*le devenir femme*) in her writing – but 'not to the same extent' as Henry James, D. H. Lawrence, or Henry Miller.[24]

Women writers are even more implausibly absent from the women theorists' texts. While the specificity of the female subject (and even that of a vague, never-named female *writing subject*) is a major question in many of their texts, women writers are not. Cixous, the leading figure of 'Psychanalyse et Politique' and its women's bookstore Des Femmes, is perhaps the foremost theoretician in France on the specificity of 'feminine writing' (which does not mean writing by a woman). Yet it is not women writers who are the focus of her work. Her focus is on the male poets (Genet, Hölderlin, Kafka, Kleist, Shakespeare) and on the male theoreticians (Derrida, Heidegger, Kierkegaard, Lacan, Nietzsche). Because in the past women have always written 'as men,' Cixous hardly ever alludes to women writers; one recent exception is her reading and public praise of Clarice Lispector (whose narrative is more 'traditional' than one might have expected).[25] Irigaray and Kristeva are uniquely concerned with analyzing the male tradition: from Freud to the philosophers to the avant-garde. The women disciples of all of these theorists do sometimes mention contemporary women writers (Michèle Montrelay mentions Chantal Chawaf, Marguerite Duras, and Jeanne Hyvrard),[26] but such references are not in any way central to their theses.

The (very American) kind of empirical categorizing of texts in which I have just indulged is perhaps ultimately not very useful. But this lack of textual reference to women should at least be pointed out, given our 'intersections.' For the second reason that gynesis is not necessarily about women is more abstract: within traditional categories of thought, women can (have) exist(ed) only as opposed to men. Indeed, women, especially feminists, who continue to think within those categories are, henceforth, seen as being men by many of the theorists mentioned thus far. It is perhaps this particular conclusion that renders the work in question the most suspect for feminist theoreticians, for it explicitly negates their own status as readers.

But there is one final reason for the absence of an alliance between traditional feminism and modernity: the theoretical writing in question does not enjoy a valorized position in the vast majority of French and American critical circles, while feminism, especially as linked to women's studies in the United States, is one of the few viable critical discourses around. Ironically, this situation would seem to be due in part to the 'feminine status' of the texts of modernity themselves. These intensive explorations of gynesis, especially by male theorists, have themselves been genderized as feminine and treated accordingly; the connotative threads that make up the actual fabric of gynesis have problematized the gender and hence critical handling of these writers' own texts.

All of the questions presented here hover at the very limits of representability. Can or should feminism be something other than an attention to the *representation* of women (in several senses of the word)? If gynesis as process has most certainly always been marginally at work in the West, especially in religious and literary texts, in what ways are its more visible links to modernity subject to feminist analysis? Is feminist theory as a search for the female self (most characteristic of Anglo–American criticism) in complete contradiction with the, strictly speaking, antifeminist insistence in France on the liberating potentiality of losing the self? Might there be a way to imagine a new kind of feminist hermeneutics able to give up its quest for truth; capable of self-reflection on its own complicity with inherited systems of represen-tation? If feminism is to remain radical and not become but patchwork for a patriarchal fabric ripped apart by the twentieth century, what kinds of alliances will it be able to form with the most radical modes of thought produced by that century? These are indeed a set of historical intersections.

For Modern Man does seem to be crossing some kind of Great Void. There is a Track to be followed and he has been told that the map to the Oasis is inscribed on her Body. Is it a question, as with the Biblical Zachary, of reconstructing the Empty Temple evoked by Goux as but a prelude to a new Messianic Era? Or does Zachary know that, deaf and blind, his Quest is already historically amiss, and that, always already Oedipalized, he would not recognize the Image of his Father at *any* crossroads? Most important, is Track to accompany him in his quest? If yes, in what way? And if no, where is it that she would like to go instead? What will she ultimately make of this unexpected twist in the patriarchal story? Perhaps . . .

> It was to be the last time he saw her.
> Are you thinking of going back to Blitlu, he asked?
> Can I drop you here . . . I don't want to run into your Uncle, she said.

My uncle . . . How do you know my uncle?
He's everybody's uncle, she said, condescendingly.[27]

NOTES

1. Walter Abish, 'Crossing the Great Void,' in *In the Future Perfect* (New York: New Directions, 1977), pp. 98–113. All further page references in text.
2. Annette Kolodny, 'Some Notes on Defining a "Feminist Literary Criticism,"' *Critical Inquiry* 2:1 (Fall 1975): 75.
3. She also mentions a third category: 'any criticism written by a woman, no matter what the subject' (Kolodny, p. 75), but does not pursue it, implying its inadmissibility to any feminist.
4. Kolodny, 'Some Notes,' p. 75.
5. Now classical feminist readings of the repetition seemingly inherent to male fictions are those of Simone de Beauvoir and Kate Millet. Recent books in the United States (e.g., Nancy Miller, *The Heroine's Text*) and in France (e.g., Anne-Marie Dardigna, *Le châteaux d'éros*, and Claudine Herrmann, *Les voleuses de langue*), while based in this gesture, go beyond it through their use of structuralist and poststructuralist reading strategies.
6. See, for example, Annette Kolodny's response to William Morgan's 'feminist' objections to her 'separatism': 'The Feminist as Literary Critic,' *Critical Inquiry* 2:4 (Summer 1976): 821–32.
7. Three of the perhaps best known book-length studies on the possibilities of a female literary tradition include: Ellen Moers, *Literary Women* (London: Women's Press, 1963); Elaine Showalter, *A Literature of Their Own*; and Gilbert and Gubar, *The Madwoman in the Attic*. Other widely read studies include: Susan Koppelman Cornillon, *Images of Women in Fiction* (Bowling Green: Bowling Green State University Press, 1972); Judith Fetterley, *The Resisting Reader* (Bloomington: Indiana University Press, 1978); Jacobus, ed., *Women Writing and Writing about Women*; Patricia M. Spacks, *The Female Imagination* (New York: Avon, 1972). There are, of course, many others, as well as countless important article-length studies; as a parallel gesture, anthologies, biographies, and histories of more and lesser-known women writers are increasing.
8. Kolodny, 'Some Notes,' p. 79.
9. Another helpful article, first published in Germany, addresses many of the same questions: Silvia Bovenschen, 'Is There a Feminine Aesthetic?' *New German Critique*, no. 10 (Winter 1977): 111–37.

   I should also mention here, early on, that it is this side of Anglo-American feminist criticism that has been most fervently attacked in France as being humanistic rather than political. *Humanistic* in that it looks for an unknown 'specificity of the woman writer' to be given *expression*; whereas it would be *political* to look at the words 'specificity,' 'woman,' 'writer,' each in the structure of its definition, and work to change that structure. See Stephen Heath's 'Difference.'
10. Shulamith Firestone, *The Dialectic of Sex* (New York: Bantam, 1970), p. 159.
11. Miller, *The Heroine's Text*, p. 154.
12. Kolodny, 'Some Notes,' pp. 89–90. I continue to use Kolodny's article here only in an exemplary mode – one that is inevitably unfair to one of our finest feminist critics.
13. The expression 'feminist style' is that of Josephine Donovan, 'Feminist Style Criticism,' in *Images of Women in Fiction: Feminist Perspectives*, ed. Susan Koppelman Cornillon. If this is a goal of feminist criticism, it has been reached.
14. Annette Kolodny, 'The Feminist as Literary Critic,' p. 821.
15. I refer here to Luce Irigaray.
16. Michel Foucault, 'What is an Author?' trans. Josué N. Harari, in *Textual Strategies*, ed. Josué Harari (London: Methuen, 1980), p. 143.
17. Ibid., p. 160; my emphasis.
18. Here I follow Juliet Mitchell and others in maintaining the distinction in English between 'fantasies' (conscious) and 'phantasies' (unconscious).
19. Julia Kristeva, *La révolution du langage poétique*, p. 318.
20. Ibid., pp. 352–53.

21. Why these particular writers? They all three deal with woman and women explicitly and therefore openly lend themselves to our questions. Other writers, such as Roland Barthes and Michel Foucault, for example, might have done as well; but in their texts, the signifiers woman and women are a very present absence – much more difficult to excavate. In general, the questions posed here are relevant to any modern text in which there is 1) a desire to increase the signifiable; 2) an explicit problematization of gender; and 3) a pronounced ambivalence towards the mother's body.

22. '[Elle] s'avère savoir sans moi ce que j'enseigne.' Jacques Lacan, 'Hommage à Marguerite Duras,' in *Marguerite Duras* (Paris: Albatros, 1979).

23. Excluding Marie Bonaparte – essential to Derrida's critique of Lacan in 'The Purveyor of Truth,' *Yale French Studies* 52 (1975) – I can find only three oblique exceptions to this observation. The exceptions are especially oblique in that a *particular woman* is never named in them. They are: a footnote to 'Violence and Metaphysics': 'On this subject, let us note in passing that *Totally and Infinity* pushes the respect for dissymmetry so far that it seems to us impossible, essentially impossible, that it could have been written by a woman.' (*Writing and Difference*, trans. Alan Bass [Chicago: University of Chicago Press, 1978], pp. 320–21); his references to an article by Barbara Johnson in 'Envois' (*La carte postale* [Paris: Flammarion, 1980], pp. 162–64); and his dialogue with Barbara Johnson apropos her paper on Mary Shelley's *Frankenstein* in *Les fins de l'homme*, ed. Philippe Lacoue-Labarthe and Jean-Luc Nancy (Paris: Galilée, 1981), pp. 75–88.

24. Gilles Deleuze and Claire Parnet, *Dialogues* (Paris: Flammarion, 1977), esp. pp. 55–60.

25. Cf. Hélène Cixous, 'L'approche de Clarice Lispector,' *Poétique* 40 (November 1979). The reader might also want to refer to her discussion with Michel Foucault on Marguerite Duras: 'A propos de M. D.,' *Cahiers Renaud–Barrault*, no. 89.

26. Michèle Montrelay, *L'ombre et le nom* (Paris: Editions de Minuit, 1977). One feminist critic has devoted a major study to a woman writer: Marini, *Territoires du féminin avec Marguerite Duras*.

27. Abish, 'Crossing the Great Void,' p. 107.

20

NANCY K. MILLER

'Changing the Subject: Authorship, Writing and the Reader'

In the spring of 1985 I wrote 'Changing the subject' for two conferences that provided me with an occasion after 'Arachnologies' to elaborate my thinking about the woman writer and her feminist reader in relation both to questions of feminist theory and to the various poststructuralist discussions of writing and sexual difference. The first of these events was held at the Pembroke Center, Brown University, in March 1985; its agenda was flagged in the punctuation of its title, 'Feminism/theory/politics'; the second, held at the Center for Twentieth-Century Studies of the University of Wisconsin-Milwaukee in April 1985, was entitled 'Feminist studies: reconstituting knowledge'.

The session at which I spoke at the Pembroke conference was called 'The feminist politics of interpretation', and the panellists were asked to reflect upon a crux of issues very similar to the general charge of the Milwaukee conference as Teresa de Lauretis described it in her opening remarks (now the introduction to Feminist Studies/Critical Studies*). Both call for an interrogation of the current state of feminist projects: 'What is* specifically *feminist* about the *varieties of feminist critical practice? Are feminist strategies of reading written and visual texts transferable to the study of such things as social and political institutions?' (Pembroke conference, emphasis added). In de Lauretis's letter to participants: 'there are a general uncertainty, and among feminists, serious differences as to what the specific concerns, values and methods of feminist critical work are, or ought to be . . . Speakers will seek to identify the* specificity of feminism *as a critical theory' (Milwaukee conference, emphasis added).*

These are not easy questions, and in this essay I have not attempted to describe the specificity of feminist theory and practice directly. Instead I have chosen to rehearse a certain number of positions against, from, and through which feminist critical theory might define itself as it emerges within the discourse of literary studies. This rehearsal identifies two chronologies, poststructuralist and feminist; two rhetorics, dilatory and hortatory; and, to return to the figure of the 'exquisite dance of textual priorities' named by Hortense Spillers and evoked by de Lauretis at the opening of the conference (13), two moves, or rather a hesitation between, say, the calls of a square dance and the ritual of a minuet, as the dance searches for the right steps and rhythm, perhaps the waltz satirised by Dorothy Parker, or as one of the participants suggested after the conference, the foxtrot (which has interesting possibilities).[1]

Though I may indeed be looking for a third tropology (in the feminist spirit of always mapping the territory of future perspectives), I want just as strongly to leave the hesitation in place, and refuse the temptation of a synthesis, because the question forming before us is none other than the question of female subjectivity, the formation of female critical subjects. And this, in face of the current trend towards the massive deconstitution of subjectivity, is finally the figure I'm looking for.

AUTHORSHIP, WRITING AND THE READER

The question of authorship has been on the agenda of intellectuals and literary critics in France since at least 1968, a date that also marks a certain theoretical repositioning in political and social chronologies. In 1968, for example, Roland Barthes contended in 'The death of the author' that the author, as we have known him, has lost what was thought to be a 'natural' authority over his work. The author gives way to *writing*, a theory and practice of textuality which, Barthes argued then, 'substitutes language itself for the person who until then had been supposed to be its owner' (p. 143). From such a perspective, the emergence of this disembodied and ownerless *écriture* in fact requires the author's suppression.[2] In the structuralist and poststructuralist debates about subjectivity, authority, and the status of the text that continue to occupy and preoccupy the critical market-place, the story of the author's disappearance has remained standard currency.

Now, to the extent that the author, in this discourse, stands as a kind of shorthand for a whole series of beliefs about the function of the work of art as (paternally authorised) monument in our culture, feminist criticism in its own negotiations with mainstream hegemonies might have found its positions joined by the language of those claims. It is, after all, the author anthologised and institutionalised who by his (canonical) presence excludes the less-known works of women and minority writers and who by his authority justifies the exclusion. By the same token, feminist criticism's insistence on the importance of the reader – on positing the hypothesis of her existence – might have found affinities with a position that understands the Birth of the Reader as the necessary counterpoint to the Death of the Author. (Barthes actually puts it a good deal more apocalyptically: 'the birth of the reader must be at the cost of the death of the Author' (p. 148).)

The political potential of such an alliance, however, has yet to be realised. The removal of the author has not so much made room for a revision of the concept of authorship as it has, through a variety of rhetorical moves, repressed and inhibited discussion of any writing identity in favour of the (new) monolith of anonymous textuality or, in Foucault's phrase, 'transcendental anonymity' (p. 120). If 'writing', then, as Barthes describes it, 'is that neutral, composite, oblique space where our subject slips away, the negative where all identity is lost, starting with the very identity of the body writing' (p. 142), it matters not *who* writes. In the same way, the shift that moves the critical emphasis from author to reader, from the text's origin to its destination, far from producing a multiplicity of addressees, seems to have reduced the possibility of differentiating among readers altogether: 'the reader', Barthes declares, 'is without history, biography, psychology' (p. 148). What matters who reads? The reader is a space and a process. The reader is only *'someone'* written *on*. (I also think that the failure of an effective critical alliance is more generally due to the fact that the relationship between mainstream feminism and the practices and positions that have come to be grouped together under the label of deconstruction or poststructuralism in US academic scenes has not been one of a *working* complicity: of fighting the same institutional battles. But this deserves a discussion of its own.)

I want none the less to make a distinction between the asymmetrical demands generated by different writing identities – male and female, or more perhaps more usefully, hegemonic and marginal. It is inarguable that the destabilisation of the paternal – patriarchal, really – authority of authorship (Milton's, for example) brought about through deconstruction has been an enabling move for feminist critics. But it does not address the problem of his 'bogey' at the level of subjectivity formation. The effect of his identity and authority on a female writing identity remains another matter and calls for other critical strategies. The psychological stress of that negotiation in literature for the nineteenth-century woman writer has been formulated dramatically by Gilbert and Gubar in Madwoman in the Attic. *Here I am trying to resituate that question at the level of theory itself, or rather theory's discourse about its own project.*

So why remember Barthes, if this model of reading and writing by definition excludes the question of an identity crucial to feminist critical theory? Well, for one thing because Barthes' interest in the semiotics of literary and cultural activity – its pleasures, dangers, zones, and codes of reference – intersects thematically with a feminist emphasis on the need to situate, socially and symbolically, the practices of reading and writing. Like the feminist critic, Barthes manoeuvres in the spaces of the tricky relations that bridge the personal and the political, the personal and the critical, the interpersonal and the institutional (his seminar, for example). Barthes translates seductively from within French thought the more arduous writings of Derrida, Lacan, Kristéva, for or into literature; and in the same gesture represents metonymically outside the Parisian scene (or in North American literature departments) most of the concepts that animate feminist (and other) literary critics not hostile to Theory's stories: currently, the poststructuralist epistemologies of the subject and the text, the linguistic construction of sexual identity.

In the preface to *Sade, Fourier, Loyola* (1971) Barthes returns to the problem of authorship: 'For if,' he writes, 'through a twisted dialectic, the Text, destroyer of all subjects, contains a subject to love – *un sujet à aimer* – that subject is dispersed, somewhat like the ashes we strew into the wind after death' (p. 8). And he continues poignantly in the same sentence, 'were I a writer, and dead [*si j'étais écrivain, et mort*] how I would love it if my life, through the pains of some friendly and detached biographer, were to reduce itself to a few details, a few preferences, a few inflections, let us say: to "biographemes"' (p. 9). What interests me here, more than yet another nomination, another code, is Barthes' acknowledgement of the persistence of the subject as the presence in the text of perhaps not some*one* to love in person, but the mark of the need to be loved, the persistence of a peculiarly human(ist?) desire for connection. It is as though thinking of a writer's life – a 'life' of Sade, a 'life' of Fourier appended to a reading of their writing – generated a thinking of self: for Barthes then imagines himself 'a writer'.[3] But we have just seen the writer is already dead, his ashes scattered to the winds; and the self fatally dispersed. Thus no sooner is the subject restored metaphorically to a body through love, than he is dispersed figuratively through death. If one is to find the subject, he will not be in one place, but modernly multiple and atopic.

Will *she*?

The postmodernist decision that the Author is Dead and the subject along with him does not, I will argue, necessarily hold for women, and prematurely forecloses the question of agency for them. Because women have not had the same historical relation of identity to origin, institution, production that men have had, they have not, I think, (collectively) felt burdened by *too much* self, ego, cogito, etc. Because the female subject has juridically been excluded from the polis, hence decentred, 'disoriginated', deinstitutionalised, etc., her relation to integrity and textuality, desire and authority, displays structurally important differences from that universal position.

In Breaking the Chain, *Naomi Schor takes up Barthes' analysis in S/Z of the cultural discourse on 'femininity', which he locates for the sake of argument in a passage from Balzac's* Sarrasine. *Curiously, this is also the passage that serves as the opening citation of 'The death of the author': 'This was woman herself . . .' (etc.). Following Schor's lead, it is interesting to puzzle the connections that for Barthes join écriture and 'woman' in a definition of textuality that refuses a coherent subjectivity.*

In 'Mapping the postmodern' Andreas Huyssen asks: 'Isn't the "death of the subject/author" position tied by mere reversal to the very ideology that invariably glorifies the artist as genius, whether for marketing purposes or out of conviction and habit? . . . [D]oesn't poststructuralism, where it simply denies the subject altogether, jettison the chance of challenging the ideology of the subject *(as male, white, and middle-class) by developing alternative and different notions of subjectivity?' (p. 44).*

In 'Women Who Write Are Women', Elaine Showalter, arguing against Cynthia Ozick's belief (subsequently rearticulated by Gail Godwin in the same publication) that 'writing transcends sexual identity, that it takes place outside of the social order', pointedly observes that in the gender asymmetry of dominant culture 'the female witness, sensitive or not, is still not accepted as first-person universal' (p. 33).

It seems to me, therefore, that when the so-called crisis of the subject is staged, as it generally is, within a textual model, that performance must then be recomplicated by the historical, political, and figurative body of the woman writer. (That is, of course, if we accept as a working metaphor the location of women's subjectivity in female authorship.) Because the discourse of the universal historically has failed to include the testimony of its others, it seems imperative to question the new doxa of subjectivity at this juncture of its formation.

Feminist critics in the United States have on the whole resisted the fable of the author's demise on the grounds that stories of textuality which trade in universals – the author or the reader – in fact articulate marked and differentiated structures of what Gayatri Spivak has called masculine 'regulative psychobiography'. Feminist critics, I argue in

'The text's heroine', have looked to the material of the female authorial project as the scene of perhaps a different staging of the drama of the writing subject. But what does it mean to read (for) the woman writer when the Author is Dead? Or, how can 'reading as a woman' – a deconstructionist phrasing of a reconstructionist feminist project – help us rethink the act of reading as a politics? I'd like to see a more self-conscious and deliberate move away from what I think remains in dominant critical modes, a *metaphysics* of reading. As Foucault asks in 'What is an author?': 'In granting a primordial status to writing (*écriture*), do we not, in effect, simply reinscribe in transcendental terms the theological affirmation of its sacred origin?' (p. 120).

In her presentations at both the Pembroke and the Milwaukee conferences, Spivak contrasted the psychobiography of a male subjectivity based on naturalised access to dominant forms of power with that of the 'postmodern female subject' created under late capitalism (emblematised by the hegemony of the computer chip): women of colour whom imperialism constructs as a permanent casual labour force doing high-tech work for the multinationals. Her relation to networks of power is best understood through the concept of 'women in the integrated circuit', which Donna Haraway describes as 'the situation of women in a world . . . intimately restructured through the social relations of science and technology' (pp. 84–5). It is not self-evident what form testimony would take in such an economy.

Speaking from within a certain 'new French feminism', Hélène Cixous makes a homologous argument for the need to recognise a deuniversalised subjectivity: 'until now, far more extensively and repressively than is ever suspected or admitted, writing has been run by a libidinal and cultural – hence political, typically masculine – economy' (p. 879). This definition of a sexually 'marked writing' that expresses and valorises masculine access to power emerges from the critique of phallogocentrism, but because of its place in the network of Derridean operations, it remains at odds with the reconstructive impulses of much feminist literary criticism in the United States: the analysis of canon formation and reformation through the study and valorisation of women's writing.

Thus, in his concluding remarks to the section of On deconstruction *devoted to feminist criticism, Jonathan Culler builds on Peggy Kamuf's troping of signature and identity in 'Writing as a woman': 'For a woman to read as a woman is not to repeat an identity or an experience that is given but to play a role she constructs with reference to her identity as a woman, which is also a construct, so that the series can continue: a woman reading as a woman reading as a woman' (p. 64). The question for feminist critical theory is how to imagine a relation between this logic of deferral and the immediate complexities of what Adrienne Rich calls 'a politics of location'* (Blood, bread, and poetry, p. 215).

I want to offer one kind of political reading with a passage from a famous account of a female 'psychobiography'. I take it as an example of what has been characterised as the 'first moment' or first stage of feminist criticism, a criticism Jonathan Culler describes as 'based on the presumption of continuity between the reader's experience and a woman's experience' (p. 46). The account is Adrienne Rich's 'When we dead awaken: writing as re-vision', which, she explains in a retrospective frame, was originally given as a talk on 'The woman writer in the twentieth century' in a forum sponsored by the Commission on the Status of Women in the Profession at the MLA in 1971. I cite Rich's return to the context of her talk by way of suggesting that we review these issues *both* in 'women's time' and in men's, the Eastern Standard Time of mainstream events. (I'm referring here to Elaine Showalter's personal take on the history of feminist criticism.)[4]

Rich notes:

> A lot is being said today about the influence that the myths and images of women have on all of us who are products of culture. I think it has been a peculiar confusion to the girl or woman who tries to write because she is peculiarly susceptible to language. She goes to poetry or fiction looking for *her* way of being in the world, since she is looking eagerly for guides, maps, possibilities; and over and over . . . she comes up against something that negates everything she is about: she meets the image of Woman in books written by men. She finds a terror and a dream, she finds a beautiful pale face, she finds La Belle Dame Sans Merci, she finds Juliet or Tess or Salomé, but precisely what she does not find is that absorbed, drudging, puzzled, sometimes inspired creature, herself, who sits at a desk trying to put words together. (p. 39)

Rich's woman 'susceptible to language', like Roland Barthes, goes to literature as a *writing subject*: she does not, however, find there 'un sujet à aimer'. She finds instead, a terror and a dream. To find 'somebody to love', as the song goes, Rich, like Barthes, would have to find someone somehow *like her* in her desire for a place in the discourse of art and identity from which to imagine and image a writing self – 'absorbed, drudging, puzzled' – at a desk. For the girl 'susceptible to language' the words have established a split she cannot overcome: Woman whose image, whose 'beautiful pale face' has installed in her place a regime of the specular and excluded her from production.[5] Woman leaves the woman poet in exile.

In her 1983 essay, 'Blood, bread, and poetry: the location of the poet' (where she outlines the borders of scenes of writing in North America and in Central America), Rich returns to the biography of her reading, or the history of its subject, to develop in more explicitly political terms the implications of the split between the girl and the poet, 'the girl who wrote poems, who defined herself in writing poems, and the girl who was to define herself by her relationships with men' (p. 40). To close 'the gap between poet and woman', Rich argues here, the fragmentation within the writing subject requires the context of a 'political community' (p. 536). For Rich, on *this* side of identity, the condition of dispersal and fragmentation Barthes valorises (and fetishises) is not to be achieved, but overcome:

> I write for the still-fragmented parts in me, trying to bring them together. Whoever can read and use any of this, I write for them as well. I write in full knowledge that the majority of the world's illiterates are women, that I live in a technologically advanced country where forty per cent of the people can barely read and twenty per cent are functionally illiterate. I believe that these facts are directly connected to the fragmentations I suffer in myself, that we are all in this together. (p. 540)

In 'Blood, bread, and poetry', Rich maps the geopolitics of a poetics of gender. This vision of a global context for women's writing emerges from a programme of text production as a collective project. In the 1960s, under the logic of 'the personal is the political', the communication with the community involved writing 'directly and overtly as a woman, out of a woman's experience', taking 'women's existence seriously as theme and source for art' (p. 535). In 'When we dead awaken', Rich had contrasted this euphoric turn to feminocentric production – a more prosaic, or rather less lyrical account of the agenda valorised by Cixous (in 'The laugh of the Medusa') – with the anxieties of the 1950s where, she writes, 'I began to feel that my fragments and scraps had a common consciousness and a common theme, one which I would have been very unwilling to put on paper at an earlier time because I had been taught that poetry should be "universal", which meant, of course, nonfemale' (p. 44). In the 1980s, the formula 'the personal is the political' requires a redefinition of the personal to include most immediately an interrogation of ethnocentrism; a poetics of identity that engages with the 'other woman'.[6] If for Rich in 1971 the act of women's reading as a critique of the dominant literature was seen not merely as 'a chapter in cultural history' (p. 135) but as 'an act of survival', in 1983 the act of women's writing became inseparable from an expanded definition of, and expanded attention to, the social field in which the practices of reading and writing are located and grounded. Now the question arises, if the ethics of feminist writing involve writing for the woman who doesn't read – to push this model to its limits – then what would be required of a responsive, responsible feminist reading?

The question will remain open and generate other questions. Does the specificity of feminist theory entail reading for the other woman? Would this mean reading *as* the other woman? In her place? Wouldn't this assumption reinstate a universal or an interchange ability of women under the name of woman and thereby 'collapse', as Denise Riley put it to me at the Pembroke conference, 'the different temporalities of "women"' which she glosses as 'the uneven histories of the different formations of different categories of "women" from the side of politics'? In more strictly literary terms, I would now say that we must think carefully about the reading effects that derive from a poetics of transparence – writing directly from one's own experience, especially when doubled by an ethics of wholeness – joining the fragments.

Rich speaks in this essay of her discovery of the work of contemporary Cuban women poets in a book edited by Margaret Randall called Breaking the silences. *And it is in part because of reading this book (her* tolle e lege*) that she decides to go to Nicaragua (a decision which provides the occasion for* 'Blood, bread, and poetry'*). To what extent does this active/activist model of reading establish the grounds for a prescriptive esthetics – a 'politically correct' programme of representation – of the sort that shaped the arguments of Barbara Smith and Sondra O'Neale at the Milwaukee conference?*[7]

Against the necessarily utopian rhetoric of an unalienated art that Rich reads in Cuban women poets ('the affirmation of an organic relation between poetry and social transformation') (p. 537), I want now to juxtapose the discourse with which I began this discussion of critical strategies. On the back jacket to *Sade, Fourier, Loyola* Barthes states the 'theoretical intention' of his project. It is a kind of self-referential challenge: to discover 'how far one can go with a text speaking only of its writing (*écriture*); how to suspend its signified in order to liberate its materialist deployment'. 'Isn't the social intervention achieved by a text', he asks rhetorically, located in the 'transport' of its writing, rather than in the 'message of its content'? In the pages of the preface, Barthes addresses the problem of the 'social responsibility of the text', maintaining that since there is 'today no language site outside bourgeois ideology', 'the only possible rejoinder' to, say, the establishment, is 'neither confrontation, nor destruction, but only theft: fragment the old text of culture, science, literature, and change its features according to formulae of disguise, as one disguises (*maquille*) stolen goods' (p. 10). We see here the double move we saw earlier in 'Death of the author': on the one hand disperse the subject, on the other, fragment the text, and repackage it for another mode of circulation and reception.

Dispersion and fragmentation, the theft of language and the subversion of the stereotype attract Barthes as critical styles of desire and deconstruction, rupture and protest. Certain women writers in France like Hélène Cixous, Luce Irigaray, and I would argue, paradoxically, Monique Wittig, have also been attracted to this model of relation: placing oneself at a deliberately oblique (or textual) angle to intervention. Troped as a subversion – a political intertextuality – this positionality remains in the end, I think, a form of negotiation within the dominant social text, and ultimately, a local operation.

Because it is also my sense that the reappropriation of culture from within its own arenas of dissemination is still a political urgency, I will recast my earlier question about the female subject in feminist theory to ask more narrowly now: what does it mean to read and write as a woman *within* the institutions that authorise and regulate most reading and writing in the university?

'OUBLIEZ LES PROFESSEURS'

In Charlotte Brontë's *Villette* acute attention is paid to the construction of female subjectivity, and in particular to the way in which female desire as quest aligns itself uneasily with the question of mastery (including, importantly, mastery of the French language), mastery and knowledge within an academy necessarily, in 1853, a female one. In the scene I will review here, the heroine, Lucy Snowe, is dragged off to be examined by two professors, 'Messieurs Boissec and Rochemorte' (the etymology is of course motivated). This examination perceived by Lucy as a 'show-trial' set up to prove that she indeed was the author of a remarkable essay the men suspected their colleague M. Emmanuel, Lucy's professor/friend, of having written for her (forging her signature in order to document his pedagogical agency) provides us with a vivid account of the institutional power arrangements that historically have constructed female experience. These two specimens of dead-wood interrogate Lucy:

> They began with classics. A dead blank. They went on to French history. I hardly knew Mérovée from Pharamond. They tried me in various 'ologies, and still only got a shake of the head, and an unchanging 'Je n'en sais rien.' (p. 493)

Unwilling or unable to reply, Lucy asks permission to leave the room.

> They would not let me go: I must sit down and write before them. As I dipped my pen in the ink with a shaking hand, and surveyed the white paper with eyes half-blinded and overflowing, one of my judges began mincingly to apologize for the pain he caused. (p. 494)

They name their theme: 'Human Justice'.

> Human Justice! What was I to make of it? Blank, cold abstraction, unsuggestive to me of one inspiring idea . . . (p. 495)

Lucy remains blocked until she remembers that the two examiners were in fact known to her; 'the very heroes' who had 'half frightened (her) to death' (p. 495) on the night of her arrival in Villette. And suddenly, thinking how little these men deserved their current status as judges and enforcers of the law, Lucy falls, as she puts it, 'to work'.

> 'Human Justice' rushed before me in novel guise, a red, random beldame with arms akimbo. I saw her in her house, the den of confusion: servants called to her for orders or help which she did not give; beggars stood at her door waiting and starving unno-ticed; a swarm of children, sick and quarrelsome, crawled round her feet and yelled in her ears appeals for notice, sympathy, cure, redress. The honest woman cared for none of these things. She had a warm seat of her own by the fire, she had her own solace in a short black pipe, and a bottle of Mrs Sweeny's soothing syrup; she smoked and she sipped and she enjoyed her paradise, and whe-never a cry of the suffering souls about her pierced her ears too keenly – my jolly dame seized the poker or the hearthbrush . . . (pp. 495–6)

Writing 'as a woman', Lucy Snowe domesticates the public allegories of Human Justice. Her justice is not blind (hence serenely fair), but deaf to the pathetic cries that invade her private space: arbitrary and visibly self-interested, marked not by the sword and scales of neo-classical iconography, Lucy's 'red, random beldame' smokes her pipe and sips her syrup.

However perversely, I am tempted to take this scene in which a woman is brought forcibly to writing as a parable of – which is not to say a recommendation for – the conditions of production for female authorship (or for the practice of feminist criticism). Because she reappropriates the allegory of timeless indifference particularised through the identification of the men and fictionalised through the imagined body of an ageing woman, Lucy both overcomes the terror of the blank page and undermines the regime of a universal self-reference.

I should perhaps have mentioned that the chapter in which this writing out takes place opens with a line rich in implications for the conclusion of my argument: 'Oubliez les professeurs'. Now in context, this imperative is a warning issued by Mme Beck that Lucy not think of M. Paul for herself. But clearly in this collegial psychodrama the relation to *him* is not only a question of female rivalry and the love plot. As I have just suggested, the scene asks more generally the question of women's relation to the arbitrariness of male authority, to the grounds of their power and their laws.

Lucy, we know, can't forget her particular professor, for she is moved more than she will say by his offer of friendship. But in her apprenticeship to the world of work, she has learned to make distinctions. To accept M. Paul does not mean that she accepts the system of institutional authorisation in which their relation is inscribed. Nor is the point of her essay, its style, lost on M. Paul who, having read the exam paper, calls her 'une petite moqueuse et sans coeur' (p. 496). Lucy's mockery, which is the flip side of her pathos, could also be figured as irony, which is, I think, a trope that by its status as the marker of a certain distance to the truth, suits the rhetorical strategies of the feminist critic.[8]

The chapter in which the scene of writing is staged is called 'Fraternity', for it is here that M. Paul asks Lucy to be the 'sister of a very poor, fettered, burdened, encumbered man'. His offer of 'true friendship' (p. 501), of a 'fraternal alliance' (p. 503), while not exempt from its own ironies, none the less announces a less depressing mode of relations between women and institutional authorities than that of the 'daughter's seduction' diagnosed by Jane Gallop, for it figures a working ground of parity.[9] At the end of Brontë's novel, through the enabling terms of the alliance, Lucy Snowe has not only her own seat by the fire but her own house and school for girls. Within that space, she makes Paul a 'little library'; he whose mind, she had said earlier, was her library, through which she 'entered bliss' (p. 472). And of course, in his absence, and in his place, she writes the narrative of *Villette*.

This being said, one might, in the final analysis, do better to restore to the fraternal its historical dimensions. Women writers' idealisation of fraternity belongs to a long and vexed tradition of feminist discourse about equality and difference that in 1949 provided Simone de Beauvoir with the last words of *The second sex*: 'To gain the supreme victory, it is necessary . . . that by and through their natural differentiation men and women unequivocally affirm their brotherhood' (*fraternité* (p. 814).

SUBJECT TO CHANGE

In 1973, in an essay called 'Toward a woman-centered university', Adrienne Rich described her vision of a future for feminist studies. In it we read: 'The university I have been trying to imagine does not seem to me utopian, though the problems and contradictions to be faced in its actual transformations are of course real and severe' (p. 153). Yet looking back over the past ten to fifteen years of women's studies, can we say that 'masculine resistance to women's claims for full humanity' (as Rich defines the project) has been overcome in any serious way? Nothing could be less sure.

In fact, I think that though we may have our women's studies programmes, our centres, journals, and conferences, feminist scholars have not succeeded in instituting the transformative claims we articulated in the heady days of the mid-1970s. Supported by the likes of William Bennett, Rochemorte and Boissec are going strong: they continue to resist, and to attack, feminism's fundamental understanding that the deployment of the universal is inherently, if paradoxically, partial and political. And the M. Pauls, who like Terry Eagleton *et al.* offer friendship and the promise of 'fraternal alliance', seem to be saying at the same time: 'feminism is theoretically thin, or separatist. Girls, shape up!' (Spivak, 'The politics of interpretations', p. 277). More serious, perhaps, because it is supported by the prestige of philosophy, the ultimate purveyor of universals, is the general failure on the part of most male theorists, even those most interested in 'feminine identity', to articulate sufficiently in the terms of their own enunciation what Rosi Braidotti calls 'the radical consciousness of one's own complicity with the very power one is trying to deconstruct' (Ms.). Like the humanists, they have not begun to question the grounds on which they stand, their own relation to the 'sexual differential' that inhabits '*every* voice' (Spivak, p. 277); their own difference from the universal, from the institution which houses them and from which they speak.

But we have of course participated in our own failure to challenge the 'ologies' and their authorities in a significant way. Our greatest strength in the 1970s, I would argue, was our experience, through consciousness raising, of the possibility of a collective identity resistant to but intimately bound up with Woman – in fact our account, analysis, and valorisation of experience itself (de Lauretis makes the point forcefully at the end of *Alice doesn't*). For reasons I cannot fully articulate here, but which have to do on the one hand with the difficulty of constructing theoretically the discourse of women's experience, a difficulty derived in part from the feminist bugaboo about essentialism – which can only be understood in relation to a massively theorised 'antiessentialism' (Russo, p. 228); and on the other, particularly for those of us working in things French, with the prestige of a regime of accounts of post-gendered subjectivities, we seem to have become stuck between two varieties of self-censorship.

In the face of a prevailing institutional indifference to the question of women, conjoined with a prevailing critical ideology of the subject which celebrates or longs for a mode beyond difference, where and how to move? On what grounds can we remodel the relations of female subjects to the social text? In the issue of *Tulsa Studies* devoted to the current state of feminist criticism (republished in *Feminist Issues in Literary Scholarship*) there is at least one pressing call to forget the professors, theorists masculine and feminine, to 'reject male formalist models for criticism' in the belief, Jane Marcus writes, that 'the practice of formalism professionalizes the feminist critic and makes her safe for academe' ('Still practice', p. 90). We must, I think, see this as too simple. Not only because, as Nina Auerbach argues in the same issue, 'whether we like it or not, we live in one world, one country . . . one university department with men' (p. 155), but because we don't. If women's studies is to effect institutional change through critical interventions, we cannot afford to proceed by a wholesale dismissal of 'male' models. Rather, like Lucy in the school play (in another forced performance), who refuses to play a man's part dressed in men's clothes and instead assumes '*in addition*' to her 'woman's garb' the signifiers of masculinity (p. 209, emphasis added), the effectiveness of future feminist intervention calls for an ironic manipulation of the semiotics of performance.[10]

Earlier in *Villette*, Ginevra pressed Lucy to explain herself, to reveal some deeper truth that seems to elude her grasp: 'Who *are* you, Miss Snowe?' And Lucy, 'amused at her mystification', replies, 'Who am I indeed? Perhaps a personage in disguise. Pity I don't look the character' (pp. 392–3). But Ginevra is not satisfied with this flip account: 'But *are* you anybody?' This time Lucy is slightly more forthcoming, supplying information, at least, about her social insertion: 'Yes . . . I am a rising character: once an old lady's companion, then a nursery-governess, now a school-teacher' (p. 394). Ginevra persists in thinking there is more to Lucy than Lucy will say, but Lucy will offer nothing more. If we take Lucy Snowe's account of herself at face value, not persisting like Ginevra in a hermeneutics of revelation that is structured, Barthes has taught us, on oedipal narratologies, we begin to take the measure of Brontë's radical achievement in this novel: creating a heroine whose identity is modulated through the cadences of work; through the effects of institutions. This is not to suggest that Lucy's subjectivity is recontained by a work history, circumscribed by its hierarchies of class. On the contrary, we have seen Ginevra's conviction that despite the institutional inscription, Lucy somehow continues to escape her, not only because Ginevra is looking for a social language she can under-stand – 'a name, a pedigree' – but because in some palpable and troubling way, Lucy, like the Lacanian subject she anticipates, also resides elsewhere in the 'field of language' which constitutes her otherness to herself (Mitchell, p. 241).

I want to float the suggestion, then, and by way of a gesture towards closure, that any definition of the female writing subject not universal-ised as Woman that we try to theorise now must include Lucy Snowe's ambiguities: in work, in language. This is a process that recognises what Elizabeth Weed describes as the 'impossible . . . relation of women to Woman' (p. 74) and acknowledges our ongoing contradic-tions, the gap and (and perhaps permanent) internal split that makes a collective identity always a horizon, but a necessary one.[11] It is a fragmentation we can, however, as feminist readers work with and through. This is the move of resistance and production that allows Lucy to find language 'as a woman' despite the power of the ''ologies', despite the allegory of *human* justice.

At the end of 'Femininity, narrative, and psychoanalysis' (1982), an essay in which she takes as her example Emily Brontë's Wuthering heights, Juliet Mitchell outlines a question by way of providing herself with a solution of closure to her discussion of the female (writing) subject and a critique of Kristéva's valorisation of the semiotic, the heterogeneous space of the subject-in-

process. To her own question of what identity and text might mean construed along the lines of such a theoretical model – 'in the process of becoming what?' *– Mitchell responds: 'I do not think that we can live as human subjects without in some sense taking on a history; for us, it is mainly the history of being men or women under bourgeois capitalism. In deconstructing that history, we can only construct other histories. What are we in the process of becoming?'* (p. 294).

Mitchell shrewdly leaves the question open, but since this is my essay and not hers, I have felt it important to risk a reply. At the Pembroke conference, I ended by saying: I hope we are becoming women. Because such a reply proved too ironic to occupy the privileged place of the last word, I will now say: I hope we are becoming feminists. In both phrases, however, the hope I express for a female future is a desire for all that we don't know *about what it might mean to be women beyond the always already provided identity of Women with which we can only struggle; the hope for a negotiation that would produce through feminism a new 'social subject', as de Lauretis puts it in* Alice doesn't (p. 186), *and that I have figured here as the work of female critical subjects.*

NOTES

N.B. With the exception of the introductory remarks, which I read in slightly different form at Milwaukee, the material that appears in italics was written after the events of the paper as discursive endnotes; not so much as side issues, as asides pointing to the limits of the essay's rhetorical space. Its place here in dialogic relation to the main body of the text is the result of an experiment brought about by the always imaginative critical judgement of the editor of the volume in which it first appeared, *Feminist Studies/Critical Studies*, Teresa de Lauretis. Once I saw it in print, I decided to reproduce it here in that form, with a few editorial changes of my own.

1. The foxtrot is defined in Webster's Third as 'a ballroom dance in duple time that includes slow walking steps, quick running steps, and two steps'. What appeals to me here is the change of pace, the doubleness of moves within the shape of the dance, and the collaborative requirement. The latter will re-emerge at the end of this paper, but really runs through the argument: the dead-endedness of the one-way street that bears the traffic (to mix a few metaphors) between feminist and dominant critics.

    This figuration of the problem bears a certain resemblance to my discussion of shoes and tropes in 'The text's heroine' (Chapter 3 in my *Subject to Change*). My current position has been reformulated for me by Biddy Martin, who said at the Milwaukee conference that indeterminacy (what I am thematising here as the denegation and denigration of identity) is no excuse for not acting; that we must find a way to ground indeterminacy so that we can make political interventions. The question before us then becomes how to locate and allow for particularities within the collective.

2. Barthes' essay should be situated within the discussion of changing definitions of art in conjunction with the laws governing authorship in France, in particular a 1957 law which attempted to account for new kinds of artistic and authorial production not covered by the copyright law (*droits d'auteur*) of 1793. I am indebted to Molly Nesbit's 'What was an author?', for an illuminating explanation of this material. Nesbit points out that the death of the author for Barthes seems to have meant 'really the imprinting author of 1793'; she also describes the original occasion for the essay: 'in 1967 in America for *Aspen* magazine, nos. 5 + 6 . . . dedicated to Stéphane Mallarmé'. It is boxed (literally) along with all kinds of authorial work, much of it technologically based' (pp. 241–3). See also 'Le Droit d'auteur s'adapte à la nouvelle

économie de la création', in *Le Monde*, 3 August 1985. These are pieces of a more contextual history of criticism.

3. At the Cerisy colloquium of which he was the 'prétexte', this phrase drew a certain amount of attention. In his comments on the meaning of the phrase Barthes situated his own relation to the historical context of writing *Sade/Fourier/Loyola*: 'It was the heyday of modernity and the text; we talked about the death of the author (I talked about it myself). We didn't use the word writer (écrivain): writers were slightly ridiculous people like Gide, Claudel, Valéry, Malraux' (pp. 413–14).

4. In 'Women's time, women's space: writing the history of feminist criticism,' Showalter adopts Julia Kristéva's 'genealogy' of subjectivity; of a *space* of generation which is both 'European *and* trans-European' (p. 15). In writing the history of American feminist criticism, she wants 'to emphasize its specificity by narrating its development in terms of the internal relationships, continuities, friendships, and institutions that shaped the thinking and writing of the last fifteen years' (p. 30). As examples of asymmetrical events in these non-parallel chronologies, Showalter contrasts the 1966 conference on 'the Structuralist Controversy and the Sciences of Man' (Johns Hopkins University) with 'the first feminist literary session at the Chicago MLA in 1970' (p. 32), neither of which I attended. In 1971 I was reading Roland Barthes, not Adrienne Rich. The discovery of Rich, for me a belated one, comes from being involved with a women's studies programme; this trajectory, I think, figures an inverse relation to the reading habits of much mainstream American feminist criticism, while remaining outside the classical reading patterns of women in French; which may or may not explain the feeling people have had that I am mixing things – Barthes and Rich – that somehow don't belong together. What is worrisome to me is the way in which conferences in literary studies continue to follow their separate paths: though women are invited to English Institute (for which Showalter wrote this essay), Georgetown, etc., and men to Pembroke and Milwaukee, there is no evidence yet that feminist critical theory has affected dominant organisations and theorisations.

5. The stories of readers and writers emerge in both Rich and Barthes from a gendered poetics of sexual difference and family romances. For Barthes, like Rich, the author is male, and in his effects, patriarchal: 'As an institution, the author is dead: . . . dispossessed, his (identity) no longer exerts the formidable paternity over his work that literary history, teaching, opinion had the responsibility of establishing . . . but in the text, in a certain way *I desire the author*: I need his figure (which is neither his representation, nor his projection)' (*The Pleasure of the Text*, p. 27). In Barthes' model of desire the reader and the writer participate in a system of associations that poses the masculine experience as central and universal. This 'I' who desires the author, and desires to be desired by him, who worries about the return of the father (having banished him), who takes his pleasure in a fragmented subjectivity, desires, worries, enjoys within an economy as (he of course says it himself) a son. The failure to differentiate (the question, for example, of the daughter's desire) becomes more than a matter of philosophy or style when allied with the authority – of the intellectual, writer, teacher – that supports the concept of indifference in the first place. On the politics of indifference, see Naomi Schor's 'Dreaming dissymmetry: Barthes, Foucault and sexual difference'.

6. This move corresponds to Gayatri Spivak's insistence on 'a simultaneous other focus: not merely who am I? but who is the other woman? How am I naming her? How does she name me' 'French feminism in an international frame', p. 179. On the 'other woman', see also Jane Gallop's 'Annie Leclerc writing a letter, with Vermeer'.

7. Smith wrote in her 1977 essay, 'Towards a black feminist criticism', from which she read at the Milwaukee conference: 'I finally want to express how much easier both my waking and sleeping hours would be if there were one book in existence that would tell me something specific about my life. One book based in black feminist and black lesbian experience, fiction or nonfiction. Just one work to reflect the reality that I and the black women who I love are trying to create. When such a book exists then each of us will not only know better how to live, but how to dream' (p. 184). For O'Neale's position, see her 'Inhibiting midwives, usurping creators: the struggling emergence of black women in American fiction'.

In the *New York Times Book Review*, 2 June 1985, Gloria Naylor, in a survey of writers' favourite opening passages, comments on the beginning of Toni Morrison's *The bluest eye*.

Naylor writes: 'While the novel handles a weighty subject – the demoralization of black female beauty in a racist society (also the subject – of O'Neale's paper) – it *whispers* in the mode of minimalist poetry, thus resulting in the least common denominator for all classics: the ability to haunt. It alerts my students to the fact that fiction should be about storytelling, the 'why' of things is best left to the sociologists, the 'how' is more than enough for writers to tackle . . .' (p. 52). It seems to me that we are in desperate need of a specifically text-based discussion between black and white feminist critics and writers on the relations between the why and the how, between reference and representation. Without it we run the risk of a devastating repolarisation of the sort that at times during the Milwaukee conference resulted in bitter asides and accusations of racism.

8. At the Milwaukee conference Jane Gallop asked about the implicit risk one runs that irony can misfire. In *A handlist of rhetorical terms* Richard Lanham describes this problem under the rubric of 'rhetorical irony' (p. 61). He points out that the 'relationship of persuader and persuaded is almost always self-conscious to some degree', and goes on to make the claim that 'every rhetorical posture except the most naive involves an ironical coloration, of some kind or another of the speaker's *Ethos*'. To the extent that the ethos (character, disposition) of feminism historically has refused the doubleness of 'saying one thing while it tries to do another' (the mark of classical femininity one might argue), it may be that an ironic feminist discourse finds itself at odds both with itself (its identity to itself), and with the expectations its audience has of its position. If this is true, then irony, in the final analysis, may be a figure of limited effectiveness. On the other hand, since non-ironic, single, sincere, hortatory feminism is becoming ineffectual, it may be worth the risk of trying out this kind of duplicity on the road.

   In 'A manifesto for cyborgs', Donna Haraway, calling for a greater use of irony 'within socialist feminism', argues: 'Irony is about contradictions that do not resolve into larger wholes, even dialectically, about the tension of holding incompatible things together because both or all are necessary and true' (p. 65).

9. The task of 'dephallicizing the father', as Gallop puts it in *The daughter's seduction*, to succeed must break out of the limits of the family circle (p. xv).

10. If Lucy in the classroom writes her way out of humiliation and into agency, on stage the use of language becomes a question of voice. The difficulty, Lucy discovers, once she begins to speak, lies not in the audience but in her performance: 'When my tongue got free, and my voice took its true pitch, and found its natural tone, I thought of nothing but the personage I represented' (p. 210). In both instances, Lucy's performative subjectivity is structured through a text and in another language. I have a more sustained analysis of this phenomenon in the Chapters 7 and 9 of *Subject to change*, on *Corinne* and *The vagabond*.

11. In 'A man's place', a talk she gave at the 1984 MLA session on 'Men in feminism', which has been published in the volume *Men in feminism*, Elizabeth Weed brilliantly outlined many of the issues with which I struggle here.

REFERENCES

Auerbach, Nina (1984), 'Why communities of women aren't enough', *Tulsa Studies in Women's Literature*, 3, 1–2 (spring–autumn), 153–7; rpt. (1987) in Shari Benstock (ed.), *Feminist issues in literary scholarship* (Bloomington: Indiana University Press).

Barthes, Roland (1971), *Sade, Fourier, Loyola* (Paris: Seuil); trans. Richard Miller (1976), *Sade–Fourier–Loyola* (New York: Hill and Wang).

Barthes, Roland (1977), 'The death of the author', in *Image/text/music*, trans. Stephen Heath (New York: Hill and Wang).

Beauvoir, Simone de (1976), *Le deuxième sexe* (Paris: Gallimard-Folio); trans. H. M. Parshley (1970), *The second sex* (New York: Bantam).

Braidotti, Rosi, 'Patterns of dissonance: women and/in philosophy' (manuscript).

Brontë, Charlotte (1983; 1st ed., 1853), *Villette* (New York: Penguin).

Cixous, Hélène (1976), 'The laugh of the Medusa', trans. Keith Cohen and Paula Cohen, *Signs*, pp. 1, 4, 875–94.

Culler, Jonathan (1982), *On deconstruction* (Ithaca: Cornell University Press).

De Lauretis, Teresa (1984), *Alice doesn't: feminism, semiotics, cinema* (Bloomington: Indiana University Press).

De Lauretis, Teresa (ed.) (1986), *Feminist studies/critical studies* (Bloomington: Indiana University Press).

Foucault, Michel (1980), 'What is an author?', in Donald F. Bouchard (ed.), *Language, counter-memory, practice* (Ithaca: Cornell University Press).

Gallop, Jane (1982), *The daughter's seduction* (Ithaca: Cornell University Press).

Gallop, Jane (1986), 'Annie Leclerc writing a letter, with Vermeer', in Nancy K. Miller (ed.), *The poetics of gender* (New York: Columbia University Press).

Gilbert, Sandra and Gubar, Susan (1979), *The Madwoman in the attic: the woman writer and the nineteenth-century literary imagination* (New Haven: Yale University Press).

Haraway, Donna (1985), 'A manifesto for cyborgs: science, technology, and socialist feminism in the 1980s', *Socialist Review* 15, 2 (March–April), pp. 65–107.

Huyssen, Andreas (1984), 'Mapping the postmodern', *New German Critique*, 33 (autumn), pp. 5–52.

Kamuf, Peggy (1980), 'Writing like a woman', in Sally McConnell-Ginet, Ruth Borker and Nelly Furman (eds), *Women and language in literature and society* (New York: Praeger).

Lanham, Richard A. (1969), *A handful of rhetorical terms* (Berkeley and Los Angeles: University of California Press).

Marcus, Jane (1984), 'Still practice, a/wrested alphabet: towards a feminist aesthetic', *Tulsa Studies in Women's Literature* pp. 3, 1–2 (spring–autumn), pp. 79–98; rpt. (1987) in Shari Benstock (ed.), *Feminist issues in literary scholarship* (Bloomington: Indiana University Press).

Mitchell, Juliet (1984), 'Femininity, narrative, and psychoanalysis', in *Women: the longest revolution* (New York: Pantheon).

Naylor, Gloria (1985), 'Famous first words', *New York Times Book Review*, 2 June, p. 52.

Nesbit, Molly (1987), 'What was an author?', *Yale French Studies* pp. 73, 229–57 (special issue on 'Everyday life', ed. Alice Y. Kaplan and Kristin Ross).

O'Neale, Sondra (1986), 'Inhibiting midwives, usurping creators: the struggling emergence of black women in American fiction', in Teresa de Lauretis (ed.), *Feminist studies/critical studies* (Bloomington: Indiana University Press).

Rich, Adrienne (1979), 'When we dead awaken: writing as revision (1971)' and 'Towards a woman-centered university (1973–74), in *On lies, secrets, and silence: selected prose, 1966–1978* (New York: Norton).

Rich, Adrienne (1986), 'Blood, bread, and poetry: the location of the poet', in *Blood, bread, and poetry: selected prose, 1979–1985* (New York: Norton).

Russo, Mary (1986), 'Female grotesques: carnival and theory', in Teresa de Lauretis (ed.), *Feminist studies/critical studies* (Bloomington: Indiana University Press).

Schor, Naomi (1985), *Breaking the chain: women, theory, and French realist fiction* (New York: Columbia University Press).

Schor, Naomi (1987), 'Dreaming dissymmetry: Barthes, Foucault, and sexual difference', in Alice Jardine and Paul Smith (eds), *Men in feminism* (New York and London: Methuen).

Showalter, Elaine (1984), 'Women's time, women's space: writing the history of feminist criticism', *Tulsa Studies in Women's Literature* pp. 3, 1–2 (spring–autumn), pp. 29–44; rpt. (1987) in Shari Benstock (ed.), *Feminist issues in literary scholarship* (Bloomington: Indiana University Press).

Showalter, Elaine (1984), 'Women who write are women', *New York Times Book Review*, 16 December, pp. 1, 31–3.

Smith, Barbara (1977), 'Towards a black feminist criticism', *Conditions: Two*, 1, 2 (October); rpt. (1985) in Elaine Showalter (ed.), *The new feminist criticism: essays on women, literature, theory* (New York: Pantheon).

Spivak, Gayatri Chakravorty (1981), 'French feminism in an international frame', *Yale French Studies*, pp. 62, 154–84.

Spivak, Gayatri Chakravorty (1982), 'The politics of interpretations', *Critical Inquiry*, 9, 1 (September), pp. 259–78.

Weed, Elizabeth (1987), 'A man's place', in Alice Jardine and Paul Smith (eds), *Men in feminism* (New York and London: Methuen).

Section 2

Ideologies and Authorship

Ideologies and Authorship

Whatever its cast, political criticism is generally united in opposing the idea of the author as an autonomous creator who transcends history and ideology. The high authorial role has been demystified through urging a conception of authorship as specific political praxis: rather than representing a universal truth, the author is thought to speak committedly for a particular moment of historical change. Outside of the reductive practice of Soviet Realism, this commitment was rarely encouraged in tendentious terms, and as far back as Engels the author was urged not to produce overtly didactic statements of Marxist belief. Walter Benjamin and Bertolt Brecht emphasised that the writer should exist in solidarity with the proletariat but registered such commitment as a radical refashioning of the modes of artistic production. A Marxist such as Georg Lukács, on the other hand, overrode the intentionalist issue of writerly commitment altogether: for Lukács, a reactionary writer such as Balzac reflects the truth of a moment in dialectical history no less vividly for his ideological blindnesses.

The authorial function has also been materialised by seeing the writer as a producer caught up in the same nexus of economic relations as any other worker. Marx himself had recognised that authorship is bound up with the economic and social forms of production, and this levelling process was developed in Walter Benjamin's recasting of the question in terms not of the author's relation *to* socio-economic conditions but of his existence *within* such conditions. With the advent of structural Marxism, language came to be viewed as constitutive of ideology: commitment was invested in the critic who *exposes* rather than the author who *opposes* ideology. Poststructural and cultural materialist modes of ideological critique renew interest in authorship not in terms of the individuals who occupy its space but with regard to the ideological implications of its function as an inexorable category within the discursive field.

Jean-Paul Sartre's ideas on authorship represent one of the last significant statements from an era in which it was felt that the social engagement of the author offered the potential for genuine political change. As novelist, playwright, philosopher, political activist and literary journalist, Sartre speaks to modern authorship from a vantage comparable only to that of Voltaire and Rousseau in the late eighteenth century. Though tempestuously involved with the official left, Sartre remained a radical socialist throughout his life. His version of Marxist theory is distinguished by an existential commitment to individual choice and freedom. Since, for Sartre, the self is never determined, authorship extends beyond the text to govern the individual's fundamental mode of being-in-the-world. In developing existentialist philosophy, Sartre accepted Heidegger's notion of man as radically immersed within history and developed phenomenological situatedness in a model of authorial commitment or engagement which entails both political responsibility for the future and continual responsiveness to contemporary social conditions. The subject for Sartre is absolute but only in relation to its epoch and milieu. The notions of transcendence and impersonality therefore have no place within the Sartrian picture of authorship: historical change becomes possible not from a panoramic or Lukácsian consciousness but through situated historical agency. In 'Writing For One's Age' Sartre outlines the seemingly paradoxical notion that historical groundedness gives rise to a literature all the more reflective thereby of the absolute. As well as constituting a vivid statement of Sartre's concept of the engaged author, 'Writing For One's Age' is also a suggestive reflection on writing and history, authorship and mortality.

In 'Creation and Production', Pierre Macherey replaces the praxis of the politically-committed author with the practice of ideological criticism. Macherey's general insistence that the importance of texts lies not with what is said or meant by a work but with what is unsaid renders authorial intention insignificant: the work of literature is constituted by determinate conditions of which the author is no more than a product. Macherey's work shows the influence of Benjamin's 'The Author as Producer', which opposes to the romantic notion of a writer's creative genius an artisanal view of authorship as analogous to any act of socio-economic production. Macherey thus extends Louis Althusser's recognition of an anti-humanism always implicit in Marx by (dis)placing the individual in a network of ideological relations. The term 'creation' is seen as complicit with a theological/humanist definition of man as autonomous, generative subject. Macherey's argument thus looks forward to Barthes's 'The Death of the Author' and might be said to share the latter's over-simple identification of God, man and author.

Though neither avowedly structuralist nor Marxist, Michel Foucault's enquiry into the social construction of Western knowledge had also issued in anti-humanist conclusions. In his work, *The Order of Things*, Foucault declares the death of man as consequent upon a linguistic revolution which heralds the close of anthropological modernity. In 'What is an Author?', though, Foucault refuses simply to celebrate the disappearance of the subject and instead separates the ontologies of man and author via the category of the 'author-function'. Foucault sees such a function as historically and structurally variable according to the cultural assumptions of specific systems of discursive arrangement. Foucault interprets the expanded sense of authorship from the late eighteenth century onwards in terms of discursive ownership: potentially transgressive discourses became subject to policing via the quasi-juridical procedures of attribution and accountability. In analysing authorship as a discursive function, Foucault reduces the ontological significance of authorship while enlarging its textual remit: his identification of a unique class of 'fundamental' authors such as Marx and Freud who have founded, defined and delimited discursive fields accedes nothing to authorship as presence and everything to the power of the proper name's corpus. The separation of author and biographical subject thereby identifies a space of authorship which exceeds the empirical presence or history of its signatory. This recognition of authorship as a central category in the circulation, appropriation and judgement of discourses was to influence the emergence in the 1980s of political textualisms such as the New Historicism and Cultural Materialism.

In 'What Was an Author?', Molly Nesbit literally takes up where Foucault left off by grounding the conceptual in the cultural, the epistemological in the legal. Contending that the law is the blind spot in Foucault's analysis, Nesbit shows how the sense of authorship has been explored via cultural, political and legal events such as exhibitions, militancy and copyright laws. Foucault had allowed that his essay 'should have spoken of the 'author-function' in painting, music, technical fields', and Nesbit correspondingly discusses authorship in the broadest terms as representative of the occupation of cultural space. Showing how various changes or modifications in the *droit d'auteurs* expand the category to include photographers, draughtsmen, inventors of computer games, and modes of corporate authorship such as film production, Nesbit exceeds Walter Benjamin in situating authorship as a socio–economic activity common to all the creative sites of human endeavour. Everywhere asserting that the complexities of the artist's role in society are all the more reason for expanding rather than closing the question of authorship, she traces the field from the close of patronage and the French Copyright Law of 1793, through to post-modern interrogations of ownership and subjectivity.

Donald Pease similarly asserts the continuing cultural relevance of authorship in an historical account which challenges the aesthetic construction of the debate. Written as a entry for an introductory handbook on theoretical terms, Pease's 'Author' analyses authorship as a cultural and political site unique to the postmedieval world. Pease sees the author as arising from the decline in authority of the Medieval *auctores* upon the discovery of the New World. Faced with a cultural 'other' which contradicted the world-pictures enshrined within the *auctores*' texts, a class of authors developed whose authority no longer stemmed from divine revelation but from their own creative powers. The move from *auctoritas* to authorship signalled the separation of the cultural and political: the writer's responsibility no longer consisted in participating within culture but in originating alternative worlds in an attempt to transcend the political. Pease reads the separation of author and text in the twentieth century as the consequence of a division of cultural labour parallel to the partitioning of the economic realm. With the New Criticism, for example, the critic becomes an expert govern-ing the scene of a text's reception once the authorial work of production has been completed. Pease thus diagnoses the Death of the Author as politically disabling, arguing that 'only a return to an enabling conception of the author' can produce a progressive transformation in the politics of discourse. Relating the division of human subjectivity to the conservative separation of cultural realms, Pease identifies author-ship as central to the development of a positive materialist practice.

What unites structural, poststructural and Cultural Materialist modes of political critique is their overwhelming concern with the ideology of authorship at the expense of the author's relation to ideology. During the late 1980s, however, this latter issue reasserted itself in the largely negative contexts of the controversies surrounding Martin Heidegger's involvement with National Socialist politics, Paul de Man's collaborationist journalism, and Salman Rushdie's perceived sacrilege against the Islamic creed. Hard cases certainly make bad law, if any law at all, but all three instances show in very different contexts the enduring ethical demand for authorial accountability. I will of course refrain from commenting on my own 'The Ethics of Signature' except to say that it was written as an attempt to mediate between a punitive and a responsible use of the signature in the construction of ethical fora.

Máire ní Fhlathúin's survey of responses to the Rushdie affair highlights the ethico-political dangers of divesting an author of any power to respond authoritatively to the reading of his text. Her article 'Postcolonialism and the Author' demonstrates that the aesthetic credo of separating text and intention denies the author any political power to distance himself from the attribution of erroneous, blasphemous or criminal motives. Readers are thus empowered to construct their own sense of the author from the text, a construction which will often be used to consolidate antagonistic ideological positions. Ní Fhlathúin's article sees Rushdie as stranded between the competing claims of an aesthetic postmodern and a political postcolonialism in a literary culture for which determinate meaning of a traditional or Hirschian kind can no longer be upheld, and yet one in which 'the postcolonial author, unlike his text, is not allowed the attribute of indeterminacy'. This conflict between the postmodern dispersal of agency and its requirement within a postcolonial politics perhaps suggests that neo-political criticism has implied a return to agency and authorship without calibrating the form which such a return should take. Ní Fhlathúin's exploration of the abyssal constitution of the author-within-the-text reveals a network of textual indeterminacy that parallels the uncertain juridical construction of the author-of-the-text – the question of political agency being every bit as prohibitively complex as that of narrative authority within *The Satanic Verses*.

While the Rushdie affair is complicated by the relation of fictional and ideological declaration, our expectations of the philosophical author tend to rest on a clearer equation of discursive intention and political statement. There is a greater demand that the philosophical author should existentially affirm what his or her text declares. This demand can be retraced to Plato, to the irreducible unity of life and teaching exemplified by Christ, and to the late-Medieval insistence that an *auctor* should be a moral exemplar as well as a religious authority. It also implies a different placement of the author in generic terms: in discourses which make unmediated truth claims, the writer cannot so easily be displaced in terms of narrative distance, implied authorship or irony.

Richard Rorty, in a review article entitled 'Taking Philosophy Seriously', responds to further biographical evidence of Heidegger's support of National Socialist politics. So far from challenging the evidence against Heidegger, Rorty accepts it fully in an argument which seeks to defend the Heideggerian text against the effects of its author's life: such a situation is quite the converse of that confronting Rushdie, whose life has been literally endangered by his text. Rorty argues that an author's biography should in no way bear upon the evaluation of the system of thought which the author propounds. Knowledge of moral character can only be relevant to estimation of the personality of the author and not to the system of beliefs advanced in the author's name. While Rorty's argument is unquestionably valid in prohibiting *evaluation* on these grounds, it fails to account for the relevance of the biographical findings in the *interpretation* of Heidegger's work and its relation to his epoch. Providing such information is used at the level of causal questioning and is not driven to axiological ends, it would seem entirely pertinent in the interrogation of an era which saw so many of Europe's most esteemed minds drawn to fascist politics. Holding writers to political account for what they have written is doubtless regrettable in many cases and problematic in all, but remains an inescapable consequence of discourse's inscription within the social. Similar issues arise in the next section with regard to Nietzsche's autobiographical confession to implication in events that would take place more than three decades after his death.

SUGGESTED FURTHER READINGS

Adorno, Theodor, 'Commitment', in *Aesthetics and Politics: Debates Between Bloch, Lukács, Brecht, Benjamin, Adorno* (London: Verso, 1977), pp. 177–95.

Althusser, Louis, *For Marx* (London: Allen Lane, 1969).

Appignanesi, Lisa and Sara Maitland (eds), *The Rushdie File* (London: Fourth Estate, 1989).

Benjamin, Walter, *Understanding Brecht* (London: New Left Books, 1973).

Bhabha, Homi K., *The Location of Culture* (London: Routledge, 1994).

Biriotti, Maurice and Nicola Miller (eds), *What is an Author?* (Manchester: Manchester University Press, 1993).

Derrida, Jacques, *The Ear of the Other* (New York: Schocken Books, 1986).

—— *Of Spirit: Heidegger and the Question* (Chicago, IL: University of Chicago Press, 1989).

Farias, Victor, *Heidegger and Nazism* (Philadelphia, PA: Temple University Press, 1989).

Hamacher, Werner, *Responses: On Paul de Man's Wartime Journalism* (Lincoln, NB: University of Nebraska Press, 1989).

Marx, Karl and Friedrich Engels, *On Literature and Art: A Selection of Writings*, ed. Lee Baxandall and Stefan Morawski (New York: International General, 1973).

Kamuf, Peggy, *Signature Pieces: On the Institution of Authorship* (Ithaca, NY: Cornell University Press, 1988).

Lukács, Georg, *Writer and Critic* (London, 1970).

Jameson, Fredric, *Postmodernism, or the Cultural Logic of Late Capitalism* (London: Verso, 1991).

Spivak, Gayatri Chakravorty, 'Three Women's Texts and a Critique of Imperialism', *Critical Inquiry* 12 (Autumn, 1985), pp. 243–61.

—— 'Reading *The Satanic Verses*', in Biriotti and Miller (eds), *What is an Author?* (Manchester: Manchester University Press, 1993), pp. 103–34.

—— 'Can the Subaltern Speak?', in *Colonial Discourse and Post-Colonial Theory: A Reader*, ed. Patrick Williams and Laura Chrisman (Hemel Hempstead: Harvester, 1993), pp. 66–111.

Wolff, Janet, *The Social Production of Art* (London and Basingstoke: Macmillan, 1981).

21

JEAN-PAUL SARTRE

'Writing For One's Age'

We assert against certain critics and against certain authors that salvation is achieved on this earth, that it is of the whole man and by the whole man and that art is a meditation on life and not on death. It is true that for history talent alone counts. But I haven't entered into history and I don't know how I shall enter it; perhaps alone, perhaps in an anonymous crowd, perhaps as one of those names they put into footnotes in literary handbooks. At any rate, I do not have to bother myself with the judgements that the future will bring to bear upon my work since there's nothing I can do about them. Art cannot be reduced to a dialogue with the dead and with men not yet born; that would be both too difficult and too easy; and I see in this a last remnant of Christian belief in immortality: just as man's stay here below is presented as a moment of trial between limbo and hell or paradise, in like manner, for a book there is a transitory period coinciding approximately with that of its efficacity; after which, disembodied and gratuitous as a soul, it enters eternity. But at least, among Christians, it is this stay upon earth that decides everything and the final beatitude is only a sanction. Whereas it is commonly believed that the course run by our books, when we no longer exist, refers back to our life to justify it. This is true from the viewpoint of the objective mind. In the objective mind one classifies according to talent. But our descendants' view of us is not a privileged one, since others will come after them and will judge them in turn. It is obvious that we write out of a need for the absolute, and a work of the mind is indeed an absolute. But here one commits a double error. First of all, it is not true that a writer transmits his sufferings and his faults to the absolute when he writes about them; it is not true that he saves them. It is said that the unhappily married man who writes about marriage with talent has made a good book *with* his conjugal woes. That would be too easy: the bee makes honey *with* the flower because it operates on the vegetal substance of *real* transformations; the sculptor makes a statue *with* marble. But it is with words and not with his troubles that the writer makes his books. If he wants to keep his wife from being disagreeable, it is a mistake to write about her; he would do better to beat her. One no more *puts* one's misfortunes into a book than one puts a model on the canvas; one is inspired by them, and they remain what they are. One gets perhaps a passing relief in placing oneself above them in order to describe them, but once the book is finished, there they are again. Insincerity begins when the artist wants to ascribe a meaning to his misfortunes, a kind of immanent finality, and when he persuades himself that they are there *in order* for him to speak about them. When he justifies his own sufferings by this ruse, he invites laughter; but he is contemptible if he seeks to justify those of others. The most beautiful book in the world will not save a child from pain; one does not redeem evil, one fights it; the most beautiful book in the world redeems itself; it also redeems the artist. But not the man. Any more than the man redeems the artist. We want the man and the artist to work their salvation together, we want the work to be at the same time an act; we want it to be explicitly conceived as a weapon in the struggle that men wage against evil.

The other error is just as grave. There is such a hunger for the absolute in every heart that eternity, which is a non-temporal absolute, is frequently confused with immortality, which is only a perpetual reprieve and a long succession of vicissitudes. I understand this desire for the absolute; I desire it too. But what need is there to go looking for it so far off: there it is, about us, under our feet, in each of our gestures. We produce the absolute as M. Jourdain produced prose. You light your pipe and that's an absolute; you detest oysters and that's an absolute; you join the Communist Party and that's an absolute. Whether the world is mind or matter, whether God exists or whether He does not exist, whether the judgement of the centuries to come is favourable to you or hostile, nothing will ever prevent your having passionately loved that painting, that cause, that woman, nor that love's having been lived from day to day; lived, willed, undertaken; nor your being completely committed to it. Our grandfathers were right in saying, as they drank their glass of wine, 'Another one that the

Prussians won't get.' Neither the Prussians nor anyone else. They can kill you, they can deprive you of wine to the end of your days, but no God, no man, can take away that final trickling of the Bordeaux along your tongue. No relativism. Nor the 'eternal course of history' either. Nor the dialectic of the sensible. Nor the dissociations of psychoanalysis. It is a pure event, and we too, in the uttermost depths of historical relativity and our own insignificance, we too are absolutes, inimitable and incomparable, and our choice of ourselves is an absolute. All those living and passionate choices that we are and that we are constantly making with or against others, all those common enterprises into which we throw ourselves, from birth to death, all those bonds of love or hatred which unite us to one another and which exist only in so far as we feel them, those immense combinations of movements which are added to or cancel out one another and which are all lived, that whole discordant and harmonious life, concur in producing a new absolute which I shall call the *age*. The age is the intersubjectivity, the living absolute, the dialectical underside of history . . . It gives birth in pain to events that historians will label later on. It lives blindly, distractedly, and fearfully the enthusiasm and the meanings that they will disengage rationally. Within the age, every utterance, before being a historical byword or the recognized origin of a social process, is first an insult or an appeal or a confession; economic phenomena themselves, before being the theoretical causes of social upheavals, are suffered in humiliation or despair, ideas are tools or evasions, facts are born of the intersubjectivity and overwhelm it, like the emotions of an individual soul. History is made with dead ages, for each age, when it dies, enters into relativity; it falls into line with other dead centuries; a new light is shed upon it; it is challenged by new knowledge; its problems are resolved for it; it is demonstrated that its most ardent pursuits were doomed to failure, that the results of the great undertakings of which it was so proud were the reverse of what it anticipated; its limits are suddenly apparent, and its ignorance too. But that is *because* it is dead; the limits and the ignorance did not exist 'at the time'; no deficiency was seen; or rather the age was a constant surpassing of its limits towards a future which was *its* future and which died with it; it was *this* boldness, *this* rashness, *this* ignorance of its ignorance; to live is to foresee at short range and to manage with the means at hand. Perhaps with a little more knowledge our fathers might have understood that a certain problem was insoluble, that a certain problem was badly stated. But the human condition requires us to choose in ignorance; it is ignorance which makes morality possible. If we knew all the factors which condition phenomena, if we gambled on a sure thing, the risk would disappear; and with the risk, the courage and the fear, the waiting, the final joy and the effort; we would be listless gods, but certainly not men. The bitter Babylonian disputes about omens, the bloody and passionate heresies of the Albigenses, of the Anabaptists, now seem to us mistakes. At the time, man committed himself to them completely, and, in manifesting them at the peril of his life, he brought truth into being through them, for truth never yields itself directly, it merely appears through errors. In the dispute over Universals, over the Immaculate Conception or Transubstantiation, it was the fate of human Reason that was at stake. And the fate of Reason was again at stake when American teachers who taught the theory of evolution were brought to trial in certain states. It is at stake in every age, totally so, in regard to doctrines which the following age will reject as false. Evolution may some day appear to be the biggest folly of our century; in testifying for it against the clerics, the American teachers *lived* the truth, they lived it passionately and absolutely, at personal risk. Tomorrow they will be wrong, today they are absolutely right; the age is always wrong when it is dead, always right when it is alive. Condemn it later on, if you like; but first it had its passionate way of loving itself and lacerating itself, against which future judgements are of no avail. It had its taste which it tasted alone and which is as incomparable, as irremediable, as the taste of wine in our mouths.

A book has its absolute truth within the age. It is *lived* like an outbreak, like a famine. With much less intensity, to be sure, and by fewer people, but in the same way. It is an emanation of intersubjectivity, a living bond of rage, hatred or love among those who produce it and those who receive it. If it succeeds in commanding attention, thousands of people reject it and deny it: as everybody knows, to read a book is to re-write it. *At the time* it is at first a panic or an evasion or a courageous assertion; at the time it is a good or bad *action*. Later on, when the age is done with, it will enter into the relative, it will become a message. But the judgements of posterity will not invalidate those that were passed on it in its lifetime. I have often been told about dates and bananas: 'You don't know anything about them. In order to know what they are, you have to eat them on the spot, when they've just been picked.' And I have always considered bananas as dead fruit whose real, live taste escapes me. Books that are handed down from age to age are dead fruit. They had, in another time, another taste, tart and tangy. *Émile* or *The Persian Letters* should have been read when they were freshly picked.

Thus, one must write for one's age, as the great writers have done. But that does not mean that one has to lock oneself up in it. To write for one's age is not to reflect it passively; it is to want to maintain it or change it, thus to go beyond it towards the future, and it is this effort to change it that places us most deeply within it, for it is never reducible to the dead ensemble of tools and customs; it is in movement; it is constantly surpassing itself; the concrete present and the living future of all the men who compose it coincide rigorously within it. If, among other features, Newtonian physics and the theory of the noble savage concur in sketching the physiognomy of the first half of the eighteen century, it should be borne in mind that one was a sustained effort to snatch some shreds of truth from the mists, to approach, beyond the state of contemporary knowledge, an ideal science in which phenomena might be mathematically deduced from the principle of gravitation, and that the other implied an attempt to restore, beyond the vices of civilization, the state of nature. They both drew up a rough sketch of a future; and if it is true that this future never became a present, that we have given up the golden age and the idea of making science a rigorous chain of reasons, still the fact remains that these live and deep hopes sketched out a future beyond everyday concerns and that, in order to interpret the meaning of the everyday, we must go back to it *on the basis* of that future. One cannot be a man or become a writer without tracing a horizon line beyond oneself, but the self-surpassing is in each case finite and particular. One does not surpass *in general* and for the proud and simple pleasure of surpassing; Baudelairean dissatisfaction represents only the abstract scheme of transcendence and, since it is dissatisfaction with everything, ends by being dissatisfaction with nothing. Real transcendence requires one to want to change certain specific aspects of the world, and the surpassing is coloured and particularized by the concrete situation it aims to modify. A man puts himself entirely into his project for emancipating the negroes or restoring the Hebrew language to the Jews of Palestine; he puts himself into it entirely and thereby realizes the human condition in its universality; but it is always on the occasion of a particular and dated enterprise. And if I am told, as by M. Schlumberger, that one also goes beyond the age when one aims at immortality, I shall reply that this is a false surpassing: instead of trying to change an intolerable situation, one attempts to evade it and seeks refuge in a future which is utterly foreign to us, since it is not the future that we are making, but the concrete present of our grandchildren. We have no means of action upon this present; they will live it on their own account and as they like; *situated in*

their age, as we are in ours, if they make use of our writings, it will be
for ends which are proper to them and which we had not foreseen, as
one picks up stones along the way in order to throw them into the face
of an aggressor. An attempt on our part to burden them with the
responsibility of prolonging our existence would be vain; it is no duty
or concern of theirs. And as we have no means of action over these
strangers, it is as beggars that we shall present ourselves before them
and that we shall beg them to lend us the appearance of life by using us
however they like. If Christians, we shall accept humbly, provided
they still speak of us, that they make use of us to testify that faith is
inefficacious; if atheists, we shall be quite content if they are still
concerned with our anguish and our faults, be it to prove that man
without God is miserable. Would you be satisfied, M. Schlumberger, if
our grandsons, after the Revolution, saw in your writings the most
obvious example of the conditioning of art by economic structures?
And if you do not have this literary destiny, you will have another
which will hardly be worth more. If you escape dialectical materialism,
it will be perhaps to become the subject of psycho-analysis. At all
events, our grandchildren will be orphans who have their own
concerns; why should they concern themselves with us? Perhaps Céline
will be the only one of all of us to remain; it is highly improbable, but
theoretically possible that the twenty-first century may retain the name
of Drieu and drop that of Malraux; at any rate, it will not take up our
quarrels, it will not mention what we call today the treason of certain
writers; or, if it mentions it, it will do so without anger or contempt.
But what does that matter to us? What Malraux, what Drieu are for us,
that's the absolute. There is an absolute of contempt for Drieu in certain
hearts, there was an absolute of friendship for Malraux that a hundred
posthumous judgements will be unable to blemish. There was a living
Malraux, a weight of hot blood in the age's heart; there will be a dead
Malraux, a prey to history. Why does anyone expect the living man to
be concerned with fixing the features of the dead man he will be? To be
sure, he lives beyond himself; his gaze and his concerns exceed his death
in the flesh. What measures the *presence* and weight of a man is not the
fifty or sixty years of his organic life, nor the borrowed life he will lead
throughout the centuries in minds foreign to his; it is the choice he
himself will have made of the temporal cause which goes beyond him.
It was said that the courier of Marathon had died an hour before
reaching Athens. He had died and was still running; he was running
dead, announced the Greek victory dead. This is a fine myth; it shows
that the dead still act for a little while as if they were living. For a little

while, a year, ten years, perhaps fifty years; at any rate, a *finite* period; and then they are buried a second time. This is the measure we propose to the writer: as long as his books arouse anger, discomfort, shame, hatred, love, even if he is no more than a shade, he will live. Afterwards, the deluge. We stand for an ethics and art of the finite.

22

PIERRE MACHEREY

'Creation and Production'

The proposition that the writer or artist is a creator belongs to a humanist ideology. In this ideology man is released from his function in an order external to himself, restored to his so-called powers. Circumscribed only by the resources of his own nature, he becomes the maker of his own laws. He creates. What does he create? Man. Humanist thought (everything by man, everything for man) is circular, tautological, dedicated entirely to the repetition of a single image. 'Man makes man' (in this sense Aristotle is the theoretician of humanism): by a continual unbroken investigation he releases from within himself what is already there; creation is self-multiplication. There seems to be a radical difference between theology and anthropology: man can create only in continuity, by making the potential actual; he is excluded, by his nature, from originality and innovation. But this difference is an adaptation.

Anthropology is merely an impoverished and inverted theology: in the place of the god-man is installed Man, god over himself, eternally repeating the destiny he already bears within him. In the terms of this inversion, the opposite of man-as-creator is alienated man: deprived of himself, become other. To become other (alienation), to become oneself (creation): the two ideas are equivalent in so far as they belong to the same problematic. Alienated man is man without man: man without God, without that God who is, for man, man himself.

Formulated thus, the question of 'man' involves unresolvable contradictions: how can man change without becoming other? So he must be protected, allowed to remain as he is: forbidden to transform his condition. The ideology of humanism is spontaneously and profoundly reactionary both in theory and in practice. The only activity allowed to the man-god is the preservation of his identity. The only possible legitimate changes are those which give man what already belongs to him: his property, even if he has never actually owned it. The Declaration of Human Rights, the monument of humanism, is not an institution but a declaration; it abolishes the distance which separates man from his universal, necessary and external rights. Man has been changed from what he is (the humanist ideology's explanation of 'religious alienation'): it is enough to change him back, to restore everything to its former place. Alienation is not in itself damaging, but only because of the direction in which it leads; it is enough to change the direction to release the truth which it contains but ignores. Humanism is only a very superficial critique of religious ideology; it does not contest the ideological as such, merely a specific ideology which it wishes to replace.

The purest product of humanism is the religion of art: Roger Garaudy – whose purpose is to give back to man his 'expectations', by starting him on the 'voyage' to the limitless space (if that were all it required!) of himself – is the supreme ideologue of artistic creation. Borrowing a careless phrase from Gorky (careless because it is merely a phrase, unsupported by any argument, and completely mistaken from a theoretical point of view), 'aesthetics is the ethics of the future', he proposes the liberation of man by a return to the religion of art, without seeing that art, exploited thus, is only an impoverished religion. Now, art is not a man's creation, it is a product (and the producer is not a subject centred in his creation, he is an element in a situation or a system): different – in being a product – from religion, which has chosen its dwelling among all the spontaneous illusions of spontaneity, which is certainly a kind of creation. Before disposing of these works – which can only be called theirs by an elaborate evasion – men have to *produce* them, not by magic, but by a real labour of production. If man creates man, the artist produces works, *in determinate conditions*; he does not work on himself but on that thing which escapes him in so many ways, and never belongs to him until after the event.

The various 'theories' of creation all ignore the process of making; they omit any account of production. One can create undiminished, so, paradoxically, creation is the release of what is already there; or, one is witness of a sudden apparition, and then creation is an irruption, an epiphany, a mystery. In both instances any possible explanation of the change has been done away with; in the former, nothing has happened; and in the latter what has happened is inexplicable. All speculation over man the creator is intended to eliminate a real knowledge: the 'creative process' is, precisely, not a process, a labour; it is a religious formula to be found on funeral monuments.

For the same reasons, all considerations of genius, of the subjectivity of the artist, of his soul, are *on principle* uninteresting.

You will understand why, in this book, the word 'creation' is suppressed, and systematically replaced by 'production'.

23

MICHEL FOUCAULT

from 'What Is an Author?'

. . .

It is obviously insufficient to repeat empty slogans: the author has disappeared; God and man died a common death.[1] Rather, we should reexamine the empty space left by the author's disappearance; we should attentively observe, along its gaps and fault lines, its new demarcations, and the reapportionment of this void; we should await the fluid functions released by this disappearance. In this context we can briefly consider the problems that arise in the use of an author's name. What is the name of an author? How does it function? Far from offering a solution, I will attempt to indicate some of the difficulties related to these questions.

The name of an author poses all the problems related to the category of the proper name. (Here, I am referring to the work of John Searle,[2] among others.) Obviously not a pure and simple reference, the proper name (and the author's name as well) has other than indicative functions. It is more than a gesture, a finger pointed at someone; it is, to a certain extent, the equivalent of a description. When we say 'Aristotle,' we are using a word that means one or a series of definite descriptions of the type: 'the author of the *Analytics*,' or 'the founder of ontology,' and so forth.[3] Furthermore, a proper name has other functions than that of signification: when we discover that Rimbaud has not written *La Chasse spirituelle*, we cannot maintain that the meaning of the proper name or this author's name has been altered. The proper name and the name of an author oscillate between the poles of description and designation, and, granting that they are linked to what they name, they are not totally determined either by their descriptive or designative functions.[4] Yet – and it is here that the specific difficulties attending an author's name appear – the link between a proper name and the individual being named and the link between an author's name and that which it names are not isomorphous and do not function in the same way; and these differences require clarification.

To learn, for example, that Pierre Dupont does not have blue eyes, does not live in Paris, and is not a doctor does not invalidate the fact that the name, Pierre Dupont, continues to refer to the same person; there has been no modification of the designation that links the name to the person. With the name of an author, however, the problems are far more complex. The disclosure that Shakespeare was not born in the house that tourists now visit would not modify the functioning of the author's name, but, if it were proved that he had not written the sonnets that we attribute to him, this would constitute a significant change and affect the manner in which the author's name functions. Moreover, if we establish that Shakespeare wrote Bacon's *Organon* and that the same author was responsible for both the works of Shakespeare and those of Bacon, we would have introduced a third type of alteration which completely modifies the functioning of the author's name. Consequently, the name of an author is not precisely a proper name among others.

Many other factors sustain this paradoxical singularity of the name of an author. It is altogether different to maintain that Pierre Dupont does not exist and that Homer or Hermes Trismegistes have never existed. While the first negation merely implies that there is no one by the name of Pierre Dupont, the second indicates that several individuals have been referred to by one name or that the real author possessed none of the traits traditionally associated with Homer or Hermes. Neither is it the same thing to say that Jacques Durand, not Pierre Dupont, is the real name of X and that Stendhal's name was Henri Beyle. We could also examine the function and meaning of such statements as 'Bourbaki is this or that person,' and 'Victor Eremita, Climacus, Anticlimacus, Frater Taciturnus, Constantin Constantius, all of these are Kierkegaard.'

These differences indicate that an author's name is not simply an element of speech (as a subject, a complement, or an element that could be replaced by a pronoun or other parts of speech). Its presence is functional in that it serves as a means of classification. A name can group together a number of texts and thus differentiate them from others. A name also establishes different forms of relationships among texts. Neither Hermes not Hippocrates existed in the sense that we can say Balzac existed, but the fact that a number of texts were attached to a single name implies that relationships of homogeneity, filiation, reciprocal explanation, authentification, or of common utilization were established among them. Finally, the author's name characterizes a particular manner of existence of discourse. Discourse that possesses an author's name is not to be immediately consumed and forgotten; neither is it accorded the momentary attention given to ordinary, fleeting words. Rather, its status and its manner of reception are regulated by the culture in which it circulates.

We can conclude that, unlike a proper name, which moves from the interior of a discourse to the real person outside who produced it, the name of the author remains at the contours of texts – separating one from the other, defining their form, and characterizing their mode of existence. It points to the existence of certain groups of discourse and refers to the status of this discourse within a society and culture. The author's name is not a function of a man's civil status, nor is it fictional; it is situated in the breach, among the discontinuities, which gives rise to new groups of discourse and their singular mode of existence.[5] Consequently, we can say that in our culture, the name of an author is a variable that accompanies only certain texts to the exclusion of others: a private letter may have a signatory, but it does not have an author; a contract can have an underwriter, but not an author; and, similarly, an anonymous poster attached to a wall may have a writer, but he cannot be an author. In this sense, the function of an author is to characterize the existence, circulation, and operation of certain discourses within a society.

In dealing with the 'author' as a function of discourse, we must consider the characteristics of a discourse that support this use and determine its difference from other discourses. If we limit our remarks to only those books or texts with authors, we can isolate four different features.

First, they are objects of appropriation; the form of property they have become is of a particular type whose legal codification was accomplished some years ago. It is important to notice, as well, that its status as property is historically secondary to the penal code controlling its appropriation. Speeches and books were assigned real authors, other than mythical or important religious figures, only when the author became subject to punishment and to the extent that his discourse was considered transgressive. In our culture – undoubtedly in others as well

– discourse was not originally a thing, a product, or a possession, but an action situated in a bipolar field of sacred and profane, lawful and unlawful, religious and blasphemous. It was a gesture charged with risks long before it became a possession caught in a circuit of property values.[6] But it was at the moment when a system of ownership and strict copyright rules were established (towards the end of the eighteenth and beginning of the nineteenth century) that the transgressive properties always intrinsic to the act of writing became the forceful imperative of literature.[7] It is as if the author, at the moment he was accepted into the social order of property which governs our culture, was compensating for his new status by reviving the older bipolar field of discourse in a systematic practice of transgression and by restoring the danger of writing which, on another side, had been conferred the benefits of property.

Secondly, the 'author-function' is not universal or constant in all discourse. Even within our civilization, the same types of texts have not always required authors; there was a time when those texts which we now call 'literary' (stories, folk tales, epics, and tragedies) were accepted, circulated, and valorized without any question about the identity of their author. Their anonymity was ignored because their real or supposed age was a sufficient guarantee of their authenticity. Texts, however, that we now call 'scientific' (dealing with cosmology and the heavens, medicine or illness, the natural sciences or geography) were only considered truthful during the Middle Ages if the name of the author was indicated. Statements on the order of 'Hippocrates said . . .' or 'Pliny tells us that . . .' were not merely formulas for an argument based on authority; they marked a proven discourse. In the seventeenth and eighteenth centuries, a totally new conception was developed when scientific texts were accepted on their own merits and positioned within an anonymous and coherent conceptual system of established truths and methods of verification. Authentification no longer required reference to the individual who had produced them; the role of the author disappeared as an index of truthfulness and, where it remained as an inventor's name, it was merely to denote a specific theorem or proposition, a strange effect, a property, a body, a group of elements, or pathological syndrome.

At the same time, however, 'literary' discourse was acceptable only if it carried an author's name; every text of poetry or fiction was obliged to state its author and the date, place, and circumstance of its writing. The meaning and value attributed to the text depended on this information. If by accident or design a text was presented anonymously, every effort was made to locate its author. Literary anonymity was of interest only as a puzzle to be solved as, in our day, literary works are totally dominated by the sovereignty of the author. (Undoubtedly, these remarks are far too categorical. Criticism has been concerned for some time now with aspects of a text not fully dependent on the notion of an individual creator; studies of genre or the analysis of recurring textual motifs and their variations from a norm other than the author. Furthermore, where in mathematics the author has become little more than a handy reference for a particular theorem or group of propositions, the reference to an author in biology and medicine, or to the date of his research has a substantially different bearing. This latter reference, more than simply indicating the source of information, attests to the 'reliability' of the evidence, since it entails an appreciation of the techniques and experimental materials available at a given time and in a particular laboratory.)

The third point concerning this 'author-function' is that it is not formed spontaneously through the simple attribution of a discourse to an individual. It results from a complex operation whose purpose is to construct the rational entity we call an author. Undoubtedly, this construction is assigned a 'realistic' dimension as we speak of an individual's 'profundity' or 'creative' power, his intentions or the original inspiration manifested in writing. Nevertheless, these aspects of an individual, which we designate as an author (or which comprise an individual as an author), are projections, in terms always more or less psychological, of our way of handling texts: in the comparisons we make, the traits we extract as pertinent, the continuities we assign, or the exclusions we practice. In addition, all these operations vary according to the period and the form of discourse concerned. A 'philosopher' and a 'poet' are not constructed in the same manner; and the author of an eighteenth-century novel was formed differently from the modern novelist. There are, nevertheless, transhistorical constants in the rules that govern the construction of an author.

In literary criticism, for example, the traditional methods for defining an author – or, rather, for determining the configuration of the author from existing texts – derive in large part from those used in the Christian tradition to authenticate (or to reject) the particular texts in its possession. Modern criticism, in its desire to 'recover' the author from a work, employs devices strongly reminiscent of Christian exegesis when it wished to prove the value of a text by ascertaining the holiness of its author. In *De Viris Illustribus*, Saint Jerome maintains that homonymy is not proof of the common authorship of several works, since many individuals could have the same name or someone could have perversely appropriated another's name. The name, as an individual mark, is not sufficient as it relates to a textual tradition. How, then, can several texts be attributed to an individual author? What norms, related to the function of the author, will disclose the involvement of several authors? According to Saint Jerome, there are four criteria: the texts that must be eliminated from the list of works attributed to a single author are those inferior to the others (thus, the author is defined as a standard level of quality); those whose ideas conflict with the doctrine expressed in the others (here the author is defined as a certain field of conceptual or theoretical coherence); those written in a different style and containing words and phrases not ordinarily found in the other works (the author is seen as a stylistic uniformity); and those referring to events or historical figures subsequent to the death of the author (the author is thus a definite historical figure in which a series of events converge). Although modern criticism does not appear to have these same suspicions concerning authentication, its strategies for defining the author present striking similarities. The author explains the presence of certain events within a text, as well as their transformations, distortions, and their various modifications (and this through an author's biography or by reference to his particular point of view, in the analysis of his social preferences and his position within a class or by delineating his fundamental objectives). The author also constitutes a principle of unity in writing where any unevenness of production is ascribed to changes caused by evolution, maturation, or outside influence. In addition, the author serves to neutralize the contradictions that are found in a series of texts. Governing this function is the belief that there must be – at a particular level of an author's thought, of his conscious or unconscious desire – a point where contradictions are resolved, where the incompatible elements can be shown to relate to one another or to cohere around a fundamental and originating contradiction. Finally, the author is a particular source of expression who, in more or less finished forms, is manifested equally well, and with similar validity, in a text, in letters, fragments, drafts, and so forth. Thus, even while Saint Jerome's four principles of authenticity might seem largely inadequate to modern critics, they, nevertheless, define the critical modalities now used to display the function of the author.[9]

However, it would be false to consider the function of the author as a pure and simple reconstruction after the fact of a text given as passive material, since a text always bears a number of signs that refer to the author. Well known to grammarians, these textual signs are personal pronouns, adverbs of time and place, and the conjugation of verbs.[10] But it is important to note that these elements have a different bearing on texts with an author and on those without one. In the latter, these 'shifters' refer to a real speaker and to an actual deictic situation, with certain exceptions such as the case of indirect speech in the first person. When discourse is linked to an author, however, the role of 'shifters' is more complex and variable. It is well known that in a novel narrated in the first person, neither the first person pronoun, the present indicative tense, nor, for that matter, its signs of localization refer directly to the writer, either to the time when he wrote, or to the specific act of writing; rather, they stand for a 'second self'[11] whose similarity to the author is never fixed and undergoes considerable alteration within the course of a single book. It would be as false to seek the author in relation to the actual writer as to the fictional narrator; the 'author-function' arises out of their scission – in the division and distance of the two. One might object that this phenomenon only applies to novels or poetry, to a context of 'quasi-discourse,' but, in fact, all discourse that supports this 'author-function' is characterized by this plurality of egos. In a mathematical treatise, the ego who indicates the circumstances of composition in the preface is not identical, either in terms of his position or his function, to the 'I' who concludes a demonstration within the body of the text. The former implies a unique individual who, at a given time and place, succeeded in completing a project, whereas the latter indicates an instance and plan of demonstration that anyone could perform provided the same set of axioms, preliminary operations, and an identical set of symbols were used. It is also possible to locate a third ego: one who speaks of the goals of his investigation, the obstacles encountered, its results, and the problems yet to be solved and this 'I' would function in a field of existing or future mathematical discourses. We are not dealing with a system of dependencies where a first and essential use of the 'I' is reduplicated, as a kind of fiction, by the other two. On the contrary, the 'author-function' in such discourses operates so as to effect the simultaneous dispersion of the three egos.[12]

Further elaboration would, of course, disclose other characteristics of the 'author-function,' but I have limited myself to the four that seemed the most obvious and important. They can be summarized in the following manner: the 'author-function' is tied to the legal and institutional systems that circumscribe, determine, and articulate the realm of discourses; it does not operate in a uniform manner in all discourses, at all times, and in any given culture; it is not defined by the spontaneous attribution of a text to its creator, but through a series of precise and complex procedures; it does not refer, purely and simply, to an actual individual insofar as it simultaneously gives rise to a variety of egos and to a series of subjective positions that individuals of any class may come to occupy.

I am aware that until now I have kept my subject within unjustifiable limits; I should also have spoken of the 'author-function' in painting, music, technical fields, and so forth. Admitting that my analysis is restricted to the domain of discourse, it seems that I have given the term 'author' an excessively narrow meaning. I have discussed the author only in the limited sense of a person to whom the production of a text, a book, or a work can be legitimately attributed. However, it is obvious that even within the realm of discourse a person can be the author of much more than a book – of a theory, for instance, of a tradition or a discipline within which new books and authors can proliferate. For convenience, we could say that such authors occupy a 'transdiscursive' position.

Homer, Aristotle, and the Church Fathers played this role, as did the first mathematicians and the originators of the Hippocratic tradition. This type of author is surely as old as our civilization. But I believe that the nineteenth century in Europe produced a singular type of author who should not be confused with 'great' literary authors, or the authors of canonical religious texts, and the founders of sciences. Somewhat arbitrarily, we might call them 'initiators of discursive practices.'

The distinctive contribution of these authors is that they produced not only their own work, but the possibility and the rules of formation of other texts. In this sense, their role differs entirely from that of a novelist, for example, who is basically never more than the author of his own text. Freud is not simply the author of *The Interpretation of Dreams* or of *Wit and its Relation to the Unconscious* and Marx is not simply the author of the *Communist Manifesto* or *Capital*: they both established the endless possibility of discourse. Obviously, an easy objection can be made. The author of a novel may be responsible for more than his own text; if he acquires some 'importance' in the literary world, his influence can have significant ramifications. To take a very simple example, one could say that Ann Radcliffe did not simply write *The Mysteries of Udolpho* and a few other novels, but also made possible the appearance of Gothic Romances at the beginning of the nineteenth century. To this extent, her function as an author exceeds the limits of her work. However, this objection can be answered by the fact that the possibilities disclosed by the initiators of discursive practices (using the examples of Marx and Freud, whom I believe to be the first and the most important) are significantly different from those suggested by novelists. The novels of Ann Radcliffe put into circulation a certain number of resemblances and analogies patterned on her work – various characteristic signs, figures, relationships, and structures that could be integrated into other books. In short, to say that Ann Radcliffe created the Gothic Romance means that there are certain elements common to her works and to the nineteenth-century Gothic romance: the heroine ruined by her own innocence, the secret fortress that functions as a countercity, the outlaw-hero who swears revenge on the world that has cursed him, etc. On the other hand, Marx and Freud, as 'initiators of discursive practices,' not only made possible a certain number of analogies that could be adopted by future texts, but, as importantly, they also made possible a certain number of differences. They cleared a space for the introduction of elements other than their own, which, nevertheless, remain within the field of discourse they initiated. In saying that Freud founded psychoanalysis, we do not simply mean that the concept of libido or the techniques of dream analysis reappear in the writings of Karl Abraham or Melanie Klein, but that he made possible a certain number of differences with respect to his books, concepts, and hypotheses, which all arise out of psychoanalytic discourse.

Is this not the case, however, with the founder of any new science or of any author who successfully transforms an existing science? After all, Galileo is indirectly responsible for the texts of those who mechanically applied the laws he formulated, in addition to having paved the way for the production of statements far different from his own. If Cuvier is the founder of biology and Saussure of linguistics, it is not because they were imitated or that an organic concept or a theory of the sign was uncritically integrated into new texts, but because Cuvier, to a certain extent, made possible a theory of evolution diametrically opposed to his own system and because Saussure made possible a generative grammar radically different from his own structural analysis. Superficially, then, the initiation of discursive practices appears similar to the founding of any scientific endeavor, but I believe there is a fundamental difference.

In a scientific program, the founding act is on an equal footing with its future transformations: it is merely one among the many modifications that it makes possible. This interdependence can take several forms. In the future development of a science, the founding act may appear as little more than a single instance of a more general phenomenon that has been discovered. It might be questioned, in retrospect, for being too intuitive or empirical and submitted to the rigors of new theoretical operations in order to situate it in a formal domain. Finally, it might be thought a hasty generalization whose validity should be restricted. In other words, the founding act of a science can always be rechanneled through the machinery of transformations it has instituted.[13]

On the other hand, the initiation of a discursive practice is heterogeneous to its ulterior transformations. To extend psychoanalytic practice, as initiated by Freud, is not to presume a formal generality that was not claimed at the outset; it is to explore a number of possible applications. To limit it is to isolate in the original texts a small set of propositions or statements that are recognized as having an inaugurative value and that mark other Freudian concepts or theories as derivative. Finally, there are no 'false' statements in the work of these initiators; those statements considered inessential or 'prehistoric,' in that they are associated with another discourse, are simply neglected in favor of the more pertinent aspects of the work. The initiation of a discursive practice, unlike the founding of a science, overshadows and is necessarily detached from its later developments and transformations. As a consequence, we define the theoretical validity of a statement with respect to the work of the initiator, whereas in the case of Galileo or Newton, it is based on the structural and intrinsic norms established in cosmology or physics. Stated schematically, the work of these initiators is not situated in relation to a science or in the space it defines; rather, it is science or discursive practice that relate to their works as the primary points of reference.

In keeping with this distinction, we can understand why it is inevitable that practitioners of such discourses must 'return to the origin.' Here, as well, it is necessary to distinguish a 'return' from scientific 'rediscoveries' or 'reactivations.' 'Rediscoveries' are the effects of analogy or isomorphism with current forms of knowledge that allow the perception of forgotten or obscured figures. For instance, Chomsky in his book on Cartesian grammar[14] 'rediscovered' a form of knowledge that had been in use from Cordemoy to Humboldt. It could only be understood from the perspective of generative grammar because this later manifestation held the key to its construction: in effect, a retrospective codification of an historical position. 'Reactivation' refers to something quite different: the insertion of discourse into totally new domains of generalization, practice, and transformations. The history of mathematics abounds in examples of this phenomenon as the work of Michel Serres on mathematical anamnesis shows.[15]

The phrase, 'return to,' designates a movement with its proper specificity, which characterizes the initiation of discursive practices. If we return, it is because of a basic and constructive omission, an omission that is not the result of accident or incomprehension.[16] In effect, the act of initiation is such, in its essence, that it is inevitably subjected to its own distortions; that which displays this act and derives from it is, at the same time, the root of its divergences and travesties. This nonaccidental omission must be regulated by precise operations that can be situated, analysed, and reduced in a return to the act of initiation. The barrier imposed by omission was not added from the outside; it arises from the discursive practice in question, which gives it its law. Both the cause of the barrier and the means for its removal, this omission – also responsible for the obstacles that prevent returning to the act of initiation – can only be resolved by a return. In addition, it is always a return to a text in itself, specifically, to a primary and unadorned text with particular attention to those things registered in the interstices of the text, its gaps and absences. We return to those empty spaces that have been masked by omission or concealed in a false and misleading plenitude. In these rediscoveries of an essential lack, we find the oscillation of two characteristic responses: 'This point was made – you can't help seeing it if you know how to read'; or, inversely, 'No, that point is not made in any of the printed words in the text, but it is expressed through the words, in their relationships and in the distance that separates them.' It follows naturally that this return, which is a part of the discursive mechanism, constantly introduces modifications and that the return to a text is not a historical supplement that would come to fix itself upon the primary discursivity and redouble it in the form of an ornament which, after all, is not essential. Rather, it is an effective and necessary means of transforming discursive practice. A study of Galileo's works could alter our knowledge of the history, but not the science, of mechanics; whereas, a reexamination of the books of Freud or Marx can transform our understanding of psychoanalysis or Marxism.

A last feature of these returns is that they tend to reinforce the enigmatic link between an author and his works. A text has an inaugurative value precisely because it is the work of a particular author, and our returns are conditioned by this knowledge. The rediscovery of an unknown text by Newton or Cantor will not modify classical cosmology or group theory; at most, it will change our appreciation of their historical genesis. Bringing to light, however, *An Outline of Psychoanalysis*, to the extent that we recognize it as a book by Freud, can transform not only our historical knowledge, but the field of psychoanalytic theory – if only through a shift of accent or of the center of gravity. These returns, an important component of discursive practices, form a relationship between 'fundamental' and mediate authors, which is not identical to that which links an ordinary text to its immediate author.

These remarks concerning the initiation of discursive practices have been extremely schematic, especially with regard to the opposition I have tried to trace between this initiation and the founding of sciences. The distinction between the two is not readily discernible; moreover, there is no proof that the two procedures are mutually exclusive. My only purpose in setting up this opposition, however, was to show that the 'author-function,' sufficiently complex at the level of a book or a series of texts that bear a definite signature, has other determining factors when analysed in terms of larger entities – groups of works or entire disciplines.

Unfortunately, there is a decided absence of positive propositions in this essay, as it applies to analytic procedures or directions for future research, but I ought at least to give the reasons why I attach such importance to a continuation of this work. Developing a similar analysis could provide the basis for a typology of discourse. A typology of this sort cannot be adequately understood in relation to the grammatical features, formal structures, and objects of discourse, because there undoubtedly exist specific discursive properties or relationships that are irreducible to the rules of grammar and logic and to the laws that govern objects. These properties require investigation if we hope to distinguish the larger categories of discourse. The different forms of relationships (or nonrelationships) that an author can assume are evidently one of these discursive properties.

This form of investigation might also permit the introduction of an historical analysis of discourse. Perhaps the time has come to study not only the expressive value and formal transformations of discourse, but its mode of existence: the modifications and variations, within any culture, of modes of circulation, valorization, attribution, and appropriation. Partially at the expense of themes and concepts that an author places in his work, the 'author-function' could also reveal the manner in which discourse is articulated on the basis of social relationships.

Is it not possible to reexamine, as a legitimate extension of this kind of analysis, the privileges of the subject? Clearly, in undertaking an internal and architectonic analysis of a work (whether it be a literary text, a philosophical system, or a scientific work) and in delimiting psychological and biographical references, suspicions arise concerning the absolute nature and creative role of the subject. But the subject should not be entirely abandoned. It should be reconsidered, not to restore the theme of an originating subject, but to seize its functions, its intervention in discourse, and its system of dependencies. We should suspend the typical questions: how does a free subject penetrate the density of things and endow them with meaning; how does it accomplish its design by animating the rules of discourse from within? Rather, we should ask: under what conditions and through what forms can an entity like the subject appear in the order of discourse; what position does it occupy; what functions does it exhibit; and what rules does it follow in each type of discourse? In short, the subject (and its substitutes) must be stripped of its creative role and analysed as a complex and variable function of discourse.

The author – or what I have called the 'author-function' – is undoubtedly only one of the possible specifications of the subject and, considering past historical transformations, it appears that the form, the complexity, and even the existence of this function are far from immutable. We can easily imagine a culture where discourse would circulate without any need for an author. Discourses, whatever their status, form, or value, and regardless of our manner of handling them, would unfold in a pervasive anonymity. No longer the tiresome repetitions:

'Who is the real author?'

'Have we proof of his authenticity and originality?'

'What has he revealed of his most profound self in his language?'

New questions will be heard:

'What are the modes of existence of this discourse?'

'Where does it come from; how is it circulated; who controls it?'

'What placements are determined for possible subjects?'

'Who can fulfill these diverse functions of the subject?'

Behind all these questions we would hear little more than the murmur of indifference:

'What matter who's speaking?'

NOTES

1. Nietzsche, *The Gay Science*, III, 108.
2. John Searle, *Speech Acts: An Essay in the Philosophy of Language* (Cambridge: Cambridge University Press, 1969), pp. 162–74.
3. Ibid., p. 169.
4. Ibid., p. 172.
5. This is a particularly important point and brings together a great many of Foucault's insights concerning the relationship of an author (subject) to discourse. It reflects his understanding of the traditional and often unexamined unities of discourse whose actual discontinuities are resolved in either of two ways: by reference to an originating subject or to a language, conceived as plenitude, which supports the activities of commentary or interpretation. But since Foucault rejects the belief in the presumed fullness of language that underlies discourse, the author is subjected to the same fragmentation which characterizes discourse and he is delineated as a discontinuous series; for example, see *L'Ordre du discours*, pp. 54–55 and 61–62.
6. In a seminar entitled 'L'Epreuve et l'enquête,' which Foucault conducted at the University of Montreal in the spring of 1974, he centered the debate around the following question: is the general conviction that truth derives from and is sustained by knowledge not simply a recent phenomenon, a limited case of the ancient and widespread belief that truth is a function of events? In an older time and in other cultures, the search for truth was hazardous in the extreme and truth resided in a danger zone, but if this was so and if truth could only be approached after a long preparation or through the details of a ritualized procedure, it was because it represented power. Discourse, for these cultures, was an active appropriation of power and to the extent that it was successful, it contained the power of truth itself, charged with all its risks and benefits.
7. Cf. *The Order of Things*, p. 300; and above, 'A Preface to Transgression', pp. 30–33.
8. Foucault's phrasing of the 'author-function' has been retained. This concept should not be confused (as it was by Goldmann in the discussion that followed Foucault's presentation) with the celebrated theme of the 'death of man' in *The Order of Things* (pp. 342 and 386). On the contrary, Foucault's purpose is to revitalize the debate surrounding the subject by situating the subject, as a fluid function, within the space cleared by archaeology.
9. See Evaristo Arns, *La Technique du livre d'après Saint Jerome* (Paris, 1953).
10. On personal pronouns ('shifters'), see R. Jakobson, *Selected Writings* (Paris: Mouton, 1971), II, 130–32; and *Essais de linguistique générale* (Paris, 1966), p. 252. For its general implications, see Eugenio Donato, 'Of Structuralism and Literature,' *MLN*, 82 (1967), 556–58. On adverbs of time and place, see Emile Benveniste, *Problèmes de la linguistique générale* (Paris, 1966), pp. 237–50.
11. Cf. Wayne C. Booth, *The Rhetoric of Fiction* (Chicago: Univ. of Chicago Press, 1961), pp. 67–77.
12. This conclusion relates to Foucault's concern in developing a 'philosophy of events' as described in *L'Ordre du discours*, pp. 60–61: 'I trust that we can agree that I do not refer to a succession of moments in time, nor to a diverse plurality of thinking subjects; I refer to a caesura which fragments the moment and disperses the subject into a plurality of possible positions and functions.'
13. Cf. the discussion of disciplines in *L'Ordre du discours*, pp. 31–38.
14. Noam Chomsky, *Cartesian Linguistics* (New York: Harper & Row, 1966).
15. *La Communication: Hermes I* (Paris: Editions de Minuit, 1968), pp. 78–112.
16. For a discussion of the recent reorientation of the sign, see Foucault's 'Nietzsche, Freud, Marx.' On the role of repetition, Foucault writes in *L'Ordre du discours*: 'The new is not found in what is said, but in the event of its return' (p. 28).

24

MOLLY NESBIT

'What Was an Author?'

All Authors
What with the multiplication of reproductive processes, of the
means of distribution, and the complexity of the techniques of
creation, the identity of the author is more and more difficult to
grasp and define. The paternity of a work, then, indefinable?
— *Les Immatériaux* (1985)

The French definition of the author has gone vague: the author is a
general case, an orphan, some say corpse. It is a definition too diffuse to
be useful; worse, it strips the author of distinction. As if in flight from
such a fate, lately French authors have become authors by doing other
things besides write; they may make music, psychoanalysis, Sartres,
maps. Whatever the result, it is diffused, scattered across an immense
accumulation of spectacle, the 'magazine covers, illustrations, ads, slick
and pulp fiction, comics, Tin Pan Alley music, tap dancing, Hollywood
movies, etc.,' Greenberg's kitsch.[1] Those who go looking for authors
must devise the means by which to recognize not only the worker but the
work; at some point, perhaps by night, culture was camouflaged.

The situation of positive unclarity regarding the author has given rise
to a growing body of criticism, full of dire pronouncements about the
plight of culture, author death, and postmodern conditions; apocalypse
weighs on the wind.[2] And yet, bourgeois culture has not changed all
that much in the past two hundred years. Historically, bourgeois
culture was always a little too crude to be believed. Where others cried
vulgar, we rather lamely call vague. This crudeness so essential and so

troubling is not difficult to find: we need only pose the question about what the author was.

Many have worked on an answer to the author question. They have usually been concerned with two kinds of evidence: the explicit statements written out by the authors themselves and the implicit, quiet assertions made in authorial practice. Like Mallarmé's explicit variation on the subject, written in 1895:

> The pure work involves the disappearance of the poet's voice, ceding initiative to the words mobilized by the clash of their disparity; they illuminate one another in reciprocal reflections like a virtual trail of sparks on gem stones, replacing the breathing perceptible in the old lyric inspiration or the personal, enthusiastic direction of the phrase.[3]

. . . In order to gauge the full extent of authorship, it is necessary to move outside the author's house. A more reliable standard of measurement must be found. Fortunately such a standard exists: we find it in the law.

Authors of all kinds have for a long time been flatly equated in the law, though the equation is not made using the familiar terms like creativity, genius, and ancient lyric breath. It is instead an equation of rights. The legal definition of the author is windless, dry, and plain: the author is given rights to a cultural space over which he or she may range and work; all authors share the same cultural space; they are defined by their presence there as well as by their rights to it. Through the law, then, we can gauge the author and the work. But let us not look to the law for the easy answer: the same law that defines the author is responsible for much of the confusion about what authors were and are. French copyright law dates from the Revolution; the landmark law on author's rights was enacted in 1793; it governed *droits d'auteur* until 1957, when it was revised. In 1985 it was revised again.

> The law of 1793 gave authors privileges that ordinary men did not enjoy: The authors of every kind of writing, the composers of music, the painters and draughtsmen who have their paintings and drawings engraved, will enjoy the exclusive and lifetime right to sell, to have sold and to distribute their work in the territory of the Republic and to cede the same in toto or in part.[4]

In other words, authors retained property rights over the fruits of their labor even after their work was sold to somebody else. That was the essence of the privilege. The rights themselves could be ceded or sold but this took a separate operation and was not assumed to be the natural part of any deal. The *droits d'auteur* were applied to any work done in the designated media, writing, music composition, painting, drawing, and engraving, basically those media that could be worked up into forms of high culture like poems, sonatinas, and red chalk sketches. The law did not even try to draw lines between good and bad work in these media and it did not presume to erect criteria for aesthetic quality. Slipshod failures and drawn reproductions were covered by the same rights as the masterpiece: a hack and a Mallarmé would both be called authors; an engraver of Salon paintings had just as much claim to the title as an Ingres.[5] The cultural field is broad, said the law. It covered kitsch, avant-garde, low, high, and middle brow work with equal justice. Authors were not necessarily artists.

The law did not divide culture into states. It set out a single field where standards were blurred and the different hierarchies of the arts eroded, irrelevant. Others in academies and newspaper columns and university lectures could and did quibble, insisting on other definitions of culture with genres, standards, traditions, and rules. The law let these storms erupt around it. It held like bedrock, content to make only basic distinctions. It entered the Napoleonic Code and as the nineteenth century progressed, it acquired more nuance in the courts. But historically the law of 1793 set a breathtaking precedent that was not to be undone. Its definitions of culture survived all the others: the collapse of the hierarchy of genres and the slow death of the Salon made no difference to it; neither did the rise of the mass-produced, printed forms of culture. The law had already leveled the academic distinctions; in its very practical, authoritative terms, culture was flat.

In the law, the term author did not and does not carry with it a mark of supreme distinction, nor did it designate a particular profession, like poet. It was only meant to distinguish a particular kind of labor from another, the cultural from the industrial. This is the gist, the germ, the deep essential crudeness. According to the law, the privileged, cultural form of labor exhibited certain qualities. First, it took shape only in the certified media. Second, its privilege was justified by the presence of a human intelligence, imagination, and labor that were legible in the work, meaning that such work was seen, a little more crudely, to contain the reflection of the author's personality.[6] The cultural forms of labor could, conversely, be identified from the material used and by the imprint of the author's personality which would follow from working in this material. These two qualities of material and reflected personality were linked; they became inseparable. In the nineteenth century there was only one exception made to this marriage between matter and spirit; drawing, divided in two because technical drawing had been compromised. The compromises were produced by industry; they resulted in the technical drawing's fall from grace. The compromises also point to something clear in the broad and blurry cultural field: they are the black marks that show where the edge of culture lay.

The technical drawing fell from culture because it had participated in the manufacture of industrial objects. In this exceptional case, drawing, the material, was *not* felt to reflect the personality of the draughtsman. The bond between matter and spirit had been broken. In fact these sentiments were motivated by the basest instincts: industry did not want authors in its ranks; it wanted control over the property rights to every phase of production, from technical drawing to finished commodity. In 1806, the silk manufacturers of Lyon obtained this distinction in law from Napoleon: this had the effect of exiling the technical drawing from the cultural field and exempting its maker from *droits d'auteur*; its status was thereafter defined by another set of laws protecting industrial design.[7] Still, for our purposes, the episode is instructive. Clearly the authorial media were not naturally, as it were, cultural; one saw what one wanted in them; one refused to see a self-reflecting author in the technical drawing. Later in the century, in 1891, the courts refused to see the author in the poster; no matter if there was an established artist involved.[8] And so, in France manufactured goods, designs and objects alike, were not officially allowed to embody the personality of their makers or the signs of abstract human labor: they were not to display any evidence of the commodity's fetishism.[9] manufactured goods were to be magically simple, not self-centered, not meant to serve the spiritual needs of the community the way books and pictures did. They served material needs. In essence the law of 1806 recorded the limits of a modern culture, limits which were inscribed in the economy.

Modern culture existed as an economic distinction, in effect a protected market that functioned within the regular economy. Authored work was always understood to be circulating in the market, generally in printed form. This had already been an element of the 1793 law, which had been necessary in the first place because the market for culture needed to be policed. Yet after 1793 authors were unlike other laborers: the law had given them some rights to their work; even as it moved through the economy, their work remained their property. The law played a critical, though largely unrecognized, role in the definition of modern culture. Daily the law stood by to arbitrate, to provide a practical definition of what an author was and where cultural work was to be done. It conceived of the cultural field as a marketplace and it was precisely in this place where culture (modernism too) would perforce develop. Time strengthened the law. For the duration of the nineteenth century, its terms remained sacrosanct; in a series of modifications in 1844, 1854, and 1866, the author's heirs won the rights to the work for fifty years after the author's death but the rights and regulations for authors themselves did not, in the essentials, change.[10] In theory and in practice, in all sectors of daily life, the cultural was always being distinguished from its other, the industrial; culture's basic identity was always being derived from this distinction, which was always exceptional and always economic.

The copyright law regulated the market economy for culture at the same time that it set it apart from the regular economy. The law did nothing more than negotiate the dialectical movement between the two economies with a maximum of simplicity and efficiency; it was functional but servile, something of a butler. Though it furnished the apparatus so that culture could work, it had drawbacks: for example, it could not be expected to accommodate uninvited guests. These began to arrive over the course of the same nineteenth century, new technologies and new materials for word, sound, and image; it was not long before the photograph, the phonograph, and the cinematograph all became candidates for copyright. They tested the limits of the law in yet another way. To give these producers the status of authors involved granting the new technologies (the technologies we have come to associate with mass culture) the status of the materials of aristocratic culture (the culture we have come to call high). The law, for all its apparent elasticity, could not handle such a request overnight.[11] Curiously, the problem lay not with the low order of culture but with the nature of the labor involved, a labor integrally connected to machines. Printing presses were one thing, cameras quite another, and no small stumbling block; they kept the French law from granting the technological authors their rights until 1957, long after the law had been modified to take in architecture and sculpture (1902), a good seventy years behind the law of other industrialized nations.[12] But to account for the technologies, the law could not be modified; it had to be rewritten.

In their hundred-year effort to gain these privileges, those who made photographs, records, and movies were obliged to devise justifications for the value of their materials, their medium, and for their rights to use the title, author. They and their advocates argued with the law; they produced their own voluminous definition of the author.[13] Their definition follows a pattern. Generally it was maintained that a human factor overrode the mechanical process; upon close inspection, a human mark, the trace of a cultural act, could be discerned. Alphonse Lamartine wrote one such apologia: initially he had condemned the photograph as abject, a plagiarism of nature, utterly soulless; after seeing the work of Adam Salomon, he changed his mind and wrote a public retraction. He explained that the photograph needed to be seen as the result of the particular photographer's labor. This was typical enough but he went one better: the photographer worked principally with nature, to wit, the sun, Lamartine claimed, and left the machine out of it entirely.[14] Hippolyte Taine made a more pragmatic contribution to the debate: 'Photographic work,' he wrote; 'is property; it belongs to the producer under the same title that gives the engraving to the engraver, and in the two cases, the property should be protected.[15] For all the rhetoric, which culminated in the claims for photography as a fine art, the objective of the photographers was simply to occupy a place in culture; they would have been content with lowlying regions, the wetlands of the field. Listen to the photographer Bulloz in 1890 arguing for his rights:

> All that we are claiming is that a photograph can take on the character of a personal creation. There is no question here of sentiment; photographers are not demanding to be assimilated to the ranks of the master painters; none of them would dream of asking the law to declare them the equal of Baudry or Cabanel.[16]

These terms were neither academic, nor gratuitous: if they succeeded, they could have real social, legal, and market value. This is why the photographers' offensive provoked the fierce debate that is with us still. They can be accused of throwing the definition of the author permanently up in the air.

The positive, defining justifications of the photographers and their kind, not to mention the volume of photographs, records and movies they made, were read, considered, and critiqued. In the response to this invasion, we can locate another, defensive discourse on the author, a relatively negative discourse that worried. It worried over the decline of the author and the old hierarchies of the arts; it disliked the new forms of labor; it wrongly pinned the trouble on the use of the machine, seeing it as a barrier that prevented the imprint of a human being's spirit on a certified, authorial material; it mourned a mirror stage of cultural work in which the self appeared and could reflect; it saw a dark future with no guaranteed Ideal-I. The debate lengthened, still other positions were developed and these are the famous ones, the essays of Mallarmé, Benjamin, Foucault, and Barthes.[17] This discourse .had little effect upon the disposition of the law, which continued on with its duties, maintained the cultural distinctions such as they already were, and upheld its brute definition of cultural work. But while all this talk was going on, the new technologies had imposed themselves and other, newer technologies, like television, had arrived. This seemed to warrant a revision of the law. The older but not the newest culture by technology was legalized in 1957.

The 1957 law expanded the definition of the author to include those who worked in dance and pantomime, cinema and photography, translation and maps. Industrial design and advertising were denied admission. The field of culture had grown vast however and the text of the law had grown longer too:

> The disposition of the present law protects the rights of authors and covers all work of the mind, whatever the kind, the form of expression, the merit or the destination. The following are considered work of the mind: books, brochures and other literary, artistic, and scientific writing; lectures, speeches, oaths, pleas and other work of this nature; drama and musical theatre; choreography and pantomime when the work is recorded in writing or otherwise; musical compositions with or without words; cinema and work obtained by an analogous process; drawing, painting, architecture, sculpture, engraving, lithography; artistic and documentary photography and work obtained by an analogous process; the applied arts; illustrations, maps; plans, sketches and models related to geography, topography, architecture or the sciences. The authors of translations, adaptations, transformations or arrangements of works of the mind enjoy protection under this law, without prejudice to the rights of the author of the original work. The same follows for those authors of anthologies or collections of diverse work who by the choice and arrangement of the material do the work of intellectual creation.

Titles were protected as well as works and even the name of the author was covered:

> The author enjoys this right with respect to his name, his quality, and his work. This right is attached to his person.[18]

Authorship still covered all levels of culture, high and low, but it had now spread to many media and to the separate signifiers of authorial work, like the title and the name of the author. The author's name alone could signal the body of his work so effectively that even in a detached state, the name was covered with *droits*.

After 1957 authorship was identified by more than a happy combination of a medium and a person: it could designate a rather immaterial position, a reputation and a generalized cluster of forms, stereotypes, trademarks. It was not so clear where one should be looking to find the reflection of the author's self. Authorship had become patently defined now by the reproduction of the work; it had taken on many of the characteristics of overtly commercial, brand name products; in many cases there was no single original. The law tried to cover all possible situations; it made special provision for collaborative work, such as cinema, where there was no single author.

Cinema, in fact, needed special consideration by the law. It bestowed author's rights on directors, and in this way only served the *politique des auteurs* that had been mounted during the 1950s by the *Cahiers du Cinéma*, but it also gave rights to some of the other members of the film crew, notably to the writers and the composers, and it gave control over the finished work to the production company.[19] This denied the contribution made by those who worked on the image itself and it had the effect of submitting all the authors to the will of the producer. It amounted to an authorial control by capital. The law recognized the open exploitation of the cultural field by a culture industry, as Bernard Edelman has brilliantly demonstrated; it furthermore made cultural property, the fantasmic cinema no less, take on some of the characteristics of ordinary, gritty, factory-made work. The modernization of the law in 1957 began to undermine the old, clear distinction between culture and industry.

The law ushered in a new level of *ennui* for those wanting to understand what an author is. It had cut into the mass media, pulling Hollywood film and news photography in and leaving advertising out, making the legal distinction between culture, the culture industry, and industry even more arbitary than before. It made it more difficult to conceive of a single mass culture. The new law's definition of the author did not adequately explain what constitutes creative work or what separates it from the run of the mill. It did not explain the privileged economic dynamic of the cultural field. It did not explain that this field is actually industry's inner sanctum. It did not explain that cultural forms can be industrially produced. It did not help us to make a clear distinction between the cultural subject and the industrial subject. The law however is not supposed to explain itself. That work takes place elsewhere. Explanations were not slow in coming but they were seldom adequate. The author question has kept coming up. Michel Foucault was led to ask it once again in 1969.

Foucault did not call in the law to supply answers to his essay question, 'What is an Author?'; oddly, he did not even mention it. He was more concerned to see what knowledge had made of the author and to understand why most intellectuals were calling the author a dead letter. Foucault therefore undertook to measure the disappearance of the author, though much of what he measured is actually the difference between the old law and the new. The sum of these differences, according to Foucault, amounted to this:

> We can conclude that, unlike a proper name, which moves from the interior of a discourse to the real person outside who produced it, the name of the author remains at the contour of texts – separating one from the other, defining their form, and characterizing their mode of existence. It points to the existence of certain groups of discourse and refers to the status of this discourse within a society and culture. The author's name is not a function of a man's civil status, nor is it fictional; it is situated in the breach, among the discontinuities, which gives rise to new groups of discourse and their singular mode of existence. Consequently, we can say that in our culture, the name of an author is a variable that accompanies only certain texts to the exclusion of others: a private letter may have signatory, but it does not have an author; a contract can have an underwriter but not an author; and, similarly, an anonymous poster attached to a wall may have a writer, but he cannot be an author. In this sense, the function of an author is to characterize the existence, circulation, and operation of certain discourses within a society.[20]

Foucault's essay turns on some of the law's new points, notably the name of the author and its separate existence, its ability to designate what Foucault calls an author-function. But when he separated the authors from the writers, he was not technically correct: one remained an author so long as one did not abandon one's rights; certain kinds of employment, underwriting and some kinds of journalism, for example, involved such an abdication. And when Foucault described the circulation and operation of discourses, he neglected to explain that this takes place within a market economy even though this economic condition, we have seen, defined the author in the first place. But the economy is Foucault's blind spot. His author had to exist in a

disembodied, non reflecting, dispersed state, in knowledge, not in
the world. This led him to posit an author disconnected from the
procedures of everyday life, something which experience tells us is
simply not true. Authors function, whether the state of knowledge
recognizes their existence or not.

   . . .

In 1982 the French legislature had to concern itself with yet another
negotiation between the zones of culture and industry, the trouble at
the border caused this time by the appearance of new technological
materials and a new stage in industrial production, late capitalism. On
the surface of it, the new copyright law, passed in July 1985, looks to be
an amendment of the old: rights are extended to some neglected
groups, the performers, including circus performers and puppeteers,
and the typographic designers, and to two new media, to what is in
France called the audiovisual (in America video) and to computer
software.[21] Certain clarifications in the drawing up of contracts have
made it possible to acquire a kind of copyright for advertising. But the
extension of rights is a cosmetic change compared to the rest. The
culture set forth by the law is regulated by a group of lengthy sections
on contracts that set up the administrative procedures for cultural
business; in those sections it is apparent that certain parcels of the
cultural field are to be opened up to wholesale industrial exploitation.
Which is to say that within the law itself, the old integrity of the zones,
culture and industry, has been compromised; culture has been quickly,
easily, incomprehensibly invaded. As Bernard Edelman complained
during a colloquium on the new law:

> The status of the author has been profoundly shaken. In effect we
> no longer have a single author but a multitude of authors, of which
> each represents their own economic interests. This multiplication
> of status will carry with it a multiplicity of interpretations, once
> again, according to the special interests – the advertising industry,
> the cinema, television, the recording industry, the computer
> business . . . I pity the judges who will find themselves in the
> presence of such a melting pot and will have to sharpen inter-
> pretations that are at once heterogeneous and coherent! If you
> will, I find that this law will get us lost on the way to unlikely
> horizons . . .[22]

The French definition of the author has gone vague for a reason.

The Ministry of Culture, which under Jack Lang was responsible for shepherding the new law through the legislature, saw the industrialization of culture as part of a deliberate modernization of France moving towards the time when culture would go peacefully, hand in hand, with both state and capital. A new official culture has emerged and a ministerial communiqué offered up a sketch of it:

> Guardian of the cultural patrimony, promoter of recognized, traditional culture (opera, museum, classical music, dance, theatre), the Ministry of Culture suddenly saw itself taken by the emergence of the new movements (song, rock, jazz, but also advertising, fashion, design) in the new technologies (computer, cable) and assumed a strategic role in the renewal of French industry. At this point, the Ministry of Culture becomes a sort of 'Ministry of the Culture Industry' in which its politics becomes integrated into the global strategy of the French government.[23]

These are the conditions generally recognized as the postmodern ones for culture. But they are subject to interpretation. Fredric Jameson in an article published the same summer as the communiqué, the summer of 1984, dramatically reversed the usual reading of the scenario, where industry steps in and authors die.[24] Where others saw the industrialization of culture, Jameson saw the acculturation of industry, an aesthetic production blasting out into commodity production generally and seeming to know no bounds. Culture, rather than submit to invasion, escapes.

It turns up at the Beaubourg. For much the same, euphoric, Jamesonian sense of culture was put forward in the summer of 1985 by Jean-François Lyotard and Thierry Chaput in their great exhibition, *Les Immatériaux*, or, *The Immaterials*, sponsored by the Centre pour la Création Industrielle of the Centre national d'art et de culture Georges Pompidou. The new technologies provide the raw materials of the postmodern condition: owing to their newness, no governing model for culture is available, only slippery categories and an absence of borders; even the human body is shown to break down (artificially induced genders and layers of skin grafts were part of the proof). The different confrontations between the human being and the new technologies were laid out over a labyrinth of rooms, niches, and hallways, each dedicated to the exploration of a certain subject, like the simulated smell, the angel, the second skin, the hurried eater, the invisible man, the inverted reference, the words that are objects, living speech . . .

The role of the individual author in this dematerializing complex was never too clear, though Lyotard, like Jameson, heroically declared the collapse into vagueness to be a sign of liberty. Body, mind, and object were let loose into a tumultous libidinal economy with a past and a present. In the old, modern days, parents had genders and authors spoke using the name of the father. Postmodernity offers another sexual order (significantly Lyotard's version of Genesis is devoid of sin) and endless potential for discourse (the myth of total communication).[25] Insofar as there was a parental economy of the modern, it was the market economy but here Lyotard tumbled backward into the old clichés, notably the one where an economy limits the classic concept of freedom: painting done in collaboration with the market economy is understood simply as prostitution.[26] The bustling, not-so libidinal economy behind postmodernism could not be articulated without dampening the freedom hypothesis. The law was not invoked.

The law was in the process of being written while the exhibition was being prepared; it was not perhaps the best time to make an appeal. But its presence was felt. As part of the exhibition, twenty-six French intellectuals were installed in front of word processors and asked to supply a data base with the material for keywords, like author. An artificially induced, rather laconic, debate was transacted by microchip and published as so many fragmentary passages in the part of the catalogue called *Epreuves d'écriture, or Writing Samples*. In the meditations on the word author, the juridical definition actually makes several entrances, though it is more an abstract point of reference than a real help. It is simply one definition among many, neither authority nor butler; it exits as quickly as it entered. Jacques Derrida, in his contribution to the definition of the author put it well:

> Up until what point are we the authors of our texts on the author? We have submitted ourselves to the necessity of a concept and to a rule for the game, to a list of words as well and of other authors, whereby the author in the end remains fairly indeterminate, disappearing. Is there an author in this common enterprise? Who? Where? The so-called disappearance of the author still passes perhaps by the experience of a certain sociotechnical factor (the word processor, an anonymous central telephone system, etc.) which reflects now what has been happening in the 'cultural world' for a long time, forever. Unless, through the immaterials' machine, losing tone and hand, in renouncing for all time our old mirrors, we did not again seek a supplementary authority, an oh so

symbolic authority, it is true, so that neither the image nor any other living thing any longer came back to us. But let us not forget, all is still signed, no one has the right to touch the text of another, our copyright is well protected just like in the good old days of modernity (seventeenth to twentieth centuries).[27]

The law was present, yes, but as an irony.

The new copyright law is capable of much more. Its terms remind us that a cultural distinction still exists, complicated by its business dealings, but distinct nonetheless, and legally binding. Furthermore it puts postmodern culture of the new technologies into some kind of order, and articulates its limits and taboos. The law reveals the constraints that have been placed on cultural liberty. It cuts out culture from industry in specific ways that can be defined, that are material, and that lack euphoria. The law shows clearly that the cultural field has been invaded by industrial interests, but that the markets have not merged. Culture remains apart, resting on its contracts.

The contractual obligations of authors vary but they give structure to the amorphous postmodern. The rules governing contracts prescribe different rules for different venues. The author of a novel, for example, can make claims that the author of a screenplay or the author of a computer game cannot. When it comes to the actual negotiation of contracts, authors' rights are and have in actual practice long been variable, subject to the contractor, the firm, the special interests as Edelman calls them, which is to say, in the case of the culture being made with the new technologies, industrial interests. Now it should be noted that in practice copyright was always subject to invasion by other interests: artists had to permit museums, for example, to charge reproduction fees for works in their collection and by the turn of the century abuses of artists' copyright were so flagrant that a special law had to be passed declaring that authors did not automatically abandon their reproduction rights when the work was sold.[28] But the new law recognizes the potential of bigger, telescoping markets that can be exploited by a number of means, satellite transmission, cabling, cassettes, disks; so it becomes necessary, more profitable for all concerned, to define the author contractually as part of a collective effort. This shuffling of the contracts makes for a noisy, contorted, rather too discriminating law which has been much discussed, one deputy, Alain Richard, admitting that, especially when it came to the software legislation, there was 'hair on the soup.'[29]

One might say that too many cooks have spoiled the copyright law; certainly the simple mediation it used to perform is a thing of the past. The software sections are so full of exceptions that they begin to resemble patent rather than the traditional, unilaterally generous copyright. The author of the computer program written while in the service of an employer has no rights whatsoever over the work; the employer becomes the author, though in the case of software the rights are only good for twenty-five years after the copyright has been filed. It so happens that this part of the law was written to conform to recent developments in international law, notably in the United States, and yet the law wavers elsewhere too. The author's rights for the performer do not get passed on after death to the heirs. Those who work within the context of an audiovisual production can expect the producer to divy up the rights money according to the conventions of the profession. This entails larger cuts for well-known actors and writers, lesser gains for the other authors on the team. The law is still not clear about the rights of those who actually make the image for the piece. Authorial distinction now varies with the terms of the deal. If one reads the new law through to the contracts, culture can no longer be mapped as the same flat land.

The mediating function of the new law, because of its very complexity, opens up inequalities, uneven developments, gaps, and, with them, new critical distances. They shed light on vagueness. The cultural object can be seen as the sum of so many interests and so much labor, a sum that busily pedals about the marketplace in search of reception. The cultural object is more often than not the work of a team of authors; it exhibits the tensions and the struggles of the collaboration. Texts, images, stars, directors, and producers all have different degrees of power, different investments in the piece, different roles to play that will register in the work itself. By dissecting the authorial parts of a work, it is possible to cut into the illusion of seamlessness, so powerful in the rhetoric around the new technologies and to propose roles for the individual subject.[30] It is possible to plot a politics of cultural labor and possible to imagine a collective of authors, individuals who do not lose themselves when working with others. All of which assumes the existence of authors who have left their mirrors for more responsible positions. It also assumes the continuing necessity of a cultural politics.

NOTES

1. Clement Greenberg, 'Avant-Garde and Kitsch', Art and Culture (Boston: Beacon, 1961), 9.
2. Roland Barthes, 'The Death of the Author,' in *Image – Music – Text*, ed. and trans. by Stephen Heath (New York: Hill & Wang, 1977), 142–48. The French version was first published in Mantéia, v. 5 (1968). My thinking on this subject was initially stimulated by Michel Foucault's essay, 'What is an Author?', in English in the collection *Language, Counter-Memory, Practice*, ed. Donald F. Bouchard, trans. Donald F. Bouchard and Sherry Simon (Ithaca: Cornell University Press, 1977), 113–38. The French version was first published in 1969 and should be read in conjunction with Foucault's book appearing the same year, *The Archaeology of Knowledge*, trans. A. M. Sheridan Smith (London: Tavistock, 1972). Brian O'Doherty and Barbara Novak showed me the relevance of *Aspen* 5+6 for this issue and to them I am grateful. My essay has also benefitted greatly from careful reading by André Rouillé, Adrian Rifkin, Leila Kinney, Carol Duncan, Kristin Ross, and Alice Kaplan; without them it would not have been the same.
3. Stéphane Mallarmé, 'Variations sur un sujet,' *La Revue blanche* (February–November 1895, September 1896), reprinted in his *Oeuvres complètes*, ed. Henri Mondor and G. Jean-Aubry (Paris: NRF, 1945), 366.
4. Loi 19 July 1793, given in Georges Chabaud, *Le Droit d'auteur des artistes & des fabricants. Législation – Jurisprudence – Projets de réforme* (Paris: Librairie des Sciences politiques et sociales, Marcel Rivière, 1908), ii. Chaubaud's appendix gives the texts of the laws from 1777 to 1902 and his book gives a close reading of them.
5. Those interpreting the law would not mince words: See Eugène Pouillet, *Traité theorique et pratique de la propriété littéraire et artistique et du droit de représentation* (3rd ed.; Paris: Marchal et Billard, 1908), 97: 'La loi récompense et protège toute composition due à un effort de l'esprit humain et se rapportant aux beaux-arts. Elle ne considère ni l'importance ni la beauté de l'oeuvre; elle n'envisage que le fait de la création; c'est pour cela qu'elle protège au même degré le tableau de Raphaël et l'image sortie des fabriques d'Epinal.' [The law protects and rewards all work developing from an effort of the human mind and relating to the fine arts. It does not consider its importance nor does the beauty of the work matter, only the fact of creation. It is for this reason that it protects a painting by Raphael to the same extent as the images coming out of the factories of Epinal.] Unless otherwise indicated, all translations are my own.
6. For a good summary of the evolution of this point of law, see *Dalloz. Encyclopédie juridique. Répertoire de droit civil*, dir. Pierre Raynard et Marguerite Vanel, v. 6 (Paris: Dalloz, 1975), 'Propriété littéraire et artistique.' Charles Aussy thought the point important enough to argue in his book, *Du droit moral de l'aute   sur les oeuvres de littérature et d'art* (Auxerre: Pigelet, 1911), 5.
7. The law on design and patent is separated: the laws on design: loi 18 mars 1806, 14 juillet 1909, 12 mars 1952; the laws on patent: 5 juillet 1844 and 2 janvier 1968. See *Dalloz, Encyclopédie juridique. Répertoire de droit commercial* (Paris: Dalloz, 1986).
8. Pataille, *Annales de la propriété industrielle, artistique et littéraire* (1894), 48–55.
9. Bernard Edelman, *Ownership of the Image. Elements for a Marxist Theory of Law*, trans. Elizabeth Kingdom (London: RKP, 1979), *passim*. Edelman does not distinguish between the privileged, special nature of this market and the regular market but his book remains a fine discussion of how the laws for photography and cinema reveal the property relations between people.
10. Lois 3 août 1844, 8–19 avril 1854, and 14 juillet 1866.
11. Or for that matter anyone else. See especially: Greenberg, op. cit.; Walter Benjamin, 'The Work of Art in the Age of Mechanical Reproduction,' *Illuminations*, ed. Hannah Arendt, trans. Harry Zohn (New York: Schocken, 1969), 217–51; Thomas Crow, 'Modernism and Mass Culture in the Visual Arts,' in *Modernism and Modernity. The Vancouver Papers*, ed. Benjamin H. D. Buchloh, Serge Guilbaut, and David Solkin (Halifax: Nova Scotia College of Art and Design, 1984), 215–64. On the law's evolution, see *Dalloz*, op. cit. The full texts of the laws in question are given in the *Recueil Sirey*.
12. The late arrival of architecture and sculpture to copyright stems from the fact that these professions were not of academic parentage. The institutions supporting the various cultural

professions were at odds with one another in the Ancien Régime and the law of 1793 records those differences. For more on this subject see Pouillet, *Traité théorique et pratique de la propriété littéraire et artistique*. It should also be noted that the entrance of architecture and sculpture into this law in 1902 speaks worlds about the new legitimacy of that work by the end of the nineteenth century: it was part of the national culture, often represented a culture of the state, and consequently merited much more than simple legal protection. The 1902 law is a symptom of the widening authority of the so-called industrial arts.

13. A number of these texts have been anthologized by André Rouillé in his book, *La Photographie en France 1839–1870. Les principaux textes* (Paris: Macula, 1986). For a discussion of the debates during the Paris World's Fair of 1855 over whether photography was art or industry see his article, 'La Photographie française à l'Exposition Universelle de 1855,' *Le Mouvement social*, no. 131 (April–June 1985), 87–103.

14. Alphonse Lamartine, 'Entretien 36. La littérature des sens. La peinture. Léopold Robert,' *Cours familier de littérature*, vols. 6–7 (Paris: chez l'auteur, 1858), 411 and 43 respectively.

15. Quoted without reference by A. Bigeon, *La Photographie et le droit* (Paris: Mendel, 1894), 18.

16. J.-E. Bulloz, *La Propriété photographique et la loi française* (Paris: Gauthier-Villars, 1890), 3. See also M. E. Potu, *La Protection des oeuvres photographiques. Extraits de la Revue Trimestrielle de Droit Civil* (Paris: Sirey, 1912) and Léon Vidal, *Absence d'un texte légal réglant les droits d'auteur afférents aux oeuvres des arts mécaniques de reproduction. Diversité d'opinions relatives à cette question. Solution qui semble la plus rationnelle. (Extrait des Mémoires de l'Académie de Marseilles)* (S.l.: s.d).

17. Mallarmé, Foucault, Barthes, op. cit.; Walter Benjamin, 'The Author as Producer,' from *Understanding Brecht*, trans. Anna Bostock, introduction by Stanley Mitchell (London; NLB, 1977), 85–103.

18. Loi 11 mars 1957, *Recueil Sirey*, 1957, 124.

19. *Cahiers du Cinéma. Ecrits. La politique des auteurs. Entretiens avec dix cinéastes*, préface de Serge Dancy (Paris: Editions de l'Etoile-Cahiers du Cinéma, 1984). See also *Theories of Authorship*, ed. John Caughie (London: RKP, 1981).

20. Foucault, op. cit., 123–24.

21. Loi 3 juillet 1985. A useful copy of the law, which prints it alongside the 1957 one in adjacent columns, may be found in *Droit d'auteur et droits voisins. La loi du 3 juillet 1985. Colloque de l'IRPI sous le haut patronage de M. Jack Lang (Paris, 21 et 22 novembre 1985)* (Paris: Libraires techniques, 1986), Annexe II.

22. Ibid., 168.

23. Dominique Wallon, 'Culture et industries culturelles,' communication présentée à la réunion de clôture des Rencontres franco-québecoises, juin 1984, document reprographié, Ministère de la Culture. Cited in Bernard Miège, Patrick Pajon, Jean-Michel Salaün, *L'industrialisation de l'audiovisuel. Des programmes pour les nouveaux médias* (Paris: Aubier, 1986), 23.

24. Fredric Jameson, 'Postmodernism, of the Cultural Logic of Late Capitalism,' *New Left Review*, no. 146 (July–August 1984): 53–92. See also Clive Dilnot, 'What is the Post-Modern?', *Art History*, v. 9 (June 1986): 245–63.

25. Jean-François Lyotard, 'Maternité,' *Les Immatériaux. Inventaire* (Paris: CCI, 1985).

26. Lyotard, 'négoce peint,' op. cit.

27. Jacques Derrida, 'Auteur 139,' in *Les Immatériaux. Epreuves d'écriture* (Paris: Centre national Georges Pompidou, 1985), 19.

28. Loi 9 Avril 1910. For more on this point, see Edouard Cooper, *L'art et la loi* (Paris: Achille, 1903).

29. The admission was made during the conference, *Droit d'auteur et droits voisins. La loi du 3 juillet 1985*, 176.

30. See Marc Guillaume, 'Téléspectres', *Traverses*, no. 26 – Rhétoriques de la technologie (October 1982), 18–28.

25

DONALD E. PEASE

'Author'

In common usage the term 'author' applies to a wide range of activities. It can refer to someone who starts up a game, or invents a machine, or asserts political freedom, or thinks up a formula, or writes a book. Depending on the activity and the application, the term can connote initiative, autonomy, inventiveness, creativity, authority, or originality. A common procedure whereby an anonymous agent turns into an individual binds the term to these different activities.

In turning anyone in general into someone in particular, the term 'author' carries along with its common usage some long-standing debates over what is at stake in this transformation. These debates have continued over centuries and have taken place with different emphases in different fields. But certain questions, no matter whether they were asked by politicians, economists, theologians, philosophers, or artists, remained constant. Is an individual self-determined or determined by material and historical circumstances? Is the human self infinite or finite? Can an individual ground political authority on individual creativity? What is the basis for human freedom? Can any artist claim absolute originality?

These questions as well as different cultures' responses to them have accompanied the term from its inception. The variety of these responses constitute the meaning of the term. Like other items that answer to a variety of applications, 'author' will sometimes sanction utterly contradictory usages. At the time of its inception, for example, the word 'author' was used interchangeably with its predecessor term 'auctor,' which did not entail verbal inventiveness, as 'author' did but the reverse – adherence to the authority of cultural antecedent. A good way to sort out the various, sometimes contradictory, meanings of this term might be by way of historical narrative. Like most historical narratives, this one will cover an immense trajectory of time in a short space. Consequently, only the broad outlines of its historical development will become apparent. And only some of the questions which have shaped that development will be addressed.

Another question and the contemporary debate surrounding it will provide a conclusion to this brief narrative. Is the 'author' dead? The question was asked by Roland Barthes in an essay 'The Death of the Author,' a title which presumes the answer. But Michel Foucault disagreed with this answer and wrote an essay 'What Is an Author?' which raises in the terms of recent continental criticism some of the issues addressed in the following narrative. Because their debate recapitulates and advances those issues, a discussion of its implications for the continued usage of the term will conclude the history.

The idea of authorship has a lengthy and somewhat problematic genealogy. From the beginning this genealogy has been associated with that of a related figure, the individual 'subject.' Unlike other works referring to a writer's activity – such as essayist, or poet, or dramatist – the term 'author' raises questions about authority and whether the individual is the source or the effect of that authority. The word 'author' derives from the medieval term *auctor*, which denoted a writer whose words commanded respect and belief. The word *auctor* derived from four etymological sources: the Latin verbs *agere*, 'to act or perform'; *auieo*, 'to tie'; *augere*, 'to grow'; and from the Greek noun *autentim*, 'authority.' In the Middle Ages every discipline in the *trivium* had *auctores* (Cicero in rhetoric, Aristotle in dialectic, the ancient poets in grammar) and similarly in the *quadrivium* (Ptolemy in astronomy, Constantine in medicine, the Bible in theology, Boethius in arithmetic) (see Minnis 1984, 1–73). *Auctores* established the founding rules and principles for these different disciplines and sanctioned the moral and political authority of medieval culture more generally. Over the centuries the continued authority of these founding figures derived from medieval scribes' ability to interpret, explain, and in most cases resolve historical problems by restating these problems in terms sanctioned by *auctores*.

Such restatements commanded authority because they organized otherwise accidental events into an established context capable of making them meaningful. The continued authority to make events meaningful in customary or traditional ways provided all the evidence necessary to sustain the *auctores'* power. In the Middle Ages, the relationship between these authoritative books and the everyday world was primarily an allegorical one. Worldly events took place in terms sanctioned by an authoritative book or were not acknowledged as having taken place at all. To experience an event in allegorical terms was to transpose the event out of the realm of one's personal life into the realm of the applicable authority. Following such a transposition, the event became impersonal – everyone's spiritual quest rather than one individual's personal biography. The benefit of this transposition for the individual was indeed a spiritual one – the ability to experience an event in one's life as a reenactment of a sacred custom. Any event, or thing, or emotion, or thought which made this transference into the realm of the *auctores* possible continued their cultural authority. Whereas individuals within medieval culture could interpret their lives in terms that elaborated or reenacted the sayings of the ancient *auctores*, only the monarch, as God's representative, could claim divine sanction for his everyday actions. By correlating the divine basis for his rule with auctorial precedents, the medieval ruler sanctioned the *auctores'* cultural authority. As the source, the beneficiary, and the agent of the culture's authoritative books, the monarch was the perfected cultural form of the *auctor*. His rule was his book, and his subjects were compelled to submit their world to the edicts of that book.

Auctorial sanction and monarchical rule remained more or less unquestioned until late in the fifteenth century, with the discovery of a New World whose inhabitants, language, customs and laws, geography, and plant and animal life did not correspond to referents in the *auctores'* books. Unlike events and persons in medieval Europe, the inhabitants and environment of the New World could *not* be explained in customary terms. Explorers could not find precedents in the work of *auctores* for what they discovered in the New World. Instead of returning to their culture's ancient books for allegorical prefigurations, many New World explorers described what they discovered by making up words of their own (or borrowing terms from the natives). One result of this breakdown was the addition to the English language of such words as hurricane, canoe, skunk; another was the loss of cultural authority for the *auctor*. A related effect was the appearance of what Renaissance historians now refer to as 'new men,' individuals within Renaissance culture who turned the 'news' sent home from freshly discovered lands into forms of cultural empowerment for unprecedented political actions and their personification by new agents within the culture. Among these new cultural agents were 'authors,' writers whose claim to cultural authority did not depend on their adherence to cultural precedents but on a faculty of verbal inventiveness. Unlike the medieval *auctor* who based his authority on divine revelation, an author *himself* claimed authority for his words and based his individuality on the stories he composed.

More precisely, authors exploited the discontinuity between the things in the New World and the words in the ancient books to claim for their words an unprecedented cultural power, to represent the new. Authors rose to cultural prominence in alliance with other individuals who exploited this dissociation between worlds: explorers, merchants, colonists, traders, reformers, and adventurers. Like all these other 'new' men, authors depended on what was newly discovered in the new lands as the basis for their cultural authority. The new lands were the source of news, and the news facilitated social mobility and cultural change. The recognition of what was new depended on an acknowledgment of the inadequacy of allegory as the source of cultural knowledge. Whereas medieval allegory subsumed a culture's persons and their actions – no matter how various or qualified – within its unchanging typologies, what was new asserted its difference from, rather than its correspondence with, these cultural typologies. By inventing new words to describe things in the New World, authors declared their right to be represented on their own terms rather than in the words of the ancient books. And their writings produced readers who also learned how to define themselves in their own terms.

From the fifteenth century through the first half of the twentieth century, the term 'author' enjoyed a more or less constant rise in social prestige. The beneficiary of the esteem that cultures had previously bestowed on their *auctores*, the author and his work signified a break from the cultural constraints imposed by feudal kings. Authors maintained this affiliation with cultural freedom through the creation of alternative worlds wherein individual human subjects could experience the autonomy denied them in their cultural world.

This rise to cultural prominence of the author was correlated from the beginning with the *auctores'* fall. Like the autonomous human subject, the author was an emergent political and cultural category, which was initially differentiated from the culturally residual category of the *auctor* as an example of *self*-determination. The author guaranteed the individual's ability to determine his own identity and actions out of his own experiences in a culture he could reform rather than endorsing the auctorial aim of transcending culture.

The *auctor* based his authority on divine revelation; the author derived his authority from the discovery of new worlds whose native environments contradicted the *auctores*' mandates. The *auctores* produced a culture which reproduced their mandates; authors at first produced themselves out of the alternative world-pictures they used to explain (and imaginatively inhabit) other lands.

During the years when feudal Europe was undergoing a fundamental transformation, the author was never defined apart from this process of transformation. Once the work of cultural transformation was considered complete, however, the concept of the 'author' underwent a fundamental change. Having helped effect the historic change from a feudal and predominantly agricultural society and through a variety of other political and economic arrangements to a democratic and predominantly industrial Europe, the author was no longer part of an emergent cultural process. Following the realization of an alternative culture he had earlier only envisioned, the author's work underwent a related change – from a reciprocal workaday relationship with other cultural activities into the realm of 'genius,' which transcended ordinary cultural work.

Like the medieval *auctor*, the 'genius' identified the basis for his work with the laws of the Creator. Consequently, the realm of genius was defined as utterly autonomous. Free from determination by any cultural category other than the absolutely free constructions of his creative imagination, the genius broke down the reciprocal relationship between the author and the rest of culture.

But while the genius occupied a realm that transcended culture, he nevertheless served a cultural function. As an example of the perfection that could be achieved by an inhabitant of the culture, the genius sanctioned the political authority of the culture in which he appeared. But, like the medieval *auctor*, he defined this authority as the ability to transcend the entire cultural milieu.

Whereas the author developed within the culture he helped to develop, the genius claimed to be different from the rest of the culture. So defined, the work of genius provided a politically useful contrast to other forms of labor in an industrial culture. In producing his *own* work out of materials in his own imagination, the genius performed 'cultural' as opposed to 'industrial' labor. Industrial workers did not control the means and product of their labor but worked with materials and produced commodities owned by someone else. In correlating non-alienated labor with his work rather than with the work of an ordinary laborer, the genius provided a tacit justification for the class distinctions separating those individuals who owned their labor from those who did not. If nonalienated labor defined the category of genius, it became a cultural privilege, a benefit accrued in the cultural realm rather than in the ordinary workaday world.

The difference between the genius who creates other, 'original' worlds and the author who cooperates in the emergence of an alternative culture underscores at least two contradictory impulses the author shared from the beginning with that other emergent cultural category, the 'autonomous subject.' Both the author and the individual collaborated with emergent collective processes in social life. The author and the individual shared a tendency to become alienated from society once these collective social processes were fully materialized. Although associated with the more inclusive social movements that led to revolution and civil war, the author's creative work was not separable from the collective work of these social movements. Only after an emancipatory social movement succeeded in establishing an alternative form of government with its own rules of law could an author's creative efforts be dissociated from a vital collective life – as the work of a 'genius.' As the authoritative source of the creative life, the genius marked the return of the role of the *auctor* to the postmedieval cultural world.

To understand how the *auctor* returned, we need to recall how the *auctor* was first overthrown. The *auctor* had formerly been supplanted when the Europeans, in confronting humans they believed to be of a nature other than their own, recognized their own capacity to be other. The basis for a successful transformation in a European's nature was the discovery in the New World of natural phenomena utterly inexplicable in terms of the *auctores*. These truly alien phenomena produced an 'other nature' *within* the Renaissance men who discovered them.

This 'other' within ultimately became the basis for the autonomous subject. But when it made its first appearance, this 'other nature' was put into service by the new men of commerce, who were able to gratify its appetites with the foodstuffs, spices, and goods brought over from the New World. The qualities in this other nature not put to commercial use led to a different form of government in Europe. Using the New World as tacit backdrop for their arguments, political theorists like Hobbes and Locke argued that man in nature was like a 'savage' in the New World. Prepolitical, protosocial, deprived of protection against an enemy, natural man required a social contract with the monarch to preserve 'natural' rights and liberties.

These theories eventually led to civil wars and revolutions through-out Europe. But all of them traded on an identification within European individuals of another nature that was no longer subject to the rule of either feudal monarchs or their *auctores* but in need of an alternative European political system for its fulfillment. In its process of emergence, this new political system demanded accounts of its workings quite different from those of *auctores*.

As we have seen, the transformation of the *auctores'* models into alternative accounts of alternative worlds resulted in the appearance of authors. As long as the author was involved in the process of bringing new persons and new laws into existence, his creative powers were affiliated with a collective political imagination designed to realize a body politic that did not yet exist. It was through this collective imagination that the author addressed the other within the reading public. When the author addressed the collective imaginative capacity of Europeans to make the world they wanted out of the world they inherited, the result was revolution or civil war.

Once these civil wars succeeded in establishing alternative forms of government, the author underwent an unrelated transformation. When the author's work could no longer be correlated with an emancipatory social movement, it was defined as an emancipation from the political life. The term 'genius' enabled this separation of the cultural from the political realm. As the legatee of a previous cultural identification, affiliating the *auctor*'s creative power with a founder's power to establish a city-state, the genius established a cultural realm utterly dissociated from either the political or the economic realms. He called this realm a 'Republic of Letters.' In this realm the works of genius recovered the authority previously exercised by medieval *auctores* and were elevated into exemplars and sources of value for the entire culture.

With the installation of the genius as the *auctor* ruling over the Republic of Letters, the author's function shifted accordingly – from that of producing an alternative political world to that of producing a cultural alternative to the world of politics. After the cultural sphere distinguished its workings from those within the different worlds of politics and economics, the cultural realm became increasingly self-referential.

During the political and industrial revolutions of the eighteenth and nineteenth centuries the cultural realm could not be fully distinguished from the economic and political realms. But in the twentieth century the author's genius was invoked to explain the irrelevance of economic and political issues to questions of strictly cultural interest. The genius's putative freedom from material constraints authorized this separation of the cultural from the economic realm. Following this separation, the economic, political, psychological, and historical conditions that provided the material environment for an author's work were denied any determining relationship with it.

This separation of the cultural from the political and economic realms produced an even more fundamental division within the cultural realm, separating the author from his work. The cultural figure who supervised this division was neither the genius, nor the author, but the literary critic. Produced out of this division of labor within the cultural realm, the literary critic supervised further differentiation within the cultural realm and policed the boundaries distinguishing what was literary from what was not.

The division of cultural labor distinguishing the critic's function from the author's replicated the division of industrial labor within the economic realm. What alienated the author from his work's means of production, however, was not a factory owner but the literary critic who claimed a power to understand it greater than the author's own. The critic proved this power by interpreting the work in such a way that the author seemed an effect of the critic's interpretation rather than the cause of the work.

In an essay entitled 'The Intentional Fallacy' (1954), Wimsatt and Beardsley, two American New Critics, turned the demotion of the author to a function of the critic's text into an explicit part of critical practice: 'There is a gross body of life, of sensory and mental experience, which lies behind and in some sense causes every poem, but can never be and need not be known in the verbal and hence intellectual composition which is the poem.' (See Wimsatt and Beardsley 1954, 12) In distinguishing the critic's text from the author's work, the New Critics successfully displaced the author's 'genius' as the ruler within the cultural sphere. In the process the New Critics produced a cultural artifact, the 'autotelic' or 'autonomous' literary text that they defined as utterly separate from the surrounding environment. In separating the literary text from the control of the author, the New Critics only completed a movement that had begun in the cultural realm a century earlier, when the word 'genius' separated the author's work from the socioeconomic world.

As the word 'autotelic' text implies, the New Critics positioned their newly won texts in a realm apart from every limitation other than the rules, conventions, and constraints of a purely textual milieu. In the same postwar period in which the New Critics constructed the division separating a textual milieu from a social world, however, other critics located a critical dimension within the author's work. Instead of distinguishing the critic's work from the author, those critics using historicist, Marxist, Frankfurt school, and feminist frameworks have restored the critical dimension to the author's work, thereby linking the author and critic in a shared project. These critics returned the author's work to the social, economic, political, and gendered contexts which the New Critics separated off from their autotelic texts. In restoring the historical context to the author's works, these critics have rescinded the New Critics' claim that the genius's texts transcend historical contexts. Their criticism turns the genius back into an individual subject, determined by the social and economic forces whose shapes he reflected or altered in his work. In analyzing the complex relationship between the market economy and what was formerly described as the 'free creative play' of genius, Marxist critics in particular have restored the explicit relationship between any author's work and the anticipated reception for it. Psychoanalytic, phenomenological, and feminist critics have likewise restored crucial psychosocial contexts. In thereby turning the transcendent genius back into a culturally situated human subject, these critics have attempted to reverse some of the effects of the divisions of labor within the cultural realm. Unlike the New Critics' approach, their criticism takes place at that moment within an author's work when the author becomes critically aware of determinant social, psychological, and political forces.

These critics have restored psychosocial relationships between the author and culturally committed critics by representing the author and the critic as participants in a still-emergent social process rather than as representative figures within a fully established culture or as partial selves within a textual environment.

But these revisionist efforts have more recently been opposed by still newer critics who construe the text as isolated from every context other than a purely textual one and consider the term 'author' and the history of its cultural usages to be impediments to the workings of the textual environment. Since the controversy between two of the newer critics has resulted in a consideration of the cultural value of the term 'author,' it will function as a conclusion to this brief narrative genealogy.

In order to separate the text from contamination by an author, such newer critics as Roland Barthes have declared the author dead. By the 'author,' Barthes means the demands – or psychological consistency, meaning, unity – that an autonomous subject would exact from a textual environment. In the wake of the author's death, Barthes has proposed a new definition of literature: a discursive game always arriving at the limits of its own rule, without any author other than the reader (or 'scriptor' as Barthes refers to him), who is defined as an effect of the writing game he activates.

Whereas Barthes declares that the author is dead, the text he thereby produces is not without an author. In Barthes' criticism the author returns – but in the displaced form of Barthes' metatextual account of the writing activity. In this view, then, the critic is the real beneficiary of the separation of an author from a text. It is the critic rather than the author or the reader who can render an authoritative account of the structure of the work, the internal relationships among the various textual strands and levels, and the shift from author to what Barthes names 'scriptor.' Without the author to demand the resolution of contradictory textual lines into an intended unity, the critic is free to reconstitute the text according to his own terms.

In an essay published one year after Barthes' 'The Death of the Author,' and contentiously entitled 'What Is [rather than *was*] an Author,' Michel Foucault reactivates the controversy between post-structuralists (who believed only in the environment of textuality) and historicists (who believed in a sociopolitical context for the literary work) over the cultural function of the author. Unlike Barthes, Foucault acknowledges the persistence of the author as a function within the commentary of poststructuralists who deny the author as agent.

To elucidate the crucial part the author continues to play in the material life of a culture, Foucault takes Barthes' 'death of the author rule' as a literal ethical imperative and imagines what would happen if authors actually disappeared from culture. For one thing, there would then be no warrant for criticism. Critical language (its vocabulary of accusation, defense, judgement) depends on the legal system (and the cultural systems affiliated with it) for its warrant. Without Foucault's name to connect with the words in, say, *Les mots et les choses* there would be no one to be held accountable for them and, hence, no way to justify a critique of them (or any other commentary). The name of the author turns discourse into legal property, and the notion of legal property in turn supports and is supported by related discourses concerning entitlements, liberties, duties, rights, constraints, impediments, obligations, and punishment. The name of the author saturates the entire network of legal relations, thereby empowering the attribution of discourses to the procedures that result from them.

For Foucault, the author is finally neither an individual existing apart from a discursive practice, nor a subject acting within any specific practice, but what might be called a 'subjecting' function. As the sanction for the rules within any specific practice, and as a function of the relations between them, the author for Foucault oversees and regulates all the diverse situations in which *any cultural subject* can act. Produced by the practices whose reproduction it guarantees, the name of the author turns otherwise unrelated discursive practices into a coherent cultural realm over which it maintains jurisdiction.

If the author disappeared, Foucault claims, so would the entire cultural realm under the author's jurisdiction. But Foucault postulates a different kind of author to explain figures (like Marx and Freud) whose work is discontinuous with the cultural realm. Such authors do not function within already existing discursive practices but are instead fundamental in a double sense: they found disciplines that are discontinuous with previous ones; and, unlike other cultural subjects, 'fundamental' authors produce writing practices discontinuous with the practices that follow from them.

In ending his essay with a description of the fundamental author, Foucault gives his readers the appropriate way to understand his own authorship. More interestingly for our narrative, he gives them a way to put Barthes' text to strategic cultural use. The 'fundamental' author, insofar as he begins a discipline that is discontinuous with its owns rules, gratifies what Barthes describes as the fundamental impulse of the writing practice. But, unlike Barthes, Foucault's 'fundamental' author does not make the mistake of turning this impulse into the normative imperative that the author 'die' into this discontinuity.

This controversy between Barthes and Foucault clarifies an important function that the author plays in contemporary culture. While they both write about the author as if the term has arrived at its limits as an enabling concept, their debate returns the 'author' to its relationship with another term, the 'autonomous subject.' The author replicates the difficulties of the cultural subject who feels as much *ruled by* as *ruler of* the writing activity in which he is situated. Barthes' solution to the subject's dilemma is the radical one of situating the subject in a discourse (the text) that brings rules *and* their ruler (the authors) to an end. Foucault exposes the rule governing this discourse, then proposes a discursive practice – that of the 'fundamental' author – that will enable every subject to experience the dilemma (of feeling ruled by the discourse he should be ruling) as its own solution. In the discourse inaugurated by a 'fundamental' author, every apparently derivative position a later practitioner of that discourse occupies turns out to be originative.

Foucault's 'fundamental' author opens up the cultural sphere by transforming the self-referential qualities underwritten by the author into a kind of planned heterogeneity. In a sense, the 'fundamental' author conflates the cultural duties of the traditional author (who initiates a new cultural practice) and the critic (who exposes the limits, inconsistencies, and unwarranted assumptions of the new practice). Insofar as he initiates both his own practice as well as the revisionary (implicitly critical) practices discontinuous with it, however, the fundamental author simply incorporates an otherwise separate *critical* discourse into his means of elaborating the internal differentiations vital to this continued cultural life of new disciplines.

Foucault's redefinition of the author has not actually introduced a new form of cultural agency for the author; in fact, it has merely restored to the author a cultural power so general in its deployment (what ongoing cultural practices cannot claim to be an activation of function discontinuous with prior practice?) and so pervasive in its effect that the work of the 'fundamental' author cannot be distinguished from any other exercise of power in the cultural sphere.

Whereas Foucault intended the 'fundamental' author as an alternative to the traditional author, the practices of the fundamental author only reactivate what we have already recognized as the inescapable dilemma at work in the term. Foucault's reactivation of that dilemma gives me the occasion to recapitulate the historical narrative I have been writing.

The term 'author' originally arose out of the sense of constraint experienced by the finite human subject. The authorial subject claimed the power at once to produce and to supersede those limitations. The historical result of this power was the autonomous cultural sphere. But here an imaginary scenario transpired in which the finite individual subject was instructed by the authorial subject to exclude as foreign to the cultural sphere any reminder of finitude in the form of economic, political, or material interests. When confronted with the alternative of being completely determined by material conditions, the authorial subject (as 'genius') claimed the power to represent, and then find itself transparently represented in, the material conditions of human finitude. Producing in his work what previously had claimed to produce it, the authorial subject claimed the power to transcend these limitations to the subject's power and, then, along with the commentators who collaborated in the production, proved the effectiveness of this power by recognizing it in the unity, coherence, and regularity of the work of art.

The cost of the autonomy of the author's work was the separation of the socioeconomic from the textual environment and the recognition, at the time of that separation, of the conditions of textual production (rules, conventions, generic assumptions) as the only rules applicable to the text. As historicist critics have reminded us, these textual rules were themselves rarefied versions of nontextual economic and political forces. And the division of the textual from the sociopolitical realm reproduced within the text the pervasive opposition between the determining and the determined subject informing the notion of the author.

Barthes suggests one way to resolve this opposition. By identifying with the critical subject (who can articulate the rules that determine the author's moves) until that subjectivity witnesses the disappearance of the author into the writing processes that determined his work, Barthes produced a subjectivity that was effected by the activity it engaged. Determined by the process it determined, the writing self is only a textual version of what historicist critics described as the emergent author, who was determined by the collective movement the author helped determine.

As Foucault pointed out, the expense of Barthes' vision was the recovery of the author as a function at the precise moment that the author was displaced by the writing process as a controlling force. But then instead of resituating the 'author' within a socioeconomic (as opposed to purely textual) process, Foucault identifies the fundamental mechanism at work in the writing process – the 'displacement with a difference' of what preceded it – with the political practice of the 'fundamental' author.

In so doing, Foucault has not confronted the perennial dilemma of the author; instead, he defines the conditions of textual finitude – the revisionary activity of the writing process itself – as the determining cultural practice of the fundamental author. And the fundamental author then does, in Foucault's text what the genius had earlier done in the genealogy of the term 'author'; that is, he claims a power to determine (in the form of a willed discontinuity from his practice) what otherwise would determine him.

Once transposed into the rarefied realm of revisionary discursive practices, Foucault's fundamental author can supervise a cultural domain organized like a textual or discursive milieu. His 'fundamental' author, in other words, performs the historic role of the author as genius. He polices the boundary separating the cultural realm from contamination by those material and economic conditions no author can claim to have produced. It was this very separation of the cultural sphere from the political that produced the separation of the text from the author in the work of the New Critics. Insofar as he could be influenced by nontextual considerations (by the market economy, social movements, and such) the author had to be separated from the work (which by definition could not be influenced by non-textual matters). Following this *ultimate* separation of the work from its author (usually accompanied by a revolutionary rhetoric like Barthes' borrowed from social movements) a work no longer had to be addressed in anything other than textual terms.

The utterly textual milieu of the poststructuralists is ruled by the critic, or the authorless subject, as opposed to the author. In this domain the critic can do what the author cannot; that is, expose the rules that structure the language games productive of the textual environment. But at least one of these language games, the tendency of the textual environment to generalize its domain back into the political and economic spheres (as discourses), can reactivate the countermovement earlier described.

The authorless subject is not a fact of modern existence but only an effect of the discursive practices constitutive of subjectivity. Like every other discursive effect, the authorless subject depends on a critic's metatext for an elucidation of the operative rules of these practices. But if the critic's position has been identified with the rules of these discursive practices in the process of self-revision, the critic cannot transform these practices. Following the saturation of the cultural, economic, and political realms by the critic's text, only the return of an enabling concept of the author can facilitate a genuine transformation. In order to be enabling, the term 'author' can no longer remain divided into partial subjects (the *auctor*, the author, the reader, the critic, the determining-determined subject). The controversy surrounding the term 'author,' however, may actually produce a material practice able to overcome the division in cultural realms that depends on such a partitioning of human subjectivity.

26

MÁIRE NÍ FHLATHÚIN

'Postcolonialism and the Author: The Case of Salman Rushdie'

In a profession which deals with the power and manipulation of images, it may be unwise to speak too glibly of the death of the author – particularly since it is in practice impossible to separate the author as literary force from the author as legal entity or human being. The affair of *The Satanic Verses*[1] has emphasised the change imposed by publication on the relations between the author and his text. One of the axioms of 'The Intentional Fallacy' states that a work of literature 'is not the author's (it is detached from the author at birth and goes about the world beyond his power to intend about it or control it)'.[2] The disempowering of the author, however, is not accompanied by any diminution in his responsibility for what he has written. Indeed, Wimsatt and Beardsley's companion axiom, that the 'thoughts and attitudes' of the text should be imputed 'immediately to the dramatic *speaker*' rather than to the author, becomes in the light of Rushdie's experience a clear instance of wishful thinking. In fact, he is in the worst possible situation: his stated intentions are not considered relevant to a reading of his work, but the text is used to ascribe intentions, desires and crimes to its author. By an ironic reversal of the intentional fallacy, the author becomes the creation of the text. In the aftermath of the novel's publication, a major concern for many participants in this affair has been the construction of an author to fit a particular reading of the book. There are ascribed to the name of Salman Rushdie some personal characteristics which are given as reasons for his actions, and justification for the reading.

These characteristics are, naturally, variable and often contradictory.

The Maududist opponents of the book portrayed in October 1988 an author, in the course of 'a continuous striptease, from soft to hard and even harder porn', dashing off his book in a fit of bad temper: '[Rushdie] . . . had hoped to win the Booker Prize once more. He was cross when he did not and set about putting together his Satanic Verses. Combining all his skills in writing, acting and imagining and remembering his credo 'I will show them all' he has achieved an enormous success in outrage and sacrilege.'[3] In February 1989, a broadcast on Tehran home service moved the focus from Rushdie's personal character to his supposed status as a representative of Western society:

> Materialism and all kinds of political forces . . . chose this method of action – choosing a person who seemingly comes from India, apparently is separate from the Western world and who has a misleading name . . . All this speaks of an organised and planned effort . . . This is a confrontation to break the sanctity of Islam and all that is sacred in Islam.[4]

Alan Yentob, at a March 1989 conference at the Institute of Contemporary Arts, gave an utterly contrasting view, presenting Rushdie as a man of 'dedication and commitment' who had worked on his book 'for five years, well before talk of advances or prizes or publishers' rights'. He went on to say: 'It's also important to note that Rushdie is a man who has always seen himself as part of two worlds and has always spoken eloquently on behalf of the immigrant culture which he feels is an important part of the community'.[5]

Other readers, again on both sides, stressed the importance of the author's presumed intentions, and constructed these intentions on the basis of his ascribed status as one familiar with Islam. In an open letter to Rushdie, S. Nomanul Haq accuses him of deliberately mutilating history:

> Most of your Western readers are unable to gauge the acuteness of your blow to the very core of the Indian subcontinental culture. They cannot estimate the seriousness of the injury because they do not know the history of the aggrieved.
>
> You do know it and therefore one feels that you foresaw, at least to some extent, the consequences.[6]

The same idea was echoed by Roald Dahl, in a letter to *The Times* which characterised Rushdie as 'a dangerous opportunist'. According to Dahl, Rushdie clearly had 'profound knowledge of the Muslim religion and its people and . . . must have been totally aware of the deep and violent feelings his book would stir up among devout Muslims. In other words he knew exactly what he was doing and he cannot plead otherwise.'[7] Avoiding mention of Rushdie's career, but invoking instead his inmost thoughts, the *Independent on Sunday* printed an editorial preface to his essay 'In Good Faith' which balanced the whole affair on the question of his intentions: 'But has the novel simply been misread and misunderstood? Salman Rushdie believes that it has'[8] As Richard Webster remarks, it is surprising that Rushdie himself should forsake the textual subtleties of his book and fall back on the idea that there was a meaning which was misapprehended: 'Rushdie suddenly rediscovers a naive faith in the conscious intentions of the artist and appears to believe that if he proclaims his own holy intentions loudly enough the unholy results of the publication of *The Satanic Verses* will be annihilated, or neutralised'.[9] It could be argued, however, that the one person who has a right to claim knowledge of his conscious intentions is the author himself, even though his text might betray or transcend them.

In any case, we are still left with the question of why so much effort should have been invested in the construction of an author of recognisable and consistent character. Certainly, there is a legal and physical subject to serve as a focus for action, and there exists a historical record and material presence who answers to the appropriate name. Also, the fact that most of the Muslim activists had not read a great deal of the work they condemned, and indeed were forbidden to read it, meant that the author was a more obvious target of their attention. But apart from this consideration, which is more cultural than literary, I would argue that the readers' construction of the author is a response to the nature of this text, *The Satanic Verses*, and the postcolonial writing tradition of which it has become the defining example.

The text is postmodern, written in a style which takes apart the conventions of representational story-telling. Within the framing narrative of a quest for self and love, the conflicting and intertwining lives of Gibreel and Saladin, there are rewritings of other stories (of the cinema, of Islam, of immigrants' lives in London, of the butterfly pilgrimage), and in all the stories names and characters double and replicate themselves. The destabilising of the narrative form can itself be read as part of the content: '[Rushdie's] texts offer truths which are narrated as lies and thus anticipate and expose the official lies which are mediated as truths. They offer resistance, difference, fragmentation and change where in the real world and the world depicted constancy and homogeneity are propagated.'[10] While such descriptions of the novel are to be found throughout the criticism, readers and critics seem oddly reluctant to accept the idea of instability. Instead, they tend to choose one particular thread of narrative or imagery, extrapolating from that to create a meaning for the whole.[11] Feroza Jussawalla declares that 'Rushdie has become a victim not of the Muslim world so much as of the indeterminacy, which is the condition of post-modernism, whereby authority has been completely wrested from the author and in his absence has been placed in the hands of warring factions of readers'.[12] The indeterminate text is taken as a ground for the carving of an argument, as the rest of the article traces allusions and makes connections to stop Rushdie's attempts 'to escape the responsibilities of the monstrosities he perpetuates'. Selected characters are named by Jussawalla as the carriers of Rushdie's opinions: 'Mr. Rushdie, through the voice of Saladin Chamcha, seems to disapprove of the Black British rallying around their leaders . . .', and later, 'Mr. Rushdie chooses to hide behind the figure of Salman' – but these characters are also termed 'morally shady womanizers and whores of whom Mr. Rushdie, the author, clearly disapproves'.[13] It seems that a fragmented text, an area of indeterminacy, is construed as an invitation to assign meaning arbitrarily; not so much to discover a picture as to impose one. '[T]he reader is tempted to try and find an underlying pattern because of the way in which details in the different stories echo each other.'[14] If there is no obvious pattern, the reader's attention will be directed not towards the text but through it, to the only apparent source of all the fragments, the consciousness which created it:

> It was so it was not in a time long forgot
> Well, anyway goes something like this
> I can't be sure because when they came to call I wasn't myself no yaar not myself at all some days are hard how to tell you what sickness is like something like this but I can't be sure
> Always one part of me is standing outside screaming no please don't no but it does no good you see when the sickness comes
> I am the angel the god damned angel of god . . . (*sv* 544)

The only connecting thread in Gibreel's meditation, which contains scraps and references to all the narratives of the *Satanic Verses*, is his own identity. So, in the text, in microcosm, Gibreel's story, 'which was also the end of many stories' (*sv* 543), is read as representing Gibreel's mind, his deranged synthesis of the events which took place around him. And, through the text, outside it, M. H. Faruqi declares, 'It matters little if this entire sequence happens in a dream, fictional dream, of a fictional character, because here we are dealing with the creator of that so-called fiction.[15] The focus of the reading has changed: no longer concerned with the complexities of the text, it has become a reading of the author:

> I repeated the argument about context, pointing out that the sequences Muslims found so objectionable happened in dreams to a character suffering a psychotic breakdown. The language might be offensive, but surely Rushdie had set things up in such a way as to make it quite clear there was no authorial endorsement?
>
> 'The argument doesn't wash,' said Anwar. 'Supposing Punch exposes himself in front of the children, the man in the booth who pulls all the strings cannot say, 'It's not me, it's the puppet!' Everything in that show is created by the puppeteer – the man who wrote the novel.[16]

But where is the author? Part of the text's effect is to displace him: the Author/God is summoned into the narrative, characterised as a figure 'of medium height, fairly heavily built, with salt-and-pepper beard cropped close to the line of the jaw' (*sv* 318) – bearing, Gayatri Spivak considers, a distinct resemblance to Salman Rushdie.[17] This Author/God has renounced responsibility for his creations, refusing to make any pattern clear: 'Whether We be multiform, plural, representing the union-by-hybridization of such opposites as *Oopar* and *Neechay*, or whether We be pure, stark, extreme, will not be resolved here' (*sv* 319). Later, as the plot becomes more chaotic, he still insists: 'I'm saying nothing' (*sv* 408).

When the Author/God is divested of his authority, characterised, there is immediately a space left, the space to be filled by the newly-implied, further-back meta-author who created the first one. In this space, the readers quoted above created their separate images, their versions of the author, and Salman Rushdie must, it seems, assume responsibility for all of them.

He also has to choose where his own allegiance lies. The postcolonial author, unlike his text, is not permitted the attribute of indeterminacy. The defining location of postcolonial writing is on the ground of conflict between societies, between nations, coloniser and colonised, oppressor and oppressed. The author is marked by his political surroundings as well as his literary productions. Homi Bhabha draws on the work of Lacan and Hannah Arendt to locate agency in postcolonial writing 'outside the sentence',[18] in the space described by Lacan as 'the area of signifying convention' which allows meaning to be ascribed to signs.[19] In this area, meanings and consequences are, in Bhabha's term, 'contingent', not determined, and agency is not held solely by the author:

> The contingency of closure socializes the agent as a collective 'effect' through the distancing of the author. Between the cause and its intentionality falls the shadow. Can we then unquestionably propose that a story has a unique meaning in the first place? To what end does the series of events tend if the author of the outcome is not unequivocally the author of the cause? Does it not suggest that agency arises in the return of the subject, from the interruption of the series of events as a kind of interrogation and reinscription of before and after?[20]

Read in this way, the outraged reaction to *The Satanic Verses* is a perfect example of 'the return of the subject', as the process of rewriting, interpreting and interrogating the author and his work is carried out by those who felt themselves subjects of his satiric invention. In the postcolonial 'area of signifying convention' the author's race and his nationality are signs, as is the language in which he writes, the audience he writes for, and the literary or material rewards he expects. Edward Said remarks: 'That the novel dealt with Islam in English and for what was believed to be a largely Western audience was its main offense'.[21] Authors are identified, and identify themselves, with the politics and strategies of decolonisation. Their choice of language and subject becomes significant of their commitment to the cause, as Ngugi wa Thiong'o knows when he declares that his 'writing in Gikuyu language, a Kenyan language, an African language, is part and parcel of the anti-imperialist struggles of Kenyan and African peoples'.[22] The author is constructed in the mirror of his audience and history, denied the escape of plurality:

> There is only one God, to whom we shall all return. I would like to inform all the intrepid Muslims in the world that the author of the book entitled *The Satanic Verses*, which has been compiled, printed and published in opposition to Islam, the Prophet and the Koran, as well as those publishers who were aware of its contents, have been sentenced to death.[23]

While that statement was made in obedience to a political and religious imperative, the construction of an author does not necessarily involve a non-literary misreading of the novel. The text does not remain entirely unresolved; it moves towards the partial closure achieved in the end of one cycle, which is the beginning of another. The narrative opens with infinite promise, on the images of rebirth from the seed-pod of the jumbo jet on New Year's Day (*sv* 3–10). As it progresses, the plot moves the characters away from these possibilities, towards imprisonment in other people's obsessions. Gibreel's note on page 13 proclaims freedom, the capacity to change, leave behind the old self and reshape the new: '*We are creatures of air, Our roots in dreams And clouds, reborn In flight. Goodbye.*' But the meaning cannot remain indeterminate; it is at once rewritten: 'FARISHTA DIVES UNDERGROUND . . . GIBREEL FLIES COOP'. Gibreel's self changes outside his control, more than he knows, and avenues of possibility close against him until he lies 533 pages later, trapped in madness and his friend's satanic verses, victim and murderer: 'Gibreel put the barrel of the gun into his own mouth; and pulled the trigger; and was free'. The concept of freedom, mutability, takes its natural course into the fixity of death – which is itself, according to the text, the beginning of life. The end of the novel, like that of *Finnegans Wake*,[24] impels the reader to start again: the night, the moon and the 'miraculous lands' of the last pages move on to the 'brief and premature sun', and the 'universal beginning' of the novel's opening. 'To be born again, first you have to die' (*sv* 3) – like the characterised Author/God, the novel refuses to conclude, refuses to explain, follows a track of indeterminacy into 'an infinite regress of negations'[25] until the reader interrupts, recalls the author to ask him the question of agency: '*Che vuoi*? You are telling me that, but . . . what are you aiming at?'[26]

NOTES

1. Salman Rushdie, *The Satanic Verses* (Harmondsworth: Viking, 1988). Page references have been included in the text.
2. W. K. Wimsatt and Monroe C. Beardsley, 'The Intentional Fallacy', in Wimsatt, *The Verbal Icon: Studies in the Meaning of Poetry* (1954; London: Methuen, 1970), p. 5.
3. 'Anti-Islam's New Find: "Simon Rushton" a.k.a. Salman Rushdie', *Impact International*, 28 October 1988, quoted in Malise Ruthven, *A Satanic Affair: Salman Rushdie and the Wrath of Islam* (London: The Hogarth Press, 1991), p. 93.
4. Transcript of a recording by Hashemi-Rafsanjani, 15 February 1989, quoted in Lisa Appignanesi and Sara Maitland, *The Rushdie File* (London: Fourth Estate, 1989), pp. 85–6.
5. Alan Yentob, edited version of speech on 19 March 1989, quoted in Appignanesi and Maitland, pp. 196–7.
6. S. Nomanul Haq, letter, *International Herald Tribune*, 24 February 1989, quoted in Appignanesi and Maitland, p. 233.
7. Roald Dahl, letter, *The Times*, 28 February 1989, quoted in Appignanesi and Maitland, pp. 217–18.
8. Introduction to 'In Good Faith', by Salman Rushdie, *Independent on Sunday*, 4 February 1990, quoted in Richard Webster, *A Brief History of Blasphemy: Liberalism, Censorship and 'The Satanic Verses'* (Suffolk: The Orwell Press, 1990), p. 89.
9. Webster, p. 89.

10. Aleid Fokkema, 'Post-Modern Fragmentation or Authentic Essence?: Character in The Satanic Verses', in C. C. Barfoot and Theo D'haen (eds), *Shades of Empire in Colonial and Post-Colonial Literatures* (Amsterdam; Atlanta, GA: Rodopi, 1993), p. 56.

11. See, for example, Srinivas Aravamundan's account of the '420 confidence trick' in ' "Being God's postman is no fun, yaar": Salman Rushdie's *The Satanic Verses*', *Diacritics* 19.2 (1989), pp. 3–20; and Ishrat Lindblad, 'Salman Rushdie's *The Satanic Verses*: Monoism *contra* Pluralism', in Anna Rutherford (ed.), *From Commonwealth to Post-Colonial* (Sydney: Dangaroo Press, 1992), pp. 83–90.

12. Feroza Jussawalla, 'Resurrecting the Prophet: The Case of Salman, the Otherwise', *Public Culture* 2.1, p. 107.

13. Jussawalla, pp. 109, 111.

14. Lindblad, p. 87.

15. M. H. Faruqi, 'Publishing Sacrilege is Not Acceptable', Impact International, 28 October 1988, quoted in Ruthven, p. 94.

16. Ruthven, p. 138.

17. Gayatri C. Spivak, 'Reading The Satanic Verses', in Maurice Biriotti and Nicola Miller (eds), *What is an Author?* (Manchester: Manchester University Press, 1993), p. 112.

18. Homi K. Bhabha, 'The Postcolonial and the Postmodern', *The Location of Culture* (London: Routledge, 1994), p. 184.

19. Jacques Lacan, 'The insistence of the letter in the unconscious', in David Lodge (ed.), *Modern Criticism and Theory* (London: Longman, 1988), p. 102.

20. Bhabha, p. 190.

21. Edward W. Said, 'Figures, Configurations, Transfigurations', in Rutherford (ed.), p. 6.

22. Ngugi wa Thiong'o, *Decolonising the Mind: The Politics of Language in African Literature* (London: James Currey, 1986), p. 28.

23. Ayatollah Khomeini's *fatwa* of 14 February 1989, *Observer*, 19 February 1989, quoted in Appignanesi and Maitland, p. 84.

24. There are allusions to Joyce's work, especially *Ulysses*, throughout the novel; and Rushdie's use of Joycean (or sub-Joycean) word-play occasionally seems to be considered an offence compounding his original crime. See Webster, p. 94; Jussawalla, pp. 107–8.

25. Wayne C. Booth, *A Rhetoric of Irony* (Chicago, IL and London: University of Chicago Press, 1974), p. 59.

26. Bhabha, p. 184.

27

SEÁN BURKE

'The Ethics of Signature'

> if the spirit opens to him the *signature*, then he understands the speech of another . . . (Jacob Boehme, *Signatura Rerum*)

Recent events in literary and philosophical culture have lent a desperate urgency to the question 'Who is speaking?' In very different ways, the cases of Paul de Man and Heidegger on the one side, and Salman Rushdie on the other, have shown that we are a long way from the indifference which Foucault recommended as a virtual discursive ideal.[1] Societies retain a passionate, sincere and sometimes savage interest in retracing a discourse to its author or producer though the principles governing this procedure are still largely unformulated. In what does this interest consist? In what manner is it right and proper to oppose this demand? What are the ethics of signature?[2]

The issue of the ethical relationship between a discourse and its subject was first raised through Plato's condemnation of writing in the *Phaedrus* and *The Seventh Letter*.[3] Few Platonic moments are better known in literary studies today, but copious deconstructive attention to its metaphysical thematics registers little of the ethical force of Plato's argument, nor does it unearth the questions of signature which implicitly guide the equation of discursive responsibility with the presence of the subject. For Plato, the dialectical forum guarantees the perpetual and vigilant presence of a discourse's author to its audience and thereby establishes what we might call a signatory contract based upon the signature as performative. As the *Phaedrus* puts the matter:

once a thing is committed to writing it circulates equally among
those who understand the subject and those who have no business
with it; a writing cannot distinguish between suitable and unsuit-
able readers. And if it is ill-treated or unfairly abused it always
needs its parent to come to its rescue; it is quite incapable of
defending or helping itself. (275e)

Clearly, the ethical concerns which motivate Plato are still of the
highest moment – the reception histories, for example, of the Marxist
and Nietzschean discourses commend themselves to our attention
precisely within the ethical problematic marked out here. A graphic
culture – in which discourses circulate independently of the presence of
their subject – relinquishes the dialectical structure of response and
counter-response which supposedly ensures that discourses will not be
misprised or irresponsibly interpreted. A culture dominated by 'external signs', opens up an ethical abyss in which no system of responsible
discursive transmission can be instated in terms of a text's reception,
appropriation, legacies or the pedagogic relations between its subject
and audience.

Curiously, within many areas of postmodern thought the graphic
signature has been undermined according to principles almost exactly
the reverse of those articulated by Plato. While Plato maintained the
opposition of objective truth and subjective signature in the interests
not of sundering text and subject but of preserving their ideal, self-
present union *before the graphic signature*, a number of postmodern and
poststructuralist theorists have wished to suspend the signature so as to
increase the distance between discourse and subject. This sundering has
often been justified on the understanding that the notion of the subject
is itself somehow unethical. Ironically, then, at a time in which the
specificity of discourses is stressed within critical theory, the function of
the signature has yet to be generally readdressed. This rather tangled
state of affairs has arisen from a confusion of generic and authorial
subjects so that the legitimate ethical objections to autonomist and
universalising notions of subjectivity have been conflated with the
function of the signature which in fact works contrariwise to affirm
the *specificity* of subjecthood. How, we might ask by way of simplifica-
tion, can this latter function of the subject be regarded as ethically
troublesome? How can this dominant contractual and discursive
institution be characterised as unethical?

The most common arguments advanced in an ethical sense against
the signature serve a protective function: in the first instance, to protect

the signatory from the effects of the text; in the second, to protect the texts against the effects of the signature. This former position is upheld by Foucault when he claims that 'Speeches and books were assigned real authors . . . only when the author became subject to punishment and to the extent that his discourse was considered transgressive'.[4] And to be sure, it is easy to see a number of ethical advantages to be gained from the removal of the author-function and the consequent anonymous circulation of discourse. In a world without proper names, the publication of Descartes's *Le Monde* would not have been consigned to the posthumous estate, nor that of David Hume's *Dialogues Concerning Natural Religion*; nor again need so many women writers have dissimulated the homonym behind male pseudonyms, nor need countless authors have faced the threat or reality of persecution on the basis of what they had written.

However, in assessing anonymity in general ethical terms, we are caught between the poles of responsible discursive accountability and a punitive discursive policing; between, that is, proper attribution (as in the case of Heidegger) and improper retribution (as in the case of Rushdie). It is difficult to see how anonymity can in itself be asserted as an ethical goal since our ideas about the circulation of discourses tend to be subordinate to broader ethico-political considerations. At one and the same time, the same person might well be in favour of discursive anonymity in the case of a text like the *Dialogues Concerning Natural Religion* while declaring a social right and need to identify the author of a text such as *The Garden of Fascism*. Indeed, the higher ethical demand in the case of persecuted authors is not for a rearguard policy of anonymity but to ensure that an individual may write onymously without threat of reprisal: pseudonymity and dissimulation being within the grasp of most authors, the freedom to identify oneself as the author of a particular discourse is commonly assumed as a right of citizenship. To recommend anonymity *per se* is complicit with or at least acquiescent before the very totalitarian forces that provoke such a consideration in the first place. Anonymity and pseudonymity therefore recommend themselves not as ethical demands in themselves but as measures provisional upon the development of society towards a more enlightened perspective, just as the events of a comedy anticipate an ethical resolution in which justice is established and the proper name can disclose itself. One could as easily argue for onymity on the basis of Foucauldian reasoning: in a society where it did not matter who was speaking, the proper name could be appended without risk. Certainly, in any case, the right to sign is the *a fortiori* ethical assertion here.

The second argument commonly raised against the tethering of text and signatory is concerned to guard against *ad hominem* readings: such a position both complements and reverses the direction of the former in seeking to protect the text against violation from its author's personal life or beliefs. The debate which this position promotes commonly presents itself as an unyielding opposition between those who wish to assert the relevance of an author's personal life to the appraisal of his or her work and those who prefer to establish an absolute hiatus between a subject's discourse and actions. Certainly there is everything to be said for avoiding crudely *ad hominem* attacks. While personal information may be invaluable in determining the degree of sincerity with which a person upholds a system of beliefs, it cannot in any way determine the status of that system itself.

However, this entirely principled resistance to *ad hominem* arguments should in no wise compel us to establish a forcefield between text and author. It is only necessary to remind ourselves that the conjunction of life and work opens a channel of interpretation and enquiry rather than evaluation. The causal and genitive issues raised by the confrontation of an author's life and work remain tenable even though the procedure of assessing the value of that work is fallacious. While an enquiry into the relationship between a discourse and its producer is conducted in responsible ethical terms (i.e. given that it enquires into biographical and historical circumstances by and within which an ethically problematic discourse was composed) and is not driven to axiological ends (e.g. the use of Paul de Man's wartime collaborationism to discredit or evaluate his later work), then the sundering of text and signatory is ethically regressive. As with the case of a putative discursive anonymity, to close off the domain of ethical enquiry simply to avoid *ad hominem* arguments is as unnecessary in its own terms as it is unintelligible in those of an ethical criticism: it amounts to little more than a confusion of means and ends in that it installs strategies of questionable efficacy in the place of the ethical aims to whose service they have been subalterned. Plainly, then, everything depends not upon the properties of signature but upon the discrimination with which readers or societies treat the signature and the lines of ethical enquiry established on its basis.

Naturally, such debates concerning discursive propriety or the ethics of allowing biographical factors to influence reading are only raised with intensity during moments of ethical crisis: the very different cases of Heidegger, de Man and Rushdie attest to this with awesome clarity.

Indeed, the profound interrelation of ethics and the signature is borne out by the fact that questions of the signature are among the first to be raised in the context of an ethically troublesome text: 'Who wrote this discourse?' 'At what point in history?' 'Under what circumstances?' 'Who today will take responsibility for this discourse?' As a general principle, the necessity of properly attributing a text to a signatory and of holding the signatory or the signatory's heirs to account asserts itself in direct proportion to the perceived gravity of the ethico–political issues raised by that text. Such situations of ethical crisis, in spite of and because of their extremity, reveal that an ethical contract has always already been put in place on the basis of the relationship of signatory to text. The act of signing a text thus carries with it an intricate substructural set of ethical assumptions and opens an enduring channel of enquiry. This substructure subtends the texts of triviality as surely as those of persecution: whether or not the channel is activated or reopened depends solely upon whether an ethical demand or interrogation is made of the text.

The primary ethical function of the signature is therefore to set up a structure of resummons whereby the author may be recalled to his or her text. As with the legal signature, the textual mark is addressed to the future; to mortality and to the afterlife of the written sign. In particular, it offers itself to any tribunal which may be subsequently established upon on the basis of the signatory's text in relation to as yet unrealised historical circumstances. The signature accedes to this tribunal whose shape, agendas and composition will necessarily be unknown at the time of signing but whose distinctive form will in some sense be predicated upon the manner of signature and the relation of the signatory to what has been signed, much as a sculpture lies within unhewn stone awaiting the event which will liberate as actuality what exists *in potentia*. An act of signature thus establishes the chain connecting the author to his contemporaneous estate or to her post-humous estate. Thereby, the signature binds the text respectively to the still-living author, to the legacy and legatees of the dead author, to whatever traditions might have been established *in nomine auctoris* and to the posthumous reconstructions of authorial intention, biography and any system of oeuvre effects which might influence the ethical rereading of the text in question. This entire threadwork of recall through which the text may be reprised and reassessed in relation to its signatory and to its histories, those by which it was promoted and those which it promotes – this threadwork is woven in the distance marked by the graphic signifier and the empirical absence of the signatory: it bridges the chasm which formerly opened and closed in the pause between an ephebe's question and the dialectician's response.

Naturally the graphic signature cannot ensure the safe transmission of authorial intentions, but it does not differ in this respect from the dialectical signature: the trial of Socrates itself demonstrates that an orally-signed discourse is open to all the perils of misreception. The hazards of discourse are common to both, and everything is determined by the ethos with which one signs and the ethos of the audience which countersigns a discourse. In this regard, the signature puts in place channels of accountability, responsibility and enquiry which attend to the specific concerns which haunted Plato's vision of a graphic culture. Indeed, Plato's denunciations of writing will only seem hyperbolic to us today because he did not consider this space of ethical recall that is activated by the signature. The true Platonic nightmare would indeed be an anonymous discourse, a discourse genuinely orphaned, irresponsible and without any ethical trackback whatsoever.

The signature in fact decisively supplements the ethical critique of writing in the *Phaedrus*. It enacts a double logic similar to that of the *pharmakon* in that it staunches the wound that its very possibility opens, unites text and signatory as it marks their separation, acts as the trace or track between a discourse and its departed subject. The ground which it liberates unfolds between the ephemerality of spoken discourse and the potential ethical irresponsibility of anonymous graphic discourse, allowing to a culture the advantages (ethical and otherwise) of the *scripta manent* while ensuring that discourse remains accountable and retraceable in principle to its agent. In so doing, the signatory act installs the ethical within the graphic, making an ethics of reading and of writing possible in accordance, respectively, with the ethical categories of accountability and enquiry. Like the Chinese character for trust, which depicts a man standing by speech, signature is an intrinsically ethical and fiduciary institution. Just as there is no contract without signatories, so too there can be no ethics of discourse which does not take proper measure of the signature and the deep structure of ethical relationships which it registers. In order to affirm our ethical concerns as readers and writers, we should therefore uphold a concept of the signature beyond that of a paraph or flourish decorating the covers of a text, as an excess which encompasses text, signatory and an ethical future of reading. *Why* we should do so, of course, is the first concern of a metaethics and remains another question, another country.

NOTES

1. See Michel Foucault, 'What is an Author?' in idem, *Language, Counter-Memory Practice: Selected Essays and Interviews*, ed. Donald Bouchard, trans. Donald Bouchard and Sherry Simon (Ithaca, NY: Cornell University Press, 1977), pp. 113–138: pp. 137–38

2. The question of the signature has been raised in Peggy Kamuf, *Signature Pieces: On the Institution of Authorship* (Ithaca, NY: Cornell University Press, 1988), but the clearest connection of the act of signing and ethical responsibility emerges in Jacques Derrida's finely suggestive reading of the Nietzschean legacy – see Jacques Derrida, *The Ear of the Other: Otobiography, Transference, Translation: Texts and Discussions with Jacques Derrida*, translated by Peggy Kamuf and Avital Ronnel (New York: Schocken Books, 1986). The issue of the signature and legacy is also raised in Derrida's oneiric reading of Freud's attempts to found a familial legacy *in nomine auctoritas* – see Jacques Derrida, *The Post Card: From Socrates to Freud and Beyond*, trans. Alan Bass (Chicago, IL and London: University of Chicago Press, 1987), pp. 257–409. In this discussion, I will only be dealing with the homonym and that category of pseudonym – 'George Eliot', for example – whose connection with the homonym has been thoroughly naturalised.

3. Cf. Plato, *Phaedrus and the Seventh and Eighth Letters*, translated by Walter Hamilton (Harmondsworth: Penguin Books, 1973). Page references are supplied parenthetically within the text.

4. Michel Foucault, 'What is an Author?', op. cit., p. 124.

28

RICHARD RORTY

'Taking Philosophy Seriously'

At the beginning of 1933, Martin Heidegger was the most admired and celebrated philosopher in Germany, a country that takes its philosophers seriously. Hitler became chancellor on January 30 of that year. The young Leo Lowenthal, and a lot of other politically active Jewish academics, did not go home on the night of the 30th. Lowenthal walked the streets until he could board an early morning train across the frontier. By February 21 Thomas Mann had left the country, and by March 21 Friedrich Ebert (the first chancellor of post-World War I Germany) was in a concentration camp. On April 7 all Jews were expelled from the civil service (which included all professorial positions in the German universities). On April 16 a Social Democrat who had been elected to the post the previous year was installed as rector (chief administrative officer) of the University of Freiburg. He was quickly dismissed, by order of the Nazi authorities. Heidegger accepted election as his successor on April 22.

Heidegger joined the Nazi party on May 1. On May 26 he addressed a rally in memory of a proto-Nazi, Albert Schlageter, who had just been named 'the first National Socialist German soldier.' Schlageter, Heidegger told the students, had drawn strength for his martyrdom from the granite of the Black Forest landscape, the landscape in which Heidegger himself had grown up. On May 27 he delivered his inaugural address as rector: 'The Self-determination of the German University.' Self-determination, in the sense in which Heidegger used the term, had nothing to do with 'academic freedom,' a notion Heidegger mentioned only in order to sneer at it. He defined self-determination as 'the university's primordial and communal will to attain its own essence,' and as 'the will to *Wissenschaft* [roughly: science and scholarship], conceived of as the will to carry out the historical and spiritual mission of the German people, a people that achieves self-consciousness through its State.'

A principal concern of the rectorial address was to reject the cosmopolitan, universalistic overtones of the word *Wissenschaft*. Another was to emphasize the unity of *Wissenschaft* and the role of the philosopher as the person who grasps this unity: 'all *Wissenschaft* is philosophy,' Heidegger said, 'whether it wants to be or not.' Hitler and the Nazis are not mentioned in the rectorial address, although there are a lot of passages that the Nazi students would have misheard as echoes of their own rhetoric: for example, 'The German students are on the march. They seek leaders through whom their own commitment to grounded truth will be exalted.' The Nazis would have misheard because the sort of leader Heidegger had in mind in his constantly repeated invocation of 'the leaders and protectors of the destiny of the German people' was not Hitler, but himself. The rectorial address puts forward, in entire seriousness, the claim that only Heideggerian philosophy can bring the universities into the service of this destiny. One cannot exaggerate the degree to which Heidegger took philosophy, and himself, seriously.

For the rest of 1933 Heidegger fought like a tiger to become the official philosopher, the intellectual leader, of the National Socialist movement. His dream was to become head of a governmental body that would first reorganize, and then control, all the German universities. His big idea was to combine university study with lots of hiking, camping, ROTC-style drills, and WPA-type work in the forests (and also with a lot of teaching in adult education courses, getting the new national spirit across to the non-academics). He wanted to bring the future leaders and protectors of the destiny of the German people back to the rootedness in landscape (the granite, the forests, the mountain trails) that the ancient Greeks had once enjoyed.

Thanks to Christianity and modern science – two phenomena that Heidegger distrusted almost equally because they had contributed to 'the forgetfulness of Being' – the modern world had lost this rootedness. But the Nazi movement was a chance to regain it. In the manner of the Southern Agrarians of the '30s, who explained that those who had never gone coon hunting could not grasp the 'organic' (albeit racially segregated) character of Deep South society, Heidegger explained that the rootless, cosmopolitan, academic mandarins whom he hoped to depose were out of touch with 'the real Germany.' A good old boy from the Black Forest, who was also the leading philosopher of Europe and the incarnation of pre-Socratic 'primordial essentiality,' was the obvious candidate for the spiritual leadership of Germany.

Heidegger gave this effort his best shot. In the course of 1933 he was all over the place, making speeches to gatherings of his fellow scholars and to student rallies, writing memoranda to government authorities and articles for the press. In November, in an uncharacteristically self-abnegatory article in the Freiburg student newspaper, he concluded, 'Do not let principles and "ideas" be the rules of your life. The Führer himself, he alone, is the German reality of today and of the future. He is the law of that reality . . . Heil Hitler!' In December he was helping to organize the publication in five languages of a volume that would show the scholars of other countries that German *Wissenschaft* was united behind Hitler.

By early 1934, however, it was all over. Heidegger found himself outflanked by lesser men – philosophy professors who were more cunning, better connected, more willing to lick boots and to bait Jews. Hikes in the mountains, combined with stirring talk about the pre-Socratics around the evening campfire, seemed to harder heads an unlikely basis on which to reorganize the German university system. Also, although Heidegger had dutifully enforced most of the anti-Jewish regulations sent down from the Ministry of Culture, he had made a fuss about a few of them, and this gave ammunition to his rivals. In February Heidegger stepped down from his rectorship, into political obscurity. The dream was dreamt out.

Eleven years later, when World War II was over, Heidegger was whitewashed by the University of Freiburg de-Nazification commission, but still forbidden to lecture by the French military occupation authorities. This helped him to pretend to a sort of martyrdom (the good, gray, sadly muzzled teacher) and helped set the stage for the claim, by his disciples, that the year-long 'Nazi episode' had been an unfortunate mistake, which told little about Heidegger's philosophy or his character.

Heidegger himself heartily endorsed this view in an interview he gave in 1969 (published after his death in 1976). In that interview, which he intended to be his only, definitive statement on the matter, he explained that he had mistakenly and briefly been convinced that the Nazis were Germany's only hope. He refrained, however, from any expression of regret concerning his allegiance to them. He spoke of his extravagant praise of Hitler as a necessary 'compromise'. Neither there nor elsewhere did he make reference to the Holocaust, but instead spent considerable time complaining about having himself been, after 1934, harassed by Nazi functionaries. When asked about the deletion of the dedication to Husserl (Heidegger's former patron and friend) from some of the editions of *Being and Time* published under the Nazis, Heidegger seemed to think it obvious that he had behaved sensibly by deleting a dedication to a Jew rather than letting his book go out of print.

That interview did great harm to Heidegger's reputation, not least because he stupidly thought it would do good. Harm had also been done earlier by the republication (by Guido Schneeberger, in 1962) of various documents he had written in 1933, including the tribute to Hitler cited above. But his disciples and admirers continued to insist that Heidegger was basically a man of good character, as well as a profoundly original and important thinker. They tried to portray him as a man whose vision of a redeemed, re-Hellenized Germany blinded him to certain political realities – as a man whose mind was elsewhere, who did not notice things he should have noticed.

Victor Farias's book [*Heidegger et le Nazisme*] should put an end to all such attempts. The book makes perfectly clear that, as a human being, Heidegger was a rather nasty piece of work – a coward and a liar, pretty much from first to last. Farias, a teacher of philosophy in Berlin, put in years of work digging up dirt about Heidegger from various obscure government archives and collections of letters. He found a lot, enough to paint a picture that makes plain how utterly disingenuous Heidegger's public statements on the topic were, enough to explain why the Heidegger family has refused to let Heidegger's letters be read until the middle of the next century.

There is doubtless a lot more incriminating evidence to be found, not only in those letters but, closer to hand, in the archives of the University of Freiburg for the Nazi years – archives that, shamefully, are still closed to scholars. In the meantime, Farias has given us a good sketch of what happened. His book includes more concrete information relevant to Heidegger's relations with the Nazis than anything else available, and it is an excellent antidote to the evasive apologetics that are still being published. (The book appeared first in French because Farias was initially unable to find a German publisher. Fischer Verlag has now taken on the job, and it is to be hoped that their German edition, and an English translation, will appear shortly. Both, incidentally, would benefit from enlarged footnotes; Farias's references are sometimes too sparse to help one run down what exactly is being cited.)

Why should anyone care whether Heidegger was a self-deceptive egomaniac? A good reason for caring about such matters is that the details about the attitudes of German intellectuals towards the Holocaust are important for our own moral education. It pays to realize that the vast majority of German academics, including some of the best and brightest, turned a blind eye to the fate of their Jewish colleagues, and to ask whether we ourselves might not be capable of the same sort of behaviour.

A bad reason for caring is the notion that learning about a philosopher's moral character helps one evaluate his philosophy. It does not, any more than our knowledge of Einstein's character helps us evaluate his physics. You can be a great, original, and profound artist or thinker, and also a complete bastard. Van Gogh, Keats, and Einstein were nice guys; Wagner, Milton, and Newton were not. Among philosophers, Bertrand Russell was a decent (if sometimes ducally arrogant) man, but he got most of his good ideas (as opposed to his bad, British empiricist ones) from the great founder of formal semantics and mathematical logic, Gottlob Frege, a vicious anti-Semite and proto-Nazi. Paul Tillich talked the same jargon of 'authenticity' that Heidegger had used in *Being and Time*, yet Tillich was an honest man and a good Social Democrat, and prudently scarpered, on Lowenthal's heels, in 1933.

There is no way to correlate moral virtue with philosophical importance or philosophical doctrine. Being an original philosopher (and Heidegger was as original a philosopher as we have had in this century) is like being an original mathematician or an original microbiologist or a consummate chess master: it is the result of some neural kink that occurs independently of other kinks. The only reason we think that good moral character is more important for professors of philosophy than for professors of other subjects is that we often use 'philosopher' as the name of an ideal human being: one who perfectly unites wisdom and kindness, insight and decency. All of us, perhaps, unconsciously hope to find such a guru – someone who will be everything our parents were not. But 'philosopher' is not the right name for this ideal. That name has been appropriated for other purposes, to name the people who write about, for example, Plato, Aristotle, Kant, and Hegel, or about the issues these men discussed. In this latter sense, Frege and Heidegger were equally great and original philosophers (though the issues they discussed were very different). That greatness is unsullied by their moral indecency.

Still, even if we grant that philosophical talent and moral character swing free of each other, it is tempting to think that we can classify philosophies by reference to the moral or political message they convey. Many people think that there is something intrinsically fascistic about the thought of Nietzsche and Heidegger, and are suspicious of Derrida and Foucault because they owe so much to these earlier figures. On this view, fascism is associated with 'irrationalism,' and a decent democratic outlook with 'confidence in reason.' Aristotle's casual acceptance of slavery as natural and proper is taken to be central to his moral outlook; Heidegger's blood-and-soil rhetoric is taken to be central to his 'history of Being'; Nietzsche's elitist swaggering is taken as central to his ethic of self-creation; 'deconstruction' is condemned on the basis of the young Paul de Man's opportunistic anti-Semitism.

Such attempts to simplify the thought of original thinkers by reducing them to moral or political attitudes should be avoided, just as we should avoid thinking of Hemingway as simply a bully, of Proust as simply a sissy, of Pound as simply a lunatic, of Kipling as simply an imperialist. Labels like 'irrationalist' or 'aesthete' are of no use when dealing with authors of the complexity and originality of a Heidegger or a Proust. They are merely excuses for not reading them.

'Irrationalism,' for example, has been diagnosed in everybody from William of Ockham to William James. As it happens, James was as decent a man as ever gave a philosophy lecture, as well as being Whitman's heir in the visionary tradition of American democracy. Yet that did not prevent Julien Benda (the Allan Bloom of the 1910s) from including James in his list of treasonous clerks – the people who were undermining the moral fabric of our civilization. (Heidegger and James shared the same doubts about traditional philosophical accounts of Reason and Truth – the sort of doubt that Benda found intolerable – despite having no political hopes in common.) Karl Popper, in *The Open Society and Its Enemies*, did a good job of showing how passages in Plato, Hegel, and Marx could be taken to justify Hitlerian or Leninist takeovers, but to make his case he had to leave out 90 percent of each man's thought. Such attempts to reduce a philosopher's thought to his possible moral or political influence are as pointless as the attempt to view Socrates as an apologist for Critias, or Jesus as just one more charismatic kook. Jesus was indeed, among other things, a charismatic kook, and Heidegger was, among other things, an egomaniacal, anti-Semitic redneck. But we have gotten a lot out of the Gospels, and I suspect that philosophers for centuries to come will be getting a lot out of Heidegger's original and powerful narrative of the movement of Western thought from Plato to Nietzsche.

If there is something anti-democratic in Christianity, or Islam, or Platonism, or Marxism, or Heideggerianism, or 'deconstruction,' it is not any particular doctrine about the nature of Man or Reason or History, but simply the tendency to take either religion or philosophy too seriously. This is the tendency towards fundamentalism, the assumption that anybody who disagrees with some given religious or philosophical doctrine is a danger to democratic society. No specific doctrine is much of a danger, but the idea that democracy depends on adhesion to some such doctrine is.

John Rawls, in *A Theory of Justice*, takes religious toleration as paradigmatic for a democratic political outlook: insofar as people can manage to treat their Catholic, Mormon, or atheist neighbors as full-fledged fellow citizens, insofar as they can privatize their own and others' religious beliefs, a pluralist society becomes a real possibility. More recently Rawls has suggested that democratic social theory should develop the same sort of tolerance for alternative philosophical doctrines – for example, towards such secular accounts of the point of human life as those offered by Aristotle, Spinoza, Baudelaire, Nietzsche, Proust, Hemingway, or Heidegger. As Rawls puts it, democratic social theory 'should stay on the surface, philosophically speaking.' It should stop looking for philosophical 'foundations' of democracy. It should content itself with articulating the moral sensibility that enables us to be fair to people with whom we have little in common, rather than trying to ground that sensibility on something more basic.

This Rawlsian attitude is the diametrical opposite of Heidegger's. Heidegger thought that the scientific, cultural, and political life of a society was simply the working-out of a set of ideas that some great philosopher had formulated. He believed that not only all *Wissenschaft* but all significant human activity was philosophy, whether it knew it or not. He carried over into philosophy the attitude characteristic of religious prophets: that their own voice is the voice of some greater power (God, Reason, History, Being), a power that is about to make all things new, to bring on a new age of the world.

Such an attitude on the part of the prophets leads their natural followers – the people who take the idea of 'essence' or 'foundation' seriously – to the adoration that many Shiites have for Khomeini and many Marxists have had for Lenin. Such people worry about the 'authentic interpretation' of their guru's words, about whether they have caught 'the essence' of his thought. Conversely, they see their guru's competitors as false prophets (Antichrist, The Great Satan, Goldstein, the Philosopher of Fascism, the Apologist for Bourgeois Ideology). The works of those competitors are to be burned, or mocked, or ignored, but certainly not studied.

The contrasting view is to assume that the works of anybody whose mind was complex enough to make his or her books worth reading will not have an 'essence,' that those books will admit of a fruitful diversity of interpretations, that the quest for 'an authentic reading' is pointless. One will assume that the author was as mixed-up as the rest of us, and that our job is to pull out, from the tangle we find on the pages, some lines of thought that might turn out to be useful for our own purposes. This attitude towards books is an extension of the sort of pluralistic tolerance that Rawls thinks basic to the theory, as well as to the practice, of democracy. If one adopts it, one will not think of Heidegger as a symbol of something wonderful or of something terrible, but as one more original and interesting writer, as one more source for a description of our experience, to be woven together with all the other descriptions we have encountered.

Without such a reading, we risk falling back into Heidegger's own attitude. We risk becoming philosophical fundamentalists and cultists. Heidegger and Hitler had a lot in common: blood-and-soil rhetoric, anti–Semitism, self-deception, a conviction that philosophy must be taken seriously, and the desire to found a cult. Both men's desires were, alas, gratified. But the proper reaction is not to treat Heidegger as Hitler's philosophical equivalent. It is to read his books as he would not have wished them to be read: in a cool hour, with curiosity, and an open, tolerant mind.

Part 3

Writing the Self

Writing the Self

When Arthur Rimbaud declared 'Je est un autre', he served to remind us that one cannot easily equate author and self. Indeed, in extreme cases, the act of authorship can present itself as self-deflection or indeed as the creation of an aesthetic identity which seeks to transcend or negate the biographical subject. Both spiritual and sceptical notions of selfhood themselves refuse the notion of the self as a fixed or given entity. From a spiritual viewpoint, the self is perceived as quest, as an ideal attainable only when the individual is united with the Divine Will. Contemporary theorists have produced a materialist variation on this theme by asserting the idea of the subject-in-process, often taking their lead from David Hume's more radical thesis that the self is nothing more than a sequence of sensations for which no necessary causal connection or ontological unity can be claimed. If not quite a lie against time, the humanist assumption of an enduring literary self certainly simplifies the complex relations of author, historical subject and text, as does that anti-humanism which seeks to collapse the play of subjectivity into a generalised writing.

The trials of the self are particularly acute in literature since, according to an older view, literature is the medium *par excellence* in which a continuous selfhood can be asserted against evanescence and mortality: on a more modern perspective, it thence becomes the specialised arena in which the failure or impossibility of so doing is dramatised. Naturally, the will towards self-representation varies according to genre and historical period. In epic and drama, self-concealment was often the more appropriate aim until Wordsworth attempted to adapt the epic form to autobiography and expressionist dramatists saw the theatre as a viable setting for the dramatisation of personality. With lyric and romantic poetry, the quests of the self have ever been pronounced: for the novel, self-representation is not a generic commitment in realist modes but asserts itself in the *Bildungsroman* and various species of autobiographical novel. In all these genres, however, the difficulties of self-writing can be ironically thematised or mediated through the construction of an aestheticised self. Within conventional autobiography (*autos*: self; *bios*: life; *graphe*: writing), though, such problems are compounded by the absence of an ostensible narrator or a poetic speaker through which agency the author is formally distanced from the subject of representation. The peculiar compulsion to achieve an ideal union between author (subject writing) and subject (subject written about) characteristic of autobiography is thwarted on the one side by the impossibility of reducing self to language; on the other, by the conditions of temporality: autobiography as genre requires the recapturing of a self lost in time past and renewable only through memory. Hence the issues of time and memory have occupied the great autobiographers from Augustine, through Rousseau to the novelist Marcel Proust. Among the many ways in which an autobiographer can seek to overcome the divisions in the subject, we might list the following:

1. a mystical conception of the past as contemporaneous with the present which seeks to erase the distinction between subject-writing and subject-written-about;
2. a view of the self as spiritually completed and unified in the narratives of confession and conversion;
3. the postulate of an unifying ego which assures the self-identity of the subject through time;
4. the imposition of narrative destiny or a general teleological frame-work.

   The texts represented here are chosen not for their generic purity but for their refusal of generic and subjective reassurances. In their jagged relations to the autobiographical 'proper', it is hoped that they will foreground rather than conceal the enigmatic boundaries between the no less enigmatic categories of author, self and writing.

   Modern autobiography is generally considered to have commenced with Jean-Jacques Rousseau's monumental *Confessions*. While the modernity of Rousseau's text stems in part from its organisation in terms of a unifying romantic ego, Michel de Montaigne's *Essays* show a thoroughgoing scepticism about the possibility of uniting author and subject. While owing something to Augustine, the *Essays* unfold in a secular setting and reflect the development of Renaissance humanism: Montaigne takes for his interlocutor not a Divine addressee but rather any reader with a sympathetic ear for this humane self-portrait. 'Each man bears within himself the entire form of man's estate', Montaigne declares, and his text has cancelled the gap between implied and historical reader for audiences spanning more than four centuries. Indeed, the role which it assigns to the reader as collaborator and producer of the text makes Montaigne's text uncannily modern. Its elegant omission of conjunctions and logically implied stages of argument invite the reader to supplement the sense of the text at every turn. Written over a period of twenty years, the *Essays* are always alert to the division within the autobiographical subject both in theory and practice. In the short extract included here, Montaigne's text shows itself entirely aware of the fact that the subject of the enunciation (the 'Montaigne' who writes) can never become one with the subject of the utterance (the 'Montaigne' who is written about): the autobiographical 'I' is constantly divided in its search of a past self which is ever in flight. Lacking both the potential for a spiritually reunited self that we find in Augustine's *Confessions*, or the egoic unification of the Rousseauian subject, the conceptual bases of Montaigne's 'humanism' perhaps discover their strongest resonances in Roland Barthes's ironic and self-undoing attempt at self-representation in *Roland Barthes by Roland Barthes*.

Montaigne's scepticism concerning the unity of the self is taken to radical lengths by René Descartes, whose pre-emptive method of doubt provided the prototype for the modern view of subjectivity. Descartes's 'Second Meditation' is presented in an informal tone reminiscent of the *Essays* and similarly incorporates the reader within the very performative structure of its argument. Obviously, Descartes's demonstration is not offered in the context of this reader to rigorous philosophical scrutiny but as a unique act of autobiography and self-authorship. The Cartesian *cogito* affirms existence as a performative function of consciousness – only in the act of thinking does the meditating subject assure his own existence which is affirmed independently of the body or an external world. Within this demonstration, the author indeed 'enters into his own death' (to use Barthes's phrase) – or rather the author sends the narrative 'I' to its death to be reconstituted as an impersonal thinking substance. The narrative subject of the *Meditations* cannot therefore be identified totally with its author since the latter actively divests the former of any sense of self. Thus does Descartes generate an autobiographical act which – so far from assuming a full self – suspends altogether the notion of selfhood in the form of an empty consciousness open to occupation by any reader who wishes to instantiate him or herself within the meditating 'I' for the time of the reading. The Cartesian *cogito* has exercised an inestimable influence on modern philosophy in terms of Kantian epistemology, the phenomenological investigations of consciousness and the tradition of transcendental idealism in general. On the negative side, the dualism which effectively promotes consciousness over matter, mind over body, has been the focus of intense opposition within theoretical schools for whom the Body occupies a primacy in relation to which consciousness is a mere by-product.

The anti-rationalist 'return to the body' often takes as its starting point Nietzsche's insistence that all thought is an autobiographical act prompted by a biologistic will-to-power. Nietzsche was himself the first thinker to announce the philosopher as author and *creator* (rather than rationally-elevated recipient) of a perspectival 'truth'. In his last completed text, *Ecce Homo*, Nietzsche offers an autobiographical self-summation in which he takes up the role of prophetic critic to his own work. Reversing spiritual and confessional traditions, Nietzsche declares himself as the great Dionysian immoralist, a secular Anti-Christ. In 'Why I Am a Destiny', Nietzsche offers a peculiar justification of the book's intention to show 'how one becomes what one is' by presenting himself as the author of the political future, viewing the events that collide within his own biography as the most profound and terrible shift in European thought since the advent of Christianity. With an uncanny foresight of the (mis)use which Nazi propagandists would make of his teaching in the promulgation of fascist ideology, Nietzsche affirms an unprecedented confessional paradigm in seeking not to exculpate himself from the crimes of the past but to implicate himself – with neither restraint nor misgiving – in those of the future. If not an invitation to monstrous readings, then at least a refusal to programme correct interpretations in advance, 'Why I Am a Destiny' adopts a cajoling and virtually disdainful tone towards the common reader in its appeal to an as yet unborn elect of aristocratic radicals.

The text also poses a slightly more conventional question of authorship in that Nietzsche's mental health was at breaking point during the writing of *Ecce Homo*. Are we then to take this text to occupy a place within the Nietzschean oeuvre equal to that of the soberly propounded *The Genealogy of Morals*? Is there an 'essential

Nietzsche' on the basis of which we might decide? Such a dilemma poses questions of biography as well as those of oeuvre: to what extent are we justified in allowing the salient biographical detail of Nietzsche's mental collapse to determine our ethical and evaluative economies of the texts assembled under his proper name?

Nietzsche's status as philosophical author is very much complicated by the curious intermingling of self-declaration and philosophical reflection, literary creation and intellectual critique in his work. The Argentine writer Jorge Luis Borges has developed a metafictional variation on this paradigm of the critic as author by turning essay into story, story into essay. In 'Pierre Menard: Author of the *Quixote*', Borges engineers the fantastic scenario in which a fastidious twentieth-century aesthete from Nîmes manages to rewrite sections of Cervantes's chivalrous text without reference to the original. Borges plays off the frisson of creative and replenishing disjunction against the dull chime of coherence between an author's life and work. Borges's playful aesthetic strategies of 'the deliberate anachronism and the erroneous attribution' lampoon the positivist procedures of textual scholarship while pointing up the inevitable gap between what the *Quixote* means for a contemporary readership and what Cervantes intended it to mean for his seventeenth-century audience. Radically removed in place (France rather than Spain) as in time, the figure of Menard represents 'the *reader* of the *Quixote*' in a device which dramatically registers the lacuna between Cervantes's original meaning and the text's contemporary significance. *Don Quixote* can neither mean what its author meant it to mean nor can it again reach the audience for which it was intended: as readers, we inevitably participate in *authoring* the *Quixote* for our own age. Needless to say, 'Pierre Menard' should also be read with a keen ear for *its* author's coruscating humour.

'Kafka and his Precursors' is similarly concerned with the ways in which the present *authors* the past. Borges here takes up the temporal inversion of tradition, arguing that the latecomer is not the product of his precursors but their creator. Structural rather than personal or even influential relations determine the discursive cluster: as Borges puts it, the later Kafka is prefigured less by the early Kafka than by Robert Browning. The essay may also be read as parasitic upon T. S. Eliot and prophetic of Harold Bloom or – in line with the reversal of chronological perspective which it proposes – as learning from Bloom and prefiguring Eliot.

'Everything and Nothing' explores the equation between creative empathy and the void of the creating self. Taking bardolatry to its conceptual extreme, Borges's parable of the metaphysics of authorship ironically juxtaposes the emptiness of the Divine Creator with that of his most revered literary counterpart. The narrator holds over the proper name to examine the arid and uncertain biography speculated on the basis of its oeuvre. At the close, Borges reveals that Shakespeare – who had dreamt of being so many but was nothing in himself – is a dreamer within a dream, a creator who is a creation, an author whose part and its plays have been scripted in advance by the Divine and dreaming Author.

'Borges and I' further illuminates the vertiginous labyrinth of authorship in a parable which delicately enacts the mysterious commerce between the proper name and its bearer. Sliding between almost imperceptible deictic references, the Borgesian 'I' follows the elegiac disappearance of biographical self into both time past and the reservoir of the authorial name which inherits from the flesh. The dilemma of its closing sentence will, I trust, remain beyond resolution even as it is decipherable, like those of author and self, self and text, dreamer and dream.

SUGGESTED FURTHER READINGS

Augustine, St, *Confessions* (Oxford: Oxford University Press, 1992).

Aurelius, Marcus, *The Meditations* (Oxford: Oxford University Press, 1989).

Barthes, Roland, *Roland Barthes by Roland Barthes* (London: Macmillan Press, 1977).

Benstock, Shari (ed.), *The Private Self: Theory and Practice of Women's Autobiographical Writings* (Chapel Hill, NC: University of North Carolina Press, 1988).

Bruss, Elizabeth W., *Autobiographical Acts* (Baltimore, MD: Johns Hopkins University Press, 1976).

Corngold, Stanley, *The Fate of the Self: German Writers and French Theory* (New York: Columbia University Press, 1986).

Dennett, Daniel C., 'Self-Invention', *Times Literary Supplement*, 16–22 September 1988, pp. 1,016, 1,028–9.

Derrida, Jacques, 'Roundtable on Autobiography', in idem, *The Ear of the Other* (New York: Schocken Books, 1986).

Eakin, Paul John, *Fictions in Autobiography: Studies in the Art of Self-Invention* (Princeton, NJ: Princeton University Press, 1985).

Gunn, Janet Varner, *Autobiography: Towards a Poetic of Experience* (Philadelphia, PA: University of Philadelphia Press, 1982).

Hume, David, *A Treatise of Human Nature*, Book 1, Part IV (Oxford: Clarendon Press, 1978).

Olney, James (ed.), *Autobiography: Essays Theoretical and Critical* (Princeton, NJ: Princeton University Press, 1980).

Proust, Marcel, *Remembrance of Things Past* (London: Chatto and Windus, 1981).

Rousseau, Jean-Jacques, *The Confessions of Jean-Jacques Rousseau* (Harmondsworth: Penguin Books, 1953).

Ryan, Michael, 'The Act', *Glyph II* (1978), pp. 64–87.

Wordsworth, William, *The Prelude*, ed. E. de Selincourt (Oxford: Oxford University Press, 1926).

29

MICHEL DE MONTAIGNE

from *Essays*

. . .

Others form man; I tell of him, and portray a particular one, very ill-formed, whom I should really make very different from what he is if I had to fashion him over again. But now it is done.

Now the lines of my painting do not go astray, though they change and vary. The world is but a perennial movement. All things in it are in constant motion – the earth, the rocks of the Caucasus, the pyramids of Egypt – both with the common motion and with their own. Stability itself is nothing but a more languid motion.

I cannot keep my subject still. It goes along befuddled and staggering, with a natural drunkenness. I take it in this condition, just as it is at the moment I give my attention to it. I do not portray being: I portray passing. Not the passing from one age to another, or, as the people say, from seven years to seven years, but from day to day, from minute to minute. My history needs to be adapted to the moment. I may presently change, not only by chance, but also by intention. This is a record of various and changeable occurrences, and of irresolute and, when it so befalls, contradictory ideas: whether I am different myself, or whether I take hold of my subjects in different circumstances and aspects. So, all in all, I may indeed contradict myself now and then; but truth, as Demades said, I do not contradict. If my mind could gain a firm footing, I would not make essays, I would make decisions; but it is always in apprenticeship and on trial.

I set forth a humble and inglorious life; that does not matter. You can tie up all moral philosophy with a common and private life just as well as with a life of richer stuff. Each man bears the entire form of man's estate.

Authors communicate with the people by some special extrinsic mark; I am the first to do so by my entire being, as Michel de Montaigne, not as a grammarian or a poet or a jurist. If the world complains that I speak too much of myself, I complain that it does not even think of itself.

But is it reasonable that I, so fond of privacy in actual life, should aspire to publicity in the knowledge of me? Is it reasonable too that I should set forth to the world, where fashioning and art have so much credit and authority, some crude and simple products of nature, and of a very feeble nature at that? Is it not making a wall without stone, or something like that, to construct books without knowledge and without art? Musical fancies are guided by art, mine by chance.

At least I have one thing according to the rules: that no man ever treated a subject he knew and understood better than I do the subject I have undertaken; and that in this I am the most learned man alive. Secondly, that no man ever penetrated more deeply into his material, or plucked its limbs and consequences cleaner, or reached more accurately and fully the goal he had set for his work. To accomplish it, I need only bring it to fidelity; and that is in it, as sincere and pure as can be found. I speak the truth, not my fill of it, but as much as I dare speak; and I dare to do so a little more as I grow old, for it seems that custom allows old age more freedom to prate and more indiscretion in talking about oneself. It cannot happen here as I see it happening often, that the craftsman and his work contradict each other: 'Has a man whose conversation is so good written such a stupid book?' or 'Have such learned writings come from a man whose conversation is so feeble?'

If a man is commonplace in conversation and rare in writing, that means that his capacity is in the place from which he borrows it, and not in himself. A learned man is not learned in all matters; but the capable man is capable in all matters, even in ignorance.

In this case we go hand in hand and at the same pace, my book and I. In other cases one may commend or blame the work apart from the workman; not so here; he who touches the one, touches the other. He who judges it without knowing it will injure himself more than me; he who has known it will completely satisfy me. Happy beyond my deserts if I have just this share of public approval, that I make men of understanding feel that I was capable of profiting by knowledge, if I had had any, and that I deserved better assistance from my memory.

Let me here excuse what I often say, that I rarely repent and that my consience is content with itself – not as the conscience of an angel or a horse, but as the conscience of a man; always adding this refrain, not perfunctorily but in sincere and complete submission: that I speak as an ignorant inquirer, referring the decision purely and simply to the common and authorized beliefs. I do not teach, I tell.

. . .

30

RENÉ DESCARTES

'Second Meditation'

The nature of the human mind, and how it is better known than the body

So serious are the doubts into which I have been thrown as a result of yesterday's meditation that I can neither put them out of my mind nor see any way of resolving them. It feels as if I have fallen unexpectedly into a deep whirlpool which tumbles me around so that I can neither stand on the bottom nor swim up to the top. Nevertheless I will make an effort and once more attempt the same path which I started on yesterday. Anything which admits of the slightest doubt I will set aside just as if I had found it to be wholly false; and I will proceed in this way until I recognize something certain, or, if nothing else, until I at least recognize for certain that there is no certainty. Archimedes used to demand just one firm and immovable point in order to shift the entire earth; so I too can hope for great things if I manage to find just one thing, however slight, that is certain and unshakeable.

I will suppose then, that everything I see is spurious. I will believe that my memory tells me lies, and that none of the things that it reports ever happened. I have no senses. Body, shape, extension, movement and place are chimeras. So what remains true? Perhaps just the one fact that nothing is certain.

Yet apart from everything I have just listed, how do I know that there is not something else which does not allow even the slightest occasion for doubt? Is there not a God, or whatever I may call him, who puts into me the thoughts I am now having? But why do I think this, since I myself may perhaps be the author of these thoughts? In that case am not I, at least, something? But I have just said that I have no senses and no body. This is the sticking point: what follows from this? Am I not so bound up with a body and with senses that I cannot exist without them? But I have convinced myself that there is absolutely nothing in the world, no sky, no earth, no minds, no bodies. Does it now follow that I too do not exist? No: if I convinced myself of something then I certainly existed. But there is a deceiver of supreme power and cunning who is deliberately and constantly deceiving me. In that case I too undoubtedly exist, if he is deceiving me; and let him deceive me as much as he can, he will never bring it about that I am nothing so long as I think that I am something. So after considering everything very thoroughly, I must finally conclude that this proposition, *I am, I exist*, is necessarily true whenever it is put forward by me or conceived in my mind.

But I do not yet have a sufficient understanding of what this 'I' is, that now necessarily exists. So I must be on my guard against carelessly taking something else to be this 'I', and so making a mistake in the very item of knowledge that I maintain is the most certain and evident of all. I will therefore go back and meditate on what I originally believed myself to be, before I embarked on this present train of thought. I will then subtract anything capable of being weakened, even minimally, by the arguments now introduced, so that what is left at the end may be exactly and only what is certain and unshakeable.

What then did I formerly think I was? A man. But what is a man? Shall I say 'a rational animal'? No; for then I should have to inquire what an animal is, what rationality is, and in this way one question would lead me down the slope to other harder ones, and I do not now have the time to waste on subtleties of this kind. Instead I propose to concentrate on what came into my thoughts spontaneously and quite naturally whenever I used to consider what I was. Well, the first thought to come to mind was that I had a face, hands, arms and the whole mechanical structure of limbs which can be seen in a corpse, and which I called the body. The next thought was that I was nourished, that I moved about, and that I engaged in sense-perception and thinking; and these actions I attributed to the soul. But as to the nature of this soul, either I did not think about this or else I imagined it to be something tenuous, like a wind or fire or ether, which permeated my more solid parts. As to the body, however, I had no doubts about it, but thought I knew its nature distinctly. If I had tried to describe the mental conception I had of it, I would have expressed it as follows: by a body I understand whatever has a determinable shape and a definable location and can occupy a space in such a way as to exclude any other body; it can be perceived by touch, sight, hearing, taste or smell, and can be moved in various ways, not by itself but by whatever else comes into contact with it. For, according to my judgement, the power of self-movement, like the power of sensation or of thought, was quite foreign to the nature of a body; indeed, it was a source of wonder to me that certain bodies were found to contain faculties of this kind.

But what shall I now say that I am, when I am supposing that there is some supremely powerful and, if it is permissible to say so, malicious deceiver, who is deliberately trying to trick me in every way he can? Can I now assert that I possess even the most insignificant of all the attributes which I have just said belong to the nature of a body? I scrutinize them, think about them, go over them again, but nothing suggests itself; it is tiresome and pointless to go through the list once more. But what about the attributes I assigned to the soul? Nutrition or movement? Since now I do not have a body, these are mere fabrications. Sense-perception? This surely does not occur without a body, and besides, when asleep I have appeared to perceive through the senses many things which I afterwards realized I did not perceive through the senses at all. Thinking? At last I have discovered it – thought; this alone is inseparable from me. I am, I exist – that is certain. But for how long? For as long as I am thinking. For it could be that were I totally to cease from thinking, I should totally cease to exist. At present I am not admitting anything except what is necessarily true. I am, then, in the strict sense only a thing that thinks; that is, I am a mind, or intelligence, or intellect, or reason – words whose meaning I have been ignorant of until now. But for all that I am a thing which is real and which truly exists. But what kind of a thing? As I have just said – a thinking thing.

What else am I? I will use my imagination. I am not that structure of limbs which is called a human body. I am not even some thin vapour which permeates the limbs – a wind, fire, air, breath, or whatever I depict in my imagination; for these are things which I have supposed to be nothing. Let this supposition stand; for all that I am still something. And yet may it not perhaps be the case that these very things which I am supposing to be nothing, because they are unknown to me, are in reality identical with the 'I' of which I am aware? I do not know, and for the moment I shall not argue the point, since I can make judgements only about things which are known to me. I know that I exist; the question is, what is this 'I' that I know? If the 'I' is understood strictly as we have been taking it, then it is quite certain that knowledge of it does not depend on things of whose existence I am as yet unaware; so it cannot depend on any of the things which I invent in my imagination. And this very word 'invent' shows me my mistake. It would indeed be a case of fictitious invention if I used my imagination to establish that I was something or other; for imagining is simply contemplating the shape or image of a corporeal thing. Yet now I know for certain both that I exist and at the same time that all such images and, in general, everything relating to the nature of body, could be mere dreams <and chimeras>. Once this point has been grasped, to say 'I will use my imagination to get to know more distinctly what I am' would seem to be as silly as saying 'I am now awake, and see some truth; but since my vision is not yet clear enough, I will deliberately fall asleep so that my dreams may provide a truer and clearer representation.' I thus realize that none of the things that the imagination enables me to grasp is at all relevant to this knowledge of myself which I possess, and that the mind must therefore be most carefully diverted from such things if it is to perceive its own nature as distinctly as possible.

But what then am I? A thing that thinks. What is that? A thing that doubts, understands, affirms, denies, is willing, is unwilling, and also imagines and has sensory perceptions.

This is a considerable list, if everything on it belongs to me. But does it? Is it not one and the same 'I' who is now doubting almost everything, who nonetheless understands some things, who affirms that this one thing is true, denies everything else, desires to know more, is unwilling to be deceived, imagines many things even involuntarily, and is aware of many things which apparently come from the senses? Are not all these things just as true as the fact that I exist, even if I am asleep all the time, and even if he who created me is doing all he can to deceive me? Which of all these activities is distinct from my thinking? Which of them can be said to be separate from myself? The fact that it is I who am doubting and understanding and willing is so evident that I see no way of making it any clearer. But it is also the case that the 'I' who imagines is the same 'I'. For even if, as I have supposed, none of the objects of imagination are real, the power of imagination is something which really exists and is part of my thinking. Lastly, it is also the same 'I' who has sensory perceptions, or is aware of bodily things as it were through the senses. For example, I am now seeing light, hearing a noise, feeling heat. But I am asleep, so all this is false. Yet I certainly *seem* to see, to hear, and to be warmed. This cannot be false; what is called 'having a sensory perception' is strictly just this, and in this restricted sense of the term it is simply thinking.

From all this I am beginning to have a rather better understanding of what I am. But it still appears – and I cannot stop thinking this – that the corporeal things of which images are formed in my thought, and which the senses investigate, are known with much more distinctness than this puzzling 'I' which cannot be pictured in the imagination. And yet it is surely surprising that I should have a more distinct grasp of things which I realize are doubtful, unknown and foreign to me, than I have of that which is true and known – my own self. But I see what it is: my mind enjoys wandering off and will not yet submit to being restrained within the bounds of truth. Very well then; just this once let us give it a completely free rein, so that after a while, when it is time to tighten the reins, it may more readily submit to being curbed.

Let us consider the things which people commonly think they understand most distinctly of all; that is, the bodies which we touch and see. I do not mean bodies in general – for general perceptions are apt to be somewhat more confused – but one particular body. Let us take, for example, this piece of wax. It has just been taken from the honeycomb; it has not yet quite lost the taste of the honey; it retains some of the scent of the flowers from which it was gathered; its colour, shape and size are plain to see; it is hard, cold and can be handled without difficulty; if you rap it with your knuckle it makes a sound. In short, it has everything which appears necessary to enable a body to be known as distinctly as possible. But even as I speak, I put the wax by the fire, and look: the residual taste is eliminated, the smell goes away, the colour changes, the shape is lost, the size increases; it becomes liquid and hot; you can hardly touch it, and if you strike it, it no longer makes a sound. But does the same wax remain? It must be admitted that it does; no one denies it, no one thinks otherwise. So what was it in the wax that I understood with such distinctness? Evidently none of the features which I arrived at by means of the senses; for whatever came under taste, smell, sight, touch or hearing has now altered – yet the wax remains.

Perhaps the answer lies in the thought which now comes to my mind; namely, the wax was not after all the sweetness of the honey, or the fragrance of the flowers, or the whiteness, or the shape, or the sound, but was rather a body which presented itself to me in these various forms a little while ago, but which now exhibits different ones. But what exactly is it that I am now imagining? Let us concentrate, take away everything which does not belong to the wax, and see what is left: merely something extended, flexible and changeable. But what is meant here by 'flexible' and 'changeable'? Is it what I picture in my imagination: that this piece of wax is capable of changing from a round shape to a square shape, or from a square shape to a triangular shape? Not at all; for I can grasp that the wax is capable of countless changes of this kind, yet I am unable to run through this immeasurable number of changes in my imagination, from which it follows that it is not the faculty of imagination that gives me my grasp of the wax as flexible and changeable. And what is meant by 'extended'? Is the extension of the wax also unknown? For it increases if the wax melts, increases again if it boils, and is greater still if the heat is increased. I would not be making a correct judgement about the nature of wax unless I believed it capable of being extended in many more different ways than I will ever encompass in my imagination. I must therefore admit that the nature of this piece of wax is in no way revealed by my imagination, but is perceived by the mind alone. (I am speaking of this particular piece of wax; the point is even clearer with regard to wax in general.) But what is this wax which is perceived by the mind alone? It is of course the same wax which I see, which I touch, which I picture in my imagination, in short the same wax which I thought it to be from the start. And yet, and here is the point, the perception I have of it is a case not of vision or touch or imagination – nor has it ever been, despite previous appearances – but of purely mental scrutiny; and this can be imperfect and confused, as it was before, or clear and distinct as it is now, depending on how carefully I concentrate on what the wax consists in.

But as I reach this conclusion I am amazed at how <weak and> prone to error my mind is. For although I am thinking about these matters within myself, silently and without speaking, nonetheless the actual words bring me up short, and I am almost tricked by ordinary ways of talking. We say that we see the wax itself, if it is there before us, not that we judge it to be there from its colour or shape; and this might lead me to conclude without more ado that knowledge of the wax comes from what the eye sees, and not from the scrutiny of the mind alone. But then if I look out of the window and see men crossing the square, as I just happen to have done, I normally say that I see the men themselves, just as I say that I see the wax. Yet do I see any more than hats and coats which could conceal automatons? I *judge* that they are men. And so something which I thought I was seeing with my eyes is in fact grasped solely by the faculty of judgement which is in my mind.

However, one who wants to achieve knowledge above the ordinary level should feel ashamed at having taken ordinary ways of talking as a basis for doubt. So let us proceed, and consider on which occasion my perception of the nature of the wax was more perfect and evident. Was it when I first looked at it, and believed I knew it by my external senses, or at least by what they call the 'common' sense – that is, the power of imagination? Or is my knowledge more perfect now, after a more careful investigation of the nature of the wax and of the means by which it is known? Any doubt on this issue would clearly be foolish; for what distinctness was there in my earlier perception? Was there anything in it which an animal could not possess? But when I distinguish the wax from its outward forms – take the clothes off, as it were, and consider it naked – then although my judgement may still contain errors, at least my perception now requires a human mind.

But what am I to say about this mind, or about myself? (So far, remember, I am not admitting that there is anything else in me except a mind.) What, I ask, is this 'I' which seems to perceive the wax so distinctly? Surely my awareness of my own self is not merely much truer and more certain than my awareness of the wax, but also much more distinct and evident. For if I judge that the wax exists from the fact that I see it, clearly this same fact entails much more evidently that I myself also exist. It is possible that what I see is not really the wax; it is possible that I do not even have eyes with which to see anything. But when I see, or think I see (I am not here distinguishing the two), it is simply not possible that I who am now thinking am not something. By the same token, if I judge that the wax exists from the fact that I touch it, the same result follows, namely that I exist. If I judge that it exists from the fact that I imagine it, or for any other reason, exactly the same thing follows. And the result that I have grasped in the case of the wax may be applied to everything else located outside me. Moreover, if my perception of the wax seemed more distinct after it was established not just by sight or touch but by many other considerations, it must be admitted that I now know myself even more distinctly. This is because every consideration whatsoever which contributes to my perception of the wax, or of any other body, cannot but establish even more effectively the nature of my own mind. But besides this, there is so much else in the mind itself which can serve to make my knowledge of it more distinct, that it scarcely seems worth going through the contributions made by considering bodily things.

I see that without any effort I have now finally got back to where I wanted. I now know that even bodies are not strictly perceived by the senses or the faculty of imagination but by the intellect alone, and that this perception derives not from their being touched or seen but from their being understood; and in view of this I know plainly that I can achieve an easier and more evident perception of my own mind than of anything else. But since the habit of holding on to old opinions cannot be set aside so quickly, I should like to stop here and meditate for some time on this new knowledge I have gained, so as to fix it more deeply in my memory.

31

FRIEDRICH NIETZSCHE

'Why I Am a Destiny'

1

I know my fate. One day my name will be associated with the memory of something tremendous – a crisis without equal on earth, the most profound collision of conscience, a decision that was conjured up *against* everything that had been believed, demanded, hallowed so far. I am no man, I am dynamite.[1] – Yet for all that, there is nothing in me of a founder of a religion – religions are affairs of the rabble; I find it necessary to wash my hands after I have come into contact with religious people. – I *want* no 'believers'; I think I am too malicious to believe in myself; I never speak to masses. – I have a terrible fear that one day I will be pronounced *holy*: you will guess why I publish this book *before*; it shall prevent people from doing mischief with me.[2]

I do not want to be a holy man; sooner even a buffoon. – Perhaps I am a buffoon. – Yet in spite of that – or rather *not* in spite of it, because so far nobody has been more mendacious than holy men – the truth speaks out of me. – But my truth is *terrible*; for so far one has called *lies* truth.

Revaluation of all of values; that is my formula for an act of supreme self-examination on the part of humanity, become flesh and genius in me. It is my fate that I have to be the first *decent* human being; that I know myself to stand in opposition to the mendaciousness of millennia. – I was the first to *discover* the truth by being the first to experience lies as lies – smelling them out. – My genius is in my nostrils.

I contradict as has never been contradicted before and am nevertheless the opposite of a No-saying spirit. I am a bringer of glad tidings like no one before me; I know tasks of such elevation that any notion of them has been lacking so far; only beginning with me are there hopes again. For all that, I am necessarily also the man of calamity. For when truth enters into a fight with the lies of millennia, we shall have upheavals, a convulsion of earthquakes, a moving of mountains and valleys, the like of which has never been dreamed of. The concept of politics will have merged entirely with a war of spirits; all power structures of the old society will have been exploded – all of them are based on lies: there will be wars the like of which have never yet been seen on earth. It is only beginning with me that the earth knows *great politics*.

2

You want a formula for such a destiny *become man?* That is to be found in my *Zarathustra*:

'And whoever wants to be[3] a creator in good and evil, must first be an annihilator and break values. Thus the highest evil belongs to the greatest goodness: but this is – being creative.'

I am by far the most terrible human being that has existed so far; this does not preclude the possibility that I shall be the most beneficial. I know the pleasure in destroying to a degree that accords with my powers to destroy – in both respects I obey my Dionysian nature which does not know how to separate doing No from saying Yes. I am the first immoralist: that makes me the annihilator *par excellence*.

3

I have not been asked, as I should have been asked, what the name of Zarathustra means in my mouth, the mouth of the first immoralist: for what constitutes the tremendous historical uniqueness of that Persian is just the opposite of this. Zarathustra was the first to consider the fight of good and evil the very wheel in the machinery of things: the transposition of morality into the metaphysical realm, as a force, cause, and end in itself, is *his* work. But this question itself is at bottom its own answer. Zarathustra created this most calamitous error, morality; consequently, he must also be the first to recognize it. Not only has he more experience in this matter, for a longer time, than any other thinker – after all, the whole of history is the refutation by experiment of the principle of the so-called 'moral world order' – what is more important is that Zarathustra is more truthful than any other thinker.

His doctrine, and his alone, posits truthfulness as the highest virtue; this means the opposite of the cowardice of the 'idealist' who flees from reality; Zarathustra has more intestinal fortitude than all other thinkers taken together. To speak the truth and to *shoot well with arrows*, that is Persian virtue.[4] – Am I understood? – The self-overcoming of morality, out of truthfulness; the self-overcoming of the moralist, into his opposite – into me – that is what the name of Zarathustra means in my mouth.

4

Fundamentally, my term *immoralist* involves two negations. For one, I negate a type of man that has so far been considered supreme: the good, the benevolent, the beneficent. And then I negate a type of morality that has become prevalent and predominant as morality itself – the morality of decadence or, more concretely, *Christian* morality. It would be permissible to consider the second contradiction the more decisive one, since I take the overestimation of goodness and benevolence on a large scale for a consequence of decadence, for a symptom of weakness, irreconcilable with an ascending, Yes-saying life: negating *and destroying* are conditions of saying Yes.[5]

Let me tarry over the psychology of the good human being. To estimate what a type of man is worth, one must calculate the price paid for his preservation – one must know the conditions of his existence. The condition of the existence of the good is the *lie*: put differently, not *wanting* to see at any price how reality is constituted fundamentally – namely, not in such a way as to elicit benevolent instincts at all times, and even less in such a way as to tolerate at all times the interference of those who are myopically good-natured. To consider distress of all kinds as an objection, as something that must be abolished, is the *niaiserie*[6] *par excellence* and, on a large scale, a veritable disaster in its consequences, a nemesis[7] of stupidity – almost as stupid as would be the desire to abolish bad weather – say, from pity for poor people.

In the great economy of the whole, the terrible aspects of reality (in affects, in desires, in the will to power) are to an incalculable degree more necessary than that form of petty happiness which people call 'goodness'; one actually has to be quite lenient to accord the latter any place at all, considering that it presupposes an instinctive mendaciousness. I shall have a major occasion to demonstrate how the historical consequences of *optimism*, this abortion of the *homines optimi*,[8] have been uncanny beyond measure. Zarathustra, who was the first to grasp that the optimist is just as decadent as the pessimist, and perhaps more harmful, says: '*Good men never speak the truth.*'[9]

'False coasts and assurances the good have taught you; in the lies of the good you were hatched and huddled. Everything has been made fraudulent and has been twisted through and through by the good.'[10]

Fortunately, the world has not been designed with a view to such instincts that only good-natured herd animals could find their narrow happiness in it: to demand that all should become 'good human beings,' herd animals, blue-eyed, benevolent, 'beautiful souls' – or as Mr. Herbert Spencer[11] would have it, altruistic – would deprive existence of its *great* character and would castrate men and reduce them to the level of desiccated Chinese stagnation. – *And this has been attempted!* – *Precisely this has been called morality.*

In this sense, Zarathustra calls the good, now 'the last men,'[12] now the 'beginning of the end'; above all, he considers them the most harmful type of man because they prevail at the expense of *truth* and at the expense of the *future*.[13]

'The good are unable to *create*; they are always the beginning of the end; they crucify him who writes new values on new tablets; they sacrifice the future to *themselves* – they sacrifice all man's future.

'The good have always been the beginning of the end.'

'And whatever harm those do who slander the world, the harm done by the good is the most harmful harm.'[14]

5

Zarathustra, the first psychologist of the good, is – consequently – a friend of the evil. When a decadent type of man ascended to the rank of the highest type, this could only happen at the expense of its countertype, the type of man that is strong and sure of life. When the herd animal is irradiated by the glory of the purest virtue, the exceptional man must have been devaluated into evil. When mendaciousness at any price monopolizes the word 'truth' for its perspective, the really truthful man is bound to be branded with the worst names. Zarathustra leaves no doubt at this point: he says that it was his insight precisely into the good, the 'best,' that made him shudder at man in general; that it was from *this* aversion that he grew wings 'to soar off into distant futures'; he does not conceal the fact that *his* type of man, a relatively superhuman type, is superhuman precisely in its relation to the *good* – that the good and the just would call his overman *devil*.

'You highest men whom my eyes have seen, this is my doubt about you and my secret laughter: I guess that you would call my overman – devil.'

'What is great is so alien to your souls that the overman would be terrifying to you in his goodness.'[15]

It is here and nowhere else that one must make a start to comprehend what Zarathustra wants: this type of man that he conceives, conceives reality *as it is*, being strong enough to do so; this type is not estranged or removed from reality but is reality itself and exemplifies all that is terrible and questionable in it – *only in that way can man attain greatness.*

6

There is yet another sense, however, in which I have chosen the word *immoralist* as a symbol and badge of honor for myself; I am proud of having this word which distinguishes me from the whole of humanity. Nobody yet has felt *Christian* morality to be *beneath* him: that requires a height, a view of distances, a hitherto altogether unheard-of psychological depth and profundity. Christian morality has been the Circe of all thinkers so far – they stood in her service. – Who before me climbed into the caverns from which the poisonous fumes of this type of ideal – slander of the world – are rising? Who even dared to suspect that they are caverns? Who among philosophers was a *psychologist* at all before me, and not rather the opposite, a 'higher swindler' and 'idealist'? There was no psychology at all before me. – To be the first here may be a curse; it is at any rate a destiny: *for one is also the first to despise. – Nausea* at man is my danger.

7

Have I been understood? – What defines me, what sets me apart from the whole rest of humanity is that I *uncovered* Christian morality. That is why I needed a word that had the meaning of a provocation for everybody. That they did not open their eyes earlier at this point, I regard as the greatest uncleanliness that humanity has on its conscience; as self-deception become instinctive; as a fundamental will *not* to see any event, any causality, any reality; as counterfeiting in *psychologicis* to the point of criminality. Blindness to Christianity is the crime *par excellence* – the crime against life.

The millennia, the nations, the first and the last, the philosophers and old women – excepting five, six moments in history, and me as the seventh – at this point all of them are worthy of each other. The Christian has so far been *the* 'moral being' – a matchless curiosity – and *as* the 'moral being' he was more absurd, mendacious, vain, frivolous, and more disadvantageous for himself than even the greatest despiser of humanity could imagine in his dreams. Christian morality – the most malignant form of the will to lie, the real Circe of humanity – that which *corrupted* humanity. It is *not* error as error that horrifies me at this sight – not the lack, for thousands of years, of 'good will,' discipline, decency, courage in matters of the spirit, revealed by its victory: it is the lack of nature, it is the utterly gruesome fact that *antinature* itself received the highest honors as morality and was fixed over humanity as law and categorical imperative. – To blunder to such an extent, not as individuals, not as a people, but as humanity! – That one taught men to despise the very first instincts of life; that one mendaciously invented a 'soul,' a 'spirit' to ruin the body; that one taught men to experience the presupposition of life, sexuality, as something unclean; that one looks for the evil principle in what is most profoundly necessary for growth, in *severe* self-love[16] (this very word constitutes slander); that, conversely, one regards the typical signs of decline and contradiction of the instincts, the 'selfless,' the loss of a center of gravity, 'depersonalization' and 'neighbor love' (*addiction* to the neighbor) as the *higher* value – what am I saying? – the *absolute* value!

What? Is humanity itself decadent? Was it always? – What is certain is that it has been *taught* only decadence values as supreme values. The morality that would un-self man is the morality of decline *par excellence* – the fact, 'I am declining,' transposed into the imperative, 'all of you *ought* to decline' – and not only into the imperative. – This only morality that has been taught so far, that of un-selfing, reveals a will to the end; fundamentally, it negates life.

This would still leave open the possibility that not humanity is degenerating but only that parasitical type of man – that of the *priest* – which has used morality to raise itself mendaciously to the position of determining human values – finding in Christian morality the means to come to *power*. – Indeed, this is *my* insight: the teachers, the leaders of humanity, theologians all of them, were also, all of them, decadents: *hence* the revaluation of all values into hostility to life,[17] *hence* morality –

Definition of morality: Morality – the idiosyncrasy of decadents, with the ulterior motive of revenging oneself against life – successfully. I attach value to this definition.

8

Have I been understood? – I have not said one word here that I did not say five years ago through the mouth of Zarathustra.

The uncovering of Christian morality is an event without parallel, a real catastrophe. He that is enlightened about that, is a *force majeure*, a destiny – he breaks the history of mankind in two. One lives before him, or one lives after him.

The lightning bolt of truth struck precisely what was highest so far: let whoever comprehends *what* has here been destroyed see whether anything is left in his hands. Everything that has hitherto been called 'truth' has been recognized as the most harmful, insidious, and subterranean form of lie; the holy pretext of 'improving' mankind, as the ruse for sucking the blood of life itself. Morality as vampirism.

Whoever uncovers morality also uncovers the disvalue of all values that are and have been believed; he no longer sees anything venerable in the most venerated types of man, even in those pronounced holy; he considers them the most calamitous type of abortion – calamitous because they exerted such fascination.

The concept of 'God' invented as a counterconcept of life – everything harmful, poisonous, slanderous, the whole hostility unto death against life synthesized in this concept in a gruesome unity! The concept of the 'beyond,' the 'true world' invented in order to devaluate the only world there is[18] – in order to retain no goal, no reason, no task for our earthly reality! The concept of the 'soul,' the 'spirit,' finally even '*immortal* soul,' invented in order to despise the body,[19] to make it sick, 'holy'; to oppose with a ghastly levity everything that deserves to be taken seriously in life, the questions of nourishment, abode, spiritual diet, treatment of the sick, cleanliness, and weather.[20]

In place of health, the 'salvation of the soul' – that is, a *folie circulaire*[21] between penitential convulsions and hysteria about redemption. The concept of 'sin' invented along with the torture instrument that belongs with it, the concept of 'free will,' in order to confuse the instincts, to make mistrust of the instincts second nature. In the concept of the 'selfless,' the 'self-denier,' the distinctive sign of decadence, feeling attracted by what is harmful, being unable to find any longer what profits one, self-destruction is turned into the sign of value itself, into 'duty,' into 'holiness,' into what is 'divine' in man. Finally – this is what is most terrible of all – the concept of the *good* man signifies that one sides with all that is weak, sick, failure, suffering of itself – all that ought to perish: the principle of selection is crossed[22] – an ideal is fabricated from the contradiction against the proud and well-turned-out human being who says Yes, who is sure of the future, who guarantees the future – and he is now called *evil*. – And all this was believed, *as morality! – Ecrasez l'infâme!*[23] —

9

Have I been understood? – *Dionysus versus the Crucified.* –[24]

NOTES

1. This had been said of Nietzsche in the *Berner Bund*, in J. V. Widmann's review of *Beyond Good and Evil*, September 16–17, 1886. The passage is quoted at length in Nietzsche's letter to Malwida von Meysenburg, September 24, 1886 (*Werke*, ed. Karl Schlechta, vol. III, p. 1245).
2. But *Ecce Homo* was not published until 1908, and at Nietzsche's funeral in 1900 Peter Gast proclaimed: 'Holy be thy name to all coming generations.' Even after it was published, *Ecce Homo* failed to prevent far worse mischief.
3. In *Zarathustra II*, 'On Self-Overcoming,' the text reads 'must be'; and 'evil' is followed by 'verily.'
4. Cf. *Zarathustra I*, 'On the Thousand and One Goals': '. . . "To speak the truth and to handle bow and arrow well" – that seemed both dear and difficult to the people who gave me my name . . .'
5. Although Nietzsche associates this with Dionysus, cf. also Jer. 1:10: 'See, I have this day set thee over the nations and over the kingdoms, to root out, and to pull down, and to destroy, and to throw down, to build and to plant.' But Jeremiah felt no pleasure in destruction.
6. Folly, stupidity, silliness.
7. *Schicksal*.
8. Best men.
9. Quoted from *Zarathustra III*, 'On Old and New Tablets,' section 7. There are no quotation marks in the German text.
10. *Ibid.*, section 28. Again, no quotation marks.
11. English philosopher (1820–1903).
12. In the 'Prologue,' section 5. Indeed, that section, along with the whole Prologue, may be the best commentary on the above section – though it would be more accurate to say that the above is a commentary on *Zarathustra*.
13. Those who want to abolish all hardships because they themselves are not up to them are like sick people who wish to abolish rain, no matter what the consequences might be to others and to the earth generally. Cf. Nietzsche's own remark about 'bad weather' above.
14. Both quotations are from section 26 of 'On Old and New Tablets'; but the second quotation occurs earlier in that section.
15. All three quotations, beginning with 'to soar off . . .' come from *Zarathustra II*, 'On Human Prudence.'
16. *Selbstsucht*: the word is pejorative, like 'selfishness.'
17. Nietzsche's revaluation is meant to undo the damage done by a previous revaluation: values have been stood on their head and are now to be turned right-side up again.
18. Cf. *Twilight*, Chapters III and IV.
19. Cf. *Zarathustra I*, 'On The Despisers of the Body.'
20. Cf. 'Why I am So Clever,' above.
21. Manic-depressive insanity.
22. Cf. *The Antichrist*, section 7.
23. Voltaire's motto – crush the infamy – in his fight against the church.
24. The best commentary is section 1052 of *The Will to Power*.

32

JORGE LUIS BORGES

'Pierre Menard, Author of the *Quixote*'

The *visible* work left by this novelist is easily and briefly enumerated. Impardonable, therefore, are the omissions and additions perpetrated by Madame Henri Bachelier in a fallacious catalogue which a certain daily, whose *Protestant* tendency is no secret, has had the inconsideration to inflict upon its deplorable readers – though these be few and Calvinist, if not Masonic and circumcized. The true friends of Menard have viewed this catalogue with alarm and even with a certain melancholy. One might say that only yesterday we gathered before his final monument, amidst the lugubrious cypresses, and already Error tries to tarnish his Memory . . . Decidedly, a brief rectification is unavoidable.

I am aware that it is quite easy to challenge my slight authority. I hope, however, that I shall not be prohibited from mentioning two eminent testimonies. The Baroness de Bacourt (at whose unforgettable *vendredis* I had the honour of meeting the lamented poet) has seen fit to approve the pages which follow. The Countess de Bagnoregio, one of the most delicate spirits of the Principality of Monaco (and now of Pittsburgh, Pennsylvania, following her recent marriage to the international philanthropist Simon Kautzsch, who has been so inconsiderately slandered, alas! by the victims of his disinterested manoeuvres) has sacrificed 'to veracity and to death' (such were her words) the stately reserve which is her distinction, and, in an open letter published in the magazine *Luxe*, concedes me her approval as well. These authorizations, I think, are not entirely insufficient.

I have said that Menard's visible work can be easily enumerated.

Having examined with care his personal files, I find that they contain the following items:

a) A Symbolist sonnet which appeared twice (with variants) in the review *La conque* (issues of March and October 1899).

b) A monograph on the possibility of constructing a poetic vocabulary of concepts which would not be synonyms or periphrases of those which make up our everyday language, 'but rather ideal objects created according to convention and essentially designed to satisfy poetic needs' (Nîmes, 1901).

c) A monograph on 'certain connexions or affinities' between the thought of Descartes, Leibniz and John Wilkins (Nîmes, 1903).

d) A monograph on Leibniz's *Characteristica universalis* (Nîmes, 1904).

e) A technical article on the possibility of improving the game of chess, eliminating one of the rook's pawns. Menard proposes, recommends, discusses and finally rejects this innovation.

f) A monograph on Raymond Lully's Ars *magna generalis* (Nîmes, 1906).

g) A translation, with prologue and notes, of Ruy López de Segura's *Libro de la invención liberal y arte del juego del axedrez* (Paris, 1907).

h) The work sheets of a monograph on George Boole's symbolic logic.

i) An examination of the essential metric laws of French prose, illustrated with examples taken from Saint-Simon (*Revue des langues romanes*, Montpellier, October 1909).

j) A reply to Luc Durtain (who had denied the existence of such laws), illustrated with examples from Luc Durtain (*Revue des langues romanes*, Montpellier, December 1909).

k) A manuscript translation of the *Aguja de navegar cultos* of Quevedo, entitled *La boussole des précieux*.

l) A preface to the Catalogue of an exposition of lithographs by Carolus Hourcade (Nîmes, 1914).

m) The work *Les problèmes d'un problème* (Paris, 1917), which discusses, in chronological order, the different solutions given to the illustrious problem of Achilles and the tortoise. Two editions of this book have appeared so far; the second bears as an epigraph Leibniz's recommendation '*Ne craignez point, monsieur, la tortue*' and revises the chapters dedicated to Russell and Descartes.

n) A determined analysis of the 'syntactical customs' of Toulet (N. R. F., March 1921). Menard – I recall – declared that censure and praise are sentimental operations which have nothing to do with literary criticism.

o) A transposition into alexandrines of Paul Valéry's *Le cimetière marin* (N. R. F., January 1928).

p) An invective against Paul Valéry, in the *Papers for the Suppression of Reality* of Jacques Reboul. (This invective, we might say parenthetically, is the exact opposite of his true opinion of Valéry. The latter understood it as such and their old friendship was not endangered.)

q) A 'definition' of the Countess de Bagnoregio, in the 'victorious volume'– the locution is Gabriele d'Annunzio's, another of its collaborators – published annually by this lady to rectify the inevitable falsifications of journalists and to present 'to the world and to Italy' an authentic image of her person, so often exposed (by very reason of her beauty and her activities) to erroneous or hasty interpretations.

r) A cycle of admirable sonnets for the Baroness de Bacourt (1934).

s) A manuscript list of verses which owe their efficacy to their punctuation.[1]

This, then, is the *visible* work of Menard, in chronological order (with no omission other than a few vague sonnets of circumstance written for the hospitable, or avid, album of Madame Henri Bachelier). I turn now to his other work: the subterranean, the interminably heroic, the peerless. And – such are the capacities of man! – the unfinished. This work, perhaps the most significant of our time, consists of the ninth and thirty-eighth chapters of the first part of *Don Quixote* and a fragment of chapter twenty-two. I know such an affirmation seems an absurdity; to justify this 'absurdity' is the primordial object of this note.[22]

Two texts of unequal value inspired this undertaking. One is that philological fragment by Novalis – the one numbered 2005 in the Dresden edition – which outlines the theme of a *total* identification with a given author. The other is one of those parasitic books which situate Christ on a boulevard, Hamlet on La Cannebière or Don Quixote on Wall Street. Like all men of good taste, Menard abhorred these useless carnivals, fit only – as he would say – to produce the plebeian pleasure of anachronism or (what is worse) to enthral us with the elementary idea that all epochs are the same or are different. More interesting, though contradictory and superficial of execution, seemed to him the famous plan of Daudet: to conjoin the Ingenious Gentleman and his squire in *one* figure, which was Tartarin . . . Those who have insinuated that Menard dedicated his life to writing a contemporary *Quixote* calumniate his illustrious memory.

He did not want to compose another *Quixote* – which is easy – but *the Quixote itself*. Needless to say, he never contemplated a mechanical transcription of the original; he did not propose to copy it. His admirable intention was to produce a few pages which would coincide – word for word and line for line – with those of Miguel de Cervantes.

'My intent is no more than astonishing,' he wrote me the 30 September 1934, from Bayonne. 'The final term in a theological or metaphysical demonstration – the objective world, God, causality, the forms of the universe – is no less previous and common than my famed novel. The only difference is that the philosophers publish the intermediary stages of their labour in pleasant volumes and I have resolved to do away with those stages.' In truth, not one worksheet remains to bear witness to his years of effort.

The first method he conceived was relatively simple. Know Spanish well, recover the Catholic faith, fight against the Moors or the Turk, forget the history of Europe between the years 1602 and 1918, *be* Miguel de Cervantes. Pierre Menard studied this procedure (I know he attained a fairly accurate command of seventeenth-century Spanish) but discarded it as too easy. Rather as impossible! my reader will say. Granted, but the undertaking was impossible from the very beginning and of all the impossible ways of carrying it out, this was the least interesting. To be, in the twentieth century, a popular novelist of the seventeenth seemed to him a diminution. To be, in some way, Cervantes and reach the *Quixote* seemed less arduous to him – and, consequently, less interesting – than to go on being Pierre Menard and reach the *Quixote* through the experiences of Pierre Menard. (This conviction, we might say in passing, made him omit the autobiographical prologue to the second part of *Don Quixote*. To include that prologue would have been to create another character – Cervantes – but it would also have meant presenting the *Quixote* in terms of that character and not of Menard. The latter, naturally, declined that facility.) 'My undertaking is not difficult, essentially,' I read in another part of his letter. 'I should only have to be immortal to carry it out.' Shall I confess that I often imagine he did finish it and that I read the *Quixote* – all of it – as if Menard had conceived it? Some nights past, while leafing through chapter XXVI – never essayed by him – I recognized our friend's style and something of his voice in this exceptional phrase: 'the river nymphs and the dolorous and humid Echo.' This happy conjunction of a spiritual and a physical adjective brought to my mind a verse by Shakespeare which we discussed one afternoon:

Where a malignant and a turbaned Turk . . .

But why precisely the *Quixote*? our reader will ask. Such a preference, in a Spaniard, would not have been inexplicable; but it is, no doubt, in a Symbolist from Nîmes, essentially a devoté of Poe, who engendered Baudelaire, who engendered Mallarmé, who engendered Valéry, who engendered Edmond Teste. The aforementioned letter illumináytes this point. 'The *Quixote*,' clarifies Menard, 'interests me deeply, but it does not seem – how shall I say it? – inevitable. I cannot imagine the universe without Edgar Allan Poe's exclamation:

Ah, bear in mind this garden was enchanted!

or without the *Bateau ivre* or the *Ancient Mariner*, but I am quite capable of imagining it without the *Quixote*. (I speak, naturally, of my personal capacity and not of those works' historical resonance.) The *Quixote* is a contingent book; the *Quixote* is unnecessary. I can premeditate writing it, I can write it, without falling into a tautology. When I was ten or twelve years old, I read it, perhaps in its entirety. Later, I have reread closely certain chapters, those which I shall not attempt for the time being. I have also gone through the interludes, the plays, the *Galatea*, the exemplary novels, the undoubtedly laborious tribulations of Persiles and Segismunda and the *Viaje del Parnaso* . . . My general recollection of the *Quixote*, simplified by forgetfulness and indifference, can well equal the imprecise and prior image of a book not yet written. Once that image (which no one can legitimately deny me) is postulated, it is certain that my problem is a good bit more difficult than Cervantes' was. My obliging predecessor did not refuse the collaboration of chance: he composed his immortal work somewhat *à la diable*, carried along by the inertias of language and invention. I have taken on the mysterious duty of reconstructing literally his spontaneous work. My solitary game is governed by two polar laws. The first permits me to essay variations of a formal or psychological type; the second obliges me to sacrifice these variations to the 'original' text and reason out this annihilation in an irrefutable manner . . . To these artificial hindrances, another – of a congenital kind – must be added. To compose the *Quixote* at the beginning of the seventeenth century was a reasonable undertaking, necessary and perhaps even unavoidable; at the beginning of the twentieth, it is almost impossible. It is not in vain that three hundred years have gone by, filled with exceedingly complex events. Among them, to mention only one, is the *Quixote* itself.'

In spite of these three obstacles, Mernard's fragmentary *Quixote* is more subtle than Cervantes'. The latter, in a clumsy fashion, opposes to the fictions of chivalry the tawdry provincial reality of his country; Menard selects as his 'reality' the land of Carmen during the century of Lepanto and Lope de Vega. What a series of *espagnolades* that selection would have suggested to Maurice Barrès or Dr Rodríguez Larreta! Menard eludes them with complete naturalness. In his work there are no gipsy flourishes or conquistadors or mystics or Philip the Seconds or autos da *fé*. He neglects or eliminates local colour. This disdain points to a new conception of the historical novel. This disdain condemns *Salammbô*, with no possibility of appeal.

It is no less astounding to consider isolated chapters. For example, let us examine Chapter XXXVIII of the first part, 'which treats of the curious discourse of Don Quixote on arms and letters'. It is well known that Don Quixote (like Quevedo in an analogous and later passage in *La hora de todos*) decided the debate against letters and in favour of arms. Cervantes was a former soldier: his verdict is understandable. But that Pierre Menard's Don Quixote – a contemporary of *La trahison des clercs* and Bertrand Russell – should fall prey to such nebulous sophistries! Madame Bachelier has seen here an admirable and typical subordination on the part of the author to the hero's psychology; others (not at all perspicaciously), a *transcription* of the *Quixote*; the Baroness de Bacourt, the influence of Nietzsche. To this third interpretation (which I judge to be irrefutable) I am not sure I dare to add a fourth, which concords very well with the almost divine modesty of Pierre Menard: his resigned or ironical habit of propagating ideas which were the strict reverse of those he preferred. (Let us recall once more his diatribe against Paul Valéry in Jacques Reboul's ephemeral Surrealist sheet.) Cervantes's text and Menard's are verbally identical, but the second is almost infinitely richer. (More ambiguous, his detractors will say, but ambiguity is richness.)

It is a revelation to compare Menard's *Don Quixote* with Cervantes's. The latter, for example, wrote (part one, chapter nine):

> . . . truth, whose mother is history, rival of time, depository of deeds, witness of the past, exemplar and adviser to the present, and the future's counsellor.

Written in the seventeenth century, written by the 'lay genius' Cervantes, this enumeration is a mere rhetorical praise of history. Menard, on the other, writes:

> . . . truth, whose mother is history, rival of time, depository of
> deeds, witness of the past, exemplar and adviser to the present, and
> the future's counsellor.

History, the *mother* of truth: the idea is astounding. Menard, a
contemporary of William James, does not define history as an inquiry
into reality but as its origin. Historical truth, for him, is not what has
happened; it is what we judge to have happened. The final phrases –
exemplar and adviser to the present, and the future's counsellor – are brazenly
pragmatic.

The contrast in style is also vivid. The archaic style of Menard – quite
foreign, after all – suffers from a certain affectation. Not so that of his
forerunner, who handles with ease the current Spanish of his time.

There is no exercise of the intellect which is not, in the final analysis,
useless. A philosophical doctrine begins as a plausible description of the
universe; with the passage of the years it becomes a mere chapter – if
not a paragraph or a name – in the history of philosophy. In literature,
this eventual caducity is even more notorious. The *Quixote* – Menard
told me – was, above all, an entertaining book; now it is the occasion
for patriotic toasts, grammatical insolence and obscene de luxe editions.
Fame is a form of incomprehension, perhaps the worst.

There is nothing new in these nihilistic verifications; what is singular
is the determination Menard derived from them. He decided to
anticipate the vanity awaiting all man's efforts; he set himself to an
undertaking which was exceedingly complex and, from the very
beginning, futile. He dedicated his scruples and his sleepless nights to
repeating an already extant book in an alien tongue. He multiplied draft
upon draft, revised tenaciously and tore up thousands of manuscript
pages.[3] He did not let anyone examine these drafts and took care they
should not survive him. In vain have I tried to reconstruct them.

I have reflected that it is permissible to see in this 'final' *Quixote* a
kind of palimpsest, through which the traces – tenuous but not
indecipherable – of our friend's 'previous' writing should be trans-
lucently visible. Unfortunately, only a second Pierre Menard, inverting
the other's work, would be able to exhume and revive those lost
Troys . . .

'Thinking, analysing, inventing (he also wrote me) are not anomalous acts; they are the normal respiration of the intelligence. To glorify
the occasional performance of that function, to hoard ancient and alien
thoughts, to recall with incredulous stupor what the *doctor universalis*
thought, is to confess our laziness or our barbarity. Every man should

be capable of all ideas and I understand that in the future this will be the case.'

Menard (perhaps without wanting to) has enriched, by means of a new technique, the halting and rudimentary art of reading: this new technique is that of the deliberate anachronism and the erroneous attribution. This technique, whose applications are infinite, prompts us to go through the *Odyssey* as if it were posterior to the *Aeneid* and the book *Le jardin du Centaure* of Madame Henri Bachelier as if it were by Madame Henri Bachelier. This technique fills the most placid works with adventure. To attribute the *Imitatio Christi* to Louis Ferdinand Céline or to James Joyce, is this not a sufficient renovation of its tenuous spiritual indications?

For Silvana Ocampo   *Translated by J. E. I.*

NOTES

1. Madame Henri Bachelier also lists a literal translation of Quevedo's literal translation of the *Introduction à la vie devote* of St Francis of Sales. There are no traces of such a work in Menard's library. It must have been a jest of our friend misunderstood by the lady.
2. I also had the secondary intention of sketching a personal portrait of Pierre Menard. But how could I dare to compete with the golden pages which, I am told, the Baroness de Bacourt is preparing or with the delicate and punctual pencil of Carolus Hourcade?
3. I remember his quadricular notebooks, his black crossed-out passages, his peculiar typographical symbols and his insect-like handwriting. In the afternoons he liked to go out for a walk around the outskirts of Nîmes; he would take a notebook with him and make a merry bonfire.

'Kafka and His Precursors'

I once premeditated making a study of Kafka's precursors. At first I had considered him to be as singular as the phoenix of rhetorical praise; after frequenting his pages a bit, I came to think I could recognize his voice, or his practices, in texts from diverse literatures and periods. I shall record a few of these here, in chronological order.

The first is Zeno's paradox against movement. A moving object at A (declares Aristotle) cannot reach point B, because it must first cover half the distance between the two points, and before that, half of the half, and before that, half of the half of the half, and so on to infinity; the form of this illustrious problem is, exactly, that of *The Castle*, and the moving object and the arrow and Achilles are the first Kafkian characters in literature. In the second text which chance laid before me, the affinity is not one of form but of tone. It is an apologue of Han Yu, a prose writer of the ninth century, and is reproduced in Margouliès's admirable *Anthologie raisonnée de la littérature chinoise*

(1948). This is the paragraph, mysterious and calm, which I marked: 'It is universally admitted that the unicorn is a supernatural being of good omen; such is declared in all the odes, annals, biographies of illustrious men and other texts whose authority is unquestionable. Even children and village women know that the unicorn constitutes a favourable presage. But this animal does not figure among the domestic beasts, it is not always easy to find, it does not lend itself to classification. It is not like the horse or the bull, the wolf or the deer. In such conditions, we could be face to face with a unicorn and not know for certain what it was. We know that such and such an animal with a mane is a horse and that such and such an animal with horns is a bull. But we do not know what the unicorn is like.'[1]

The third text derives from a more easily predictable source: the writings of Kierkegaard. The spiritual affinity of both writers is something of which no one is ignorant; what has not yet been brought out, as far as I know, is the fact that Kierkegaard, like Kafka, wrote many religious parables on contemporary and bourgeois themes. Lowrie, in his *Kierkegaard* (Oxford University Press, 1938), transcribes two of these. One is the story of a counterfeiter who, under constant surveillance, counts banknotes in the Bank of England; in the same way, God would distrust Kierkegaard and have given him a task to perform, precisely because He knew that he was familiar with evil. The subject of the other parable is the North Pole expeditions. Danish ministers had declared from their pulpits that participation in these expeditions was beneficial to the soul's eternal well-being. They admitted, however, that it was difficult, and perhaps impossible to reach the Pole and that not all men could undertake the adventure. Finally, they would announce that any trip – from Denmark to London, let us say, on the regularly scheduled steamer – was, properly considered, an expedition to the North Pole. The fourth of these prefigurations I have found is Browning's poem 'Fears and Scruples', published in 1876. A man has, or believes he has, a famous friend. He has never seen this friend and the fact is that the friend has so far never helped him, although tales are told of his most noble traits and authentic letters of his circulate about. Then someone places these traits in doubt and the handwriting experts declare that the letters are apocryphal. The man asks, in the last line: 'And if this friend were . . . God?'

My notes also register two stories. One is from Léon Bloy's *Histoires désobligeantes* and relates the case of some people who possess all manner of globes, atlases, railroad guides and trunks, but who die without ever having managed to leave their home town. The other is entitled 'Carcassonne' and is the work of Lord Dunsany. An invincible army of warriors leaves an infinite castle, conquers kingdoms and sees monsters and exhausts the deserts and the mountains, but they never reach Carcassonne, though once they glimpse it from afar. (This story is, as one can easily see, the strict reverse of the previous one; in the first, the city is never left; in the second, it is never reached.)

If I am not mistaken, the heterogeneous pieces I have enumerated resemble Kafka; if I am not mistaken, not all of them resemble each other. This second fact is the more significant. In each of these texts we find Kafka's idiosyncrasy to a greater or lesser degree, but if Kafka had never written a line, we would not perceive this quality; in other words, it would not exist. The poem 'Fears and Scruples' by Browning foretells Kafka's work, but our reading of Kakfa perceptibly sharpens and deflects our reading of the poem. Browning did not read it as we do now. In the critics' vocabulary, the word 'precursor' is indispensable, but it should be cleansed of all connotation of polemics or rivalry. The fact is that every writer *creates* his own precursors. His work modifies our conception of the past, as it will modify the future.[2] In this correlation the identity or plurality of the men involved is unimportant. The early Kafka of *Betrachtung* is less a precursor of the Kafka of sombre myths and atrocious institutions than is Browning or Lord Dunsany.

Translated by J. E. I.

NOTES

1. Non-recognition of the sacred animal and its opprobious or accidental death at the hands of the people are traditional themes in Chinese literature. See the last chapter of Jung's *Psychologie und Alchemie* (Zürich, 1944), which contains two curious illustrations.
2. See T. S. Eliot: *Points of View* (1941), pp. 25–26.

'Everything and Nothing'

There was no one in him; behind his face (which even through the bad paintings of those times resembles no other) and his words, which were copious, fantastic and stormy, there was only a bit of coldness, a dream dreamt by no one. At first he thought that all people were like him, but the astonishment of a friend to whom he had begun to speak of this emptiness showed him his error and made him feel always that an individual should not differ in outward appearance. Once he thought that in books he would find a cure for his ill and thus he learned the

small Latin and less Greek a contemporary would speak of; later he
considered that what he sought might well be found in an elemental rite
of humanity, and let himself be initiated by Anne Hathaway one long
June afternoon. At the age of twenty-odd years he went to London.
Instinctively he had already become proficient in the habit of simulating
that he was someone, so that others would not discover his condition as
no one; in London he found the profession to which he was predes-
tined, that of the actor, who on a stage plays at being another before a
gathering of people who play at taking him for that other person. His
histrionic tasks brought him a singular satisfaction, perhaps the first he
had ever known; but once the last verse had been acclaimed and the last
dead man withdrawn from the stage, the hated flavour of unreality
returned to him. He ceased to be Ferrex or Tamberlane and became no
one again. Thus hounded, he took to imagining other heroes and other
tragic fables. And so, while his flesh fulfilled its destiny as flesh in the
taverns and brothels of London, the soul that inhabited him was
Caesar, who disregards the augur's admonition, and Juliet, who abhors
the lark, and Macbeth, who converses on the plain with the witches
who are also Fates. No one has ever been so many men as this man who
like the Egyptian Proteus could exhaust all the guises of reality. At
times he would leave a confession hidden away in some corner of his
work, certain that it would not be deciphered; Richard affirms that in
his person he plays the part of many and Iago claims with curious
words 'I am not what I am'. The fundamental identity of existing,
dreaming and acting inspired famous passages of his.

For twenty years he persisted in that controlled hallucination, but
one morning he was suddenly gripped by the tedium and the terror of
being so many kings who die by the sword and so many suffering
lovers who converge, diverge and melodiously expire. That very day
he arranged to sell his theatre. Within a week he had returned to his
native village, where he recovered the trees and rivers of his childhood
and did not relate them to the others his muse had celebrated, illustrious
with mythological allusions and Latin terms. He had to be someone; he
was a retired impresario who had made his fortune and concerned
himself with loans, lawsuits and petty usury. It was in this character
that he dictated the arid will and testament known to us, from which he
deliberately excluded all traces of pathos or literature. His friends from
London would visit his retreat and for them he would take up again his
role as poet.

History adds that before or after dying he found himself in the
presence of God and told Him: 'I who have been so many men in vain

want to be one and myself.' The voice of the Lord answered from a whirlwind: 'Neither am I anyone; I have dreamt the world as you dreamt your work, my Shakespeare, and among the forms in my dream are you, who like myself are many and no one.'

Translated by J. E. I.

'Borges and I'

The other one, the one called Borges, is the one things happen to. I walk through the streets of Buenos Aires and stop for a moment, perhaps mechanically now, to look at the arch of an entrance hall and the grillwork on the gate; I know of Borges from the mail and see his name on a list of professors or in a biographical dictionary. I like hourglasses, maps, eighteenth-century typography, the taste of coffee and the prose of Stevenson; he shares these preferences, but in a vain way that turns them into the attributes of an actor. It would be an exaggeration to say that ours is a hostile relationship; I live, let myself go on living, so that Borges may contrive his literature, and this literature justifies me. It is no effort for me to confess that he has achieved some valid pages, but those pages cannot save me, perhaps because what is good belongs to no one, not even to him, but rather to the language and to tradition. Besides, I am destined to perish, definitively, and only some instant of myself can survive in him. Little by little, I am giving over everything to him, though I am quite aware of his perverse custom of falsifying and magnifying things. Spinoza knew that all things long to persist in their being; the stone eternally wants to be a stone and the tiger a tiger. I shall remain in Borges, not in myself (if it is true that I am someone), but I recognize myself less in his books than in many others or in the laborious strumming of a guitar. Years ago I tried to free myself from him and went from the mythologies of the suburbs to the games with time and infinity, but those games belong to Borges now and I shall have to imagine other things. Thus my life is a flight and I lose everything and everything belongs to oblivion, or to him.

I do not know which of us has written this page.

Translated by J. E. I.

Index